The Impact of the Fifth Republic on France

The Impact of the Fifth Republic on France

edited by

William G. Andrews

Stanley Hoffmann

State University of New York Press

ALBANY

Published by
State University of New York Press, Albany

Printed in the United States of America

For information, address State University of New York Press,
State University Plaza, Albany, N.Y. 12246

Library of Congress Cataloging in Publication Data
Main Entry under title:

The Impact of the Fifth Republic on France.

    Papers presented at a conference held at the State
University College at Brockport, N.Y. in June 1978.
    Includes index.
    1.   France—History—1958-
—Congresses.—
I.   Andrews, William George, 1930
II.   Hoffmann, Stanley.
DC412.146   944.083   80–14651
ISBN 0–87395–440–8

*A grant from the University Awards Program of the State
University of New York and the Research Foundation of
State University of New York assisted in paying the costs
of publishing this book.*

10 9 8 7 6 5 4 3

To Michel Debré

He came, he spoke, he conquered

Contents

Preface

The Fifth French Republic was begotten by one of contemporary history's Great Men and brought forth by civil strife and constitutional disgust, the last of the West's colonial wars as its midwife. At birth in 1958, the sickly creature seemed unlikely to survive either a settlement of the Algerian conflict or the retirement of its founder. Yet, at this writing, it has outlasted the former event by eighteen years, the latter by eleven, and shows no sign of demise in the foreseeable future.

Such confounding inspires reflection, re-examination, reconsideration, perhaps insight and new understanding. To create an opportunity for such deliberations to proceed in concentrated, collective fashion, the editors of this volume organized an academic conference of specialists on contemporary France, held at the State University College at Brockport, New York, in June of 1978. The intention was to strike a balance sheet on the impact of the Fifth Republic on France.

The conference met exactly twenty years after the return to public office of Charles de Gaulle, which had been followed by the referendum ratifying the constitution of the Fifth Republic in September 1958 and de Gaulle's election as its first president in December. By 1978, the regime had survived four presidential elections, six referendums, and six parliamentary elections. The styles and policies of three presidents could be compared. The functioning of the institutions in periods when one party dominated the National Assembly could be analyzed comparatively with periods when the Majority was split between two rival parties. Both the resurgence of the Left and its resounding fiasco of March 1978 could be discussed. The transformations of French society after the shock of May/June 1968 and the great economic take-off of the mid-1950's could be appraised. The ups and downs of economic policy could be studied for the years of rapid growth and for the lean years that began in 1973. The effects, if any, of twenty years of political stability and presidental preponderance on French cultural life could be considered. The conference participants discussed all those aspects and others of the French polity since 1958. Those were twenty years of Gaullism; de Gaulle had provided the institutions and inspiration, and even today, the Chief of State owes his election and parliamentary control to the (grudging) support of the Gaullist party and proclaims the continuity of French diplomacy and defense.

The conference brought together North American and French students of the Fifth Republic. Especially attractive was the prospect of including the second Founding Father of the regime, M. Michel Debré. As minister of justice, he had had a decisive role in the drafting of the 1958 Constitution before becoming its first Prime Minister. Having written at length about the need for institutional reform after the Liberation and with ferocious persistence about the flaws of the Fourth Republic and having played a leading role in its successor from its inception, he is the best qualified commentator on French constitutional evolution since 1958. He attended the conference, delivered a speech at its banquet that provided the perspective and critical analysis that were expected from those qualifications, and responded repeatedly to questions about many aspects of French affairs and about his long and still active (indeed ebullient) political career. Spectacularly evident at Brockport was the mixture of passion, sensitivity, generosity, candor, and personal simplicity that makes even those who have clashed with him or occasionally deplored his stands admire him as a human being and recognize him as a major statesman. We are much in his debt. This volume includes the text of his speech and an edited transcript of his dialogue with the conference participants. The editors owe many other debts. The funds that made the conference possible were contributed by the State University College at Brockport, the Center for European Studies at Harvard University, the SUNY Conversations in the Disciplines program, the Corning Glass Works Foundation, the Frank E. Gannett Newspaper Foundation, the French-American Foundation, the French government, the Council for European Studies, and the Brockport Faculty-Student Association. We are grateful for this generosity.

Our greatest debt of gratitude is reserved for the authors of the conference papers. Not only did they produce first-rate works of scholarship, but they also suffered the loss of many beloved words and phrases and precious theoretical frameworks and in a few cases the deletion of studies. They took it all with grace and patience. We are grateful for their understanding.

Some 185 specialists on contemporary French affairs attended the Brockport Conference, contributing to its success and making this volume possible. In particular the editors are grateful to Nicholas A. Wahl for his assistance in organizing the program and to the following panelists: Luther A. Allen, Pierre Aubéry, André Baeyens, Konrad Bieber, Robert Berrier, Stephen Bronstein, Bernard E. Brown, Jean-Claude Casanova, Priscilla Clark, Panayote Dmitras, Henry W. Ehrmann, Elizabeth G. Evatt, Walter O. Filley, David B. Goldey, Charles Hauss, Eli Ben-Zion Kaminsky, Carl Lankowski , Edward L. Morse, Jesse R. Pitts, Brinton Rowdybush, Jacqueline Simon, Martin Slann, Marianna Sullivan, Ronald Tiersky, Jeffrey S. Victor and Nicholas A. Wahl. The con-

Preface

ference staff itself consisted of Shirley Schuff, Paula Lieberman, and Sharon Cook. Brockport's President, Albert W. Brown, and Academic Vice-president, Vera King Davis, gave us valuable encouragement.

William G. Andrews
Stanley Hoffmann

Key to Abbreviations

ADASEA: Association Départementale pour l'Aménagement des Structures des Exploitations Agricoles
CAP: Common Agricultural Policy
CDU–CSU: (German) Christian Democratic Union-Christian Social Union
CEA: Commissariat à l'Energie Atomique
CEG: Collège d'Enseignement Général
CERES: Centre d'Etudes, de Recherches et d'Education Socialistes
CES: Collège d'Enseignement Secondaire
CFDT: Confédération Française et Démocratique du Travail
CFP: Compagnie Française des Pétroles
CFT: Confédération Française du Travail
CFTC: Confédération Française des Travailleurs Chrétiens
CGC: Confédération Générale des Cadres
CGE: Compagnie Générale d'Electricité
CGPME: Confédération Générale des Petites et Moyennes Entreprises
CGT: Confédération Générale du Travail
CGT–FO: Confédération Générale du Travail-Force Ouvrière
CGT–CFDT: Confédération Générale du Travail-Confédération Française et Démocratique du Travail
CGTU: Confédération Générale du Travail Unitaire
CIASI: Comité Interministériel pour l'Aménagement des Structures Industrielles
CID–UNATI: Comité d'Information et de Défense-Union Nationale des Artisans et Travailleurs Indépendants
CNIB: Confédération Nationale des Industries du Bois
CNIP: Centre National des Indépendants et Paysans
CNJA: Centre National des Jeunes Agriculteurs
CNPF: Confédération Nationale du Patronat Français
CODER: Commission de Développement Economique Régional
DATAR: Délégation à l'Aménagement du Terriroire et à l'Action Régionale
EDF: Electricité de France

ELF: Essences et Lubrifiants de France
EMS: European Monetary System
ERAP: Entreprise de Recherches et d'ActivitéPétrolières
FAI: Force d'Appui et d'Intervention
FASASA: Fonds d'Action Sociale pour l'Aménagement des Structures Agricoles
FBR: fast breeder reactors
FDES: Fonds de Développement Economique et Social
FEN: Fédération de l'Education Nationale
FFA: Fédération Française d'Agriculture
FGDS: Fédération de la Gauche Démocrate et Socialiste
FDSEA: Fédération Départementale des Syndicats d'Exploitants Agricoles
FILB: Fédération des Industries Lourdes du Bois
FMP: Force de Mobilisation Populaire
FNS: Force Nucléaire Stratégique
FNSEA: Fédération Nationale des Syndicats d'Exploitants Agricoles
FO: Force Ouvrière
GEC: Groupe d'Echange et de Coordination
GEPI: (Italian) Gestione Partecipazioni Industriali
IAEA: International Atomic Energy Agency
IEA: International Energy Agency
IFOP: Institut Français d'Opinion Publique
IMF: International Monetary Fund
IUT: Institut Universitaire de Technologie
IVD: Indemnité Viagère de Départ
LWR: light water reactors
MBFR: Mutual Balanced Force Reduction
MDSF: Mouvement Démocrate-Socialiste de France
MODEF: Mouvement de Défense des Exploitatants Familiaux
MRG: Mouvement des Radicaux de Gauche
MRP: Mouvement Républicain Populaire
NATO: North Atlantic Treaty Organization
OECD: Organization for Economic Cooperation and Development
OPEC: Organization of Petroleum Exporting Countries
ORTF: Office de Radiodiffusion et Télévision Française
PCF: Parti Communiste Français
PDM: Progrès et Démocratie Moderne
PR: Parti Républicain
PRI: Parti Républicain Indépendant
PRS: Parti Radical-Socialiste
PS: Parti Socialiste
PSI: (Italian) Parti Socialista Italiano

PSU: Parti Socialiste Unifié
RATP: Régie Autonome des Transports Parisiens
RGR: Rassemblement de la Gauche Républicaine
RPF: Rassemblement du Peuple Français
RPR: Rassemblement pour la République
SAFER: Section d'Aménagement Foncier et d'Etablissement Rural
SFIO: Société Française de l'Internationale Ouvrière
SMIC: Salaire Minimum Interprofessionnel de Croissance
SNFCC: Syndicat National des Fabricants de Ciments et Chaux
SPD: (German) Sozialistischedemokratische Partei Deutschlands
SUAD: Service d'Utilité Agricole de Développement
TMB: travail mécanique du bois
TNW: Tactical Nuclear Weapons
UDF: Union pour la Démocratie Française
UDR: Union des Démocrates pour la République
UER: Unité d'Enseignement et de Recherche
UNEB: Union Nationale des Exploitants du Bois
UNESCO: United Nations Economic, Social, and Cultural Organization
UNICER: Union des Chefs et Responsables d'Entreprises

The Constitution of 1958, Its Raison D'être and How It Evolved

Michel Debré

A parallel is often drawn between the American Revolution and the French Revolution; but it is important also to understand how they differ.*

In the United States, events at the end of the 18th century created a legitimacy. The citizens of the first states wanted order; the members of the Constitutional Convention in Philadelphia gave it to them. Order was born of the Constitution, society was created and power emerged.

In France, events outwardly similar, at least in the early days, brought down a legitimacy that was several centuries old. Order, society, and power in France were changed by the political rupture. And the entire 19th century attests to the difficulty France had in finding a new legitimacy consistent with the aspirations of modern times.

This effort was made more difficult still by the fact that France's relative power declined as a result of the Napoleonic wars and the slower growth of its population. On a European scale it remained a country capable of greatness, of making its presence felt in distant lands; but at the world level it had lost its supremacy.

In 1870, a few years after the War Between the States which ushered in the rise of American power, there occurred the first of three wars between France and Germany. The defeat of the Empire and the upheaval of the Commune—a brief, terrible tragedy—resulted in a republic whose constitutional laws were drafted without republican zeal or democratic fervor. The sole concern was to counter ''personal power'' until a conservative parliamentary monarchy patterned after the British could be restored.

*Translation from French by French Press and Information Service, New York.

As it happened, the fundamental political rules that were instituted on a provisional basis endured unchanged until 1940, creating a quite special type of system that I labeled some thirty years ago the assembly system.

It looked as if there were separation of power, but in reality it was different. A mercantile bourgeoisie and a landed aristocracy succeeded, either by fighting each other or pooling their efforts, in becoming the dominant political class, resulting in a system of parliamentary sovereignty: the only check on the all-powerful chamber of deputies was the senate, whose task was to cool the passions of the former. The tribute to Montesquieu concealed the triumph of Rousseau's ideology.

The chief of state was elected by both chambers. This rule of law came to mean, in fact, that the majority in parliament chose as the person to head the executive a man who would never take a major initiative and who would, above all, respect the authority of parliament.

The cabinet was responsible to the chambers. The electoral system chosen for the election of members of parliament was not the British or American one nor the majority vote sought by the early republicans. It was an election in two rounds that made it difficult to have a cohesive majority. The cabinet, which was formed from a coalition of parties, became vulnerable. Its responsibility to the assembly became submission. This submission generated crises and instability which—with few exceptions—were the hallmark of the Republic.

Laws were the expression of parliament's will. Parliament was not checked by constitutional rules simply because those who had adopted the laws wanted them to be temporary and so had not set forth any principle that legislators had to respect. To top it all off, there was silence about the judiciary whose independence lay more in the judges' minds than in the statutes.

The Third Republic had a hard time establishing its legitimacy. In the nineteenth century, France was deeply divided between monarchists and republicans, who in turn were divided among themselves. Moderate republicans opposed radical republicans, and the moderates and radicals opposed the socialists.

Nevertheless, the Republic gradually won recognition through its regulations, laws, and leaders. It was helped by a vigilant patriotism that emphasized the reconquest of Alsace and Lorraine; that wanted, through education and social legislation, to put leadership within reach of the people; and by a spirit of adventure and expansion which, in less than thirty years, increased France's presence in Africa, Asia, and the Pacific.

The Republic was badly shaken by a series of major events occurring within. The most important of these was the Dreyfus affair, which in the long run served the cause of the republic's legitimacy by imposing on the institutions and on the men who ran them, in addition to their obligation to serve the nation, the obligation to respect the rights of the individual.

Thus in 1914; first the *union sacrée,* then victory, endorsed the national legitimacy of the Republic. The Third Republic had remodeled France, had recovered Alsace and Lorraine, and had set the country on the path of modernization and social progress.

But, as is often the case in history, the consolidation of a political system coincides with the intimations of its downfall: the tragic effects of the weakness of the administration, long hidden by the quality of the civil service, began to increase.

The price of victory was heavy: politicians were slow to perceive the significance of a million and a half dead and another million and a half wounded. A decline in the population—whether due to a decline in the birth rate or a rise in mortality—lowers the quality of the population. This was especially true after a long war in which the youngest, bravest and most dedicated had fallen. Twenty years later, when the generation sacrificed would have reached the age of responsibility, the burden of their absence could be felt.

Politicians in Europe—whether British or French—found it no less difficult to understand the return of the United States to isolationism or Russia's turning inward on itself when once it had proclaimed itself the bastion of socialism.

A few years later, there was no greater perception about the consequences of the American crisis for Europe than there was courage to confront the rise in dictatorships, or the tyranny Hitler installed in Germany and around it.

In 1933, the seeds of doubt were sown first—unfortunately in too few people's minds—about the political capability of the Third Republic. No one doubted its moral legitimacy. Human rights were respected. The effort to promote human advancement and dignity went on. But moral legitimacy is not enough. There must be political legitimacy, that is, the ability to ensure the survival of the nation and the security of its citizens. In the face of economic difficulties, growing unemployment, and threats from a bloodthirsty and criminal regime, France of the 1930s looked decidedly pallid: divided at home, naive abroad.

The disaster in 1940 confirmed its impotence. The Republic went down in defeat. And for France there emerged a new crisis of legitimacy. A semblance of legal power was installed in Vichy. In a few months, it ceased to be legitimate. A semblance of illegal power was installed in London. In a few months General de Gaulle came to embody legitimacy. The legitimacy of one man, however, was not enough. There had to be a legitimacy of institutions.

In August 1944 General de Gaulle arrived in Paris. Wholly determined to restore France to the first ranks of victorious nations, he was confronted at home with the prestige of the Communist party, the after effects of Vichy highhandedness, and the haste of a political establishment impatient—to use the word of an illustrious parliamentarian of the time—to demonstrate its capacity for democracy through its capacity for ingratitude.

3

General de Gaulle seemed omnipotent. With his attention turned toward his principal goal, he kept silent on institutions. On the strength of his personal legitimacy, he wanted to gain time before giving France a new constitution. The German surrender brought a torrent of different opinions. Some urged him to return to the institutions of the Third Republic. That might have been a solution, providing it were done fast and with a few drastic changes. It was not done fast and, apart from a small number of people who had thought about it in the final months of the Resistance, there was no general agreement on what changes should be made. So General de Gaulle convened a constituent assembly and at the same time held a referendum repealing the constitutional laws of 1875.

Then, General de Gaulle committed, in my opinion, the error of not presenting a draft constitution—doubtless out of concern for democracy. I would like to interject a personal word here: I was one of the people who had thought about the institutional requirements of modern France and when I was called to assist General de Gaulle in mid-1945, I used my earlier thoughts to prepare the text of a constitution based on the three points I believed had been revealed by the inadequacy of the Third Republic. For the stability and authority of the executive I used an idea that found favor later, the idea of a republican monarch. In the second place, a genuine parliamentary system was needed, that is, a cabinet that directs the actions of the government and the work of parliament but is responsible to this body; a parliament whose activity is organized and whose will is not all powerful. And finally, a method of election which, while ensuring as cohesive a majority as possible, permits solid cooperation between the cabinet and parliament, and thus greater government stability.

These ideas were never translated into facts. The return of political parties that accompanied the rebirth of democracy resulted in a conflict which General de Gaulle predicted would have serious consequences on the political history of France. He did not want to jeopardize his legitimacy in quarrels he viewed as secondary compared to the state of the world. He withdrew. From the standpoint of institutions, he did nonetheless make one innovation: the use of the referendum which, thus, made a furtive entry into the constitutional life of the Republic and which soon became an element of its legitimacy.

Left to itself, that is, to the parties, the constituent assembly was subject to strong Socialist and Communist influence and produced a poor constitution. Underneath the apparent changes—to wit, the solemn reaffirmation of the principles of democracy, the new organization of parliament with the power of the second chamber considerably diminished in relation to the first, and rules of procedure that were supposedly designed to give the government more staying power—underneath, it was a return to the assembly system, the system of the Third Republic. In many respects its mechanisms were even worse, and consequently so were its drawbacks. These, then, were the roots of the illegitimacy

4

of a regime which, as the French people gradually came to realize, had as its sole aim setting up what General de Gaulle later called the party system. By this he meant the system in which virtually all the political power reverted to a coalition of parties which, although clever enough to get their leaders into power, were not strong enough to lead the country.

On two occasions, the people showed their impatience and distrust. The first time, they rejected the text of a constitution prepared and adopted by the constituent assembly. The second time, they adopted a text which was scarcely any different from the first, but which had the support of the parties, especially since General de Gaulle had announced his opposition to it. It was approved by only one third of the votes, with slightly less than one third of the people voting against it and a little more than one third staying away from the polls. Even this lukewarm response was obtained only after assurances were given on all sides that the draft could be revised quickly. Actually, the people never really gave the institutions their backing since they saw all too clearly how close they were to the ones that had made France ineffectual politically between the two world wars.

I said this at the time, and events proved that my fears were justified. The institutions of the Fourth Republic were unable to set up a legitimate regime because they were incapable of establishing the authority of the state, all the more so because the assembly was elected by proportional representation.

Under this system the executive, legislative, and administrative power is shared by the leadership of the parties, no one of which can ever obtain a majority and consequently ever feels responsible for the general interest. It is really a coalition of party interests which sets up camp in the state and shares its spoils. Let me add an important point, which is that this system of voting gives the Communist party a great deal of weight.

Individual merit was not much help: those leaders who were former members of the Resistance, many of whom were my friends and comrades in arms, were on the whole courageous and sincere. But when it came to dealing with world events and especially the trials awaiting France in Indochina and North Africa, this system, without a stable executive power and dominated by the all-powerful impotence of a divided assembly, demonstrated its inability to decide on a national policy, its inability even to ensure respect for human rights.

The Fourth Republic can claim some successes, which were due to the fact that deep down the French people wanted to avenge the circumstances that had brought them to such depths: the birth rate did climb and industry began to grow. The French joined in the postwar euphoria. It was not a citizenry the Republic was missing—it was leadership.

General de Gaulle immediately perceived the weakness of the new Republic. In 1947, he founded the Rally of the French People. It had immediate success both in the municipal elections and in the elections for the second chamber, later named the Council of the Republic.

Popular reaction against the parties of the Fourth Republic was so strong that in order to defend itself the administration, just prior to the decisive legislative elections of 1951, instituted an unheard-of voting system: it was proportional representation coupled with the so-called *apparentements* method in which the various parties, by combining the votes received by their tickets, could obtain a majority and thus divide the seats among themselves. Party coalition leaders and ministers explained to U.S. leaders, among others, that this method of voting was designed to reduce Communist representation. In fact, that explanation was for outsiders only. The real aim was to keep General de Gaulle from returning to power by means of election. The results were as desired. The Rally of the French People got more votes than any other party by a large margin, but its representation in parliament came to only 130 deputies out of nearly 600.

A legitimate regime that is not successful rapidly ceases to be legitimate. It was to preserve his stature that General de Gaulle withdrew a few months after this defeat.

It did not help make the Fourth Republic more legitimate, quite the contrary. Unconsciously for some, consciously for others, the Fourth Republic sought a new kind of legitimacy by trying to build a European superstate. Many were pleased by this until the plan for a 'European army' came up. The great controversy over this European Defense Community provoked a national crisis and resulted in 1954 in rejection of the proposal by the National Assembly. The Gaullists and some moderates, the Communists, and half the Socialists, joined together in rejecting the political prospects of integrating France into Europe. Sustaining a military defeat in Indochina and, close on its heels, becoming bogged down in a military situation in Algeria were the final blows to a failing regime. The government could neither bring about victory by arms nor negotiate with the rebels. Confronted with the threat of civil war, President Coty summoned General de Gaulle, and in a historic meeting in June 1958, even though the number of Gaullist deputies had been drastically reduced by the preceding elections, de Gaulle obtained the backing of all those political groups, except the Communists, that had fought so hard against him for ten years.

So legitimacy was once more, for a few months, embodied in a man, General de Gaulle. Guided by experience, despite pressing economic and financial problems, despite the difficulty of the Algerian problem, General de Gaulle made it his first priority to draft a new constitution. It took one summer.

The drafting began early in July and was completed at the end of August. The 1958 Constitution was approved by a referendum in September. The aim of the new constitution was to build a legitimate republic by creating a state

6

that was effective with regard to national exigencies while remaining faithful to the principles of democracy.

For twenty years, I have read and heard it said that this constitution was made for General de Gaulle. For twenty years, I have alerted professors of political science to the fact that this is a major analytical error. Most certainly this constitution, in the minds of those who conceived and wrote it, and I myself was foremost among them, did allow General de Gaulle to assume responsibility for French affairs for the longest period of years possible. How could we have considered doing otherwise when in every respect our domestic state of affairs, the needs of Europe, and the exigencies of the world scene called for a kind of government that only General de Gaulle, even though he was entering his later years, could lead and ensure? But in spirit, the constitution was not tailored to an individual. Its aim was to correct the inadequacies of the Republic's institutions which had been apparent for nearly a century, inadequacies which, because they were so ill-suited to national exigencies, led to the disasters of the post-World War I period and to the dangers of the decolonization period.

When summarizing my thoughts, I have often repeated an idea that I think is still true: 'The Republic had to acquire the attributes of government.' What did it need to succeed?

To my mind, three truly basic attributes were required: an executive with its own authority stemming from both its mode of selection and its powers; a parliamentary system, meaning on one hand a cabinet backed by a majority within an assembly and thus able to guide this majority as well as head the administration, but also on the other hand, a parliament that could carry out its legislative duties and act as a control without infringing on the executive: and third, an election method as close as possible to the British-American system, the one used by the first French republicans, election by majority vote.

The executive first of all had to be a chief of state worthy of the name. What do I mean by 'worthy of the name'? Well, above all he should not be selected by a nonrepresentative college in which alliances could be made. Then, he should have powers that guarantee him the ability to take responsibility for the nation's fate. Finally, he should have control over the functioning of institutions, if not directly, then in any case through his right to appeal to arbitrating bodies.

One such body is the Constitutional Council, which ensures primarily that the rules determining jurisdiction in constitutional matters are respected. But the most important arbitrating body is public opinion itself, expressed in referendums or in elections when the assembly is dissolved.

All this went into the Constitution.

The parliamentary system means above all that the cabinet is based on a majority in parliament and is responsible to that majority. The tragedy for the Republic had been its instability because the administration could constantly be challenged over any issue. This was corrected by specific measures such as controlling parliament's agenda, setting a strict procedure for the motion of censure, and making it incompatible to hold a seat in parliament and hold a cabinet position. Parliament, which is active for two three-month sessions each year, is completely free to bring matters up for consideration and put questions to ministers, but it cannot challenge the responsibility of the cabinet without using a formal procedure and this procedure cannot be invoked frequently: the motion of censure. Parliament has the right to change things, but within its jurisdiction. One major innovation in the 1958 Constitution was defining legislative limits so that the administration can keep the assembly from infringing on the administration's action, something as harmful as ministerial instability. These two phenomena—infringing on administrative action and ministerial instability—are the two main problems with the assembly system compared with a true parliamentary system. *The parliamentary system was instituted.*

I would have liked the principle of election of deputies by majority vote to be written into the constitution. I did not win on this point. The French tradition of the vote as a political instrument rather than a principle is very strong. Proportional representation was abolished but, also by reason of France's political sociology, the ordinance changing the voting method reestablished the two-ballot system, under which an absolute majority was needed to win on the first ballot. *The reform was not as strong as I would have wished.*

Four years after the 1958 Constitution, General de Gaulle wanted to make a major change and succeeded in doing so despite opposition by the leadership of all the political parties. Whereas the original text of the constitution had called for election of the president by a college of 100,000 people representing first and foremost the cities, towns, and departments, de Gaulle held a referendum which approved election of the president of the Republic by universal suffrage. This measure had not been possible while millions of people in Africa, Madagascar and even Asia had had French citizenship. Independence for countries in those parts of the world made it possible again. It was deemed necessary. This measure unquestionably reflected a personal idea of General de Gaulle. His legitimacy came from the people and, faced with the prospect of new presidential elections, he thought that as far as he was concerned he could not request renewal of his mandate without appealing to the people as a whole. But this personal idea was reinforced by two other ideas, each of them of fundamental importance.

One was an idea regarding national defense. Since 1959 France had wanted to become a nuclear power and base its defense on deterrence. One of the elements of deterrence is the credibility of an authority who would carry out the

8

terrible threat should the need arise. This credibility assumes that the chief of state has legitimacy in his own right, independent of the legitimacy of institutions. He therefore had to have the support of universal suffrage.

The second idea had to do with institutions. France is still a country where it is difficult to picture the formation of two parties which alternate in power and thus ensure the democratic functioning of the state. Extreme groups in France contest the legitimacy of the republican form of government. Because of this, the Republic still lives under the threat, despite the merit of its institutions, of once more falling into the system of coalitions of various parties which dominate the government. Basing the authority of the chief of the state on universal suffrage is a safeguard against this eventuality.

The 1962 referendum, which approved election of the president of the French Republic by universal suffrage, is interesting in another respect. Four years previously, the 1958 referendum had given the new constitution an unusually broad popular base. With the exception of the Communists, every party had recommended voting for it and it was possible to deduce that this support by the political parties had been a determining factor in shaping the vote to the wishes of General de Gaulle.

In 1962 the situation was completely different. General de Gaulle stood alone. The Communist party opposed him but he was also opposed by the Socialists, the Radicals, the Christian Democrats and the moderates. Only the Gaullists supported de Gaulle, and they seemed so isolated that when I began to campaign in support of him, people thought I showed an exceptional amount of courage! The referendum was more than 60 percent in favor. Nearly two-thirds of the French voted for General de Gaulle and, above and beyond the man, for the legitimacy of a republic that could free itself of the grip of the parties in times of major importance. This shows the extent to which the leadership of the parties can act as a screen. And the nature of the step taken by the Gaullist authors of the constitution must be clearly understood: it was to reveal the truer political reality by appealing to the people through universal suffrage. It is not a right to be abused, moreover. De Gaulle learned this cruel lesson in 1969.

Twenty years have elapsed. General de Gaulle is dead. Succeeding him for five years was one of his prime ministers, then on his death, a man who had been one of his ministers for a few years, a man whose political commitment had never been to Gaullism. The personal position of the current president is much more favorable to the old parties.

Whereas the institutions of the Third Republic acquired legitimacy only belatedly and those of the Fourth Republic never, the elections early in 1978 actually revealed the extent to which the present institutions have become established. Twenty years after 1958, the French people see them as a reflection of themselves, and the immediate and total acceptance of the results, and

9

therefore of the legitimacy of the state, is very significant. The institutions of the Fifth Republic have given the Republic its legitimacy. This is what I am most proud of, though I am not overlooking that, France being France, that is to say a country that has scarcely changed since Julius Caesar or Richelieu passed judgment on it, everything could still be brought into question again. The sanctity of institutions, which is what the public needs, is all too easily exposed to criticism, sometimes on ideological grounds, sometimes from self-interest.

Certain gains, very important ones, seem to be permanent now. Among them are the election of the president of the Republic by universal suffrage, the elimination of the danger of governmental instability and the ruling on the constitutionality of laws by the Constitutional Council. In other words—and this is what is important—the rules that check the excessive power of an assembly have become legitimate and so cannot be contravened without a veritable disruption of legitimacy.

But over and above the legitimacy that has now been acquired, it is important to consider three things that may influence for better or worse its ultimate evolution. The first, which is not unusual, is that there are two possible readings of the constitution, that is, two ways of interpreting it; the second, more disturbing, is the desire to move either closer to the presidential system or closer to the assembly system; the third, totally undesirable, is the trend on the part of numerous party leaders to seek proportional representation in elections to the National Assembly.

The president of the republic chooses a prime minister. The prime minister must have the confidence of the National Assembly. An arrangement such as this leads to two interpretations of the constitution, both completely correct.

One interpretation makes government more particularly the affair of the president. The other interpretation gives the prime minister considerable personal authority due primarily to the support of the parliament. These two interpretations have each been employed in turn.

In the early years of the present constitution, during the three years when I was prime minister, the head of state enjoyed an indisputable and undisputed preeminence in all matters pertaining to defense, foreign affairs, and Algeria, matters in which the prime minister, as his name indicates, was the principal collaborator of the head of state. Regarding all else: the whole range of internal affairs, the economy, finance, administration, education, social questions, and so forth, I the prime minister had a free hand. Then came another prime minister and General de Gaulle saw to the general operation of things. He was able to do this all the better because the elections gave his supporters an absolute majority in the National Assembly.

In 1966, after his term of office had been renewed—not the easy victory he had expected—he gave greater freedom of action to the then prime minister, Georges Pompidou, and the minister of the economy and finance that I

10

became. Our greater freedom was confirmed after the legislative elections in 1967 which marked the resurgence of the opposition. After the events in May 1968, the National Assembly was dissolved and in the ensuing elections the Gaullists won a large majority. The new prime minister, Maurice Couve de Murville, became a very strict and loyal top aide of General de Gaulle who remained at the helm until the unfortunate referendum that caused him to withdraw from public life. The presidency of Georges Pompidou lasted for five years. His first cabinet, that of prime minister Chaban-Delmas, had considerable autonomy regarding the management and general direction of national affairs. However this was not the case with his successor, Mr. Messmer. The government then became more "presidentialized"—as they say in politico-legal jargon. It has continued to be so with the cabinets designated by the current president who would have been obliged—as he acknowledged during the 1978 election campaign—to alter his line of conduct completely had the elections been won by the opposition. On the contrary, the success of the majority has enabled him to strengthen the presidential side of the constitution.

I have grave political disagreements with the current leadership of my country. In no way does that influence my constitutional judgment. The presidential system is not prohibited by our constitution and when the majority that has elected the president is the same as the one that has elected the assembly, this division of power does not run counter to the constitution.

Nevertheless, I favor France having a more parliamentary application of its constitution. Too much concentration of power in the hands of the president, at the expense of the cabinet, diminishes parliament's ability to play a proper parliamentary role and runs the risk of paralyzing it in its main function, which is to be a trusted intermediary between the government and the people. At the same time, the administration may be run less effectively by ministers who feel no personal responsibility to the assembly.

For this reason, I have serious doubts about the trends toward presidentializing the constitution in the manner of the United States. To strengthen these powers would require shortening the length of the presidential term—at the risk of shocking some, perhaps all of you, I must say that I find a four-year term rather short in a century in which nations are struggling for survival. Not to mention the fact that an increase in presidential powers is promptly countered by an increase in the powers of elected assemblies. Without dwelling on the paradox, it is important to see that the presidential system tends to be balanced by an assembly system. The United States, which is a powerful country, can combine the power of the president with that of Congress. This is a gamble you can take because of your strength and also your wealth. I do not think that France, a medium-sized nation with less wealth and constantly exposed to danger, can allow itself this luxury. There has to be a link, and also a buffer,

11

between president and assembly; this role falls to the prime minister—or to the cabinet—on whom falls a very large share of the executive power, who is responsible to parliament and whose work he must also direct.

The possibility of a return to proportional representation for deputies to the National Assembly disturbs me deeply. I can see no point in giving the Communist party maximum representation. Were this method of election followed in a country where the tradition of a multi-party system has long been established, it would achieve a real transfer of sovereignty from the people to party leaders. It would alter the parliamentary system by doing away with the concept of a united majority responsible to the electorate. In vain I have proposed to my countrymen that we should follow the British and the Americans, who praise this system of election all the more since they have decided never to use it themselves. I am not always heeded and I suspect I will have to continue the fight for the next several years.

The founding fathers of democracy, inspired by the noble idea that right should prevail over arbitrary rule, perhaps placed undue emphasis on institutions. To be sure, institutions are an important element of every republic. Throughout my life I have taken pains to say so and to make an often skeptical political establishment understand this. The definition of responsibilities, the chances of success of our leaders' initiatives, the length of time they are in office, the equilibrium of functions within the administration, the possibility of adapting these functions to circumstances are all equally essential elements in combining public well-being with public freedom, which is the supreme task of the republican state. The method of election cannot be left to circumstance; it is a fundamental element not only in the choice men make but in the general tenor of the seat of power.

Another feature that enhances the value of a constitution is its capacity to face crises, external crises of course but also internal ones, which make for the greatness and the liability of regimes founded on universal suffrage. Opposition between the executive and the legislative, change in the ruling majority, social crisis, are all inevitable when power comes from a regularly consulted electorate and when the functions of government are shared among independent authorities.

Through government stability and the principle of majority vote, the 1958 Constitution reduced the number of crises. When they did occur, the ability of the head of state to consult the people made it possible to solve them democratically.

But institutions are only one part of public life. People are also involved and they change. There are ideas, customs, the mood of the times, and these change, too.

During difficult periods, though public opinion can be mistaken, men and women are more ready to turn to those who can talk and act in the general interest. When times are less threatening, the art of theater, which is partly necessary in that phase of public life which is the quest for power, sometimes engenders illusions. Likewise, a generation of men and women that has gone through great trials is susceptible to the appeal of candidates who talk of responsibility before history. Generations that have not experienced these trials are more apt to look to flamboyant personalities, drawn by the possibility of being able to play a personal role. As for new ideas, it is sometimes difficult to separate those that are sincere aspirations from those concealing other interests. In our present age, which has been caught up in a whirlwind of innovation, new ideas always exercise a great influence; and the new ideas—not always so new as they claim to be—are not always consistent with the interests of the Republic, which itself is permanent.

For example, among the politically aware in France, some are drawn to the idea of a so-called integrated Europe without assessing either the political individuality of France on the continent or the dramatic requirements of the national state. Coupling public well-being with public freedom postulates the existence of a solidarity that has sprung up naturally. The mechanism that ensures authority through the law of the majority is a delicate instrument. It is not given to just any group to defer to the authority of one man designated by virtue of a margin over his competitor that may be less than 1 percent of the votes cast, or to a law adopted by one vote as the Third Republic was. What I am saying is that legitimacy is not decreed. It is a sign of social consensus, which is a feature of nations in general and France in particular. France has given this legitimacy its own form—highly different from the Latin, Germanic, and Anglo-Saxon worlds that surround it.

Another example of the new ideas that are more widespread in the political establishment than among the people of France is the concept of dividing sovereignty among the regions. Administrative decentralization, as long as it is complemented and supported by political, financial, and social solidarity, is a good idea but the dismemberment of power is disastrous.

In a country such as France, inequality in the distribution of income together with the profusion of local interests would quickly lead to fractured solidarity and a dispersal of power which would be the ruin of the institutions of the Republic. My satisfaction with the progress made since 1958 is tempered by my concern over the all-too-frequent failure to perceive the exigencies of the legitimacy of power in France.

I have dwelt at length on the word "legitimacy" in the course of these remarks. It is a difficult and fundamental issue that touches the very soul of the community. Nothing in public life is ever achieved permanently. But the unprecedented advances in our knowledge, like the progress in our technical capacity, do not affect the eternal behavior of men, societies and nations. The viability of institutions is an essential element in the success of this continuous

13

struggle—the political struggle, in which thought is the basis for action.

Legitimacy is loyalty to moral principles and the public interest, while respecting national sovereignty. Legitimacy requires simplicity. Everything in institutions that fosters the simple appeal to the truth of things and feelings, strengthens legitimacy: a head of state elected by the people, deputies elected by majority vote, the right to dissolve parliament in the event of conflict between the cabinet and the assembly. On the other hand, everything that tends to obscure—a complicated electoral method, power-sharing with the regions, delegations to supra-national communities—erodes legitimacy. The great merit of the Fifth Republic is having restored to the French people their right to decide their future. Never has France voted on so many issues and, what is more important, never have people gone in such numbers and so freely to the polls to cast their votes. They should now take care not to lose what they owe to tragic circumstances, which established a personal legitimacy for one man, General de Gaulle, which he, a good republican, used to restore the legitimacy of the Republic.

May those who lead our country, and educate and inform its citizens refrain from tampering with the principles of our society, with the public interest, and with our nation's sovereignty.

The Collective Political Executive Under the Gaullists

William G. Andrews

INTRODUCTION

At the time of its formation, the Fifth Republic was viewed widely as a hybrid regime with an indeterminate prognosis. The 1958 Constitution contained both parliamentarist and presidentialist characteristics. Pundits predicted the evolution of the regime into either of those basic forms or into a stable or unstable amalgam of them.

That ambivalence was institutionalized in the bicephalic quality of the executive branch. The prime minister was dependent on the National Assembly in the classic parliamentarist sense. The president of the Republic had a separate constituency in the traditional manner of presidentialist systems. Commentators speculated on the likelihood that one of those institutions would emerge dominant with the passage of time, thereby determining the constitutional destiny of the republic.

At the outset of the Fifth Republic, each of those incipient chief executives chaired a council that had some characteristics of a collective decision-making body. The prime minister met with the rest of the Government as the Cabinet Council. The president of the Republic and the government formed the Council of Ministers. The existence of both institutions in the early Fifth Republic contributed to its ambivalence.

This chapter examines the fate of those councils and shows that the ambivalence was dissolved by the extinction of the parliamentarist Cabinet Council and the establishment of the Council of Ministers as a viable instrument of presidentialist governance. Similarly, it shows that the committee structure of the executive branch evolved in the same direction. This should shed some light on the process through which the Fifth Republic brought to France a regime that is essentially presidentialist.

15

BACKGROUND

The Council of Ministers and Cabinet Council had long and varied histories in Republican France before 1958. The 1795 constitution forbade them both with a provision (Art. 151) that "the ministers shall not form a council." The 1848 Constitution implied the rehabilitation of the Council of Ministers (Art. 64), but left the Cabinet Council in limbo. The 1875 constitution reinforced the former,[1] but continued to ignore the latter. However, the 1877 rupture between the president of the Republic and the government and the resultant political eclipse of the presidency left the Council of Ministers a formal, ratifying body for decisions hammered out in the Cabinet Council.[2]

The 1946 Constitution institutionalized both councils more fully. It recognized the Cabinet council constitutionally for the first time by mentioning the "Cabinet" in five articles (12, 45, 48, 49, 52). Also, it gave more elaborate attention to the Council of Ministers (Arts. 45, 55). It gave prime ministers constitutional ascendancy over the presidents of the Republic, in addition to the political ascendancy they had held since 1877. This ensured the continued practical dominance of the Cabinet Council, although the Council of Ministers continued to function regularly and even enjoyed some modest efflorescence when the political orientations of president and government were similar and rapport between them was good.[3] Thus, the significance of the councils shifted with changes in the political importance of their chairmen and in the characters of the regimes. When the presidency of the Republic was powerful (the Second Republic and early Third Republic), so was the Council of Ministers. Otherwise, the Cabinet Council dominated. The more presidentialist the regime, the stronger the Council of Ministers; the more parliamentarist, the stronger the Cabinet Council.

THE CABINET COUNCIL

The pattern of that historical background and the Gaullists' distrust of "assembly government" suggested strongly that the balance would swing away from the Cabinet Council when de Gaulle returned to power in 1958. However, the new constitution did not make that altogether clear. It did not mention the Cabinet Council by name, though some of its many references to "the Government" were the functional equivalent. For instance, Article 7 provided that "the Government" may petition the Constitutional Council to certify "the incapacity of the President," hardly business to be transacted in the Council of Ministers with the president in the chair. In any case, the "Government" was a collective entity and it functioned collectively only as Cabinet Council and Council of Ministers. When the constitution referred to it in that latter form, it used the label "Council of Ministers." Its other references to the Government seem to mean the Cabinet Council.

16

Meeting Schedule

However the text may be read, Michel Debré, the principal author of the 1958 constitution and its first prime minister, seems to have intended that the Cabinet Council continue to function as a viable institution. He has said that he scheduled meetings for it about once a month.[4] Such an intention would seem to be consistent with his "reformed parliamentarism" concept of the Fifth Republic.[5]

The public record suggests that his intention survived for about two years of his three-year term. An inaugural meeting of his Cabinet Council held a long, serious discussion of substantive matters two days before the first session of the Council of Ministers.[6] It met, thereafter, about once a month for about one year.[7] After the fourth meeting (March 18), the government spokesman announced that "henceforth the members of the Government will meet at least twice a month in Cabinet Council....These deliberations will permit the Government to take the pulse of public opinion."[8] Apparently, the Government took that pulse by other means, for it never kept its noble resolution.[9]

Its failure to keep a bi-weekly schedule did not deter it from announcing a weekly schedule. After a meeting on February 22, 1960, Debré said that the Cabinet Council would meet weekly "to provide for better coordination of governmental activities."[10] A week later, after another Cabinet Council, the announcement was repeated.[11]

Those intentions faded fast again. The Cabinet Council met once in March, three times in April, and eight times in the last eight months of 1960. Moreover, it met only four times in 1961 and the only meeting called by Debré in 1962 was a formal farewell session after he had submitted his resignation.

Debré's successors abandoned the Cabinet Council almost completely. Pompidou's only meeting was a formality for the inauguration of his first government.[12] Couve de Murville, Chaban-Delmas, and Messmer held no meetings at all, except that Couve called three meetings during the interim presidency of Alain Poher in 1969, when the president and the government were barely on speaking terms.[13]

Meeting Contents

The Cabinet Council dealt mainly with parliamentary, political, and fiscal matters, although Couve de Murville gave a foreign affairs report at least once. The imminent opening of the parliamentary session was an especially favored occasion for the Cabinet Council to review extensively the status of the government's legislative program. Major parliamentary bills of high political sensitivity provided the grist for two noteworthy meetings in December 1959: an attempt to work out a compromise on the school-aid bill and a discussion of a bill to reform the electoral system for municipal councils.[14] Taxation and budget

17

matters were standard agenda items. Other topics that received extensive attention were administrative reform, farm prices, social security, overseas France,
judicial reform, Algeria, foreign policy, and some of the 1959 ordinances. The
topics tended to be broad, to have political sensitivity, and to involve the relations of the government with parliament.

Meeting Style and Form

The style and form of the meetings varied considerably. The session on
school-aid, for instance, included serious deliberation and negotiation. Other
meetings were entirely one-man shows. This was especially true of the pre-
parliamentary meetings. One such session was "long and important," yet consisted of a lengthy speech by Debré and written notes by ministers on their
legislative plans, but no discussion.[15] Debré told another meeting: "Each of
you may make your views known. I will gather up your reflections in order to be
able to take them into account when appropriate."[16] Two others were
"show-and-tell." Eight ministers one week and nine the next reported on their
current activities, plans to use special powers, and proposed bills for the
forthcoming parliamentary session.[17]

Conclusions

The continuance of the Cabinet Council in the early Fifth Republic reflected
the parliamentarist side of its ambivalence. Its survival could have provided the
prime minister with the organizational means to challenge or erode the
political powers of the chief of state as had happened after 1877 and in nineteenth century Britain. Debré wanted a viable Cabinet Council and tried
repeatedly to pump life into it. He announced active meeting schedules and
avoided the appearance of conflict with de Gaulle by ensuring that its agenda
skirted the "presidential reserve." He experimented with various meeting for-
mats in search of one that would suit any natural function it might develop.

Nothing worked. The Cabinet Council never really functioned. Its demise
may be seen as both cause and symptom of the evolution of the Fifth Republic
from ambivalence into a preponderantly presidentialist system. The concommi-
tant emergence of the Council of Ministers as a viable collective organ of executive leadership tended in the same constitutional direction.

COUNCIL OF MINISTERS

Constitutional Status

The 1958 Constitution referred to the Council of Ministers in eight articles
(9, 13, 21, 36, 38, 39, 49, 92). They provided that the president of the
Republic would chair its meetings, specified the conditions in which the prime

minister might serve in his stead, and required that certain executive decisions be taken in the council. Their main import was to make the council a consultative body in which key decisions of the president and government would be made officially in a formal setting with the principal officers of the executive present. However, they did not require that it function as a *collective* deliberative and decision-making body.

Membership

Decisions on categories of members for Gaullist Councils of Ministers seem to have been made with a view to strengthening it as an executive instrument of the presidency. De Gaulle departed from the practice of the Third and Fourth Republics, which had included only the president of the Republic, the prime minister, and all full ministers in its membership. Secretaries of state (junior ministers) had attended only when responsible for agenda items.[18] De Gaulle included the secretaries of state on a regular basis to reinforce governmental solidarity.[19]

Practice varied during the Pompidou presidency. The Chaban-Delmas government reverted to the practice of the preceding republics, except that the secretaries of state for the budget and as government spokesman attended regularly. The change was not explained officially, but may have resulted partly from the size of the government. Its eighteen ministers and twenty secretaries of state totaled eight more than any previous Fifth Republic government. Also, Chaban-Delmas experimented with "apprentice-ministers," secretaries of state assigned to senior members to be trained as ministers. Their solidarity with the government may have been viewed as derivative and, therefore, not requiring their presence in the Council.[20] To compensate for their absence from the council, Chaban-Delmas announced at the inception of his government that he would meet with them fortnightly to review the business transacted in the Council and to give them an institutionalized opportunity to air grievances and aspirations.[21] However, few such meetings were held and the experiment was not repeated by his successor.[22]

The first two Messmer governments restored de Gaulle's practice, but the third excluded all secretaries of state.[23] The former change was not explained officially, but Messmer gave size as the reason for the subsequent exclusions, claiming that government by sixteen rather than thirty-eight "will certainly be more rapid and consequently more effective."[24] Undoubtedly, the rapid deterioration of Pompidou's health was another factor in that change.

Also, the Council of ministers varied in size as a result of changes in the number of full ministers. Their number ranged from fifteen (Messmer III) to twenty-three (Pompidou V) and the total size of the Council from seventeen (Messmer III) to thirty-two (Pompidou V and Couve de Murville). (See Table 1.) The average total was 27.6 and the median was 29.

TABLE 1.

Size of Councils of Ministers and of Governments, 1959–74.

| | Debré | | Pompidou | | | Couve | Chaban | | Messmer | | |
	I	II	III	IV	V		a.	b.	I	II	III
President of the Republic	1	1	1	1	1	1	1	1	1	1	1
Prime Minister	1	1	1	1	1	1	1	1	1	1	1
Ministers	20	21	17	21	23	18	18	20	19	21	15
Secretaries of State attending	6	4	10	7	7	12	2	2	10	16	–
Size of Council of Ministers	28	27	29	30	32	32	22	24	31	29	17
Secretaries of State not attending [c]	–	–	–	–	–	–	18	19	–	–	13
Size of the government	27	26	28	29	31	31	39	42	30	28	29

a. As of January 23, 1969
b. As of January 7, 1971
c. Not counting the President.
All figures refer to size at the time the governments were formed.

20

Probably, the Council was too large (except Messmer III) to deliberate and make decisions collectively with optimal efficiency. The frequent changes suggest a search for that optimum. Whether the Council was being enlarged for wider "solidarity" or reduced for greater efficiency, the changes were justified as increasing its effectiveness and, therefore, as strengthening the presidentialist leg of the regime.

Another change in attendance at Council meetings served the same purpose. For the first time, a presidential staff member was present. During the Third Republic, no staff member attended. In the Fourth Republic, the general secretary of the government took minutes under the prime minister's direction, as the constitution required.[25] Under the Gaullists, he was joined by the general secretary of the presidency.

The two secretaries at adjacent small tables in a corner of the room kept notes of the proceedings but never spoke. The general secretary of the government submitted draft minutes of each meeting to the general secretary of the presidency for review and approval by the president. The minutes were confidential, the only copy being placed in the presidential archives.[26] These staff arrangements helped make the Council a more effective instrument of presidential governance.

Members rarely missed Council meetings. Official travel abroad and genuine serious illness seem to have been the only acceptable excuses for most members. Antoine Pinay was the only apparent exception. Occasionally, he simply preferred to stay home in Saint-Chamond. Presidents missed only four meetings,[27] but prime ministers Pompidou and Chaban-Delmas were absent fairly often. Donnedieu les Varbres, the general secretary of the government, missed only one meeting in ten years, an emergency session called suddenly while he was traveling abroad.[28]

Meetings

Schedule In keeping with the significance the Gaullists sought to give them, Council of Ministers meetings were scheduled to be frequent and regular. Through 1963, the schedule called for meetings at 3 p.m. every Wednesday. In practice, the Council met almost weekly, except for vacation periods, but less than two-fifths of the time (38.3 percent) on Wednesday afternoons. It missed eighteen non-vacation weeks, usually because de Gaulle was traveling. Nine times, it met twice in a single week. (See Table 2).

In January 1964, de Gaulle changed the scheduled meeting time to Wednesdays at 10 a.m.[29] Thereafter, the Council met more regularly. Nearly four-fifths of the meetings were held Wednesday mornings, more than ten times as many as any other half-day. Meetings were canceled or held twice in a week about as often as before. The regularity was broken only during May/June 1968.

TABLE 2.

Frequency and Regularity of Council of Ministers Meetings

	Mon. a.m.	p.m.	Tues. a.m.	p.m.	Weds. a.m.	p.m.	Thurs. a.m.	p.m.	Fri. a.m.	p.m.	Sat. a.m.	p.m.	Total
De Gaulle													
until 1/22/64	2	5	9	12	85	95	16	10	4	9	0	1	248
after 1/21/64	2	1	9	3	197	10	18	1	4	0	4	2	251
Pompidou	0	0	3	0	186	7	13	2	6	1	0	0	218

	Weeks Skipped Vacations	Other	Weeks With Two Meetings	Average Interval	Adjusted Average Interval	% of Weeks with 1 Meeting	Percentage of Weeks with Meetings held On Schedule
	18	9	9	7.4 days	7.7 days	89.8	35.7
	23	13	5	7.7 days	7.8 days	87.2	69.9
	21	4	1	8.0 days	8.0 days	89.7	75.7

+Omitting the second meetings in the weeks when they were held.

Sources: Newspaper clipping file at the *Fondation nationale des sciences politiques* and *Le Monde*.

Pompidou adhered to the same schedule even more closely, 85.3 percent of the meetings being held Wednesday mornings. He canceled fewer meetings and scheduled two meetings in only one week. In all three periods, two or three meetings were skipped in August and early September and one at Christmas.

The frequency and regularity of Council of Ministers meetings suggest the extent to which they were an important, institutionalized part of the Gaullist executive. The rising regularity shows how that institutionalization increased with the passage of time. That, in turn, helped to solidify the presidentialist element of the executive.

Length The Gaullist Council of Ministers consumed substantial and increasing amounts of time. About half of de Gaulle's meetings lasted two to three hours. The remainder were divided equally between longer and shorter sessions. About three-fourths of Pompidou's meetings were 2½ to 3½ hours long. Two-thirds of the remainder were longer and one-third shorter. Most of the latter occurred as he faded into his final illness.

The longest Gaullist meeting lasted six hours on February 4, 1959. It reviewed the last and largest batch of ordinances.[30] Two others lasted five hours. One concerned the 1969 referendum; the other the 1969 devaluation.[31] The shortest took thirty minutes to approve Couve de Murville's inaugural declaration to the National Assembly.[32]

The substantial length suggests substantial business. Substantial business suggests a substantial institution. That the length increased over time suggests that the Council (and presidentialism) became stronger.

Location The Council always met in the president's Elysée Palace, except that it met in the Hotel Matignon the four times that the prime minister presided. Until October 7, 1959, it met in the ground-floor Salon des Ambassadeurs, one of the three rooms it used in the Fourth Republic. Then, de Gaulle moved it to the second-floor Salon des Fêtes, much nearer his office.[33] When Pompidou wanted that room for Pierre Juillet's office, he moved the Council to the Salon Murat, another ground-floor room it used during the Fourth Republic. The frequent moves at the president's behest suggest the extent of the Council's dependence on him.[34]

The Business of the Council of Ministers . Its Basis

Constitutional. Much of the Council's business was required by explicit provisions of the constitution. It had to discuss all government bills and all decisions to pose votes of confidence. (Arts. 39, 48). All ordinances and states of siege had to be decreed there. (Arts. 38, 92, 36). So did all appointments to the highest civil and military service. (Art. 13). The Council was not required to decide these matters collectively. It simply had to discuss or be present. The president decided.

Also, the constitution conferred on "the Government" certain functions that, to the extent they were performed collectively, fell to the Council of

23

Ministers in practice. among them were to "determine and conduct the policies of the nation," to ask parliament for authority to issue ordinances, to propose referenda, to expedite reviews by the Constitutional Council, and to refer certain kinds of matters to the Economic and Social Council. (Arts. 20, 38, 11, 61, 70). If a parliamentarist system had developed, the Cabinet Council would have been the natural locus for such deliberations. As things turned out, they were consigned necessarily to the Council of Ministers.

Other constitutional functions of "the Government,"however, could not conveniently be performed collectively on a routine basis. These included declaring proposed amendments to bills non-receivable; sending bills to special committees; proposing, opposing, or accepting amendments and requiring "blocked votes"; declaring bills urgent and controlling their consideration thereafter; transferring stalled budget bills to the Senate; and setting parliamentary agendas. (Arts. 41, 43, 44, 45, 47, 48). They all involved parliamentary procedural questions, often requiring spot judgments. The general situation might be discussed in the Council of Ministers, but usually only the prime minister or the minister responsible for the bill could make the necessary decisions in catch-as-catch-can consultation with his colleagues and MPs.

Extra-constitutional. The Council of Ministers transacted substantial amounts of business not required by the constitution. The most common type was the presentation of reports and policy statements by ministers. A second type, especially under de Gaulle, was the delivery of instructions by the President of the Republic to the Council members. Finally, informal discussions of politics were held occasionally, especially under Pompidou.

The most frequent reports were those given weekly by the minister of foreign affairs and the minister for the economy and finance. Also, Council members usually gave accounts of their official trips abroad and visits by foreign dignitaries to France. The minister of the interior reported on each French election and the secretary of state for parliamentary affairs did so on each parliamentary session. Appropriate ministers reported on most other major political and governmental events.

Instruction-giving was less frequent. One example was de Gaulle's issuance of homework assignments on Algeria in 1959. Another was his order to the inaugural meeting of Pompidou III that the new ministers submit to him within two months "general reports outlining the activities of their departments and the reform projects and achievements they intend to carry out."[35]

Usually, the discussion of politics was unofficial and unreported. Only twice were such discussions mentioned in "the communiqué." The first occurred during the disorders of 1968 and the second during preparations for the 1973 elections.[36] Unofficial reports suggest that the Pompidou Council turned to politics fairly often in its more relaxed moments.[37]

24

The Types

Four basic types of business were transacted in the Council of Ministers:

Ceremonial. The first meeting of each government was devoted to taking the official group photograph, "pep talks" by president and prime minister, and basking in the glory of being among the annointed few.

Routine. The bulk of most meetings was taken up by the official tasks of the Council as they matured in the normal rhythm of governmental operations. Usually, they had been well-prepared in advance, controversies had been resolved, and the deliberations were smooth and dull.

Emergency. On rare occasions, that rhythm was disrupted in a way that required Council action too urgently to await the next scheduled meeting. One example was Prime Minister Pompidou's amnesty proposal during the student disorders of 1968.[38] However, most emergencies concerned international monetary matters.[39]

Historic. When a Gaullist president wished to consecrate an especially important policy departure, he used a special Council ritual that became part of the magic and drama of Gaullism. The ritual followed these steps: a) The Council members were informed of the terms of the issue in advance and instructed to prepare recommendations; b) during the meeting, the president polled all members individually, giving them full opportunity to present their recommendations, listening attentively, and asking probing questions; c) after all members had spoken, concluding with the prime minister, the president announced his decision and instructed the members to support that policy actively or resign immediately.[40] At least twice, two successive lengthy meetings were required to complete the ritual.

Notable examples of "historic" business are: *1959*, self-determination for Algeria, church-school subsidies, tax reform; *1962*, the Evians Accords, presidential electoral reform[41]; *1968*, the May/June disorders, education reform; *1969*, regionalization and Senate reform; *1972*, expansion of the European Community.

Conclusions. The Council agenda tended to be dominated by business requiring formal, official action. The meetings afforded scant opportunity for the working deliberations that resolve disagreements and settle problems. Those were the tasks of other organs. The purpose of the Council was to satisfy the President that those organs had done their job and to provide him an official forum in which to announce his approval. Because the president emerged as the *de facto* chief executive, his approval was substantive, rather than merely *pro forma*, and the role of the Council was enhanced.

The Conduct of the Meetings. Preparing Them

Council meetings were prepared elaborately. As business items percolated toward the top, the presidential and governmental secretaries called staff and ministerial meetings to ensure their readiness. When those meetings and appropriate telephone consultations seemed conclusive, the general secretary of the government placed the items on a draft agenda that he distributed the Friday evening preceding a Wednesday meeting to all members of the Council and to the general secretary of the presidency. The prime minister was master of the draft until it went to the president.[42]

The prime minister and president discussed the draft agendas at their regular Monday morning meetings and the two general secretaries presented a second draft to the president that afternoon. At that time, the president gave the agenda its final form, often making revisions. That final draft was distributed to all members, with special reminders to those responsible for its items. Finally, the prime minister consulted the president briefly in his office immediately before each Council meeting. Thus, the process gave the prime minister the initiative and the president the final say, unlike its parliamentarist predecessors which gave the prime minister both.

Chairing Them.

The 1958 Constitution provides that "The President of the Republic shall preside over the Council of Ministers." (Art. 9) However, it permits the prime minister, "exceptionally, to replace him as chairman of a Council of Ministers by virtue of an express delegation and for a fixed agenda." (Art. 21) In fact, the presidents almost always presided.

Prime ministers chaired only four meetings. Before de Gaulle underwent prostate surgery in 1964, he prepared the agenda for the April 22 meeting and gave Pompidou the required delegation. Pompidou chaired the meeting and the two general secretaries reported to de Gaulle in the hospital where he signed the decrees it had reviewed.[43] Similar arrangements were made for the meetings of 30 September, 1964, and 17 May, 1968, while de Gaulle was traveling in Latin America and Rumania, respectively.[44] Finally, Prime Minister Messmer presided on 14 February, 1973, when president Pompidou was ill.[45]

At least five other delegations were made or planned for meetings that were cancelled. Two were second meetings during de Gaulle's hospitalization and Latin American trip. Two had been scheduled during de Gaulle's trips to the Soviet Union and Somalia in 1966. Finally, on the evening of 2 April, 1974, three hours before he died, Pompidou signed a delegation for the April 3 meeting.

The handling of the chairmanship underlines the rising dominance of the presidency. Presidents authorized meetings in their absence only when no alternative seemed feasible. Such occasions arose rarely.

The Format

Preliminaries. Most members arrived fifteen or twenty minutes before each meeting. They prepared their papers and water glasses and chatted until the arrival of the president and prime minister was signalled by the entry of a *huissier* in formal attire. Chattering stopped and all members stood at their assigned places. The president and prime minister circled the table slowly, greeting and shaking hands with each member.

Seating was formal and hierarchical by rank of office. The president and prime minister sat directly opposite at the center of each side. Ministers of state and other super-ministers sat to the right and, then, left of the president and, then, of the prime minister. The other full ministers were arranged similarly in descending order of the traditional status of their ministries: justice, foreign affairs, interior, defense, economy and finance, etc. The secretaries of state sat at the ends of the table.[46]

Substantive. The meetings were structured in accordance with the format set in 1947. *Part A* reviewed bills and decrees that had been approved by the ministers directly concerned. If other ministers objected, they were deferred pending resolution of the disagreements. *Part B* consisted of communications by the president, the prime minister, and other ministers and of personnel appointments. *Part C* reviewed preliminary important or controversial proposed bills and decrees. Also, "historic" business and politics were discussed in Part C.

Aftermath. Immediately after each meeting, the official government spokesman used the notes of the general secretaries to prepare a communiqué reporting the official actions of the meeting, in straight-forward, factual phrases. The president reviewed, revised, and approved the communiqué and instructed the spokesman on oral comments to give the press. Information beyond the official communiqué and commentary was privileged. Finally, the general secretariat of the government prepared for the president's signature and distributed to the Council members a summary of the decisions taken.[47]

The Style

The style of discourse in Gaullist Council of Ministers meetings was stiff and formal, especially under de Gaulle. He permitted no smoking or side conversations, although notes were passed and doodling took place. Late arrivals, lengthy presentations, technical arguments or explanations, and interruptions were bad form. Each member reported on his own affairs and avoided his neighbor's. Nothing was debated; little was deliberated; few dissents were expressed; routine meetings were dull.[48] One minister, emerging from his first meeting, asked another with amazed disappointment: "So, that is how it goes?" [49] Another first-timer exclaimed, in astonishment: "No one said anything." Still another minister called the meetings "Funeral wakes with a difference: the corpse speaks."[50]

Nevertheless, de Gaulle did try to encourage discussion. He told new members: "You are not only minister of posts (for example), but a member of the government. You have the right and duty to express your views on every problem."[51] When some bold soul followed this instruction, de Gaulle lis-

27

tened attentively and spoke politely, but rarely heeded the advice.[52] Moreover, his austere presence intimidated more than his words emboldened. Also, Prime Minister Pompidou discouraged maverick comments, for they tended to disrupt the orderly presentation of business that he had arranged, often with great difficulty.[53]

President Pompidou's Council meetings were somewhat more relaxed. He allowed smoking and set the example. Ministers could leave the table to refill their water glasses. Discussion was freer, though side conversations still brought black looks from the president. Reports were presented more casually. Ministers were more prone to poach on their colleagues' domains, moves well designed to enliven meetings with debate, even squabbles.[54] Pompidou's more casual and open style lengthened the meetings. However, his control was no less complete than de Gaulle's. The agenda, the flow of business, the decisions were his as thoroughly as they had been de Gaulle's.[55]

Monologue was the standard form of discourse in both administrations. The elaborate preparations for each meeting discouraged questions and dissent. Members usually spoke only to present their reports. However, the monologues varied greatly in quality. Couve de Murville's delivery was barely audible in an austere, soporific monotone, reporting only what the daily press had published already. Nevertheless, one of his colleagues—who sat next to him—said that he added "one word, one fact, one opinion which held all of substance."[56] Giscard d'Estaing was famous for the brilliance of content and presentation of his economic reports. Even de Gaulle admired them. He was confident, competent, articulate, perfect master of his vast domain, displaying his genius with swift, precise, authoritative flourishes that sparkled with statistics, facts, and analytic sallies.[57] André Malraux's rare interventions spellbound his colleagues with his literary elegance, his sense of drama, and his resonant voice.[58] Under Pompidou, Maurice Druon took Malraux's literary and stentorian place briefly.[59]

Members differed, also, in readiness to offer dissent. In the early years, Pinay, Soustelle, Sudreau, Cornut-Gentille, and Pisani were noted for brashness.[60] Under Pompidou, Debré, Giscard d'Estaing, and Duhamel had similar reputations.[61] On the other hand, Guichard never spoke and rarely moved.[62]

A Gaullist president was challenged directly and forcefully only once in a Council of Ministers meeting. In November 1959, Minister of Finance Antoine Pinay responded to de Gaulle's comment that "Europe must organize its defense." The exchange requires reproduction in full to show why no one emulated Pinay. Two months later, he left the government:

> Pinay: M. *le Président* (not *Mon général* as de Gaulle preferred), how do you reconcile this necessity, for the Europeans to provide for their own defense, with the speech that you just delivered at the *Ecole militaire:* national defense must be

French? If I understand, you have condemned the very principle of NATO.

De Gaulle: M. le ministre des Finances is interested in problems of foreign policy?

Pinay: Yes, I am interested in problems of foreign policy. And, as few of my colleagues are informed about your speech, I will read the most interesting passages on which I hope that we may receive, if you will be so good, some light (Pinay then read several key paragraphs from the speech.) Our allies are in consternation over your speech. Do you believe that, financially, technically, and militarily, we have the means to defend ourselves? For my part, I answer *no* at once, as far as the economic and financial domain is concerned. No, we do not have the means to defend ourselves alone. In a period of intercontinental missiles, it is senseless to pretend to act in isolation. We do not have the real possibility to create a striking force and we must prevent the Americans from leaving at all costs.

De Gaulle: Of course, our defense, the establishment of the means, our conception of the conduct of war, must be combined with those of other countries. Our strategy must be coordinated with the strategy of the others. On the battlefields, it is infinitely probable that we will be side by side with our allies. But each should have his part to himself.

The discussion moved to other topics. Then, de Gaulle turned back. He reminded Pinay that when de Gaulle had removed part of the French Mediterranean fleet from NATO command and sent memoranda to Eisenhower and Macmillan proposing to reorganize NATO, *"Monsieur le ministre des finances did not raise objections."*

Pinay: I beg your pardon, *Monsieur le President,* I learned by newspaper that you were withdrawing part of the French fleet.... As to the memorandum to President Eisenhower and Mr. Macmillan, it is correct that you mentioned, in Council of Ministers, the sending of that text. Perhaps, you even said a few words about it, but you did not disclose its contents and, in any case, your decision had been taken.

Monsieur le Président, do not look for cover. You are the one who taught me the laws of ministerial solidarity.[63] All ministers are together. Ministers who are in the minority on a question yield or resign. I do not have the same conception of ministerial solidarity as you do. Decisions must be deliberated, discussed, taken in common. But we are confronted by decisions that have been taken already.

I do not want to sound you out on your intentions. I am not the depository of your thoughts. I have only one question to ask you, simple, clear, and precise. You declared at the *Ecole militaire:* 'The system of integration is over.' What does that mean?

De Gaulle, rising: Thank you, M. Pinay. Gentlemen, the meeting is adjourned.[64]

Though Pinay's persistence was unique, more moderate disagreement was not unusual. Debate was more impassioned on Algeria under de Gaulle than it had been on Indochina or Tunisia under the Fourth Republic.[65] Also, serious dissent was expressed on such issues as the 1959 school-aid bill, various agricultural issues, the 1968 university reforms, the miners' strike, and the reorganization of the Paris region.

Understandably, such dissent was more forthcoming when the presidents solicited opinions directly from individual ministers. The consideration of "historic" matters, as mentioned above, provided the most noteworthy occasions for such opportunities. However, both presidents used the device less systematically at other meetings.

Genuine deliberation was rare, if not non-existent. The 3½ hour emergency meeting in November 1968 may have been as close as a Gaullist Council came to working out a major decision collectively. The international financial community agreed that devaluation was inevitable that weekend and the French government had only its size to decide.[66]

Finance Minister Ortoli opened the discussion by reporting on his negotiations in the European Community and listing three possible decisions: a large devaluation of about fifteen percent, a small one of about ten percent, or no devaluation. He expressed no choice at that time, but later made clear his preference for no devaluation. Then, de Gaulle asked each minister to state his preference. He began with a minister whom he knew would oppose devaluation eloquently. As each minister spoke, de Gaulle, "serene and relaxed," asked questions and commented. If a minister was unclear or equivocal, he asked: "Then, are you for or against the devaluation?" Only Marcellin favored devaluation.

Immediately after the meeting, de Gaulle announced his decision not to devalue. Clearly, this had been his preference at the outset, but persuasive arguments to the contrary by most of the ministers might have changed his mind.

The presidents' polling of the Council should not be mistaken for voting. Though they might tally the results, they did not feel bound by them. For instance, only four of twenty-four members in the Chaban-Delmas government favored the posing of a vote of confidence. Yet, Pompidou approved the request.[67] Also, more than half the Council opposed reorganization of the Paris region, but de Gaulle approved it without change.[68]

The manner of concluding an item of Council business was invariable. When the president believed that a discussion had proceeded far enough, he announced the Council's decision that was, in fact, *his* decision or said that he would announce the decision after the meeting. In Pompidou's words: *"C'est moi qui décide."*[69]

Conclusion

The Council of Ministers under the Gaullist presidents became the chief collective body in the political executive, yet its real importance was difficult to assess. Most meetings were formal and routine with very little serious deliberation. Yet, its review was the culminating step in the process of governmental decision-making for the most important policy matters in the executive. It attracted substantial serious attention from the presidents and prime ministers and was an essential part of each minister's week.

Furthermore, this key executive institution became a major tool of the presidents. In earlier republics, presidents had chaired the Council formally, but, in fact, prime ministers had exercised greater control over its business. De Gaulle and Pompidou transformed formal leadership into effective and virtually complete control. To use Walter Bagehot's terminology, the Council was converted from a "dignified" to an "efficient" institution of government and became one means by which the presidentialist aspects of the Fifth Republic came to prevail over the parliamentarist features.

OTHER COUNCILS AND COMMITTEES

Introduction

Committees rule democracies. No modern legislature or political executive can operate expertly at its most general level. Presidents, prime ministers, cabinets, parliaments must rely on specialized committees to prepare their decisions.

The collective elements of the Gaulllist political executive, then, included a committee system—standing and *ad hoc* committees in both the presidential and prime ministerial spheres. Elaborate and important committee systems developed in both areas. Changes were especially significant in the presidential sphere. The establishment and growth of that presidential committee system may have been one of the key managerial factors that made presidentialism possible.

Background

Very few presidential committees existed in the Fourth Republic. The only ones of consequence were created by the 1946 Constitution. It made the president of the Republic chairman of the High Council and Committee of National Defense (Art. 33), the High Council of the Judiciary (Art. 34), the High Council of the French Union (Art. 65), and the Constitutional Committee. However, the High Council of National Defense met only rarely;[70] the High Council of the French Union did not come into existence for five years and then met only twice;[71] and the Constitutional Committee met only once.[72]

The High Council of the Judiciary was the most important presidential committee of the Fourth Republic, being responsible for ensuring the discipline and independence of French judges. It consisted of twelve other members (two appointed by the President) plus the minister of justice as vice chairman. It decided by majority vote, with the president having a casting ballot (Art. 83) and a virtual veto on appointments and promotions. Also, he exercised the right of pardon in the Council, though he was not bound by its judgment.[73]

The only other presidential standing committee of significance was the Committee of National Defense which was composed of appropriate ministers and high-ranking military officers. However, the president's chairmanship was quite formal. The prime minister controlled its composition and staff and "directs (it), under the high authority of the President of the Republic."[74] In fact, the president was expected to refrain from expressing opinions,[75] though, on occasion, he did.[76] In any case, the Committee never functioned very smoothly or effectively.[77]

In addition to those councils, Auriol called some *ad hoc* committee meetings on a few serious foreign affairs problems. However, they had little consequence and were not repeated by his successor.[78] Otherwise, no presidential committees existed in the Fourth Republic.

In contrast, prime ministerial committees were quite common in the Fourth Republic. Coalition politics thwarted an early effort to establish a system of standing committees in the government. Therefore, most of them were *ad hoc*, although some did become permanent, especially those dealing with defense and economic affairs. Usually, prime ministers appointed them to prepare matters for the Council of Ministers, to try to resolve disagreements that had surfaced in the Council of Ministers or Cabinet Council, or to coordinate the implementation of governmental decisions. Such committees were mentioned frequently in Council of Ministers meetings. However, the fragility of the governmental coalitions rendered their work quite tentative and in the latter years of the republic, an effort was made to give the committees broader bases by working through mixed governmental-parliamentary-partisan *ad hoc* committees called "round tables."[79]

In summary, then, presidential committees had very little importance in the Fourth Republic and prime ministerial committees were used much, but with mixed results. In contrast, parliamentary committees were notorious for their overwhelming strength. The reversal of that power hierarchy contributed greatly to the development of a structural basis for presidentialism in the Fifth Republic.

Presidential Committees

Amount of Activity

Although the amount of committee activity was great during the Gaullist administrations, it cannot be measured precisely. Many of the meetings were so informal that no records were kept. Also, only fragmentary data on the meetings have been published and neither of the secretariats has released additional information.

Nevertheless, the available material seems to provide a sufficiently solid basis for a generally accurate description. With respect to the presidential committees, called *"conseils restreints,"* it suggests that de Gaulle presided over an average of about 5.25 such councils per month and that Pompidou chaired many fewer, perhaps as few as about one per month on the average.[80]

Standing Committees

All presidential standing committees were created formally by official texts, constitutional provisions, laws, or decrees:

The High Council and Committee of Defense. The 1958 Constitution provided (Art. 15) that the president "shall preside over the higher councils and committees of defense." A 1959 ordinance and a decree later that year spelled out the details, creating a Higher Council of Defense, a Defense Committee, and an Inner Defense Committee *(comité de défense restreint)*, all chaired by the president, though he might delegate that authority to the prime minister for the Inner Committee.[81] The Higher Council contained as many as fifty members, including the prime minister, appropriate ministers, high-ranking military officers, civil servants, and private persons. The Defense Committee members were the prime minister; the ministers of foreign affairs, armies, interior, and finance and economic affairs; and such other ministers as the president might invite. The chairman of the joint chiefs of staff, the chiefs of staff of the three services, the general secretary of national defense, and the president's personal military chief of staff also attended its meetings and a member of the Elysée military staff served as recording secretary. The composition of the Inner Committee was decided by the prime minister who also called its meetings.[82] A "General Secretariat of National Defense" reported to the prime minister. In theory, the Higher Council undertook studies of defense problems for the government. The Defense Committee made "decisions on the general conduct of defense." The Inner Committee made "decisions on the military conduct of defense."

In practice, defense policy was made by the president in the Defense Committee and was reiterated by him in the Council of Ministers.[83] The High Council was too large and inappropriately constituted. The Inner Committee hardly functioned, having been designed as a war council for major international hostilities. The Defense Committee met about once a month during the Algerian war and four or five times a year thereafter.[84]

Initially, some doubt existed as to whether the president or prime minister was pre-eminent in defense policy. However, the committee structure favored the president. Decrees in 1960 and 1962 removed that ambiguity.[85] Of course, de Gaulle's personal qualities and background expedited the clarification, but the situation did not change appreciably under Pompidou.

Council of Algerian Affairs This institutionalized presidential council was created officially by decree during the "Barricades Crisis" of 1960, but it had developed out of earlier *ad hoc* meetings of appropriate officials on the Algerian problem.[86] Its purpose was to give the president the means to have an official, direct role in resolving the Algerian problem without resort to Article 16 emergency powers.[87] Therefore, it played an important role in French governmental affairs.

The founding decree designated as members the president, the prime minister, and the ministers of the interior and of the armies. It authorized the general delegate of the government in Algeria, the general secretary of Algerian affairs, the chief of staff of national defense, and the commanding general in Algeria to attend its meetings and empowered the president to include other members of the government. De Gaulle's principal staff advisor on Algeria says that the ministers of finance and foreign affairs were members also.[88] The general secretariats of the president of the Republic and for Algerian affairs provided the staff and administrative support. De Gaulle gave the general delegate the very unusual permanent delegation of authority to convene the other members, except the prime minister.[89] After the 1962 Evians Accords were signed, the minister of state for Algerian affairs and the high commissioner of the French Republic in Algeria replaced the ministers of the interior and the armies and the high functionaries "authorized" to attend no longer did so.[90] However, the Council met very little thereafter.[91]

The Council's mandate was to "make the decisions concerning Algeria so far as they are not taken in the Council of Ministers." In practice,

> Without replacing the Council of Ministers, the Committee prepared its deliberations and carried them further. Within it or after having consulted its members, General de Gaulle took most of his important decisions concerning Algeria.[92]

Among those decisions was the transfer of certain senior officials, the dissolution of some dissident defense units in Algeria, the suppression of the Psychological Warfare Bureau, reforms in the Algerian system of justice, the principal economic and financial policies for Algeria, the transfer of the general delegation outside Algiers, the preparation of the Evians negotiations, the creation and oversight of the Algerian *commissions d'élus*, the preparation of the 1961 referendum, and the implementation of its provisions.[93]

Council for African and Madagascan Affairs. This committee was an attempt to salvage something from the collapse of the ill-fated Franco-African "Community" of the 1958 Constitution (Title XII).[94] By an exchange of letters in 1961, Prime Minister Debré and the president of the Community Senate acknowledged officially the demise of the original Community institutions.[95] Then, de Gaulle issued executive orders converting the general secretariat of the Community into a "General secretariat to the presidency of the Republic for the Community and African and Madagascan Affairs"[96] and creating this Council.[97]

The members of the Council were the prime minister, the ministers of foreign affairs and of cooperation, the secretary of state for foreign affairs, the general secretaries of the presidency and to the presidency for the Community, and other members of the government and high civil and military functionaries invited by the president. The Council was charged with making "the decisions concerning the relations of the Republic with the African and Madagascan states that issued from the former French Union insofar as they are not taken in the Council of Ministers."

The Council fared no better than its predecessor institutions. Relations between France and her former colonies became bilateral very quickly. Also, the secretariat and the successive ministers that dealt with the "Community" states usually operated more efficiently than the Council. By 1964, the Council was virtually moribund. It met on March 23, 1965, for the last time.[98]

Council of Foreign Affairs. Still another presidential council, the Council of Foreign Affairs, was announced in March 1960.[99] De Gaulle chaired its first meeting and the foreign minister and general secretaries of the presidency and of the foreign ministry attended also. This Council completed a network of presidential committees for the policy areas in the "reserved sector" (defense, Algeria, Community, foreign affairs).

However, the Council seems to have died aborning. No founding decree was issued. No later meetings were announced. Its business seems to have wound up in the Defense Committee.[100]

High Council of the Judiciary. The 1958 Constitution followed its 1946 predecessor by placing the president of the Republic in the chair for the High Council of the Judiciary (Art. 65). However, the first president of the Court of Cassation was to take the chair when it acted as "disciplinary council for the judges." Also, the minister of justice, as vice president of the Council "may preside in place of the president of the Republic."

Despite the president's elimination from the process of disciplining judges, his authority actually increased substantially over matters within the purview of the Council. He became "the protector of the independence of the judicial authority" to be "assisted by the Council." He acquired the right to appoint all nine members of the Council (with some restrictions), rather than two of twelve as in the Fourth Republic. Finally, his authority over judicial appointments and promotions was increased at the expense of the Council.[101] Also, he retained the powers of pardon and reprieve, the Council having a consultative voice only.[102]

Ad Hoc Committees

Except the institutionalized councils described above, all Gaullist presidential committees seem to have been *ad hoc*.[103] The presidents called meetings as occasion required and invited participants as they deemed appropriate. Their appearance and growth in the Fifth Republic helped the presidency develop a decision-making infrastructure to tilt the regime toward presidentialism.

The *ad hoc* committees always included the prime minister, and, usually, the finance minister, because finance touched so many policy areas. The most frequent other participants were the ministers of foreign affairs and defense. High functionaries attended meetings on matters for which they were responsible. For instance, the planning commissioner attended most meetings on economic and social affairs.[104]

Ad hoc committees met four or five times a month under de Gaulle and about half as often under Pompidou. Initially, they had no regular schedule, but Prime Minister Pompidou tried to confine them to Tuesdays and Thursdays.

Meeting calls were initiated by the presidents or prime ministers or by members of the Elysée staff who used them to influence the ministries. Each meeting was organized by a technical councilor on the presidential staff in consultation with the prime ministerial staff. He prepared the agenda, collected necessary supporting materials, and distributed them in advance to all participants. He attended the meeting, took minutes, distributed them to the members, and was responsible for follow-up.[105]

The *ad hoc* committees met in the same room as the Council of Ministers with much the same formality, though their smaller size made them less austere. The prime minister directed the presentation of business and the president arbitrated. De Gaulle "listened much and well, asked for explanations, provoked confrontations by posing hypotheses that did not always represent his own views. He concealed neither his ignorance nor his uncertainty."[106]

Ad hoc committee meetings had three main purposes: 1) *Information*. The officials who were mainly responsible for a matter explained it to the president. 2) *Decision*. The president resolved disagreements among officials when the prime minister had failed. His decisions were submitted to the Council of Ministers for ratification later. 3) *Directive*. The president impressed upon his aides his insistence that they ensure execution of his high priority projects.

Ad hoc committees met only for Algeria, defense, and foreign affairs during the Debré premiership. Thereafter, they met in all areas of policy,[107] although they tended to concentrate on the "presidential sector" and the economy. The most frequent topics were foreign affairs, the Common Market, the State budget, the economy, international monetary matters, and education. Other examples from de Gaulle's administration were aeronautical and space questions, atomic energy, computers, agriculture, population, the Paris region, administrative reform, the ORTF, regional reform, and the judicial system.[108]

These councils rarely dealt with matters of capital importance, though their cumulative significance may have been crucial in the evolution of the regime. The decisions on self-determination for Algeria, the 1962 constitutional referendum, the withdrawal from NATO, and the aborted 1968 referendum were not taken in such meetings, though their implementation may have been discussed there. Their domain lay "at the junction of the political and the administrative."[109] In short, they gave the presidents an important instrument for ensuring that their decisions in the Council of Ministers were prepared properly and implemented loyally.

Prime Ministerial Committees

Amount of Activity

Committees chaired by the prime ministers or members of their staffs were even more active than the presidential committees. Debré and Pompidou chaired 599 committee meetings during the first seven years of the regime, an average of 7.11 per month, and members of their staffs chaired another 1,742, 16.8 per month.[110] The prime ministerial meetings showed no consistent trend in frequency, but the staff-chaired meetings became much more numerous with the passage of time. (See Table 3)

Standing Committees

As with the presidential standing committees, most prime ministerial standing committees were established by official texts. Their institutionalized character was enhanced further by assigning some of them offices and substantial staffs. Ten such committees existed in 1974, including:[111]

Interministerial Economic Committee. This committee was created by de Gaulle while he headed the Provisional Government after World War II[112] and was active and important throughout the Fourth Republic, with meetings scheduled weekly.[113]Under Debré, meetings on economic matters were scheduled every Tuesday, though they were not necessarily those of the Interministerial Economic Committee.[114] After that, the official committee declined in importance, meeting only a few times per year and being replaced by *ad hoc* economic committees, except that the standing committee was revived briefly while Debré was minister of the economy and finance in 1966–67.[115]

While Debré was premier, the standing committee was the object of a tug of war between a prime minister who "strove to be the real Minister of the National Economy"[116] and ministers who insisted on continuing the tradition that the rue de Rivoli rule the economics domain with an iron hand. The traditional view prevailed while Pinay was minister of finance, but the control of Wilfrid Baumgartner, who replaced him, was limited, though still substantial. If the committee's agenda contained only technical matters, Baumgartner presided, but if its business had political implications, Debré took over. However, Debré delegated to Baumgartner authority to "coordinate" the activities of the "technical" ministries of labor, industry, and agriculture and to arbitrate economic and financial disagreements among the other ministries.[117] Also, at that time, the committee was responsible for wage questions in the public sector.

Interministerial Committees on the Plan. Pompidou put new curbs on the finance ministry very soon after he became prime minister. He transferred the General Planning Commission from it to his office[118] and used its authority over long-term policies to control the short-term policies of the ministry. Four years later, he went a step further by replacing the *Interministerial Committee on the Plan for Economic and Social Development,* which had supervised the

37

TABLE 3.

Number of Committee Meetings Chaired by Prime Ministers and their Staffs

	1959	1960	1961	1962	1963	1964	1965	1966	1967	1968	1969	1970	1971	1972	1973	1974
PM	33	57	118	88	87	100	116	129	118	94	92	147	121	100	73	82
Staff	23	61	142	154	283	394	356	329	318	322	307	530	592	583	501	534

Sources: Dulong, *op. cit.*; Debré and Debré, *op. cit.*

Commission since 1953,[119] with three new committees.[120] He chaired all three, as he had their predecessor. The other members of the *Interministerial Committee charged with Problems of Administering the Plan* were the minister of state for the civil service, the minister of the economy and finance, the secretary of state for the budget, and the general commissioner of planning. The *Interministerial Committee charged with Public Enterprises* had the same membership, except that it omitted civil service and added the ministers of the armies, of industry, of facilities (*équipement*) and of scientific research. The *Interministerial Committee charged with Private Enterprises* was composed of the ministers of the economy and finance, of scientific research, and of social affairs; the general delegate for territorial improvement; and the general commissioner of planning. All three committees had high civil servant "*rapporteurs*."

Standing Interministerial Committee for Territorial Improvement and Regional Action. The second of Pompidou's "parallel" committees began as two committees created by Debré in 1960: the *Interministerial Standing Committee for the Paris Region*[121] and the *Interministerial Standing Committee of Regional Action and Territorial Improvement.*[122] The latter committee absorbed the former in 1963.[123] The merged committee was composed of the ministers of interior, finance and economic affairs, public works and transportation, industry, agriculture, labor, and construction, and the secretaries of state for finance and for domestic commerce. The General Commissioner of Planning attended some meetings. The committee had a secretariat.[124]

Pompidou attached the committee to an administrative agency that he created at the same time: the *Delegation for Territorial Improvement and Regional Action.*[125] The Delegation, in turn, was attached to his office. The delegate chaired the committee and had a staff of about twenty persons.

The mission of the committee was to advise the delegate whose task was to coordinate the work of the various ministers and other governmental agencies insofar as they affected "territorial improvement" and regional planning. He had the authority to require ministers to clear their programs with him, to investigate the investment programs of their ministers, to arbitrate among them on certain budget disputes, and to monitor the elaboration of the Plan. Certain key services in some ministries were placed at his disposal, though not under his direction, and some interministerial services were assigned to his administration. The Delegation had a substantial budget to promote its objectives by subsidizing the budgets of various ministries.[126]

Interministerial Committee on Tourism. The General Commission on Tourism had existed since 1935.[127] Soon after Debré became prime minister, he reorganized it to make it an instrument of control.[128] He created and chaired the committee, whose other members were the minister of state for cultural affairs and the ministers of finance and economic affairs, public works and transportation, foreign affairs, and the interior, with the general commissioner of tourism as a non-voting member. Other persons attended by invitation of the prime minister. When Pompidou became prime minister, he transferred the general commission from the ministry of public works and transportation to his office.[129] The overlap of tourism with the concerns of such ministries as transportation, public health, construction, commerce, foreign affairs, interior, and cultural affairs made the committee a useful prime ministerial tool for control and coordination.

Interministerial Committee for Questions of European Economic Cooperation. This was another Fourth Republic committee.[130] Its members were the prime minister as chair; the ministers of foreign affairs, of finance, economic affairs, and planning; and of industry and commerce: "the member of the Government charged with European affairs and all interested ministers." The committee had its own secretariat. Two "interministerial technical committees" were attached to it to deal with the implementation of the EEC, ECSC, and Euratom treaties. The finance minister chaired the EEC/ECSC committee and the prime minister or the minister charged with atomic questions chaired the other. In 1964, Pompidou brought all three committees more directly under his authority by transferring their secretariat to his office.[131] Because so many ministries were affected by European economic integration, this arrangement strengthened prime ministerial control.

Other Standing Committees. Several other prime ministerial standing committees existed during the Gaullist period. Their value for control and coordination is suggested by their titles: Scientific and Technical Research, Vocational Training and Social Advancement, Industrial Policy, Employment, the Family and Population, Atomic Energy, Protection of Nature and the Environment, Equitation, Air Space, Highway Safety, For Participation of Workers in the Growth in the Capital of Enterprises Due to Self-Financing, Foreign Investments, For Information.[132] Of course, not all were chaired by the prime minister, but all served his purposes of control and coordination.

Significance. Prime ministerial standing committees were more numerous, active, and important in the Fifth Republic than in the Fourth Republic. They were developed by Debré and even more by Pompidou as devices for centralizing control of the government in the prime minister. Not only did the prime ministers use them to work with ministers on matters where their authority converged, but also, they attached to them administrative agencies with independent authority paralleling, supplementing, and rivaling that of the ministries. Furthermore, the committees frequently included high civil servants, as well as ministers. Debré preferred to have high civil servants present, because, then, he "was more confident that the decisions would be implemented."[133]

Ad hoc Committees.

The second basic type of prime ministerial committee was the *ad hoc* committee which usually seems to have performed quite a different kind of function than the standing committee. The latter were instruments for coordination and control. The former were means for the prime minister to consult collectively, to arbitrate disagreements among his colleagues in the government, and to reach policy decisions.

The composition of the *ad hoc* committees was highly flexible. Their members were invited by the prime minister on the basis that their presence would contribute to the search for a solution. They included members of the government, high civil and military functionaries, and persons from the private sector. A prime ministerial staff member served as scribe. A presidential staff member attended all prime ministerial meetings for the purpose of keeping the Elysée informed. Debré resisted this intrusion, but Pompidou accepted it as an essential element of the character of the regime. Also, he had two very practical reasons for favoring that practice. First, it seemed to him important for the cohesion of the relationship between the presidency and the government. Secondly, it permitted him to assume that a decision reached in one of his committees had been accepted by the president if he did not hear to the contrary within two days.[134]

At least during the Pompidou prime ministership, most committee meetings lasted from one to two hours. Pompidou called on each member to express his views, then summarized them and stated his own conclusions. He spent four or five hours a day in such meetings.[135]

The list of topics covered by prime ministerial committees is virtually as long as that of the areas of governmental policy. Thus, to present a sampling here would serve little purpose. Also, no attempt can be made to discuss the even more diffuse subject of the interministerial working groups or *ad hoc* meetings not chaired by the prime minister.

CONCLUSIONS

The collective leadership elements of the Gaullist political executive evolved in ways that contribute importantly to an understanding of the character of the regime. The parliamentarist Cabinet Council withered away, despite the first prime minister's repeated efforts to keep it alive. The presidentialist Council of Ministers became more significant as a deliberative body and more thoroughly dominated by the presidents. Presidents and prime ministers developed a complex and active system of standing and *ad hoc* committees and councils. That change was especially dramatic for the presidency, which had lacked entirely such instruments of power before 1958. However, even on the prime ministerial side, the new growth had a very substantial centralizing effect.

All of those changes worked to bring governmental activities more closely under the president's control. Of course, that reduced necessarily the effectiveness of parliamentary oversight of the executive. A constitutional consequence of those changes was the dissolution of much of the original ambiguity in the system. Combined with such other significant factors as societal changes, the introduction of popular election of the President, the unifying effect of the Algerian war, the personalities of the presidents, and the emergence of a homogeneous parliamentary majority, those structural developments gave the political executive the autonomy necessary for it to emerge as a truly coordinate branch of government. They helped tilt the regime decisively toward presidentialism.

NOTES

1. Laws of 31 August, 1871, Art. 2, and 25 February, 1875, Art. 6.
2. *Documents d'études*, no. 9, October 1970 (*La III République*); Andrée Martin-Pannetier, *Institutions et Vie Politique Françaises de 1789 á nos jours*, L.G.D.J., Paris, 1971, 226 pp., p. 52. However, as late as 1913, President of the Republic Raymond Poincaré said that the "Council of Ministers deals with the more important business, the Cabinet Council with current questions of internal politics, the former meeting about twice as much as the latter." Poincaré, *How France is Governed*, T. Fisher Unwin, London, 1913, 375 pp., p. 197.
3. Serge Arné, *Le Président du conseil des ministres sous la IVe République*, Pichon and Durand-Auzias, Paris, 1962, 462 pp., p. 91; Marcel Martin, ed., *Les Institutions politiques de la France*, La documentation française, Paris, 1959, 532 pp., pp. 234-35; Philip M. Williams, *Crisis and Compromise*, Longmans, London, 1964, 546 pp., pp. 196 n., 204.
4. Interview with Michel Debré, 10 July, 1978.
5. See, for instance, his speech to the Council of State, August 27, 1958, William G. Andrews, ed., *European Political Institutions*, Van Nostrand, Princeton, 2nd ed., 1966, 587 pp., pp. 43-55.
6. *Le Monde*, January 11/12, 1959
7. Interview with Michel Debré, 10 July, 1978.
8. *Le Monde*, 20 March, 1959.
9. For accounts of other 1959 meetings, see *Le Monde*, 29 January, 3 February, 19/20 April, 15 May, 26 August, 6 October, 4, 8 December, 1959; *Combat*, 18 June, 1959. Other meetings may have been held, but not reported in the press.
10. *Le Monde*, 24 February, 1960.
11. *Le Monde, 2 March, 1960*.
12. *Le Monde*, 22 March, 24 April, 14 July, 10 November, 1960; 25 January, 29 August, 1961; *Combat*, 6, 7 April, 1960, 17 April, 1962; *Le Figaro*, 18 April, 16 May, 1961; Pierre Avril, *Le Régime politique de la Ve République*, L.G.D.J., Paris, 2nd. ed., 1967, 437 pp., p. 245. However, Pompidou did hold business luncheons to which all members of the Government were invited. Dulong, *op. cit.*, p. 142n.
13. *Le Monde*, 29 April, 16 May, 20, 21 June, 1969.
14. *Le Monde*, 4, 8 December 1959.
15. *Le Monde*, 25, 26 August, 1959; *La Croix*, 27 August, 1959.
16. *Le Monde*, 29 April, 1960.
17. *Le Monde*, 24 February, 2 March, 1960.
18. Patrice Verrier, *Les services de la présidence de la république*, PUF, Paris, 1971, 96 pp., p. 45.
19. Charles de Gaulle, *Memoirs of Hope: Renewal and Endeavor*, Simon and Schuster, New York, 1971, 392 pp., p. 272. That decision may have been motivated partly by lingering resentment over his exclusion from the Reynaud government's Council of Ministers when he was an undersecretary of state in 1940. Michel Debré and Jean-Louis Debré, *Le pouvoir politique*, Seghers, Paris, 1976, 159 pp., p. 66.

The Collective Political Executive

20.   J.L. Bodiguel, M.-Ch. Kessler, M. Sineau, "Cent ans de Secrétariats d'Etats'', pp. 51-96, in Institut française des Sciences administratives, *Les Superstructures des administrations centrales*, Ed. Cujas, Paris, 1973, 367 pp., p. 54; Claude Dulong, *A L'Elysée au temps de Charles de Gaulle*, Hachette, Paris, 1974, 265 pp.; *Le Figaro*, 26 June, 1969; Victor Silvera, "La structure du septième gouvernment de la Vème République'', pp. 444-52, in *Revue administrative*, July/August 1969, p. 445.

21.   Silvera, *loc. cit.*, p. 445.

22.   Bodiguel *et. al., loc cit.*, p. 55. For instance, no meeting was held in the first five months of 1971.

23.   Victor Silvera, "La structure du septième gouvernement de la Vème République'', pp. 484-92 in *Revue administrative*, September/October

24.   *Le Monde*, 3, 4 March, 1974. In fact, the Council of Ministers membership under Messmer III was seventeen and would have been thirty with the secretaries of state.

25.   Jean Massot, *La Présidence de la République en France*, La Documentation Française, Paris, 1977, 234 pp., 33.

26.   Dulong, *op. cit.*, pp. 121-22; Pierre Viansson-Ponté, "Les pouvoirs parallèles,'' pp. 25-31 in *L'Evénement*, March 1966, p. 30.

27.   On 22 April, 1964, when de Gaulle underwent surgery; on 30 September, 1964, during his South American trip; on 17 May, 1968, during his Rumanian trip, and on 14 February, 1973, when Pompidou was "suffering from the flu.'' Verrier, *op. cit.*, p. 45n; *Le Monde*, 18 May, 1968, 15 February, 1973.

28.   *Le Figaro*, 11 March, 1974.

29.   *Combat*, 22 January, 1964.

30.   *Combat* and *Information*, 5 February, 1959.

31.   *Le Monde*, 28 February and 30 August, 1969; *Articles et documents* (La documentation française), Nos. 1,947 and 1,973.

32.   *Le Monde*, 14, 15 July, 1968.

33.   *Le Monde*, 8 October, 1959; *Combat*, 13 August, 1959; *Chronique des jours moroses*, p. 31; Dulong, *op. cit.* p. 119.

34.   *Combat*, 26 June, 1969; Jean-Pierre Farkas, "Comment l'Elysée gouverne,'' pp. 31-34, 75, in *Paris-Match*, 19 January, 1974, p. 33; *Le Monde*, 25 June, 1969.

35.   *Le Monde*, 19, 25 August, 1959; 13 January, 1966.

36.   *Combat*, 3 June, 1968; *L'Aurore*, January 4, 1973.

37.   *Chronique des jours moroses*, pp. 280-281.

38.   Official communiqué, 21 May, 1968. *La documentation française.*

39.   *Le Monde*, 16 June, 1959, 26 November, 1968, 30 August, 1969, 20, 21 January, 1974; Raymond Tournoux, *Journal secret: Une année pas comme les autres*, Plon, Paris, 1975, 342 pp., pp. 27-28.

40.   Only one minister ever chose to resign—Sudreau on the October 1962 referendum.

41.   For the texts of the ministers' remarks on this issue, see J.R. Tournoux, *La Tragédie du général*, Plon, Paris, 1967, 697 pp., pp., 631-47.

42.   Gérard Belorgey, *Le gouvernement et l'administration de la France*, Colin, Paris, 1967, 451 pp., p. 111; Edgard Pisani, *Le Général indivis*, Albin Michel, Paris, 1974, 251 pp., p. 128; Dulong, *op. cit.*, p. 119-20; Massot, *op. cit.*, pp. 174-75.

43.   Massot, *op. cit.*, p. 175; Buron, *op. cit.*, p. 219; Belorgey, *op. cit.*, p. 111.

44.   *Le Monde*, 1 October, 1964, 18 May, 1968.

45.   *Le Monde*, 16, 18/19 February, 1973.

46.   *Chronique des jours moroses*, pp. 174, 217; Robert Buron, *Le plus beau des métiers*, Plon, Paris, 1963, 252 pp., 218-19; Dulong, *op. cit.*, pp. 120-121; *Le Figaro*, 8 October, 1973.

47.   *Le Figaro*, 8 October, 1973; *L'Organisation du Travail gouvernemental et les services du premier ministre*, La documentation française, Paris, September 1972; Massot, *op. cit.*, p. 117.

48.   Pisani, *op. cit.*, p. 131; Jacques Soustelle, *Vingt ans de Gaullisme*, J'ai lu, Paris, 1971, 432 pp., p. 181; Jacques Soustelle, *L'espérance trahie*, Ed. de l'Alma, Paris, 1962, 328 pp., p. 94; Buron, *op. cit.*, p. 220; *Chronique des jours moroses*, p. 217. For exceptions to these generalizations, see below pp. 38-39.

49.   *Vingt-huit ans de gaullisme*, p. 181.

50. Pierre Viansson-Ponté, *Histoire de la république gaullienne*, Gallimard, Paris, 1970, 2 vols., vol. I, pp. 167, 206.

51. Bernard Chenot, *Etre ministre*, Plon, 1967, 173 pp., p. 66.

52. Pisani, *op. cit.*, p. 128; Buron, *op cit.*, p. 223.

53. Pisani, *op. cit.*, p. 128.

54. *Le Figaro*, 8 October, 1973.

55. Charles Debbasch, *La France de Pompidou*, PUF, Paris, 1974, 324 pp., p. 40.

56. Pisani, *op. cit.*, pp. 129–30.

57. Pisani, *op. cit.*, pp. 130–31.

58. *Ibid.*, p. 129.

59. *Le Figaro*, 8 October, 1973.

60. Viansson-Ponte, *Histoire de la république gaullienne*, I, p. 206.

61. Jack Hayward, *The One and Indivisible French Republic*, Norton, New York, 1973, 306 pp., p. 96; *Chronique des jours moroses*, p. 31; Merry Bromberger, *Le destin secret de Georges Pompidou*, Fayard, Paris, 1965, 349 pp., p. 299.

62. *Le Figaro*, 8 October, 1973.

63. An allusion to de Gaulle's purge trials of Vichy ministers.

64. *La Tragédie du général*, pp. 315–20.

65. *Op. cit.*, p. 221.

66. *Le Monde*, 26 November, 1968.

67. Philippe Alexandre, *Exécution d'un homme politique*, Grasset, Paris, 1973, 298 pp., p.279.

68. Pisani, *op. cit.*, p. 133.

69. Debbasch, *op. cit.*, p. 40.

70. Williams, *op. cit.*, p. 198.

71. *Ibid.*, p. 294; Arné, *op. cit.*, p. 79n.

72. *Ibid.*, p. 305.

73. *Ibid.*, p. 199; Dulong, *op. cit.*, p. 146; Vincent Auriol, *Journal du Septennat, 1953-1954*, Colin, Paris, 1970, vol. I (1970), pp. lvi, 36, 60, 153, 172-73, 517.

74. Auriol, *op. cit.*, Vol. I, p. 56.

75. Dulong, *op. cit..*, p. 146.

76. Auriol, *op. cit.*, p. 239.

77. Martin, *op. cit.*, p. 239.

78. Verrier, *op. cit.*, p. 16.

79. Martin, *op. cit.*, pp. 239–40.

80. De Gaulle press conference, 9 September, 1965; *Année politique 1965*, p. 441; Dulong, *op. cit.*, p. 139; Debré and Debré, *op. cit.*, p. 60.

81. Ord. 59–147 of 9 January, 1959; D-59-942 of 31 July, 1959.

82. Dulong, *op. cit.*, p. 143. In practice, the Defense Committee came to be called the Defense Council, in keeping with the practice of using "council" when the President chaired; Massot, *op. cit.*, p. 178; Verrier, *op. cit.*, p. 48.

83. Avril, *op. cit.*, p. 229.

84. Avril, *op. cit.*, p. 229; Jean Baillou and Pierre Pelletier, *Les Affaires Etrangers*, PUF, Paris, 1962, 378 pp., p. 29; Herbert Tint, *French Foreign Policy since the Second World War*, Weidenfeld and Nicolson, London, 1972, 273 pp., p. 240; Verrier *op. cit.*, p. 48; Tricot, *Charles de Gaulle...p.* 2.

85. D. 60–1455 of November 1960 and D. 62-808 and 809 of 18 July, 1962.

86. Its official title was *"Comité des affaires algeriennes."*; D. 60-120 of 13 February, 1960.

87. Tricot, *Charles de Gaulle*, p. 3.

88. Bernard Tricot, *Les Sentiers de la Paix*, Plon, Paris, 1972, p. 142.

89. Dulong, *op. cit.*, p. 147

90. D. 62-344 of 26 March, 1962.

91. Tricot, *Charles de Gaulle...*, p. 3.

92. Tricot, *Les Sentiers* p. 142. Also, see Tricot, *Charles de Gaulle...*, p. 3.

93. De Gaulle, *op. cit.*, p. 85; Tricot, *op. cit.*, p. 142   William G. Andrews, *French Politics and Algeria*, Appleton-Century-Crofts, New York, 1962, 217 pp., p. 120.

The Collective Political Executive

94. D. 61-491 of 18 May, 1961.
95. Raymond Barillon *et. al.*, *Dictionnaire de la Constitution*, Ed. Cujas, Paris, 1976, 396 pp., p. 45.
96. Arrêté of 16 May, 1961.
97. D. 61-491 of 18 May, 1961.
98. Dulong, *op. cit.*, p. 149; de Baecque, *op. cit.*, p. 109.
99. *Le Monde*, 10 March, 1960.
100. Baillou and Pelletier, *op. cit.*, p. 29; Maurice Couve de Murville, *Une politique étrangère*, 1958-59, Plon, Paris, 1971, 499 pp; de Baecque, *op. cit.*, p. 108
101. J.A. La Ponce, *The Government of the Fifth Republic*, U. of California Press, Berkeley and Los Angeles, 1961, 415 pp, pp. 295-96.
102. The importance of this power is indicated by the fact that about 2,000 appeals for presidential grace are made each year and fifty persons received death sentences under criminal law, 1959-77, of whom thirty were reprieved. Debré and Debré *op. cit.*, p. 42.
103. The High Council of the Magistracy is not discussed here because it is not, strictly speaking, a committee of the executive, even though the president of the Republic chairs some of its meetings.
104. Dulong, *op. cit.*, pp. 50-51; Verrier, *op. cit.*, p. 50; Dulong, *op. cit.*, p. 140.
105. Tricot, *Charles de Gaulle...*, p. 6.
106. Bromberger, *op. cit.*, p. 318.; Tricot, *Charles de Gaulle...* p. 7; 123 b. *Ibid.*, p. 5
107. Interview with Michael Debré, 10 July, 1978.
108. Dulong, *op. cit.*, p. 140. For a list of the "themes" of the ad hoc councils, see Tricot, *Charles de Gaulle...*,p. 4.
109. *Ibid.*, p. 8.
110. Debré and Debré, *op. cit.*, p. 60; *Ibid;* Dulong, *op. cit.*, p. 139.
111. *Repertoire permanent de l'administration française 1968*, La documentation française, Paris, 1968, 404 pp., pp. 6-9; *Repertoire permanent... 1974*, pp. 9-13.
112. Ordinances of November 23, 1944.
113. André G. Delion, "Les Conseils et comités interministeriels", pp. 268-76, in *A.J.D.A.*, June 1975, p. 274.
114. Interview with M. Michel Debré, 10 July, 1978.
115. Delion. *op. cit.*, p. 274; *Le Monde, in passim; Fondation nationale de science politique* clipping file.
116. Langlois-Meurinne, *op. cit.*, p. 142.
117. *Le Monde*, 1 March, 1960.
118. D. 62-555 of 10 May, 1962.
119. D. 53-455 of 19 May, 1953.
120. *Combat*, 3 March, 1966.
121. D. 60-106 of 2 February, 1960; D-1187 of 31 October, 1961.
122. D. 60-1219 of 19 November, 1960; D. 61-728 of 6 July, 1961.
123. D. 63-114 of 14 February, 1963.
124. D. 60-1219 of 19 November, 1960. *JO.LD.* 20 November, 1960, p. 1063.
125. Pierre Rouanet, *Pompidou*, Grasset, Paris, 1969, 315 pp., pp. 105-106.; D. 63-114 of 14 February, 1963.
126. Guichard, *op. cit.*, p. 216.
127. Decree of 25 July, 1935.
128. D. 59-766 of 19 June, 1959.
129. D. 62-1530 of 22 December, 1962.
130. D. 48-1029 of 25 June, 1948, D. 52-1016 of 3 September, 1952, and D. 58-344 of 3 April, 1958.
131. *Repertoire permanent...1965.*
132. D. 58-1144 of 28 November, 1958, D. 60-309 of 18 March, 1960; D. 61-362 of 8 April, 1961, D. 64-182 of 26 February, 1964, Decree of 5 August, 1970; Law of 3 December, 1966; Decree of 12 May, 1970; Decree of 2 February, 1971; Decree of 12 April, 1945; D. 64-628 of 25 June, 1964; Ord. 45-2563 of 18 October, 1945; D. 45-2572 of 18 October, 1945; Decree of 2 February, 1971; *Figaro*, 28 January, 1971; Decree of 11 August, 1971; Decree of 17 December, 1971; Decree of 5 July, 1972; *Nation*, 29 June, 1972.

133. *Combat*, 10 March, 1966.
134. *Ibid.*
135. *Articles et documents*, No. 1933.
136. Interview with Michel Debré, 10 July, 1978.
137. Dulong, *op. cit.*, p. 142.
138. Bromberger, *op. cit.*, pp. 318–319.

Parliament in the
Fifth Republic

J. R. Frears

The first decade of the Fifth Republic produced an admirable and detailed study of its 'New model Parliament' by Philip Williams.[1] The purpose of this chapter is to suggest that it is time for another, and to provide some statistics which will help in drawing up a balance-sheet.

The starting point must be a clear perception of the role of a Parliament in a modern liberal democracy. We shall not parade here the lengthy literature on the 'decline of legislatures' nor examine in detail the different views of what a Parliament is for. We shall briefly suggest that its principal role is, or should be, in the words of Sir K. Wheare, 'making the government behave'.[2] Turning to the French Parliament we shall examine the limitations of its role in the political system of the Fifth Republic and review its performance as legislator and, in the more important sphere of activitiy suggested by Wheare's phrase, as a check on the use of executive power.

Un Parlement, pour quoi faire?[3] If it is possible to deduce a consensus from modern writers like Wheare, Crick, J.P. Mackintosh or Gerhard Loewenberg[5] on the role of parliaments in modern parliamentary democracies it would include, apart from representation of constituents and the redress of grievances, four main features. Parliament should be able to scrutinize and improve legislation rather than initiate or impede it. Parliament should be as prestigious as possible an arena for political debate and for the permanent electoral campaign which is part of democracy's essence. Parliament should have the means and the capacity to control executive power in the sense of information, access, powers of investigation and scrutiny, and as a final resort the power to dismiss the government. Finally, since in most parliamentary systems a majority of parliamentarians are political supporters of the government, the exercise of these functions means to a large extent ensuring that the opposition has a wide

47

range of procedural opportunities: not to prevent government from governing but to scrutinize and to criticize what it does. Let us now see to what extent the French Parliament in the Fifth Republic measures up to these requirements.

Parliaments in the Third and Fourth Republics were regarded as the main begetters of instability and ineffectiveness. No parliamentary majority ever was willing to support a government when unpopular decisions had to be faced. Parliament had unbridled powers to harrass, impede, or destroy governments. Decisive government was impossible. General de Gaulle's prescription for the country in 1958, when the Fourth Republic collapsed in impotence before a crisis in Algeria, was a greater 'separation of powers' where a strengthened executive could govern and a circumscribed Parliament could legislate. The 1958 constitution is unusual in that it lays down in minute detail innumerable aspects of parliamentary procedure—all designed to ensure that the government can govern free from parliamentary harrassment. Government business has priority on the agenda, the government can intervene in a deadlock between the two houses National Assembly and Senate, the government may ask for delegated legislative powers, the government's sphere of regulation covers anything that is not specifically legislative, and so on. The Fifth Republic remains a parliamentary regime because the National Assembly can, by a motion of censure or denial of confidence, remove the government—but the procedure for bringing this about makes it as difficult as it decently could be.

THE LEGISLATIVE ROLE OF PARLIAMENT IN THE FIFTH REPUBLIC

'Laws are made by Parliament' says Art. 34 of the constitution which then goes on to mark out the sphere of law-making in order to distinguish laws from what comes under the executive's power of regulation. Laws can be proposed by the government (*Projets de Loi*) or by parliamentarians (*Propositions de Loi*). These legislative proposals may begin either in the National Assembly or in the Senate. A bill is then considered by one of the six large permanent committees which the constitution allows to each assembly.[6] The basic legislative work is done in these committees. For each legislative proposal the committee to which it goes appoints a *rapporteur*, by no means always a government supporter, who has the services of the committee's staff to study the bill and produce a report. He contacts ministerial departments, professional organizations, sets up working groups. His report is considered by the full committee which can also ask to hear the view of the relevant government minister. Amendments are considered in the committee. when the report comes before the full assembly, it is presented by the *rapporteur* even if he personally does not agree with the committee's conclusions. The assembly decides whether to adopt the final text or send it back to the committee. When adopted by one assembly, the Bill passes to the other. If it is amended there it returns to the first assembly. To stop the '*navette*' (shuttle) going on forever, the Government may call for a

Commission Mixte Paritaire—a joint committee of National Assembly and Senate—to reach a compromise. If a compromise is accepted by both assemblies and the government, that resolves the matter. If not, the government has a variety of initiatives including inviting the National Assembly to have the final say.

Apart from its procedural options over the *Commissions Mixtes Paritaires*, the executive is in a strong position to dominate the legislative process. The constitutional primacy accorded to government business means that the government has the unfettered right to determine what bills will be discussed by Parliament and in what order. When the *order du jour prioritaire* is completed, *Propositions de Loi* not endorsed by the Government may be discussed in an *ordre du jour complémentaire*, but Parliament has made little effort to exploit this possibility.[7] Furthermore, the government can propose its own amendments to bills and can oppose the consideration of members' amendments that have not been considered by the committee. The government can also, under Art. 44 of the constitution, require an assembly to decide by a single vote the whole or part of a bill under discussion. All these procedures are clearly designed to counteract the faults of the Fourth Republic—the *ordre du jour* and endless discussion of amendments could be used to block government business. This is not very different from the British House of Commons where Governments can use their parliamentary majority to reject any amendment and to bring in a 'guillotine motion' to curtail discussion or end a filibuster. The most objectionable constraint on the powers of Parliament as legislator lies not in these procedural questions but in Art. 41 of the constitution which declares out of order any legislative proposal relating to a matter deemed to be within the sphere of the executive and not of the law as defined in Art. 34. One job of the Constitutional Council is to patrol the fence of Art. 34 and drive back any parliamentarian who ventures into the executive sphere.

Some statistics will help to illustrate the legislative activity of Parliament in the Fifth Republic.[8]

	Legislation	
	Government Origin	Parliamentary Origin
4th Republic (1946–58)	70.6%	29.4%
5th Republic*		
1959–1962	93.2%	6.8%
1963–1966	85.9%	14.1%
1967–1968	81.3%	18.7%
1969–1972	84.1%	15.9%
1973–1977	86.5%	13.5%
Total 1959–1977	86.8%	13.2%
(Great Britain 1968–76[9])	81.9%	18.1%)

*The years have been divided to correspond roughly to each legislature.

The figures in this table reveal that the parliamentarian in the Fifth Republic initiates less legislation than his predecessor of the Fourth, a little less than his government-dominated British counterpart, but more today than in the first Parliament of the Fifth Republic. The table also shows that from a legislative point of view the Fifth Republic divides between the period of the Debré government and the Algerian crisis (1958–1962), when the executive did not have the support of a stable and permanent parliamentary majority, and the more relaxed period since 1962 when it has. The same characteristic is reflected in the 'success rate' for Parliamentarians' *Propositions de Loi* (*Propositions* that become law as a percent of *Propositions* put down). In 1959–1962 the 'success rate' was 3 percent; in 1970–72 under the Pompidou presidency and a vast Gaullist parliamentary majority it was around 10 percent; in four years of the Giscard d'Estaing presidency 1974–77 it was 8 percent. In the House of Commons 1968–76 this 'success rate' was 14 percent. As far as political groups and *propositions de loi* are concerned: from 1970–77 *propositions* of Gaullists were crowned with success in 15 percent of cases, of *Giscardiens* and centrists in 9 percent, of Socialists and their allies in 7 percent, and of Communists in 4 percent. These figures confirm the observations of Phillip Williams that members of the government's majority are more able to influence ministers—through party groups, or through the presidents of parliamentary committees who invariably belong to the Majority.[10] One final note on *Propositions de Loi*: between 1959 and 1974 the Senate originated 19 percent of private member legislation and the National Assembly 81 percent.

Amendments

A better indication of parliamentarians' contributions to the legislative process can be derived from amendments proposed and adopted.

Amendments—National Assembly—1970–1977

	% of all amendments put down by*	% of all amendments adopted originated by	'success rate' %
Government	11.5	21.1	80.6
Committee	40.1	60.1	66.0
Deputies			
Gaullists	15.0	9.3	27.4
Giscardians &			
Centrists	10.2	4.5	19.8
Socialists & allies	11.6	2.6	9.8
Communists	10.3	1.2	5.1
All amendments	100.0	100.0	44.0

*including those declared out of order (communist amendments being the most inflicted) or withdrawn.

These figures reveal that parliamentarians do make a contribution in the form of amendments to legislation and that even opposition members have some modest success in gaining acceptance for their amendments. To give two brief examples: in November 1977 Communist members were able to obtain the removal of a qualifying period before claims are permissible under a new social security law, and in the following month they and the Socialists obtained a lengthening of the guarantee period for customers of the construction industry.[11] These were obtaind not by winning a vote in the Assembly but by gaining acceptance for these amendments by the reporting committee. 4 percent of all successful amendments presented by committees had the countersigned endorsement of an opposition member.

Procedural Interventions by Government in the Legislative Process

An earlier paragraph indicated some ways by which the government, under the constitution, can intervene in the legislative process. In all of these, as with legislation in general, the government is nowadays a little less inclined to act as a steamroller. Where the two assemblies do not agree, the government may demand that a joint-committee (*Commission Mixte Paritaire*—CMP) be set up. This happens fairly often (about 12 percent of all laws). When the CMP produces a report the government has the power to simply reject it—but it has never done so. It has always allowed the report to be submitted to Parliament though it has frequently used its power to propose further amendments. Also, it can eliminate the Senate at this stage: it can make the National Assembly decide on the basis of the CMP's report or of the Assembly's own last text which was not accepted by the Senate. There were 257 CMP's in the Fifth Republic through 1977. On seventy-two occasions (28 percent) the government asked the National Assembly to decide alone because agreement could not be reached. From 1974 to 1977 this happened only once—possibly reflecting the fact that under the presidencies of General de Gaulle and Pompidou the Senate was the more difficult assembly for the government. Under president Giscard d'Estaing the Gaullists in the National Assembly have been more prickly and less reliable, while the Senate is *Giscardien*.

One of the greatest constraints on the legislative role of the French Parliament is the distinction drawn by the constitution between the legislative sphere and the sphere of government regulation. Whole areas of what in England would be called secondary legislation—for instance the implementation in national law of European Community Directives and Regulations—do not come before the French Parliament at all because it belongs to the '*domaine du réglement*'.[12] If the government believes that a legislative proposal or an amendment by a deputy strays into the sphere of its own regulations it invokes Art. 41 of the constitution to prevent further discussion. This happens fairly frequently and is ruled on by the president of the assembly concerned. If he does not agree with the government's interpretation, the Constitutional Council decides. In 1977, Art. 41 was invoked five times—three times in the National Assembly where the president ruled two texts out of order, twice in the Senate (both out of order). The third case in the National Assembly, where a Communist deputy had put down a bill on social security in mines, was decided by the Constitutional Council against the government and in favor of the member. On seven other occasions the Constitutional Council had to decide whether a proposal was legislative or regulatory under Art. 37, and found them 'particularly legislative' in all but two cases. Jack Hayward has noted how in recent years the Constitutional Council was becoming much less systematically prone to decide in favor of the government.[13]

A constitutional reform, adopted by both Assemblies meeting as a congress on 21 October 1974, has given Parliament, which means in particular the opposition, an additional weapon to challenge the government over the constitutionality of its act. A law can now be submitted to the Constitutional Council before promulgation not merely by the president of the Republic, the prime minister, or the president of either assembly as in the past, but by any sixty deputies or sixty senators. This had been done nineteen times by March 1978. In six cases the Constitutional Council declared all or part of the law unconstitutional.

The final relevant instance of government intervention in the legislative procedure is the use of Art. 44—the *vote bloqué*—when Parliament can be asked to decide the whole (or part) of a Bill by a single 'package' vote. This enables the government to avoid separate votes on politically sensitive or unpopular parts of a measure. Philip Williams reports that Art. 44 was used more frequently and more harshly under the Pompidou government (1962-1968) which had a reliable majority than under the Debré government (1958-1962) which did not. Since 1974 the package vote has been used on average in the National Assembly about four times a year—a quarter of the frequency of the bad old days of the mid-1960s. Even so, in December 1977, the president of the Senate felt obliged to recall to the prime minister's attention the 'bitterness' and 'the cruel memories' aroused by the practice of the *vote bloqué*. M. Barre replied that the government had invoked Art. 44 for its recent bill to indemnify French *rapatriés* from Algeria, Tunisia, and elsewhere because there was an economic limit to what could be afforded and it could not go on accepting amendments on this emotive subject.[14]

Legislation Without The Assent Of Parliament

The legislative process can by-pass Parliament in three ways. In this respect, as in many others, the second decade of the Fifth Republic has been much less anti-parliamentary than the first. In a crisis, the president of the Republic (under Art. 16 of the constitution) takes emergency powers and can do almost anything including legislate. This has been used only once—by General de Gaulle at the time of the Algiers *Putsch des Généraux* in 1961.[15] During the operation of Art. 16, Parliament meets 'by right' and cannot be dissolved. However, it was not permitted in 1961 to question the use of presidential prerogatives under Art. 16 and, when it tried during the summer, using the fact that because of Art. 16 it was still in session, to discuss a farm-price crisis, its initiative was declared out of order. It was not related to the emergency for which Art. 16 had been invoked! Secondly, laws may be submitted to popular referendum under Art. 11. On two occasions—October 1962 and April 1969—General de Gaulle used this procedure for amendments to the constitution. This was highly irregular since Art. 89 explains that constitutional amendments have to be accepted by Parliament before submission to referendum. The first occasion was of immense importance: the people decided by referendum to have a directly-elected presidency. On the second occasion the proposals involving reform of the regions and of the Senate were defeated and General de Gaulle resigned.

The third means of non-parliamentary legislation lies in Art. 38 of the constitution. Parliament may delegate its legislative powers to the government for a limited period by a vote of special powers. This was used quite a lot in the early years of the Fifth Republic to 'protect' Gaullist MP's from having to vote for unpopular laws.[16] The constitution requires that a ratification bill for legislation of this kind be laid before Parliament. This procedure was often abused, though, because these ratification bills have usually been excluded from the Parliamentary agenda and thus not called for debate, amendment, or a vote. When ratification has been debated, as in 1968 when the government promised the labor unions that ratification of its 1967 social security reforms, decreed under Art. 38, would be discussed in Parliament, there has been considerable amendment. Art. 38 has not been invoked since 1969. Governments have had a very safe majority since 1968 and their supporters have been prepared to give support.

Ministers in the government, in addition to possessing all these procedural weapons, can intervene at any time in the proceedings of either assembly. When a minister has a piece of legislation going through he takes a very close interest and his *cabinet* staff are in touch constantly with the chairman and staff of the relevant committee, and with the deputies who belong to the government's parliamentary majority. The incompatibility rule (Art. 25 of the constitution) requires ministers to give up their parliamentary seats if they have them. This saves them from the crushing and impossible burden of British ministers who have to fulfill all their parliamentary duties, such as voting all night in divisions, as well as their government functions. It does not mean, however, that French ministers are never to be seen. The government is more attentive to the dignity of Parliament and to the feelings of its own supporters than it used to be. The big difference between the French political system of the Fifth Republic and that of the Fourth, a difference which has had a profound effect on the legislative process in particular and upon the relationship between Parliament and the Executive in general, is the emergence of a reliable parliamentary majority which sees its job as being to sustain the government and give it the means to govern effectively.

The conclusion, as far as legislative aspects are concerned, is that the government's dominant role in the legislative process is in keeping with that in other parliamentary democracies, that its powers are being used less abusively as the *fait majoritaire* begins to have an effect on political mores, and that parliamentarians are able to make a reasonable contribution to the legislative process in the form of amendments and *Propositions de Loi*. In short the first of our requirements for a modern parliament—that it should direct itself to scrutinizing and improving legislation rather than initiating or impeding it—is reasonably well fulfilled.

PARLIAMENTARY CONTROL OF THE EXECUTIVE

The other three requirements to which we referred relate more to parliamentary control of the executive. This is the real task of a modern Parliament and in this respect the balance-sheet of the Fifth Republic is rather thin. Parliament is not a particularly prestigious or even much-noticed arena for political debate—mainly because debate can never be initiated by the opposition except, as we shall see, in the drastic form of a censure motion. The status of the opposition remains low: it has little legitimacy in the eyes of government supporters or the civil service, and few procedural opportunities to deploy a parliamentary case. Parliamentary opportunities to investigate, scrutinize, or even gain information about the actions of the executive are inadequate. If we examine this last point, the shortcomings in the first two aspects of parliamentary control—Parliament as an arena, and the status of the opposition—will become apparent.

Parliamentary Questions

In Westminster Parliamentary Questions may not always penetrate the guard of a well-briefed minister, and are often the occasion of harmless indeed pointless knockabout, but they retain great prestige as an instrument of parliamentary scrutiny of the executive. A torrent of supplementary questions, succinctly put, punctuated by brief replies permits Parliamentarians to put ministers through a searching and punishing test on issues of topical concern. Question time, especially Prime Minister's Question Time which in 1978 was broadcast on radio, finds an echo in public opinion and the press and is a central arena of political combat in the nation.

The French Parliament's arrangements for Questions are very similar to those at Westminster, but the manner is quite different. Until 1969 there were three kinds of questions—written questions, which are numerous (around 8,000 replies a year) and of no political importance, oral questions without debate, and oral questions with debate.

Oral questions without debate, despite their name, are potentially quite an interesting form of scrutiny. The member develops his question for two minutes, the minister replies, the questioner returns for a further five minutes, and finally the minister can reply to the supplementary point. For instance on 9 December 1977 a junior minister for industry, M. Rufenacht, had to defend the government against communist criticism over an electricity strike and centrist criticism over the decline of the steel industry in Lorraine.

These questions find no echo in the public at large: at least a month lapses between putting down a question and receiving a reply and these questions are heard on a Friday when most parliamentarians have left Paris. On average about 150-200 questions of this type are '*inscriptibles*' on the National Assembly's *ordre du jour* but in fact only 35-40 percent actually get answered. The figure for 1977 was 69 percent, so perhaps the Conference of Presidents (group leaders and the President of the Assembly) who decide the *ordre du jour* and the government are now going to ensure that more questions are dealt with. The numbers of questions selected for presentation show no discrimination against the opposition. To establish whether politically embarrassing questions are still winnowed out would require more research.[17] There are more Questions without Debate answered in Senate—but it must be remembered that the Senate does not have the procedure of *Questions au Gouvernement* which will be reviewed in a moment.

Questions with Debate provide one of the very few occasions in the French Parliament for debate on anything but the text of a law.[18] They have almost disappeared, however, from the National Assembly since *Questions au Gouvernement* were introduced. No Questions with Debate were discussed in 1976 or 1977. The Senate has Questions with Debate—not always on a Friday—on average about fifty a year (seventy-six in 1977). The procedure makes it more a debate than a question. The author of the question speaks for half an hour. Other members wishing to speak are allowed twenty minutes each. The minister makes a speech. The original questioner may reply to the minister. No vote is taken at the end—unlike in the Fourth Republic. These questions have little political impact and are seldom on burningly topical political issues. On 4 November 1977 (a Friday) were debates on the politicisation of education and noise nuisance. On the 15th (a Tuesday) was a debate on a number of questions relating to the conditions of widows, and on the 18th (a Friday) a debate on energy policy.

In 1969, the National Assembly introduced *Questions d'actualité* supposedly modelled in the House of Commons Question Time. The aim was to have short questions on current political topics and short replies that same day or that week. In 1974 *Questions d'actualité* were dropped in favor of a new procedure *Questions au Gouvernement*. Every Wednesday, time is set aside for questions on any matter to be put to any minister. All ministers are there and there is no notice of the questions to be put. Half the time is allocated to the majority, half to the opposition. On average about 330 questions a year are put, with the ministers for industry, finance, and the interior being interrogated the most frequently. From 1974 to 1977, the four principle political groupings shared questions as follows:

Gaullists	24% of questions	(36% of Assembly membership)
Giscardiens and Centrists	24% of questions	(24% of Assembly membership)
Majority	48% of questions	(60% of Assembly membership)
Socialists and allies	28% of questions	(22% of Assembly membership)
Communists	23% of questions	(15% of Assembly membership)
Opposition	51% of questions	(37% of Assembly membership)

Thus, the opposition had a fair share of question time in proportion to their membership, though, from the point of view of parliamentary scrutiny of the executive, opposition questions should be much more important than questions from government supporters. The opposition does not seem to have drawn much blood by the use of *Questions au Gouvernement*. Questions take the form of a speech by the questioner followed by a speech in reply by the minister. There are no supplementary questions so that the minister is free to make unchallenged political capital with his reply which could be inaccurate, anodyne, evasive, or irrelevant. For example, some communist questions on 24 June 1977 were intended to reveal that the standard of living of workers was going down and that the steel industry in Lorraine was being broken up and sold to the Germans. The ministers concerned simply said they were doing an excellent job in containing inflation and planning a vigorous future for the Lorraine steel industry. On 7 December, a Socialist raised the question the right of political asylum—an important matter arising out of international terrorist activities. The Minister of Justice just explained the law on extradition and declared that France would remain a haven for political exiles. Without quickfire question and answer, without awkward supplementaries, there is no

56

drama and no real scrutiny. although the proceedings of Parliament may be televised, they seldom are, and *Questions au Gouvernement* do not appear on the screen. It is a pity parliamentary questions have so little impact—they are one of the very few opportunities deputies have to probe areas of executive action that fall outside the legislative sphere.

Committees of Enquiry and Control (*Commissions d'enquête ou de Contrôle*)

One means of great potential importance for parliamentary scrutiny of the executive are in the *Commissions d'enquête* and *Commissions de contrôle* which each assembly has the power to set up.[19] For the first few years of the Fifth Republic this procedure was hardly used but it has been gaining momentum recently.

As instruments of control and scrutiny these committees suffer from certain restrictions. A resolution to set one up has to go to the *Commission des Lois* or another permanent committee, which can stifle the demand. In the first two Parliaments (1958–1967) the *Commission des Lois* simply never reported on the resolutions put to it for *commissions d'enquête*. Since 1970, matters have improved as it is now obligatory for a report on such a resolution to be submitted. A majority of the Assembly has to support the resolution to set up one—and supporters of the government do not like to help the opposition to make life difficult for it. The time for deliberation is limited—it was four months (a real problem when Parliament only meets for two brief sessions in the year) but in October 1977 it was extended to six months. The Assembly can decide not to accept or publish the committee's report. Before October 1977, a proposal to publish the report had to be supported by a majority—not always easy. Now reports are automatically published unless a special procedure is followed to stop it. Unlike committees of the American Congress, these committees have no powers to compel witnesses to attend. Quite frequently, the government refuses cooperation: ministers refuse to attend and bar their civil servants from appearing. The most flagrant case was the denial of cooperation to a Senate committee of control which was looking into the practice of telephone tapping. On other occasions civil servants have been authorized to appear only if questionnaires have been submitted in advance. Various pretexts have been given: a matter involving judicial proceedings, a matter involving security, or 'interests of state'. Parliamentary control of the Executive has precious little meaning if the executive can refuse to be controlled. Sometimes Parliament has preferred to set up *missions d'information* which are easier to establish and not subject to the same rules of procedure. However their status and conclusions are less august.

The demands for committees of enquiry or control that were buried by the permanent committees have included some politically sensitive ones on

Algeria, on the repression of student demonstrations, on the police, or on counter-intelligence activities. The committees that have investigated and reported have included some harmless topics like lyric theatres and some that were embarrassing to the government.[20] These have included the financial and administrative scandal of the Abattoirs of la Villette, the stormy question of telephone tapping, and, more recently, an examination of the use of public funds by the aviation company owned by Gaullist deputy Marcel Dassault. The Senate has been on the whole more persistent in attempting to use this form of parliamentary control, but, as the figures show, demands for *commissions d'enquête* have recently been all the rage in the National Assembly. The demands are no longer systematically blocked—another fact suggesting that French governments feel safe enough, with their parliamentary majorities behind them, to allow Parliament a little more freedom to perform its role. The impact of the reports of these special committees is not spectacular. The non-cooperation of the government in 1973 over the telephone-tapping enquiry committee caused a small row. No motion of censure has yet been put down in the National Assembly in order to sanction the government after the revelations of a committee report. The Senate, in any case, is not even entitled to use the censure motion procedure.

		Parliaments				
		1st 1958 to 1962	2nd 1962 to 1967	3rd 1967 to 1968	4th 1968 to 1973	5th 1973 to 1978
Commissions d'enquête						
National Assembly	—demanded	6	5	6	10	59
	—established	0	0	0	1	7
Senate	—demanded	2	0	3	7	2*
	—established	0	0	0	1	0*
Commissions de contrôle						
National Assembly	—demanded	3	1	1	6	8
	—established	1	0	0	1	2
Senate	—demanded	1	1	1	3	1*
	—established	1	1	1	1	1*

*up to October 1975.

Motions of Censure and Confidence

The ultimate form of parliamentary control in a parliamentary democracy lies in the power of the legislature to dismiss the government. In the Fourth Republic this power was used so often that it made government impossible. In the Fifth Republic the procedure for Parliament to register its lack of confidence in the government is more difficult for the opposition to operate and gives the government some slightly unfair advantages, yet the power remains. That is why parliamentary elections are still so important. The president of the Republic, who is not responsible to Parliament, can exercise the policy leadership which has been characteristic of the last twenty years, only if the majority in the Assembly allows him to do so by supporting the governments he appoints. The big debate before each parliamentary election is on the issue of who would exercise policy leadership if the Left won a majority of seats in the Assembly. The answer is that the president would have to appoint a prime minister acceptable to the new majority and allow him to carry out policies acceptable to it or see the government defeated on motions of censure. So the power of Parliament to sustain or dismiss governments is an important political reality.

This power can be exercised in three situations. The prime minister may ask the Assembly for a vote of confidence on the government's programme or declaration of general policy. Secondly, the government may make the passage of a bill a question of confidence. Under this procedure the bill is passed unless a motion of censure is put down and carried. The most recent law passed in this way was the bill on direct elections to the European Parliament, carried in April 1977 because no censure motion was put down. Art. 49 of the constitution lays down the procedures for confidence and censure. A censure motion must be signed by one tenth of the Assembly's membership—fifty members—or about a quarter of the opposition, about half the Socialist group, and more than half of the Communist group. The same members cannot put down another motion in the same half-yearly session of Parliament—which means, for instance that the absolute limit for the Communist group acting alone would be two motions per year. Motions thus put down must wait forty-eight hours before being put to the vote—a procedure which destroys heat-of-the moment topicality. Only votes for the motion are counted and to be carried a majority of the whole Assembly membership must support it—anyone who is ill or absent or even a member of the majority who would have liked to show disapproval by abstaining thus counts as a supporter of the government. This certainly protects the government, as the constitution-makers rightly intended, against snap defeats on ill-attended occasions.

By mid-1979 there had been thirty-eight votes on questions of confidence or motions of censure in the Fifth Republic.[21] Only one has resulted in a defeat for

59

the government: in October 1962 almost all non-Gaullist groups in the Assembly expressed their outrage at being excluded from the proper procedure for amending the constitution when de Gaulle called a referendum on direct election of the presidency. Since the measure proposed was popular in the country, this vote of censure only helped the Gaullists to gain a solid parliamentary majority at the elections which followed the fall of the government and the referendum. Only four censure motions were initiated bt the opposition in the 1973–78 Parliament, the same number as in the first Parliament of the Republic (1958–62). This is a very good indicator of the feebleness of parliamentary opposition in France. The censure motion is about the only occasion when the opposition may initiate a debate on an important matter at a time of its own choosing. It is somewhat frustrating to be an opposition member in a political system where the opposition is regarded as scarcely legitimate, and where the person who really determines policy is not responsible to Parliament, but even so a much greater effort could have been made to ensure that the government defended its actions publicly before Parliament in debate. By the end of the spring 1978 session, the opposition had initiated no motion of censure in the National Assembly since April 1975 when a condemnation of the general policies of the Chirac government was attempted. The government periodically asks the assembly for a vote of confidence on its programme. The re-appointed Barre government did so after the elections of March 1978—thus obliging the Gaullists to show where they stood. The importance of these votes can be illustrated by the decision of President Pompidou in 1972 to dismiss his prime minister Jacques Chaban-Delmas only a few weeks after the latter had obtained a parliamentary vote of confidence! However, they provide occasions for Parliament to exercise a deliberative function and to be an arena for a major debate on public policy in which party leaders can take part.

The Senate has no powers to censure the government although it can be asked by the government (Art. 49) to express its 'approval to a declaration of general policy'. The first time it was asked was in June 1975 by the Chirac government on foreign policy. In March 1977, Raymond Barre put government policy as a whole before the Senate. Had the Senate voted against approval the consequences would have been interesting. The constitution is silent but probably the government would have felt compelled to resign. It is however no coincidence that both these occasions have occurred since the election of President Giscard d'Estaing in 1974 when what was left of the opposition centre—an element which was still quite strong in the Senate—had become part of the new President's *majorité*. The Senate is no longer the *Assemblée d'opposition* that it was for the first decade at least of the Fifth Republic.

60

THE STATUS OF THE OPPOSITION

Parliamentary control of the executive means nothing unless the opposition has the fullest opportunity to question and criticise the government and compel it to explain and to be accountable for its actions. In systems with a majority party or firm pro-government coalition one cannot expect electorally damaging criticism from the ranks of the government's own supporters. As noted, the government in France has powers to resist opposition scrutiny—an example was the resistance to *commissions d'enquête*. As noted, the government, procedurally speaking, has been behaving a little better in recent years and treating the Parliamentary right to scrutinize it a little more seriously. Also as noted—especially with regard to censure motions—the opposition seems strangely reluctant to use its opportunities to perform its parliamentary role. There are, however, other things that the opposition cannot do and this makes their parliamentary task extraordinarily difficult. There are no 'supply days' on which, in Westminster, the opposition selects the subject for debate. There are no opportunities to initiate a debate, other than in the drastic form of a censure motion or the pinprick of a *question orale avec débat*. Important subjects like foreign policy can be debated only when the foreign affairs section of the budget comes up for consideration (because foreign policy does not require much legislation) or when the government chooses to make a general declaration on it a matter of confidence. Parliament's role in foreign affairs or European Community policy is practically nil and the government is virtually unaccountable.[22]

Those in power throughout the Fifth Republic have shown an unwillingness to accept that opposition has an important constitutional role in a democracy and an unwillingness by the opposition to play one. The fiction of total systematic opposition to the regime goes on—believed by the political elite of both government majority and opposition, despite the fact that in the country as a whole no major social group is in outright opposition to the regime and its institutions. President Giscard d'Estaing has made strenuous efforts to change elite attitudes.[23] He would like to see in France as in England a 'loyal opposition' with a part to play in the functioning of institutions and a right to be briefed on broad issues like national objectives in foreign policy, and for such a role to be accepted by government supporters. He would like the opposition to be associated with international initiatives hence his invitation to some Socialist deputies to join the presidential delegation to the United Nations in 1978. The efforts to bring about '*décrispation*' or '*cohabitation raisonnable*', to coin the two phrases the president has used in his efforts to build a normal relationship with the opposition, have met with little success. The Gaullists in the National Assembly blocked his move to get one or two of the influential chairmanships of the six permanent committees allocated to the opposition after the 1978 election. The opposition would not accept a couple of token vice-chairmanships. So the bureaux of all six committees remain solidly majority, with four Gaullist RPR chairmen and two UDF (*Giscardiens*). This is regrettable because the chairmen of the six committees are extremely influential and have considerable resources at their disposal. A chairmanship of a major committee would have given the opposition real access to the administration. Outside Parliament, the opposition has been granted the right of reply to ministerial (but not presidential) broadcasts, but not much else. One difficulty is that much of the opposition consists of the Communist party, which often prefers to cooperation a posture of systematic and truculent rejection of everything, which is distrusted for its pro-Soviet attitudes and old Stalinist ways. At all events the opposition—especially the Communists but Socialists as well—tends to be treated as an untouchable caste. Civil servants deny them information.[24] Concessions made by the Executive to Parliament are those made to government supporters agreed behind closed doors.

Parliament has changed greatly during the twenty years of the Fifth Republic. The changes we have mentioned here are related to the much larger change in the party system from a fragmented, loosely-disciplined, ever-changing multi-party system to a bi-polar government and opposition arrangement. Since 1962, governments have been able to rely upon the support of a majority in the Assembly and these majorities have seen it as their job to support the government. Parties have repeatedly fought and won elections on the strength of *continuité*. This essay has not looked at the workings of parties in Parliament—their study groups, their discipline over their members, their growing propensity to vote as disciplined groups.[25] A fuller study would be needed to develop these aspects.

As time has gone on the executive, supported by its reliable and disciplined majority, has been less inclined to abuse its procedural powers in relation to Parliament. There have been no unconstitutional referenda since 1969, no delegation of legislative powers on an important matter since 1967 (none at all since 1969), less abusive use of the *vote bloqué* procedure, and less blocking of *commissions d'enquête*. There is better provision for parliamentarians to invoke the Constitutional Council, better facilities for asking questions, a genuine part for members in the scrutiny and improvement of legislation. Yet France remains a country where executive power remains almost totally immune from parliamentary scrutiny, especially the sort of power exercised by the technocratic elite in ministerial *cabinets*. The main causes are the rigid division between the domain of the law and the domain of executive regulation and the low status of the opposition. Vast areas of executive action and executive discretion remain closed to parliamentary enquiry because they do not give rise to legislation, and because parliamentary procedure as laid down in the constitution does not make it possible for the opposition to initiate regular debates. The opposition is excluded from exercising responsibility in parliamentary committees and thus from the administrative support, influence, and access that such responsibility would bring. The opposition's low status is compounded with a certain defeatism so that it does not exploit the procedural and other opportunities it has.

A deeper study of Parliament in the Fifth Republic would need to be augmented with case studies, legislative and other. Our conclusion at this stage must be that Parliament in France, except in its legislative role, fails to fulfill the four criteria we laid down. The government in France is behaving a little better these days, but not because of the effectiveness of parliamentary pressure, and it is still much too safe from scrutiny and control.

NOTES

1. *The French Parliament 1958-1967* (London. Allen and Unwin, 1968).

2. *Legislatures* (Oxford University Press, 1963) p. 114.

3. This question is the title of a book by the Socialist Deputy A. Chandernagor (Paris, Gallimard, 1967).

5. Wheare, op.cit.; Bernard Crick *The Reform of Parliament* (London. Weidenfeld & Nicholson, 1964), John P. Mackintosh and G. Loewenberg in Loewenberg (ed.) *Modern Parliaments, Change or Decline?* (Chicago, Atherton, 1971).

6. In the National Assembly: Commissions des Lois, des Finances, de la Defense Nationale, des Affaires Etrangères, de la Production et des Exchanges, des Affaires culturelles, familiales, et sociales. In the Senate: Commissions des Lois, des Finances, des Affaires Economiques, des Affaires étrangères et de la Défense, des Affaires Sociales, des Affaires culturelles. Occasionally a group of deputies or the government asks for a *Commission spéciale. Commissions spéciales* have rather gone out of fashion in the latter years of the Fifth Republic—only six have been requested since 1973 and only two established. Occasionally they were of some political importance. In 1967, for instance, much of the controversy surrounding the state's radio and television monopoly was reflected in demands for *Commissions spéciales.*

7. See F. Goguel in Loewenberg (ed.) op.cit. p. 93.

8. Sources: Bulletin de l'Assemblée Nationale (annual statistics), *Le Sénat* (Documentation Francais), Le Sénat—bulletin d'informations rapides, Jean-Luc Parodi: *Les Rapports entre le législatif et l'exécutif sous la Cinquième République* (Paris, FNSP) 1972.

9. Source S. A. Walkland & M. Ryle (eds.): *The Commons in the Seventies* (London, Fontana, 1977). p. 78.

10. in G. Loewenberg (ed.) op.cit. p. 98.

11. Assemblée Nationale 30 Novembre 1977 and 19 Décembre 1977.

12. See J. R. Frears, 'The French Parliament and the European Community' in *Journal of Common Market Studies*, December 1975, pp. 140-156.

13. *The One and Indivisible French Republic* (London, Weidenfeld and Nicholson, 1973) pp. 122-4.

14. Senate 21 Dec. 1977.

15. See M. Harrison 'The French experience of exceptional powers, 1961' *Journal of Politics* Feb. 1963, pp. 139-58, and William G. Andrews 'Constitutional dictatorship in Gaullist France'APSA Paper 1975, pp. 13-15.

16. For an excellent example see Philip Williams *The French Parliament* op.cit. pp. 85-89 ('The Social Scourges Bill, 1960') and William G. Andrews ibid pp. 16-26.

17. Philip Williams *The French Parliament* op.cit. pp. 48-9 suggests that there used to be some executive abuse but not much.

18. Another occasion (not mentioned elsewhere in this paper), but initiated by the government, lies in the procedure of '*déclarations du gouvernement*'. These may be with or without debate—usually with. The government makes on average about three declarations per year on a variety of policy areas. In 1977 there were debates on the steel industry and problems of the sea—following government declarations.

19. See J. Desandre: *les commissions parlementaires d'enquête ou de contrôle en droit francais* (Documentation Francais, 1976).

20. Full list of *commissions d'enquête et de contrôle* see Appendix A.

21. Complete list in Appendix B.

22. J.R. Frears 'The French Parliament and the European Community' *Journal of Common Market Studies* December 1975 op.cit.

23. See J.R. Frears: 'Legitimacy, Consensus, and Democracy—a Presidential analysis', *West European Politics* October 1978.

24. See Ezra Suleiman *Politics, Power, and Bureaucracy in France* (Princeton 1974), pp. 361-2. Suleiman also has a chapter (XI) on the contempt in which civil servants hold deputies in general.

25. For the latter point see F.L. Wilson and Richard White 'Parliamentary Cohesion in the first four National Assemblies of the Fifth Republic' *Legislative Studies Quarterly* November 1976. Voting cohesion is now almost total for all party groups in the Assembly except the *Giscardiens* and centrists whose Parliamentary group has an ideology of 'freedom of conscience'. But the effect on cohesion is very small. The Senate is less disciplined. For the other points see J.R. Frears *Political Parties and Elections in the Fifth Republic* (London, C. Hurst & Co., 1977) pp. 169-172.

Appendix A
Commissions d'Enquête—Committees of Enquiry 1959–79

	Subject	Proposed by	
National Assembly	Property development	Mitterrand (Soc)	10 Dec. 1971
	Pollution of Mediterranean	Barel (Comm)	27 June 1974
	Energy Situation	Mexandeau (Soc)	27 June 1974
	Oil companies	Marchais (Comm)	27 June 1974
	Building permits in Paris	Frédéric-Dupont (Ind)	18 Oct. 1974
	Meat trade	Goulet (Gaull)	18 Oct. 1974
	Public funds for Marcel Dassault companies	Defferre (Soc)	10 Nov. 1976
	'Importations sauvages'	Boudet (Cent)	18 May 1977
	'Amoco Cadiz' disaster	Darinot (Soc)	11 May 1978
	'Amoco Cadiz' disaster	Goasduff (Gaull)	5 May 1978
	Information to the public	Labbé (Gaull)	15 Mar. 1979
	Jobs and unemployment	Labbé (Gaull)	16 Mar. 1979
Senate (up to Oct. 1975)	La Villette abattoirs	Courrière (Soc)	14 Dec. 1970

Commissions de contrôle—Committees of Control 1959–1978

National Assembly	Aid to film industry	Bonnet (Rad)	11 Dec. 1961
	Radio and Television	Delmas (Soc)	20 Dec. 1971
	Telephone service	Boscher (Gaull)	29 Oct. 1973
	Radio and Television—Financial management	Labbé (Gaull)	29 Oct. 1973
	Administration of Social Security	Labbé (Gaull)	23 Dec. 1978
Senate (up to Oct. 1975)	Lyric Theatres	Roubert (Soc)	15 Dec. 1960
	Guidance and selection in education		
	Radio and Television	Gros (Ind)	21 Apr. 1966
	Implementation of 5th plan—Capital spending on health and social services	Diligent (Cent)	14 Dec. 1967
		Grand (Rad)	18 Dec. 1969
	Telephone tapping	Monory (Cent)	29 June 1973

Sources: Assemblée Nationale Statistiques (annual); J. Desandre *les commissions parlementaires d'enquête ou de contrôle en droit francais* (op.cit)

66

Appendix B

Confidence and Censure—National Assembly, 5th Republic

A—confidence (asked by government);
B—Censure motions when government makes a Bill a matter of confidence;
C—Censure motions initiated by opposition

Date	PM	Type	Subject	Signatories	Opp	Votes Gov	Abs
Jan 1959	Debre	A	Programme		56	453	29
Oct 1959	"	A	Algerian Policy		23	441	88
Nov 1959	"	B	Budget	Soc.Rad	109		
May 1960	"	C	Not recalling Parliament	Soc.Rad	122		
Oct 1960	"	B	Nuclear Deterrent	Soc.Rad,Ind	207		
Nov 1960	"	B	Nuclear Deterrent	Soc.Rad,Ind	214		
Dec 1960	"	B	Nuclear Deterrent	Soc.Rad,Ind	215		
Dec 1961	"	C	Agriculture	Soc.Rad	199		
Apr 1962	Pompidou	A	Programme		128	259	119
Jun 1962	"	C	Algeria	Ext Right	113		
Jul 1962	"	B	Nuclear Deterrent	Soc.Rad,MRP,Ind	206		
Oct 1962	"	C	Referendum	All-party	280*		
Dec 1962	"	A	General Policy	Soc,Centre	116	268	69
Oct 1964	"	C	Agriculture	Soc.Centre	209		
Apr 1966	"	C	Withdrawal from NATO	Soc.Rad	137**		
May 1967	"	B	Special Powers (Art 38)	Soc.Rad,Comm,Cent	236		
Jun 1967	"	B	Special Powers (Art 38)	Soc.Rad,Comm,Cent	237		
Jun 1967	"	B	Special Powers (Art 38)	Soc.Rad,Comm	207		
Oct 1967	"	C	Economic Policy	Soc.Rad,Comm	207		
Apr 1968	"	C	News and Information	Soc.Rad	236		
May 1968	"	C	Student Unrest	Soc.Rad,Comm	233		

Date	PM		Subject	Parties		
Sept 1969	Chaban Delmas	A	Gen Policy (New Society)		85	369
Oct 1970	,,	A	General Policy		89	382
Apr 1971	,,	C	General Government Policy	Soc, Ind	95	
May 1972	,,	A	General Policy		96	368
Oct 1972	Messmer	C	General Government Policy	Soc, Comm	94	
Apr 1973	,,	A	General Policy		206	
Oct 1973	,,	C	General Government Policy	Soc, Comm, Left-Rad	181	
Jan 1974	,,	C	Monetary policy	Soc, Comm, Left-Rad	208	
Jun 1974	Chirac	A	General policy		181	297
Dec 1974	,,	C	General Government Policy	Soc, Comm, Left-Rad	183	
Apr 1975	,,	C	General Government Policy	Soc, Comm, Left-Rad	183	
Oct 1976	Barre	B	Budget 'plan Barre'	Soc, Comm, Left-Rad	181	
Apr 1977	,,	A	Programme	Soc, Comm, Left-Rad	186	271
Apr 1978	,,	A	Programme	Soc	199	
Oct 1978	,,	C	General Government Policy	Soc	197	
Mar 1979	,,	C	European Policy	Comm	86	
Mar 1979	,,	C	General Government Policy	Soc	200	250

F1*Censure motion carried. Government Resigned.
**Censure motion not supported by Communists.

Sources: Philip Williams— *The French Parliament* (op.cit.) p.54 and Assemblée Nationale Statistiques (annual).

68

Administrative Reform and the Problem of Decentralization In the Fifth Republic

Ezra N. Suleiman

All political party platforms, all major political speeches, and all newly formed governments in France express their deep commitment to administrative reform and to the decentralization of administrative power.[1] Rare is the minister who does not attack publicly the civil servants in his own ministry,[2] proclaiming that they need to be more strictly controlled and that their work and attitude need a rather heavy dose of humanity injected into them. Even the Communist party, whose Leninist structure has scarcely been modified, openly attacks the undemocratic nature of the centralized state apparatus and has now become a believer in *autogestion*.[3] Alain Peyrefitte's *Le Mal français*, which is viewed as a severe critique of the French bureaucracy and a brief on behalf of decentralization, had no critics either on the Left or the Right. François Goguel even referred to Peyrefitte's book in a front page review in *Le Monde* as a "book of the Left."[4]

With so much agreement on the need for decentralization and reform of the administrative structure, how may one explain the almost total absence of any serious reforms? It is surely no accident that the rhetoric of administrative reform and local democracy has become a substitute rather than a program for genuine reforms. This essay attempts to explain, with reference to the evolution of the politico-administrative system under the Fifth Republic and to the "Jacobin consensus" that underlies this system, why the decentralization of the state apparatus is an elusive goal and why it is likely to remain confined to rhetoric. We suggest that an incompatibility exists between corporate interests that derive from the administrative structure and the goal of decentralization. The consequences of this incompatibility are so serious that it is likely to remain unchanged if a left-wing government were to replace the center-right majority that has governed since 1958.

POLITICAL ADMINISTRATION

The politico-administratif system works to the advantage of a small group of civil servants whose success in the state apparatus enables them to move into the political arena with relative ease. The Ecole Nationale d'Administration has become more and more a school of elite selection and less and less a school that aims to give a technical training to the state's future administrators. As François Bloch-Lainé put it: ENA *"est une machine à brasser et à classer. Ce n'est guère une machine à instruire."*[5] Far more than in the past, ENA is seen by those who succeed in gaining entry into it as a gateway to a political career. As a stepping stone to politics, it offers distinct advantages over the "apprenticeship" career-pattern of the Third Republic.

Foremost among these advantages is the rapidity with which one can win a mayorship, a seat in the National Assembly, or a ministerial portfolio. These political heights may be attained without spending many years developing a constituency in the provinces. Indeed, gradually the political career pattern is coming to be overturned: success at the national level (becoming a minister or secretary of state, for example) leads to success at the local level. Prior to the Fifth Republic, the progress of a political career developed from the local to the national level.

The law in France is very accommodating to a civil servant who wishes to enter politics. He need not resign from the civil service either while a candidate for office or when elected. While a candidate, he neither resigns nor takes a leave of absence. He continues to draw his salary exactly as if he were performing his normal duties. When he is elected to local office, he continues to function as a civil servant.[6] The *"cumul"* of two positions—administrative and political—legally inadmissible in other western countries, is sanctioned by law in France.

This form of *"cumul"* not only does little to separate the political from the administrative domain, but allows the state to subsidize, in one way or another, the political careers (or the attempts at such careers) of its privileged civil servants.

In numerous ways the higher civil servants, and most particularly those who belong to the *grands corps de l'Etat*, benefit from a state subsidy. In the first place, the state subsidizes the entry of its officials into ministerial cabinets.[7] The civil servants who enter a ministerial cabinet—who are, in other words, serving a minister who belongs to a government and, generally, a political party—continue to get paid by the corps or administration to which they belong. What occurs, in effect, is that a public institution continues to pay the salary of a civil servant who no longer works for it and has become a political apprentice.

In addition to the role that civil servants play in ministerial cabinets, they

70

also play important roles in various political movements and parties while exercising their functions as civil servants. Obviously, they cannot fulfill both tasks at the same time. Either they devote their time to their political responsibilities, in which case the state is simply providing an indirect subsidy to political movements; or, they attempt to continue to function as civil servants, in which case the requirements of neutrality and *"reserve"* are cast aside.

The contradictions in the administrative system, and the benefits which higher civil servants derive from these contradictions, become most evident in electoral periods. The civil servants become all too ready to shed the noble principles (general interest, neutrality, equality) on which they were reared and to enter the political arena with strong partisan commitments. They become candidates for national and local offices, advisors to political leaders, and party activists. They devote their time fully to political activity while receiving their state salaries. No better example can be given of the state subsidies for the political activity of its administrative elite than the way it pays the salary of members of this elite while asking little in return.[8]

Quite apart from the attraction that elections have for civil servants, it has also become customary under the Fifth Republic to elicit the support of civil servants for political movements. The Comité pour l'indépendance et l'Unité de la France, created by Michel Debré, has four members of the Conseil d'Etat; the General Secretary of this party until March 1978 was Jérôme Monod, a member of the Cour des Comptes; the Mouvement des Sociaux-Libéraux created by Olivier Stirn had as the Directeur-Général Adjoint a director of the Ministry of Interior who is a member of the corps of Ponts et Chaussées. François Mitterrand's directeur de Cabinet was Laurent Fabius, a member of the Conseil d'Etat who has now been elected to the National Assembly. Mitterrand's economic advisor is Jacques Attali, a member of the Conseil d'Etat. Until his election to the National Assembly in March 1978, Michel Rocard was at the same time an Inspecteur des Finances, a national secretary of the Socialist party, a mayor, and a candidate to the National Assembly. When elected deputy, Rocard went on leave from the Inspection des Finances, to which he will always be able to return, as he did after he lost his seat in the National Assembly in 1973.

In certain cases, the political activity of a civil servant is less than full-time. In others, his civil service attachment is a fiction that simply enables him to continue drawing his salary. For Monod, Fabius, Attali, Rocard, and scores of others, membership in a *grands corps* was purely a formality since they rendered little, if any, service to their corps. This involves three things: (1) the indirect subsidy by the state of the political activities of a privileged group; (2) the novelty that is introduced in the way that a political career is conceived; and (3) the inequalities that inhere in this system for the administration and for the society.

The manner of recruitment of the administrative elite and the guarantees for a career that knows little downward mobility give the administrative elite an extraordinary degree of liberty. The civil servants who belong to this elite scarcely need account for their activities. The *"obligation de réserve et de neutralité"* applies in practice only to the lower levels of the administrative hierarchy. The work done by the privileged civil servants and the amount of time they devote to it are left up to them.

The Fifth Republic is largely responsible for this state of affairs, even though these practices are probably the logical consequence of the French system of elite training. Nonetheless, the past two decades have witnessed an expansion of what might be called state subsidies for an elite desiring to enter politics. Several factors have contributed to an acceleration of this process: the entry of civil servants into ministerial posts and into ministerial cabinets; the increasing number of ENA graduates; the spectacular political success of some former civil servants; the imperialism of the *grand corps* who are forever on the lookout for additional sectors to conquer so as to prevent rivals from getting there first; the rapid success of members of the *grands corps* within the administrative sector, which leads them to seek outlets beyond the administration; finally, the easy success which they often attain in politics (within political party hierarchies, in ministerial cabinets, in elective posts) which makes political careers more attractive. Thus, factors inherent in the administrative structure (and in the political arena) lead civil servants to opt for political careers.

The second consequence of this extension of the state subsidies is that it alters considerably the way in which a political career is conceived. Risk is undoubtedly the main ingredient of a political career. Its insecurity is enormous, for even serving one's constituency with great devotion does not guarantee success.

Yet, the French civil servants have essentially succeeded in eliminating risk from political careers. The extraordinary facility with which they can move into and out of politics, the possibility of campaigning without resigning their positions, the liberty of testing the terrain, of joining political movements—all this they can do as easily as they can enter a ministerial cabinet. If they do not succeed they simply return to their corps. Their posts, being permanent, have been kept warm for them and they need not even accept salary losses in attempting to break into the political profession.

It is hardly surprising, therefore, that the number of candidates employed by the state was extremely high during the March 1978 legislative elections. Higher civil servants alone represented 10 percent of the candidates in the Republican party, 7.2 percent in the R.P.R., 6.9 percent in the M.R.G., and 5.2 percent in the P.S. and 1.6 percent of the P.C.[9]. Of the 480 deputies elected, 125 were civil servants.[10]

The third consequence of this system is the extreme inequality that it introduces. The inequality has nothing to do with the Left-Right division of the society. Not only those associated with the governing majority benefit from this system. On the contrary, the system is designed to benefit an elite and makes no distinction regarding the political coloration of the members of this elite. Hence, both the opposition and those in power benefit from the subsidy. The inequalities concern the strata *within* the administration. It is clear that only a very privileged group within the administration is able to profit from the subsidy. This group is made up of those who belong to the *grands corps*.

The spectacular successes of a number of former civil servants in political and other careers have become a model for the younger generation, for whom "*le sens de l'Etat*" means something very different from what it meant to the previous generation of civil servants. When Michel Debré created the Ecole Nationale d' Administration, he noted: "The training—one need not hide this—also has a moral objective. It is not one of the missions of the school to play politics or to impose a particular doctrine. But the school must also teach the future civil servants '*le sens de l'Etat*', it must make them understand the responsibilities of the administration, make them taste the grandeur and accept the servitudes of the *métier*."[11] Thirty years ago, this aim did not appear outmoded and was the expression of a generally accepted principle. However, members of the administrative elite are no longer content to remain confined to the administration. They continue to believe that they are imbued with a '*sens de l'Etat*'. Their conception of what constitutes "*l'Etat*" has, however, drastically changed.[12]

All this does not mean that the old administrative ethic has been abandoned totally. It does mean that the French administrative system, which depended on a separation of responsibilities and those who bore them, is gradually giving way to a new system. The edging toward this new system was seen over thirty years ago by Debré, who wrote:

> Our Republic is meeting its most painful failure today in the area of political independence...the independence of the State has to require an abstention from political activity, at least from activist politics...We are engaged on the most dangerous road possible for a Republican state...Politics is no less ardent than unionism: it is entering in full swing into the administration. In a period of a few months, the danger point has been passed.[13]

Debré may have had a rather idealized view of state service and state independence. The alarm he was ringing in the late 1940s, which was signaled by the era of *tripartisme* and particularly by the Communist party's colonization of certain ministries, expressed a fear about the evolution of the administrative system as it had functioned until the end of the Third Republic. It is perhaps not a minor irony that the entry of politics into administration and of administrators into politics—"*l'échec le plus douloureux*," as Debré called

73

it—owes its most rapid development to the Fifth Republic. If an irreversible trend has been created, part of the responsibility lies with the Gaullist regime.

This raises the question of why an administrative system that gives such large privileges to a small group of civil servants and that allows them to use their positions within the state apparatus as mere ports of embarcation for political careers enjoys support of such general consensus, if not in society—which remains largely ignorant of this system—at least among the various political forces. The answer is that the spoils of the system are shared by all the parties. Political party involvement—with the possible exception of membership in the Communist party—is no hindrance to benefiting from the system. For about one year preceding the 1978 legislative elections, many members of the *grands corps* were so busy with various political activities that they did not treat a single dossier. Yet, except for a few private utterances, not a single corps found this situation sufficiently irregular to warrant questioning it. Nor did any political party propose doing away with this abuse of state service. The reason is that the state becomes like a kitty into which Gaullists, Socialists, Republicans, Centrists and others can dip. Besides, to question the liberty to engage in politics is to question all other liberties that members of the *grands corps* enjoy. In short, a consensus exists among the various political forces for sustaining a system that provides privileges to all, regardless of political affiliation. The entry into politics of higher civil servants is, therefore, a consequence of the elitist system of training.

ELITISM VS. DECENTRALIZATION

This consensus about the structure of administrative institutions that serve as the only legitimating criteria for excellence and that provide liberties and privileges to a small group also has important political consequences. Foremost among these is the stumbling block that these administrative institutions pose for the decentralization of administrative power. The Club Echanges et Projets, headed by Jacques Delors, noted recently that a general agreement exists over centralization: "The French State is at once highly centralized, uniform, and fragmented whereas our changing society calls for decentralization, heterogeneity and coordination. This archaic State is ultimately a rigid world, paralyzed by an informal balance in the distribution of power, a balance that no one wants or dares to question."[14] Why is centralization such a convenient state of affairs for those who hold power? Yves Mény has noted that, while Jacobinism has disappeared from political speeches and proclamations, it remains a leitmotif and is found in guarded language in practically every political program.[15]

While every group may have reasons for preferring a particular form of decentralization or deconcentration, there seems to be little doubt that there is an intimate link between the structure of administrative institutions (particularly the *grands corps*) and the centralization of power. The ability of the various corps to preserve their power and to offer such wide liberties to their members reposes on the concentration of power. The corps, therefore, constitute one of the most powerful forces in the society opposing a genuine decentralization of the state apparatus.

This is not in the least surprising when one considers the origins of the corps and the manner in which they have survived over the past two hundred years. Each corps was created to represent the state in a specific domain and was granted a monopoly therein. The building of roads, the verification of public finances, the administration of justice, the maintenance of public order, each of these was placed in the hands of one institution that grew jealous of its power and that constantly fought off attempts to encroach on its monopoly. On the whole, most of the corps have been remarkably successful in adapting to the changing political and economic environment in which they live and in preserving their monopoly over their respective sectors.

Such long experience at adaptation has made it patently evident to all the corps (the *grands* and the less *grands*) that the monopoly over a sector is intimately linked to the centralization of the state apparatus. They recognize that decentralization—local, legislative, budgetary, and fiscal powers—poses the greatest possible threat to their autonomy. And since the administrative structure is made up of several hundred corps, it follows that the administration will always be a force against decentralization. But the fight against a genuine decentralization of power will be led by the *grands corps* because, unlike the other corps who have a monopoly over a specific sector and have been content to confine their power to that sector (corps of forestry, telecommunications, and the like), the *grands corps* have to protect far more than a monopoly over a single sector. Over the years, they have acquired control—and this characteristic distinguishes them from the other corps—over numerous other sectors. The easy mobility across different sectors, which the *grands corps* offer to their members, makes them so desirable. To abandon, therefore, the monopoly over which they exercise responsibility—a consequence that would follow naturally from a process of decentralization—would be to abandon far more than this monopoly. It would be to give up considerable power and privilege for which the monopoly serves merely as a base.

The *grands corps* have never shown much enthusiasm for decentralization. In fact, when their power was threatened by it directly they showed an incontestable hostility toward it. They tended to regard efforts at decentralization simply as attacks on their power. Usually, they found it difficult to see larger social and political issues in proposals for decentralization. The reaction of the prefectoral corps is particularly illustrative in this regard. Howard Machin has shown how hostile the prefectoral corps was to the Fifth Republic's attempts at regionalization.[16]

The prefects dragged their feet at setting up the Regionalization Conferences, or when they did set them up, they made sure that they met infre-
quently, and often did not attend the meetings. More seriously, the prefects
refused to recognize that the Regional Missions could undertake objective
economic studies of their regions. "Many Prefects refused to accept the notion
that objective criteria could be established for the determination of public investment policy. When the Mission carried out such 'objective' studies, the
results were often rejected by the Prefects."[17] What mattered more than the
needs of the regions, were the departmental interests of the prefects. The corps
was gripped by a fear of losing control over its traditional area of competence.
Ultimately, the prefects had to adapt themselves to the new regional institutions, but in doing so they were still able to preserve their traditional territory.

The case of the corps of *ponts et chaussées* is equally instructive, for it shows
the profound hostility of this corps to a devolution of power. Decentralization
is viewed by the *ponts et chaussées* as a zero-sum game, for when the localities
are strengthened the corps is weakened. Traditionally, the power of this corps
was anchored in the rural society that gradually gave way to the urban society.
The corps made the transition, not without difficulty, but ultimately rather
successfully. The *ponts et chaussées'* embrace of urbanization was accompanied
throughout by policies designed to prevent the strengthening of local collectivities. As Thoenig explains:

> If the engineers of the Ponts (et Chaussées) pushed for a more efficient State policy
> in the area of urban development, it was not, as the minister wanted, in order to
> redistribute the roles between the State and the local collectivities or to decentralize
> power from Paris to the provinces. On the contrary, it was in order to reinforce the
> hold of the State apparatus on local initiatives...For the engineers of the Ponts, it was
> crucial that the State Administration maintain its preponderant role. They did not
> want to develop new solutions in the area of urban development that would lead to a
> weakening of the administration's role...Why should the local collectivities be
> strengthened when they might end up no longer needing the *tutelle* of the Ad-
> ministration and having the possibility of creating an effective counterforce to it?[18]

What is true of the prefectoral corps and the corps of *ponts et chaussées* applies to the other major corps. The power of the *Inspection des Finances* and of
the *Cour des Comptes* would rapidly disappear if local collectivities were endowed with greater power over their financial affairs. When one considers the
interests involved in a continued centralization of the state apparatus, one
understands why decentralization has been confined (and consigned) to
political rhetoric.

The dependence of the *grands corps* on administrative centralization may be
preventing not merely the introduction of local democracy in France, but also
more efficient functioning of the administrative machine. Thoenig has criticized the *grands corps* on the grounds that they can no longer deal with the complex problems that face society.[19] The problem is not so much the efficiency of

the *grands corps* in comparison with another system. Rather, it is that their interests in the present administrative structure prevent an alternative system being tried.

ADMINISTRATIVE REFORM?

Not only does the preservation of the administrative structure require the centralization of the state apparatus. The obverse of this is true also: namely, that administrative reform will require decentralization. The only way to break the hold of the *grands corps* over the sectors that they monopolize may be to decentralize their functions. That step is perfectly logical, for decentralization would accomplish gradually and untraumatically what would require considerable political courage otherwise. François Bloch-Lainé has argued that it would be a mistake to destroy the *grands corps* without first having something equal or better to do their job. Decentralization, according to him, is the way to do this.[20]

However, Bloch-Laine's wish to see decentralization do the job of administrative reform may not be very realistic. The problem is that precisely because decentralization whittles away the power of the major administrative corps, it has been, and will continue to be, resisted and sabotaged all the way. Arguments similar to Bloch-Laine's have been made with respect to upgrading the role of the universities in the face of the prestige of the *grandes écoles*. The *grandes écoles* are necessary, it is argued, because the universities do not respond to the needs of society. When the universities have reformed themselves and taken their place besides the *grandes écoles*, the importance of the latter will diminish automatically. Yet the favored treatment which the *grandes écoles* continue to receive—treatment which is justified by the lamentable condition of the universities—makes it extremely unlikely that the universities will be able to overcome their present predicament.[21]

This is not to argue that the *grands corps* should be abolished. They perform useful functions, which other institutions would need to carry out in their absence. All that needs to be done is to ensure that the corps are confined to their own domain and are not simply used by their members as jumping-off points to other careers.[22] This could be done quite simply by limiting their use of leaves of absence.

Equally important, these privileges of the members of the *grands corps* are reinforced by the way they are recruited. The long preparation for the *concours* and the competition to which they are subjected at ENA and the Ecole Polytechnique endow them with a sense of self sufficiency and superiority that is scarcely compatible with notions of equality. They come to hold paternalistic attitudes toward the society and they justify the centralization of the State apparatus on the ground that it helps to cement a divisive society. Centralization and the unity of the state are indissoluble. Perhaps the best illustration of this belief is, paradoxically, Peyrefitte's *Le Mal Francais*, a book that owes its enormous success to its apparent attacks on the French administration, on the civil servants, and on the centralized state.

As part of his attack on the phenomenon of centralization, Peyrefitte vents his anger on those who administer the centralized state. Much of the book attacks the civil servants, their power, and their obliviousness to the everyday life of ordinary citizens. Peyrefitte blames the bureaucracy for just about everything, and one has to admit that his target can never duck shots taken at it.

But matters are never that simple. Peyrefitte claims that "political power is the prisoner of administrative power"[23] and that the state has abdicated much power to the bureaucracy, which makes decisions, tries to prevent some decisions from being taken, and refuses to apply decisions it dislikes but cannot prevent. This critique has an element of truth, but is far from the whole truth. For one thing, if the Fifth Republic is as "strong" and "solid" as Peyrefitte claims, why has it failed to control the bureaucracy? Why has it refused to take serious measures to reform this institution? Why has it not decentralized the State apparatus?

A time-honored political tactic attributes reforms to the foresight and power of politicians, and measures not undertaken or not applied to the power of bureaucrats. Peyrefitte was Minister of Education from 1967 until the student outbreaks in May 1968. The outbreaks were caused in part by the total paralysis of this ministry for at least a year preceding the events of May.[24] Was Peyrefitte "the prisoner of administrative power?" How, then, was he able to tame the bureaucracy in 1964 when, as Minister of Information, he gave the ORTF (the state-controlled television network) a statute specifically tailored to Gaullist needs? Peyrefitte, the diagnostician, criticizes the centralized censor powers of the state, but those powers used by Peyrefitte, the Minister of Information, who promised some religious orders (the promise was carried out by his successor) that the film "La Religieuse" based on the story by Diderot) would be censored? "Administrative Power" often serves as an alibi for political ineptitude or inertia. Michel Debré, a Gaullist and an *étatiste* of impeccable credentials, was not wholly off the mark when he told Peyrefitte: "No, the administration is not a power! Its role is limited to preparing, and then executing decisions! It does not make decision. Only the political authorities do. If you talk to me about bureaucracy, technocracy, or *"énarchie,"* it is because the political authorities have been negligent in their duty."[25] All this is to say that if centralization and administrative authoritarianism explain the French disease, the Gaullist regime must accept a large share of the blame not only for not curing it but also for spreading it.

To be sure, the Fifth Republic cannot be held responsible for the creation of the corps, for their centralization, or for their opposition to decentralization. But in facilitating the entry of corps members into the political arena it has undermined the political will to introduce a single major reform of the administrative structure. Equally important, in facilitating the entry of the *grands corps* into governmental positions, it has also channeled them into the opposition, thereby assuring that no political force will take seriously the need for administrative reform.

NOTES

1. An earlier version of this essay was written while the author was holding a Fellowship from the John Simon Guggenheim Memorial Foundation. Acknowledgement is also made of the support of the Joint Spanish-American Committee.

2. On being named Minister of Economy in April 1978, René Monory proclaimed, "As long as I am in the government, it is I who will command the fonctionnaires." *L'Express*, no 1396, 10-16 April 1978.

3. See Georges Marchais, *Parlons franchement* (Paris: Grasset, 1977), pp. 56-70.

4. *Le Monde*, 16 December 1976.

5. François Bloch-Lainé, *Profession: fonctionnaire* (Paris: Editions du Seuil, 1976); p. 236.

6. The only exception to this rule is that one cannot be a civil servant in the same *département* in which one holds an elective office.

7. On the extent of the penetration of ministerial cabinets by civil servants, see Jean-Luc Bodiguel, *Les Anciens élèves de l'E.N.A.* (Paris: Presses de la Foundation Nationale des Sciences Politiques, 1978), chapter 4.

8. For an elaboration of this see, Ezra N. Suleiman, "Fonction Publique et Politique," *Le Monde*, 20 July 1979.

9. G. Fabre-Rosane and A. Guéde, "Une Sociologie des candidats des grandes formations," *Le Monde*, 17 March 1978.

10. Calculated from data given in, A. Guéde and G. Fabre-Rosane, "Portrait robot du député 1978," *Le Matin*, 19 April 1978. For further data on the number of civil servants who sought office in the March 1978 legislative elections, see the above authors', "Sociologie des candidats aux élections législatives de mars 1978," *Revue Française de Science Politique*, vol. 28, no. 5 (October 1978), pp. 852-855.

11. Michel Debré, *Réforme de la fonction publique* (Paris: Imprimerie Nationale, 1946), pp. 24-25.

12. See Ezra N. Suleiman, *Elites in French Society: The Politics of Survival* (Princeton: Princeton University Press, 1978), chapters 3, 8, and 9.

13. Michel Debré, *La Mort de l'Etat Républicain*(Paris: Gallimard, 1947), pp. 115-116.

14. Echange et Projets, *La Démocratie à portée de la main* (Paris: Albin Michel, 1977), p. 66.

15. Yves Mény, "Partis politiques et décentralisation," paper presented at the conference "L'Administration vue par les hommes politiques," held at the French Senate, 10-11 February 1978, p. 6.

16. Howard Machin, *The Prefect in French Public Administration* (New York: St. Martin's Press, 1977), pp. 89-90.

17. Ibid., p. 98.

18. Jean-Claude Thoenig, *L'Ere des technocrates: le cas des Ponts et Chaussées* (Paris: Les Editions d'Organisation, 1973), pp. 102-103.

19. Jean-Claude Thoenig, "L'Exemple Français des Grands Corps," paper presented at the Eighth World Congress of the International Political Science Association, Munich, August 1970, p. 12.

20. Bloch-Lainé, *Profession: fonctionnaire*, p. 236.

21. This is discussed further in Suleiman, *Elites In French Society*, chapters 2 and 3.

22. For an elaboration of this argument, see my article in *Le Nouvel Observateur*, September 13, 1976.

23. Alain Peyrefitte, *Le Mal français* (Paris: Plon, 1977), p. 3-5.

24. On this, Peyrefitte is silent, saying only in a footnote that this would "require a special chapter" and that "the moment for telling it all has not arrived" (p. 90).

25. Cited in Peyrefitte, *Le Mal français*, p. 286.

79

Gaullism Abandoned,
Or The Costs Of Success

Peter Alexis Gourevitch

Giscard's triumph in the legislative elections of 1978 seems so obviously to have strengthened the Fifth Republic in the year that ended its second decade that it might pay to probe some difficulties which the results conceal. The major problem is that this victory has come via polarization, which, by undermining the center, destroys important mechanisms for legitimating the present distribution of power. Furthermore, the way this polarization has occurred takes the Majority farther and farther from the political strategy devised by founder of the Fifth Republic. The seeds of the present course were sown in the sixties; they germinated rapidly in the hothouse condition of *les événements,* and after, 1969, spread rapidly to cover the Hexagon with a new growth, which, while going under the old name, is a mutant indeed.

GAULLISM: THE ORIGINAL VERSION

All regimes require some way of appearing to benefit and represent most of society. Conservatives and radicals alike must appeal to a broad audience. Each must avoid being captured by the narrow conception of interests of the militant core on each side. For conservatives, this means not being seen simply as defenders of bourgeois property and privilege. Instead, broader programs must provide ways of constructing alliances with other groups.[1]

The British Conservative party does this by a mixture of nationalism, welfare, monarchism, religion, ethnicity, and social snobbery. In Germany and Italy, the legitimation has been undertaken by Christian Democracy. Whatever the D.C.'s problems, Italian politics would be profoundly different if it did not exist or were much weaker. Can one imagine the Liberals or Republicans as the principal mobilizers of resistance to the Communists or neo-Fascists? Conversely, could the Communists contemplate as readily the Historical Compromise if their interlocutor were not a party with at least some centrist and progressive credentials? Even when religious issues *per se* no longer dominate the political agenda, religion remains a powerful integrative force in Europe. Without some kind of alliance with the confessional parties, social and economic conservatives would be far weaker. Conversely, should the left succeed in attracting significant support from religious forces, it too would be strengthened greatly.[2]

In France, history has prevented the continuity needed for some version of the Conservative party.[3] Instead, such forces have relied on either Christian Democracy or Gaullism, not that most French conservatives have preferred one of these alternatives, but since the war they have never been strong enough to rely on their own political formations, and have had to make alliances.

Christian Democracy failed, partly because of the problems of decolonization (Indochina and Algeria), and partly, Gaullism destroyed it. De Gaulle undercut the MRP first with the RPF, then with the Fifth Republic and the UDR. Had de Gaulle put himself at the head of a confessional party, like Adenauer and De Gasperi, he would not have been de Gaulle, but the MRP might have evolved into a much stronger force, comparable in weight to the CDU-CSU or the DC.

Without a strong Christian Democratic movement, French conservatives turned to de Gaulle. However, Gaullism was not simply a strategy of conservative defense. In fact, conservatives had to share Gaullism with other goals and claims on its strengths: economic modernization, institutional rejuvenation, and nationalistic assertion. Still, conservatives knew that de Gaulle's other goals would not lead to a fundamental attack on private property or accumulation or on the structure of privilege. Obviously, they preferred Gaullism to socialism. But Gaullism did mean some reformism beyond what conservatives liked or would have done had they controlled politics.

De Gaulle forged an alliance of groups to support a set of interconnected policies: in foreign affairs—nationalism, defiance of the great powers, assertion of French interests and a French role; in colonial affairs—realism, cutting out impossible obligations while retaining influence via less costly means than outright colonialism; in economic policy—rationalization and modernization, consolidation of companies, increasing plant size and efficiency, squeezing inefficient peasants off the land and inefficient producers out of the marketplace, gearing up for foreign competition; in politics—a new set of institutions providing the executive with the authority to pursue these policies in a consistent manner, and a political organization capable of mobilizing support for de Gaulle without the constrains of a regular party organization.[4] The coalition which supported this package was attracted by different aspects.. Nationalitic-Loyalists were drawn primarily to the image of French grandeur and the person of de Gaulle. Modernizers wanted to rationalize the economy and society. Conservatives wanted protection from Left radicalism.[5]

81

The mixture gave de Gaulle autonomy from each piece. Left support for the anti-American/anti-Atlantic foreign policy contributed to de Gaulle's autonomy at home from the narrower "bourgeois defense" components of his constituency. The conservatives, on the other hand, provided leverage against the Left. Modernization was possible because neither side could veto it. Thus de Gaulle, along with Louis Napoleon and Bismarck, provides plenty of material for writers, neo-Marxist and non-Marxist alike, interested in "the autonomy of the state": the state promotes the long-run interests of the capitalist economy without simply being the "executive committee" of the capitalists, that is, by doing things frequently over the objections of the capitalists themselves.[6] De Gaulle also provides fuel for various debates over the functions of foreign policy in domestic politics.[7]

De Gaulle was certainly anti-Communist. He always took pains, however, to be more than that. He offered a vision and a partial reality which sought to capture some of the Communists' appeal, and to integrate them into French political life, on his terms rather than theirs. This was also his strategy toward the old Vichy right: to reintegrate it on the basis of republican nationalism, not defeatist fascism. De Gaulle constantly sought to deny the relevancy of left and right altogether. He always avoided an openly class-linked stance. This was the key to his strength: the interconnected ingredients created a whole stronger than any of the parts, capable of attracting support from all parties, all classes, all regions, all ideologies, all religious orientations. The essence of Gaullism was the judicious use of confusion and ambiguity, the presentation of many faces to many people, all the while continuing in a particular direction.

De Gaulle had, of course, certain personal qualifications for making good use of Gaullism. History had, as he put it, conferred upon him a certain legitimacy: the wartime leader of the Resistance, the refusal to be either dictator à la Franco or leader of a regular party à la Adenauer, the "*traversée du désert*," the distant public image, army officer status—these were powerful tools in public life, reinforced by the seriousness of the Algerian crisis.

Inevitably, things have been more difficult for his successors. None could draw on an historical legacy with a fund of personal charisma. None had a crisis like Algeria to make him appear the only alternative to worse options. None seemed indispensable in having no plausible successor. As a result, none of de Gaulle's followers could afford to do certain things the General could. In particular, none could disregard party organization and concrete interests. To survive without charisma, organization is necessary. To the leverage provided the Government by the Constitution had to be added that of organization and interests. Sooner or later, the Gaullist movement had to become a more conventional party, woven into the fabric of life at every level. It had to create a national staff and local headquarters. It needed card-carrying militants, professionals, and a large network of local office holders. It needed to serve the concrete interests of social factors, to distribute patronage, to grant favors, to fulfill large and small ambitions. In short, it had to become *un parti comme les autres* or go out of existence—always a possibility: functional requisites are not always met.

What such a party would be like was an open question. However inevitable a settling down may have been, the precise direction of that process was not foreordained or obvious. The internal diversity of the Gaullist movement meant it could be taken in different places. Outside the party were a variety of groups and formations with their own concerns, seeking to pull or push the Gaullists one way or another, or break it up to draw off its electorate.

Several "scenarios" of the evolution of Gaullism after de Gaulle can be imagined retrospectively. Four strategies derived from two sets of choices that had to be made by the leaders of Gaullism and of the other parties on the center and right. The first set concerns *program*: how much change; how much modernization of French society, economic structure, education, labor relations; what balance between modernization and preservation?. The second dimension deals with *leadership*: who governs? which leaders carry out these policies? Do the Gaullists and the other parties of the center and the right fight or cooperate? Do the Gaullists replace the existing elites or merge with them?

TABLE ONE

"Strategies for Survival"

LEADERSHIP	PROGRAM PRESERVATION	MODERNIZATION
Replacement	Strategy One	Strategy Two
Reconciliation	Strategy Three	Strategy Four

The principal distortion comes from omitting the third major variable—foreign policy. The major difference is between Nationalists and Atlanticists, those who want a France independent of the superpowers and dominant in Europe; and those who want to integrate France and Europe into an Atlantic bloc. Adding this distinction to the above pair makes for eight possible combinations. The first four, which stress internal politics, shall be treated here and foreign policy will be discussed at the end of the essay.

Strategy One: Conservative Policy and Gaullism as a bulwark against radical change, under new leaders.
Strategy Two: Gaullism as a means of modernizing French society, under new leaders.

83

Strategy Three: Conservatism and Reconciliation preventing radical change by means of a common front among the new Gaullists and the older political formations.
Strategy Four: Modernization and Reconciliation modernizing society through a common front of old and new elements.

Since the mid sixties France has switched from Strategy Two to Strategy Three: from modernization and the attempt to implant a new leadership group, to caution and merger with the old elites. This shift is clearest since 1969, but has earlier roots. Some support for Strategies One or Four does exist, but proved to be weak so far.

The end of the war in Algeria posed for Gaullism the problem of how to ensure its long run survival. The parties of the center and right that had supported the government during the crisis brought it down. De Gaulle beat back that challenge easily via the 1962 referendum. This assured his autonomy from *la classe politique* for a while, but not forever. Embroiled in fights with the center and right parties, aware of the UNR's organizational weakness at the local level, the Gaullists sought to remedy both problems by running their own candidates in municipal and departmental elections and by creating new structures of local government and new forms of representation to allow the passage of a "natural elite," presumably more favorable to Gaullism. Thus in the mid sixties, the Gaullists were pursuing Strategy Two: modernization combined with an attack upon the traditional notables.

This attempt to replace the old elites failed. Gaullist candidates in head-on collisions with the regular parties did not do well in the 1965 municipal elections. In the CODER (the new regional assemblies created by the 1964 decrees), the socio-professional elites were much like the other ones, not especially Gaullist. In Paris, some UDR leaders drew certain implications from this: outright confrontation would not work well. Instead, Gaullism should pursue a "Popular Front" Strategy—develop cooperative relations with the center and right formations, form and dominate a broad moderate-to-conservative coalition. A party organization would be built up, using the patronage provided by control of the state. The organizational and policy dimensions were linked; building up the organization meant servicing interests, which meant decreasing autonomy from social forces—not at all what de Gaulle had wanted. These steps were taken quietly in the period 1966–68 by Pompidou and Robert Poujade, leader of the UDR.[8]

Before 1968, the reorientation was not evident. De Gaulle dominated the scene; modernization, confrontation, nationalism were the prevailing policies. Indeed, had de Gaulle remained in office or had there been no *événements* of 1968, Strategy Two might have continued a long time, or there might have been a slow oscillation between the two with no discernible trend.

However, *les événements* sharpened the alternatives and forced a fateful choice in serveral interconnected ways. First, de Gaulle's own position received a very severe blow. His behavior during the crisis, especially his very weak speech of 24 May 1968 corroded his image of strength and efficiency. Suddenly, de Gaulle seemed to both elites and masses to have lost his touch. Second, a plausible successor emerged. Pompidou's handling of the situation was admired widely, and received credit for saving the day.

Third, the events repolarized French politics on a left-right continuum. Pompidou saved the situation only by playing a very costly card: the trump of Gaullism's political ambiguity. Pompidou mobilized Gaullism as the *parti de l'ordre*, the movement was "demystified." The slow revival of the left in mid-sixties accentuated (after the shock of 1968 wore off), and led to the very close contests of 1973–78. At the same time, many elements of French society were horrified by the events. They wanted a staunch conservative line: some moderate left votes shifted over to the right, and many center-right votes wanted a stiff no-nonsense policy, with no pointless adventurisms.[9]

This made de Gaulle's position extremely difficult. His response was a policy of reformism: the French want change—they shall have it, but orderly change, not *"chienlit."* This theme would be *"la participation"*. Its arenas would be universities, factories and local governments. Many of his own followers wanted no part of this: they sought conservatism, caution and a crackdown on the left. They saw de Gaulle as adventurist, not prudent. They could no longer be blackmailed into supporting him—they had Pompidou instead.

During the fall and winter of 1968–69 de Gaulle faced an increasingly resistive and unhappy majority in the Palais Bourbon. They challenged him consistently, and Pompidou let it be known he was available. De Gaulle had two choices. He could trim his sails to the new winds—but become the obedient leader of the majority, not the autonomous head of government he had always been. Or, he could challenge the politicians by appealing over their heads to the electorate. If he provoked them and won, he would reestablish his autonomy. Thus, the 1969 referendum. Why did de Gaulle add to the relatively popular cause of regional government and decentralization very controversial and unpopular representation of socio-professional groups and abolition of the Senate? Why did he not design a text to maximize the chances of victory? Because de Gaulle *needed* to be controversial. He needed to challenge the politicians to beat them. A tepid text would have produced an ambiguous result.[10]

GAULLISM MODIFIED: POMPIDOU

The circumstances under which Pompidou came to power marked a shift from Strategy Two to Strategy Three. His majority, while similar to de Gaulle's combined the elements differently, added some new ones to it, and dropped some. Under de Gaulle, the Nationalist-Loyalists, Modernizers, and part of the Left supported a program of reform and national assertion. Under Pompidou, the Nationalist-Loyalists joined the Conservatives and the Left dropped out. The resulting gap was filled by the parties of the center and the right. Pompidou enlarged the base of the Cabinet by taking in some centrists and the republican independents.

The quid pro quo of this "ouverture" of the majority was certain changes in policy: in foreign policy, Pompidou accepted British entry into the Common Market and moderated the anti-Americanism somewhat; in domestic policy, the brakes were put on further experimentation in the factory and the university, and concessions were made to steel businsses who had suffered from Gaullist expansionism; and in politics, reconciliation with the other parties was achieved by putting local government reform on ice. The dropping of Chaban-Delmas is revelatory: as Prime Minister, Chaban had tried to "unblock" the "Stalled Society"—not exactly radical, but too much for Pompidou's cautious line. Pompidou dominated the government, but he had limited autonomy as the leader of a coalition of interests. Pompidou spoke for conservative France in direct harmony with its own understandings. Pompidou did not suffer from this the way de Gaulle would have. His ambitions were different. He did not seek autonomy to do controversial things. He sought stability and was getting it.[11]

The trouble with this policy, indeed with Strategy Three, is that it sets loose a logic which gradually undermines it. As Gaullism becomes more openly conservative, and less nationalistic, it drives away significant sources of cross class, cross party support. This has to be replaced. Neighboring parties are drawn in, but this accentuates the importance of moderates and conservatives in the majority and decreases further the ability of the government to pursue the domestic and foreign policies needed to sustain a "movement" appeal rather than an openly partisan one or an openly "class" located one.

GAULLISM ABANDONED: GISCARD AND CHIRAC

Since 1974, Giscard has been caught in precisely this trap. Being outside the UDR, he has been less able to draw upon the Gaullist legend. His Republican Independents have strong conservative elements. He can hardly govern with "*les R.I.*" alone, so he must form a coalition. Seeking independence from the Gaullist clan, he moved toward the middle. The Giscard cabinets took in that slice of the center which had not rallied to Pompidou in 1969. Giscard spoke of *décrispation*, moderated French foreign policy, picked non-political people, and supported reforms such as abortion, but this reformism has narrow limits. The bulk of his constituency has been conservative. To move far enough left to attract the socialists would be to jettison a big chunk of the conservatives, probably including *the R.I.* The Socialists have not appeared willing to cooperate, but neither has the right. Thus, Giscard's language has been centrist, but his policies have been much more cautious. Indeed, very little domestic reform has been carried out. Pompidou could have put forward the *programme de Blois*—hardly a document to resurrect a *Troisième Force* including the Socialists. Giscard has *said* he wants a moderate Strategy Four: a broad coalition around moderate reform. In fact, he has pursued Strategy Three, drawing together the conservative Gaullists and the moderate-to-conservative non-Gaullists.

What of the Gaullists? Chirac, too, has spoken one line and followed another. As the heir to the Gaullist tradition, he claimed to be interested in Strategy Two: modernization under new leadership. In fact, he has moved toward Strategy One: preservation under new leadership.[12] Chirac has sought to assert his identity, visibility, individuality. He has refused to follow Pompidou's example: be patient, wait out the incumbent, his only possible replacement when the nation tires of him or he makes a mistake. His impatience has led him to an assertiveness which is full of risks. Like de Gaulle, he has antagonized the traditional formations of center and right. Unlike de Gaulle, he based his appeal increasingly on anti-leftism and on defense of very traditional interests. This completely disequilibrates the Gaullist movement. De Gaulle avoided too close an identification with the established groups or with simple anticommunism, in order to attract left support for his foreign policy and domestic modernization. Chirac has seriously diminished his capacity to do either. The people who attend his rallies and flock into the party do not want modernization nor flirtation with the left. Yet both require some left support, formal or tacit.

The greatest contradiction in the Chirac line appears in foreign policy. Chirac has taken the strongly nationalist stance of de Gaulle: anti-superpower, suspicious of the Common Market, assertive of French interests in all domains. This policy divides the center-right (and the left). Giscard has taken the opposite position, pro-Common Market and more Atlanticist, while exploiting any nationalist opportunity which arises, such as intervention in Africa. Thus, to replace center-right defections, the Gaullist foreign policy continues to require some left support, which contradicts Chirac's recent behavior directly. Chirac has thus failed to sustain the unity of de Gaulle's understanding: nationalism in foreign piolicy requires modernization at home, both of which require left support. That, in turn, strengthens the country by effecting a partial internal reconciliation. In this regard, Chaban-Delmas represented far greater continuity with de Gaulle. Chaban sought a compromise between Strategy Two and Strategy Three: continued reform, continued foreign policy assertiveness, but with less antagonism toward the elites of the Center and the moderate left. Thus, Giscard's victory in the "primary" of 1974 left the leadership of Gaullism open to Chirac's very different line.

GAULLISM REFOUND? THE FUTURE

The thrust of this essay has been to note weaknesses created for the present majority by the polarization of French politics. Polarization poses the identical problem for left and right: to find an integrating set of ideas, a program, a strategy, a *projet de société* which can support a broad political coalition. Such a coalition must not only win elections, but be able to carry out changes essential to sustaining its appeal. If certain coalition elements are too strong, they block change, and undermine the appeal of the whole.

De Gaulle's strategy for accomplishing this task entailed a complex juxtaposition of diverse social elements, mixing continuity and reform in policy, new and old leadership in personnel, and cross-party plus personal partisan appeals. His successors have all deviated from the original formula. Each has allowed the special chemistry of the mixture to precipitate out into its component ingredients which react quite differently to problems of policy. While this process cannot be divorced from the personalities involved, the original strategy and its alternatives can nonetheless be seen as types, among which the center-right parties have chosen and will continue to choose.

Over the next decade, any of these strategies could emerge, depending on events. If economic problems continue to be critical several scenarios are possible:

Economic tensions accentuate the decomposition of relations among the PSF and the PCF. Part of the PS breaks away and allies with the center around a policy of renewed Keynesian management of the economy: better fiscal and monetary policies, more aid to industrial reorganization, continued participation in the Common Market and a relatively open international economy. This "productivist" coalition seeks to adapt France to new conditions in the international economy. For the majority, this would be Strategy Four. Giscard is well placed to lead this alliance, as would certain reformist Gaullists.

The same economic situation prompts reliance on market forces which so raise unemployment as to prevent Socialist participation in the government. This would be Strategy Three, which is indeed what Giscard appears to have done since March 1978.

A worsening international economy produces very strong pressures for a "protectionist" response.[13] French industries suffering severely from international competition, and labor unions in those industrial branches would seek immediate help in the form of tariffs and other devices. Such policies would certainly be accompanied by a renewal of anti-Atlantic and anti-EEC nationalism, and a greater role for the State. This coalition would include elements of both business and labor, in conflict with the other cross class productivist alliance. Anti-leftism would be moderated in the service of a broad national appeal. This mobilizing nationalism used for some kind of modernization as well would be the original form of Gaullism, or Strategy Two. A more purely defensive version would be a variant of Strategy One that would render difficult the left appeal it requires. Probably, Chirac's past actions make it impossible for him to lead a Strategy Two coalition though he could continue as the main embodiment of Strategy One. Much will depend on Giscard's behavior. Too liberal a policy may permit Chirac to repair his relations with the left.

Whatever the specific individuals decide, the strategies remain permanent options. The original Gaullist formula might be possible only in times of acute crisis, when a certain sort of individual happens to be in a particular place. If so, de Gaulle will continue to fade into the history of the Fifth Republic as a lawgiver, useful in legitimation, but not as a model for imitation.

NOTES

1. The PCI understood this long ago. See Donald Blackmer and Sidney Tarrow, eds., *Communism in Italy and France* (Princeton: Princeton University Press, 1977). Also Suzanne Berger, "D'Une Boutique à L'Autre: Changes in the Organization of the French Middle Classes from the Fourth to the Fifth Republics," *Comparative Politics*, 10 (October, 1977).

2. Religion remains of great importance in shaping voting behavior. See Guy Michelat and Michel Simon, "Religion, Class and Politics,"*Comparative Politics*, 10 (October 1977). In both Italy and France, left gains in the seventies came via some partial breakthroughs in traditionally Catholic areas.

3. Robert Blake, *Disraeli* (New York: St. Martin's, 1966); Robert Blake, *The Conservative Party* (New York: St. Martin's, 1970); Paul Smith, *Disraelian Conservatism and Social Reform* (London: Routledge and Keagan Paul, 1967); P.F. Clarke, *Lancashire and the New Liberalism* (Cambridge: Cambridge University Press, 1971); Samuel Beer, *British Politics in the Collectivist Age* (New York: Random House, 1965); S.M. Lipset and Stein Rokkan, "Cleavage Structures, Party Systems and Voter Alignments: An Introduction," Party Systems and Voter Alignments (New York: The Free Press, 1967).

4. My understanding of de Gaulle and Gaullism, indeed of French politics in general, has been shaped very deeply by Stanley Hoffmann. See in particular his *Decline and Renewal* (New York: Viking, 1976).

5. For greater elaboration of the categories "Loyalists, Modernizers, and Traditionalists" within Gaullism see Peter Gourevitch, *Paris and The Provinces: The Politics of Local Government Reform in France*, (Berkeley: University of California Press, forthcoming) and Peter Gourevitch, "Reforming the Napoleonic State: The Creation of Regional Governments in France and Italy," in Luigi Graziano, Peter Katzenstein and Sidney Tarrow, eds., *Territorial Politics in Industrial Nations* (New York: Praeger, 1978), pp. 27–93.

6. For neo-Marxist views exploring the autonomy of the state and tension between "accumulation" and "legitimation" functions, see Fred Bloch, "The Ruling Class Does Not Rule: Notes on the Marxist Theory of the State," *Socialist Revolution* 33 (May-June, 1977) 6-28 David Gold, Clarence Low and Eric Olin Wright, "Recent Developments in Marxist Theories of the Capitalist State," parts 1 and 2 *Monthly Review* (October and November, 1975); Klaus Offe, "Structural problems of the Capitalist State," Klaus von Beyme, ed. *German Political Studies*(Beverly Hills: Sage, 1976); Klaus Offe and Volker Ronge, "Thesis on the Theory of the State," *New German Critique* 6 (fall 1975); James O'Connor, *Fiscal Crisis of the State* (New York: St. Martin's Press, 1977).

7. On the role of international politics in shaping domestic politics, and an explicit consideration of the "Caesarist model" in politics, see Hans-Uhlrich Wehler, "Bismarck's Imperialism, 1862-1890," *Past and Present* 48 (1970), 119-155. Also, Peter Gourevitch, "The Second Image Reversed: The International Sources of Domestic Politics," *International Organization* (fall 1978) and Peter Gourevitch "International Trade, Domestic Coalitions and Liberty: Comparative Responses to the Crisis of 1873-1896," *Journal of Interdisciplinary History* VIII: 2 (Autumn 1977), 281-313. See also the very fascinating exploration of the impact of the international trade crisis on the politics of the Weimar Republic in David Abraham, "Intraclass Conflict and the Formation of Ruling Class Consensus in Late Weimar Germany," (University of Chicago, Ph.D. dissertation, Department of History, 1977).

8. See Jean Charlot, *Le Phenomène Gaulliste* (Paris: Fayard, 1970), and *L'UDR* (Paris: Armond Colin, 1967).

9. On voting patterns, see Guy Michelat and Michel Simon, "Religion Class and Politics;" also the data given in Roy Macridis, *French Politics in Transition: The Years after de Gaulle* (Cambridge: Winthrop, 1975).

10. See JES Hayward, "Presidential Exit by Suicide," *Political Studies* (1970) and Peter Gourevitch, "Reforming the Napoleonic State."

11. See the very illuminating passages on Pompidou in Alain Peyrefitte, *Le Mal Francais* (Paris: Plon, 1976), especially ch. 48.

12. Indeed, in the past few years, Chirac has shown signs of going in several quite different directions. When he agreed to be Giscard's prime minister, it appeared he might be about to pursue Strategy Three: to lead the conservatives among the Gaullists into alliance with Giscard, along with some of the modernizers, leaving the Loyalists out, even perhaps breaking up the UDR in the process. This would have required allowing Giscard to lead, at least at present. Instead, in seeking to supplement Giscard, he Chirac has rediscovered the advantages of having one's own party base. He has also had to differentiate himself from Giscard. Thus when Giscard moved to the Atlanticist, moderate, décrispation strategy, Chirac was left with the nationalist, antagonistic one. It is not obvious that each couldn't have pursued the strategy of the other; indeed we might have predicted that from looking at the composition of their party organizations in 1974. Giscard was in a position to move first, and may have preempted certain options. Foreign policy is especially important: to take up Atlanticism required moving to the center, which in turn required décrispation. Certainly personal rivalry and ambition play a larger role in all this.

13. On international trade and coalitions see the material cited in Note 7, and the very brilliant essays by James Kurth "The Political Consequences of the Product Cycle: Industrial History and Political Outcomes," *International Organization*, 33 (winter 1979), and his equally brilliant essay "Delayed Development and European Politics" (mimeo 1977) part of which will appear as an essay in a forthcoming volume on Latin America, edited by David Collier, sponsored by the Joint Committee on Latin American Studies of the Social Science Research Council. On the political implications and the choices posed for labor of economic crises, see the stimulating work by Andrew Martin, "The Politics of Economic Policy in the United States: A Tentative View from a Comparative Perspective," *Sage Professional Papers*, Vol. 4, 1973.

The Effects of Twenty Years of Gaullism on the Parties of the Left

Georges Lavau

The title given to this conference, "Twenty Years of Gaullism," presupposes an accepted meaning of the term "Gaullism." However, there are at least three possible interpretations which, while clearly interrelated, do not necessarily overlap. Our assessments of the political consequences of these twenty years will be somewhat different, depending on whether we focus on one of them in particular or whether we consider all three simultaneously as a whole.

"Twenty years of Gaullism" may mean "twenty years of the Fifth Republic" (i.e., of the *political regime* defined specifically by the Constitution of 1958). If so, undoubtedly these years of Fifth Republic constitutional, political, and electoral procedures have had a profound impact on the entire political life of France, and the parties of the Left have felt the effects (if only because the preconditions of their action have been affected profoundly by the changes introduced by this regime). This is all the more true in that, certain modifications (some legal, others simply practical) notwithstanding, the regime has essentially undergone very few changes since its inception.

A second possible interpretation is that "twenty years of Gaullism" means "twenty years of Gaullist ideology and politics." This interpretation is less specific than the first (necessitating a somewhat detailed description of this "ideology" and this "politics"). This interpretation cannot be dismissed *a priori*, for "Gaullism" has not been simply a "political regime." It has also been an ideal, a political vision, and a certain orientation to the economy, foreign affairs, development, political relations, and ideologies. This interpretation requires more subtle distinctions than the former: firstly, because Gaullist "ideology" and "politics" have perhaps not enjoyed the same continuity and permanence as the "regime" in these twenty years; secondly—as

91

the remainder of this study will show—because the Left and the parties of the Left (or at least a segment of the Left between 1960 and 1966–68) have been affected less by these factors than by the regime iself. Be that as it may, the Left parties have withstood this "ideology" and "politics" better under the "Gaullism" of Pompidou and Giscard than under that of de Gaulle.

The third interpretation would translate "twenty years of Gaullism" as "twenty years of stable domination by a unified majority which does not include the parties of the Left." Certainly, Gaullism cannot be so reduced in character or scope, particularly prior to 1967. At the same time, this is a view which is not entirely inappropriate and which, to my mind, has carried more and more weight since the undoing of Chaban-Delmas' attempt to build a "new society" (around 1971). In any case, for the purpose of this study—namely, an analysis of the effects of "twenty years of Gaullism" on the parties of the Left—this view has equal importance with the first two.

The three interpretations have comparable validity. Moreover, even if they can be analyzed separately, they are still largely interconnected and these three facets of "Gaullism" (or these three different Gaullisms) have wrought a combined impact on political life.

The following pages shall look at the "twenty years of Gaullism" in light of these three interpretations with the understanding that, given the objective of this study, certain parts may lay more stress on one or another of them.

TWENTY YEARS:
A PERIOD WHICH HAS LEFT ITS MARK

"Gaullism," or the Fifth Republic, is twenty years old. The Fourth Republic lasted thirteen years, the Nazi Reich twelve years, and Mussolini's fascism twenty-one years. Twenty years of political continuity is the equivalent of 1937 for the USSR and 1959 for Francoism. If a regime this age is not mature, it has at least established a store of memories and experiences and partially eradicated earlier ones. This is particularly the case since, during these twenty years, the regime and its officials have sought assiduously to extirpate old political practices and have given scant attention to maintaining the old order.[1]

To grasp as firmly as possible the political effect this period has had on the generation who knew both the Fourth and Fifth Republics, after reaching the age, in 1944, at which their interests in politics had formed and their political orientations been consolidated (that is, between fifteen and eighteen years of age), we must consider not only the respective durations of these two regimes, but also the frequency of the major national electoral contests. Those who had just attained voting age in 1944 could vote seven times under the Fourth Republic (but only twice between 1947 and 1958); those same French had fourteen chances to vote between September and March 1978 (twenty-three times if we include second ballots). To weigh more accurately the impact of this electoral pattern, it must be remembered that this increase in opportunities for participation has been simultaneous with the development of television (which has both broadened electoral campaigns and turned them into "spectacles") and of public opinion polls. In addition, referenda and presidential elections have dramatized and simplified the stakes of political struggle and have polarized this struggle around the very existence of the regime, its merits, and its achievements. All of these conditions were profoundly different under the previous regime which had much less *visibility* than the Fifth Republic (this applies not only to the *regime*, but to the whole of *political life*).

The inculcation of "Gaullism" has also clearly been facilitated by factors promoting simple memorization (operating in reverse to the pattern of elections, but resulting in the same phenomenon of "visibility"): in thirteen years of the Fourth Republic, the French were permitted only a fleeting image of sixteen presidents of the Council, while in twenty years of the Fifth Republic they have familiarized themselves more readily with seven prime ministers who have been a daily presence on their television screens. The opposition, too, has benefited: from 1965, Francois Mitterrand, Jacques Duclos, Waldeck Rochet and Georges Marchais have enjoyed greater visibility than Guy Mollet, Maurice Thorez, Jules Moch, Pierre Mendès-France, Felix Gaillard, Robert Schuman, or René Mayer ever had.

The simple conclusion is that, leaving aside the respective "performances" of the Fourth and Fifth Republics, it would be surprising if "Gaullism"—for reasons of endurance, visibility, and frequency of participation opportunities alone—had not made a profound mark on those French who were adults at the beginning of the Fourth Republic and, even more so, of those who have come to political life since 1958.

Clearly, this does not mean that the political persuasions of the French have been homogenized and unified by the very fact of the regime's duration. France has continued to be divided politically and the gradual success of the Fifth Republic in building up in the minds of the French a body of *common* political representations certainly has not prevented the Left parties from keeping—and recruiting—voters, members, and militants throughout these years (both adverse and favorable). It means simply that, since the rules of the game have been changed profoundly and irrevocably, the major arenas of political struggle shifted, and the political representations of the French conditioned significantly by "Gaullist" practices, the Left parties have been more or less forced to adapt to "Gaullism" and to react within the context of new political conditions.

Their adaptation has not conformed to any regular pattern: it has quickened since 1966. It has varied in depth by party: all were not equally vulnerable to the "challenge" of "Gaullism"; some were better able to resist adaptation because they remained relatively little identified with previous regimes (e.g., the PCF and the PSU); others (e.g., the Socialist party and the Radicals) sustained the full force of the political changes since 1958.

PERIODIZATION

Let us begin with a paradox. If we consider only the very end of our period (1977-78) and look back to the Fourth Republic and even to 1921-39, it is possible to reach the opinion—a not entirely superficial and impressionistic one—that, after twenty years of Gaullism, the parties of the Left and the entire body of the Left are not in a profoundly altered situation.

A few examples: on the whole, protagonists are the same: the Communist party, the Socialists and the Radicals. True, their respective positions have changed. The PCF has lost some ground to the Socialist party (which has regained approximately the level of votes the SFIO had in 1945). The Radicals have seen the deepening of a process of division and retrenchment, which was already well under way during the Fourth Republic. None of the Left parties has disappeared fusions between them have been minimal and have involved only fractions of the non-communist Left between 1963 and 1971 (it is different for Center and Right parties: the Popular Republican Movement—MRP—has ceased to exist, the National Center of Independents and Peasants —CNIP—mainains no more than a symbolic presence, and the Union for French Democracy may perhaps absorb the Radical party, the Republican party, the Democratic Center, and the CNIP). The entire Left still represents a minority as it was from 1951 to 1955 (given that almost half of the Rally of the Republican Left, RGR, was certainly not on the Left).

Relations between the PCF and the PS from 1977 to 1978 are similar to those of 1937-38 (forty years ago!), or again of 1956-57. The trade union similarities are even greater: no accommodation between the FO, the CGT and the FEN; and the CFDT is still in profound disagreement with the CGT.

If we consider only the state of affairs in 1977-78, it would appear that the major impact of twenty years of "Gaullism" has affected only the political structures of the Right and the Center (both markedly changed), the composition of governmental personnel, institutional processes, and the behavior of the senior public administration. To all intends and purposes, the Left has been affected much less.

This can be explained by the following factors, which probably operate simultaneously (although in different degrees, depending on which political components of the Left we consider):

1) quite simply, during these twenty years, the Left has been isolated in the opposition and has thus been less immediately breached by the direct effects of "Gaullism" as a whole;

2) to a certain extent also, the parties of the Left have had the will to resist "Gaullism," neither to acknowledge its influences nor to succumb to them;

3) finally, the effects of "Gaullism" have probably been felt much more at the political, economic, and social bases of the Center and Right than at those of the Left. Despite its avowed intentions, "Gaullism" has wrought fewer changes in the conditions of the workers, the low-income wage-earners and the popular classes—which constitute the political base of the Left parties—than in those of the middle classes.

The initial impression that the Left parties remained relatively impervious to the effects of "Gaullism" is not entirely inaccurate, but, nevertheless, it becomes highly implausible as we survey the Left's reactions over the entire period of 1958–79 and break these reactions down into time periods.

As with any attempt at periodization, we face the classic choie: short or long-term periodization?

Long-term periodization highlights the important change in the conditions of the Left's struggle and leads us to situate the major break at the end of 1965 (Mitterrand's candidacy) and the beginning of 1966. Before then the Left parties had waged effectively a non-frontal, non-programmatic battle against "Gaullism." The candidacy of Mitterrand—supported by the SFIO and the PCF—marks the beginning of an electoral union which gave birth slowly to vague agreements and, then, to a common program for the Left. After this, the battle became *frontal* and rested on a *desire for a common program*.

The disjuncture is not merely formal. It also conforms, although only approximately, to deeper changes. When Mitterrand repeated that the Left regained hope from the date of his candidacy the movement of recovery began and "Gaullism" no longer appeared invulnerable, his claims were not entirely without foundation. It is also partly true—even if the process was slow and intermittent—that from this time, the old SFIO was condemned either to fail or to change and that the Union of the Left, outlined then (for the first time since 1936), could consolidate only by means of programmatic unity and, therefore, by means of an ideological rapprochement (albeit one laden with misunderstandings) between the PCF and the non-communist Left.

However, this long-term periodization ignores the contradictions inherent in each of the two major phases and does not take into account the breaks, delays, spurts and reversals in the processes. Accordingly the phase of the non-frontal, non-programmatic battle can be subdivided as follows:

1958–autumn 1962: disarray and division.
autumn 1962–December 1965: the beginning of a recovery.

and the phase of the frontal, programmatic battle as follows:

1966–May 1972: a difficult and eventful prelude.
June 1972–October 1974: the Union in action.

95

October 1974–March 1978: progress, mistrust, and defeat.

This short-term periodization seems to be more accurate.

1958–November 1962: Disarray and Division

The Algerian War, the assertion of "personal" and "reserved power" (*domaine réservé*) by the president of the Republic, the imposition of rigourous discipline over the governmental party, the reformist "Stakhanovism" implemented by the government of Michel Debré, and finally the harsh economic effects of the complete emergence of the Common Market: all these issues were paramount during this period and, in one way or another, summarily forced the Left (which had received 43.4 percent of the votes in November 1958) into highly unfavorable and hitherto unknown conditions.

Deeply divided, powerless, and stymied, the Left "arched its back." A group of voters from each of its three parties had voted for those parties which had rallied to or been associated with "Gaullism." Certain political personalities of the Center Left the extreme-left had gone over to "Gaullism."[2] The problem of the Algerian War overshadowed all others, so that no Left party (not even the PCF) could suggest a broad-sweeping program, the political strategies of the Communists and the Socialists were still completely at variance, and their leaders still had no contact or dialogue.

November 1962–December 1965: the Beginnings of a Recovery

To a certain extent, the end of the Algerian War freed the Left parties from their immediate preoccupations, while the two-fold triumph of "Gaullism" in the referendum of 28 October 1962 and the elections of 18–25 November 1962 (the Left, including the Radicals, gained only 42.2 percent of the votes) forced them to struggle more efficiently or, at least, in some way, to avoid succumbing passively to a slow process of contraction.

"Struggle more efficiently": for the PCF after the Central Committee meetings of 13–14 December 1962, meant to seek a union with the Socialist party "at any cost" through an inter-organizational agreement, which would enable them to negotiate and sign a "common governmental program of democratic unity," a line which was ratified solemnly by the 17th Congress in 1964. This line would lead the PCF to adopt gradually a less forbidding, less alienating, less pro-Soviet stance (at least, in that part of itself which it showed to its "anticipated allies"): but it led also to an even tougher stand against "Gaullism" (with exceptions allowed for certain aspects of foreign policy).

The SFIO also tried to struggle "more efficiently," but with less unanimity than the PCF. The majority of the party around Guy Mollet, adopted a much more heavily critical posture than during 1958–62 and refused generalized unity of action with the communists (and even more, a common program), confining itself to a cautious policy of *ad hoc* common actions and limited electoral agreements. A minority of the SFIO, aware that the party was growing old and becoming ideologically impoverished, aspired to a resuscitation of the "old party" (*la vieille maison*), if necessary, by means of a graft—one, however, which would change neither its "revolutionary" heritage nor its secular character.

This latter aspiration encountered another movement, albeit little organized, in the Left which found expression through the "political clubs" that began to flourish and intensify their activity precisely at this time. From diverse political tendencies and sensibilities, these clubs had picked up a following of people resigning from old Left or Center-Left parties, of union and social militants, of intellectuals inspired by a need for activism, and of senior officials for whom "Gaullism" seemed too authoritarian and too irrational (even if they found it fascinating in certain respects).[3] These clubs—this "extra-party" Left—and a minority among the minorities of the SFIO (an admixture of many differences which were in themselves far from secondary) had in common a *desire to modernize the parties of the Left*, in their structures, practices, ideology, relations to civil society, and responses to the challenge of "Gaullism." It was, in sum, a strange combination of "Gaullism" (returning to rationality), of anti-"Gaullism" (but quite distinct from the usual "leftist" critique of "Gaullism") and of "Kennedyism" (seen through Parisian eyes). This assembly of political tendencies was mobilized around the attempted candidacy of Gaston Defferre for the presidency of the Republic (early 1964–June 1965).

This desire for modernization met with opposition not only from Guy Mollet and his followers in the SFIO, but primarily from the PCF, because it implied a strategy which excluded the Communist party and promised to bring it under control either by solitary starvation in its ghetto or by rallying unequivocally around modernization and the reconquest of the Left.

In fact, the undertaking was premised on the hypothesis that it was possible to win away from "Gaullism" not only the quasi-legendary "vital forces" (*forces vives*), but also a part of the Political Center (essentially the MRP) and some Radicals, and to link them to a non-communist Left through a socialist, modernizing project.

It was a fiasco which left the field open for Francois Mitterrand and for those realists who thought that the Left should reestablish the old Union of the Left (PCF, SFIO, and Radicals), then incorporate the political clubs and try simultaneously to constitute the entire non-communist Left as a single federation.

The rallying of almost all the Left Parties around Mitterrand's candidacy in the presidential election of December 1965 marks both the first stage in this undertaking and the beginning of a process that gave the old SFIO no alternative but to change. But the road was long and difficult.

A Difficult and Eventful Prelude

The first step was the agreement between the PCF and the Federation of the Democratic and Socialist Left (FGDS) on withdrawals for the 1967 legislative elections. Meanwhile, the PCF continued to apply pressure for a programmatic agreement on a genuine union of the Left, and negotiations for more effective integration of the FGDS proceeded very slowly.

The second step was the signing on 24 February 1968, of a "Joint Declaration" between the PCF and the FGDS—still not a common program but the beginnings of one. Its development would be impeded from the time of the great crisis of May 1968 until the eve of the presidential election of June 1969. But though electoral agreement was maintained for that election, the events of May, the candidacies of Defferre and Jacques Duclos, and troubles in the FGDS revealed the manifold disagreements between the PCF and the non-communist Left and within its own ranks.

The process resumed, with difficulty, at the end of 1969 and continued almost until the Epinay Congress of the SFIO in 1971. However, three factors made progress easier:

1) firstly, the resignation of Mollet from the leadership of the SFIO and his replacement by Alain Savary who initiated a revival of the New Socialist party;

2) secondly, the municipal elections of March 1971 in which Communists and Socialists frequently drew up common lists that garnered quite good results;

3) finally, the clear abandonment by Georges Pompidou, now president of the Republic, of the visionary aspects of "de Gaulle's Gaullism." The new president unerringly chose conservative order (*l'ordre conservateur*), the support of the entire Right and of the bulk of the Center, and made the country's primary objective "industrialization." The immediate results of industralization (concentration of firms and industrial reorganization) would mean heavy economic and social costs for the Left parties' political clienteles. The "new society" proclaimed by prime minister Jacques Chaban-Delmas and his attempts to implement a broad contractual politics did not conceal for long the harsh reality of Pompidou's conservative political and social choices.

The last stage in this sub-period happened very quickly in the form of the successive publication of the Communist and Socialist parties' programs for government and of negotiations for a Common Program, signed at the beginning of June 1972 by the PCF, the PS, and the Left Radical Movement (a splinter group of the Radical party).

June 1972–October 1974: The Union in Action

This was the era of progress. Until the presidential election of 1974, progress has been slight in terms of electoral performance: in the 1973 legislative elections, the Left as a whole achieved a total no higher than in 1967; and Mitterrand's successes in the first ballot of the presidential election were rather deceptive. Progress was of a different order. To begin with, the Left parties were on the offensive constantly, while the majority was on the defensive. The Left no longer appeared disorganized, the Common Program (criticized quite sharply until 1973 by the CFDT and the PSU) was proudly mentioned, and the image of unity brought sympathizers and adherents into the fold, to the benefit of the PCF and the PS. Finally, the unity of action between the CFDT and the CGT, begun in 1966, was in perfect working order after 1973: trade union unity was following the same route as the Union of the Left.

There was scarcely a hint of disagreement among the parties of the Common Program until after the presidential election of May 1974. Their euphoria seemed to last until the round of legislative by-elections of early fall 1974. These by-elections followed the pattern that had begun in 1973: a dwindling of the majority's political and electoral reserves, from which the PS was the obvious beneficiary, while the PCF lost ground proportionately and at times absolutely.

Meanwhile, the 21st (extraordinary) Congress of the Communist party took place in October 1974. Contrary to the PCF's discourse and practice since the signing of the Common Program, this congress severely criticized the socialist partner, reproaching it for wanting to "eliminate" the Communist party, for not participating in popular struggles, and for having remained reformist and social democratic. Above all, it proclaimed that the Party must reassert its identity more clearly and maintain autonomy and independent action within the Union of the Left. It declared, as its objective, 25 percent of the vote and one million members. Henceforth, the "rival allies" would strive unceasingly to "cultivate their differences."[4]

October 1974–19 March 1978: Progress, Mistrust and Defeat

This last phase is so recent and has been analyzed so closely that I shall confine myself to some very brief observations on its contradictions and paradoxes.

In spite of some moments of clarification and improvement (notably, during campaigns for the 1976 cantonal and 1977 municipal elections), the atmosphere of relations between the PCF and the PS continued to worsen (not only at the upper level of the party apparatuses but among the base organizations), recapitulating in some ways inter-union relations among the CGT, the CFDT and the FEN.[5] However, throughout this period, the opinion polls were almost always favorable to the Left (until 6 March 1978), suggesting that the public was unmindful of the climate of disunity; and, in fact, at the time of the second cantonal, municipal, and even legislative ballots of 1978, the vote transfers between the lists or candidates of the Common Program were made under generally satisfactory conditions.

There were other paradoxes. When the PCF launched a bitter campaign among its militants to urge them to attack the PS—attacks to which the PS replied very feebly, if at all—opinion polls showed that Communist sympathizers consistently held more favorable opinions of the PS than Socialist sympathizers did of the PCF.[6]

After the electoral defeat of 1978 in which the Left gained results essentially equal to those of the second ballot of the 1974 presidential election, the Common Program no longer existed and the Union of the Left was virtually shattered.

After twenty years, the net gains were marginal. Without losing significant ground electorally, the PCF had nevertheless yielded first place on the Left to the Socialist party—by a margin of two points. But once again the PS was threatened with internal problems and risked seeings its achievements come to a standstill, if not decline. Meanwhile, the PCF reinforced its militant potential and tightened its hold over the CGT considerably, and yet it still did not seem completely free from internal crises either.

Again, twenty years of Gaullism seem to have affected the parties of the Right and of the Center (the RPR and the UDF) more than the parties to the Left.

CHANGE AND RESISTANCE TO CHANGE

It would be impossible to deny that the Left parties have *changed* in the course of these twenty years. But it is also clear that they have frequently demonstrated a *resistance* to change.

To begin with, they were forced to adapt new conditions of political struggle resulting primarily from the new constitutional framework, the new electoral system, and changes in the distribution of the loci of power. Also, new conditions resulted from the many changes in French civil society. These latter changes were more responsible than the direct effects of Gaullism for the transformations on the Left. Certainly, from the second half of the sixties onward, political Leftists could no longer view "Gaullism" as a passing phenomenon, a temporary departure from the concept of the "Republic" or as a "bad moment which would pass." But, also, it would be incorrect to say that they "learned" something from Gaullism and from the Fifth Republic (the somewhat casual beginnings of reflection and comprehension on this point within the political clubs during the years 1960–65 were nipped in the bud and never continued); they simply practiced a policy of tactical adaptation. Similarly, the "classical" Left (Communists, Socialists and Left Radicals) adopted only a few verbal and rhetorical by-products of the wave of new ideas and practices that came out of the wild explosion of May 1968, and learned to use a few second-hand catch-phrases to back them up.

Quite clearly, the Left parties underwent changes whose scope and depth shall be delineated. But we must also evaluate the effects of the Fifth Republic had on the practices, ideology and mythology of the Left. In all these aspects, as we shall see, inhibitions and inertia blocked change; but frequently there was something more: a determination to resist change.

The New Conditions of Struggle

After the dark years of disarray and division, in the field of electoral struggles the Left parties felt most comfortable and best able to take up the challenge of "Gaullism." They adapted quite well to the two-ballot majority voting system, which (if it worked against the Radical party, finding itself in more and more straitened circumstances, and the Communist party, which it always under-represented in Parliament) at least had the advantage, once national agreement upon withdrawals existed, of making the old political rules of "republican discipline" work in their favor—rules to which a growing number of socialist and radical voters had been conforming since 1967. The parties adapted equal-ly well to other electoral arrangements, no matter how harsh, such as the prere-quisite of 12.5 percent of votes that candidates had to meet in order to appear on the second ballot, and the system of closed lists for municipal elections in towns of more than 30,000 inhabitants. The presidential election (which, in 1962–65, most analysts were predicting would rout the parties of the Left) finally became—with the exception of 1969—a test which the Left (if it could reach an agreement between its constituent parts) could meet with forces almost equal to those of "Gaullism."

The relatively rapid sociological and demographic changes in the composi-tion of the electorate could have been disastrous for the Left parties. Never-theless, neither the Communist party nor the Socialist party was hurt ultimately by the significant decrease in the agricultural and rural population, or by the relative decline in the working-class population in the strict sense. The Socialist party—and even, to a certain extent, the Communist party—was able to carve out a satisfactory electoral share among the developing professional sectors: ter-tiary sector workers, technicians, engineers and middle-level executives (*cadres moyens*).

The Left parties could defend themselves effectively in electoral struggles against Gaullism because they held two trump-cards which gave them powers of resistance, and even a certain superiority over Gaullism.

The first was the organization of a part of their electorate within union and professional structures which related and extended the activities of the parties, or which at least mitigated the impact of Gaullism. This was particularly true of the trade-union organizations of wage-earners (CGT, CFDT) and of teachers (FEN), and is partially true also of the more informal networks of mutual societies, defense associations and agricultural organizations in certain regions.

The second trump card lay in the already long-standing political entrenchment of Radicals, Socialists and even Communists in the departmental and municipal assemblies. In this area, the Gaullist party had to start from scratch; and to the extent that it gradually succeeded in gaining a foothold in local power structures, it was at the expense more of the old moderate and centrist parties than of the left. Nation-wide, the Left has always gained better results in local elections than in national contests (the opposite was true for the UNR, now the RPR). The more the major issue of elections lay in the conquest of central power, the more the Left had trouble threatening Gaullism; the more the issues were situated at the level of daily and immediate concerns of the citizenry, the better the Left's performance.

Experience taught the Left parties very quickly that, while the Fifth Republic regime allowed them space for struggle in the electoral field and in the realm of municipal power—space virtually as free as before—their possibilities in the sphere of parliamentary control over the government and the president were limited very seriously by the new rules of the game. In addition, they saw almost no further possibility for interfering or for pressure, being minorities in the National Assembly, excluded from the government, and having no ally or even any benevolent spokesman in ministerial quarters, in the high administration, or in the prefectoral corps.

Such restraints entailed very little change in the Communist party's situation. But they were a source of considerable concern for the PS and the Radicals which had buttressed each other since the Third Republic in their pursuit of influence over central power.

They imposed upon the Left parties the urgent necessity—if they were to escape from semi-impotence—to take over *all* the central positions of power simultaneously: an absolute majority of seats in Parliament (in a unified and disciplined coalition), and control of the government and the presidency of the Republic. The undertaking was so difficult that—all other constrains aside—it gave the Left parties no choice but to unite firmly in an effort to rally part of the Center electorate (if not the parties themselves). In that direction they could follow different strategies. However, only the PS could attempt to build an anti-Gaullist coalition with the left Center and the right Center (forced together electorally by Gaullism since 1962), leaving the Communist party in isolation. This last strategy was abandoned after the Defferre initiative in 1964 and tried again vainly before the 1969 presidential election (in the candidacies of Poher and Defferre).

The objective of conquering all the central positions of power at one time meant that the Left parties—assuming they could convey an image of perfect unity—would have to create the public image of a challenger capable of competing with Gaullism *on its own turf.* That is to say, a challenger possessing the characteristics and qualities attributed, in all Gaullist propaganda, to men and parties who could legitimately occupy these central positions of power: the stature of statesman, a sense of national responsibility, independence from interest group pressures, political realism, ability, worldly experience, a sound familiarity with state affairs, and the support of strong teams of experts and technicians.

As we have discovered from numerous opinion polls, the Socialist party never really succeeded in creating this image, despite Mitterrand's and the party's rather belated efforts: the televised debates between Mitterrand and Valéry Giscard d'Estaing and with Raymond Barre have always hurt the Socialists *on this score.* The Communist party also tried to achieve such an image, but its efforts were always thwarted by its preference for maintaining a popular style, for keeping its reputation as defender of the "poor" and "the common people," and by its refusal to renounce on immediate, everyday claims. Most importantly, from the moment the Common Program was signed (June 1972) until the debates over its implementation (May 1977–February 1978), this document, which claimed to offer precise and final solutions to all the problems of government, *prevented* the signatories from deviating an inch from its text. It was both a strict contract and a prayer book which had only to be recited. That is why the Union of the Left began to crack when the government challenged the signatories to the Common Program to "calculate," in financial and budgetary terms, the costs and revenues of the program; it was to provoke the Left into displaying its accountability and its economic expertise. In taking up the challenge, the Left parties promptly revealed their disagreements: disagreements between the PCF and its partners, but also disagreements between the different internal wings of the PS, and finally disagreements between the CGT and the CFDT and between these unions and the Left parties.

The only positive result of these efforts—a rather dubious result—was a considerable expansion of the role of experts in these two parties. In the Socialist party "expert groups" proliferated around the National Secretariat, particularly after 1974, and this development, whose aims were publicity and an "identifying image," rather than a serious improvement of party analyses, seems to have produced only unequal and rather sloppy results. Incomparably better organized, the PCF has kept pace, directing the recruitment and the work of its experts throughout the different commissions of the Central Committee and sections of the Secretariat with its usual diligence. But here too, the major political choices of the PCF do not really seem to have come under the influence of the experts; rather they were used more often to provide justifications for decisions made in their absence.

Changes in the Parties and the Effects of Gaullism

The changes in the Communist and Socialist parties have given rise to a body of literature which is so abundant and so complex that we can only give a very incomplete synthesis of it here.

The only question to be examined—and to which I do not pretend to give a definitive answer—will be the extent to which these changes were determined, more or less directly, by the impact of twenty years of Gaullism. In other words, would these changes have taken place anyway and would they have been of the same order (or to carry it further, would they have been more sweeping?), if there had been no "Gaullism" during these twenty years?

As we have seen already, the parties of the Left were forced more or less to adapt to new conditions of struggle and to the new rules of the game of the Fifth Republic. Nevertheless, many other changes cannot be attributed to the impact of Gaullism, but have their origins either in an internal dynamic specific to each of these parties and their interrelations, or in changes in French civil society which have affected the parties.

The conclusion reached (and here we can speak with an authority based on established scientific facts) is that the latter two factors, more so than the impact of Gaullism, have been responsible for the changes within the Communist party. The case of the Socialist party is different: it has been influenced by all three agents of change.

If the Communist party committed itself more and more resolutely (at least until November 1977) to the Union of the Left and to a strict alliance with the Socialist party, it is clearly partly because isolation would have been harmful to it under the new political regime. Nevertheless, it was also simply being faithful to one of its main strategies since June 1934; and already in 1956 it had agreed to support the Mollet government, as much for its social measures as for its policy of reestablishing order in Algeria. Similarly, the ambiguities concealed in its United Left strategy from 1972 to 1978 are not fundamentally different from those which were concealed, several decades earlier, in its policy of the "Popular Front for peace, bread, and liberty" (1935–38) and the "United Front" policy (1922–34): Gaullism and the Fifth Republic were not relevant at all.

The most dramatic change by the Communist party since 1958 (and especially since 1968) has been its relative disengagement from the Communist party of the Soviet Union. Here again, the impact of Gaullism has almost nothing to do with the phenomenon (whatever our final assessment of its real extent and scope). The determinants were numerous and diverse. Among these were the gradual disintegration of the international communist movement (begun with Togliatti's "Testament" and the Sino-Soviet rift) which would eventually include the PCF; increasingly broad public awareness of the real political and economic situation in socialist countries; the death of Maurice Thorez; the growing attrition, in the ranks of the PCF, of those generations of followers associated with Bolshevization and the Second World War; and finally the "Prague Spring" tragedy in 1968. But all these factors were secondary in importance to the fact that, at least until the signing of the Common Program, the Socialists with whom the PCF wanted a secure alliance at any price, could exact a "de-Russification" from the PCF as the cost of this alliance.

There were other changes in the PCF, such as a gradual softening of the notorious "wooden speech" (*langue de bois*) in favor of a more open, more direct, and more diversified manner of speaking. These were largely due to the factors mentioned above, which were highlighted by changes in French society (changes in political language, cultural changes among the younger generations who were flocking to the PCF in ever-increasing numbers, advances in the media, and changes in the means and forms of political communication).

Likewise, there were changes in the theoretical domain: not Gaullism but the collective factors just outlined caused the PCF to give up the ideal of a single party, to accept alternation in power (even after the advent of socialism), to abandon the concept of the dictatorship of the proletariat, and to condemn the theory of a "model" of socialist society.

In short, the PCF has adapted to the new conditions, to changes in the international environment, and to those in society, but it has essentially been responsible for determining its own perspectives and objectives. It was all the easier for the PCF to remain relatively immune to the impact of Gaullism when its electoral forces—once they had recovered from the setback of 1958—were less and less amenable to Gaullism. The PCF's electoral level dropped between 1956 and 1974 by about four points and then stabilized. The Gaullist regime was, however, partly responsible for this situation, which is in itself rather significant: since 1958, the PCF has never been able to regain its electoral level of 1951-56. Certainly other factors contributed, but the new political regime clearly played a role.

There remains the question of Gaullist foreign policy. The PCF has occasionally (but not always) given its support—both overtly and discreetly according to the circumstances—but it seems impossible to claim that it was forced to adopt that position under pressure from Gaullism. On the one hand, a concern for national sovereignty and for disengagement from NATO was part of its policy before the Fifth Republic. Then again, the PCF has lent its support to Gaullist foreign policy only when and if it suited.

The situation evolved quite differently for the Socialist party, especially before 1965 and even the Epinay Congress in 1971. Experience has largely shown that part of the old Socialist electorate was aware of the attractions of Gaullism, particularly until 1965, and that this was especially true of a number of its personnel (some of whom had had careers in the Gaullist party and some even in the government). The weakness of the SFIO organization, the aging of its members, and the near-disappearance of its potential for militancy, meant that the PS did not have the same powers of resistance as the PC. It risked losing the indispensable support of the Radical party.

Accordingly, the Socialist party had to seek at any cost—but not without occasional changes of heart before 1971—a means to avoid obsolescence and domination by the PCF, as well as escaping its image as a sentimental old party from a less and less glorious past. On this count, the prolonged existence of the Fifth Republic was the *primary* cause of the changes to which it began to yield from early 1965—changes which were no really implemented until the end of 1969. Putting it very bluntly: the Fifth Republic indirectly made Mitterrand first General de Gaulle's challenger in 1965, and then the first secretary of the new Socialist party, created at Epinay in 1971, and finally the Common Program's candidate in 1974; except for the presidential election by universal suffrage—introduced by the Fifth Republic—Mitterrand would probably never have been anything more than the deputy for Chateau-Chinon.

But, of course, although Gaullism was the primary instigator of change within the Socialist party, it had much less direct influence over the means and the direction of the changes that occurred.

The Socialist party was able to survive "the gloomy years" before 1971 for two reasons. Firstly, since the Communist party almost never deviated from its "Stalinist" character during all these years, it could neither attract the traditional non-communist Left electorate, nor provide a refuge against Gaullism. This left, in spite of everything, only the Socialist party. Secondly, the electoral and political support of the SFIO lay in social bases which, on the whole, remained loyal. These bases consisted primarily of teachers and petty bureaucrats, as well as the widespread network of local socialist elected officials and their clients. This network eroded slowly and lost its powers of social and political control gradually, but nevertheless managed to endure long enough to permit the rebirth of the Socialist party. Finally, the old "republican" base made resistance possible among diverse rural and urban social strata.

Many protagonists with varied credentials were involved in the creation of the new Socialist party at the Congress of Epinay: first were Mitterrand and a small coterie of fundamentally anti-Gaullist friends, most of whom had been with him since 1964; next were most of the activists and office-holders from the old SFIO; and finally, some small groups of generally young men who were active, Marxist-oriented, and ardent supporters of an alliance with the Communist party. But until the signing of the Common Program, and especially until the 1973 elections, the Socialist party, although slowly increasing its membership, was scarcely different in composition from the FGDS during 1966-67; it was more unified, but hardly any stronger. "New blood" began to flow in after the 1973 elections, with a new and even more important vitality

106

during and after the 1974 presidential campaign, a pattern repeated in the cantonal electoral victories of 1976, the 1977 municipal elections, and triumphant public opinion polls.

All the analyses of the elections of 1973, 1974, 1976 and 1977 show that the Socialist party's gains in regions which had not been traditional strong for the SFIO were made almost always at the expense of Gaullism or of Gaullist-oriented centrist parties; the PS was building to the detriment of the Fifth Republic and Gaullism. Continuing economic crisis, unemployment, and the effects of anti-inflationary measures were instrumental in winning this electorate; but equally so was the fact that the PS continued to be seen, according to the polls, as a party that posed very little threat to the liberties or economic and social order of the country.[8]

The members and the activists who joined the PS after the Epinay Congress were clearly from different backgrounds, but only a very few were deserters from Gaullism (with some notable exceptions like Edgard Pisani and Jacques Delors who, after all, had never been part of the "Gaullist" hierarchy, despite their association with the government). The PS attracted a fraction of the unorganized extreme-left, particularly very young men and women. These young "leftists" came to the PS because it spoke a radical language, was not Communist, and seemed to offer a milieu for a free search for new political practices. To some extent, this group can be placed under the rubric of "*le courant des Assises du socialisme*" (The Assizes of Socialism, held in September 1974), which was composed of PSU deserters and CFDT militants. Another, quite different, category of sympathizers and adherents converged on the PS: all the "old soldiers" loyal to the "popular fronts" of the long-forgotten past, that is to say, all those who were attached sentimentally to the idea of socialist-communist unity and who, for so long, had taken refuge in nostalgia but were not reinspired by the signing of the Common Program. Finally, when the tide swept the PS to over 20 percent in the opinion polls, a wave of followers, variously motivated, descended on the party which was heading toward a likely victory in the 1978 elections.

In summary: the new Socialist party was distinguished from the old SFIO by four factors: the shock of the establishment of the new regime, the tenacity of Francois Mitterrand, the Union of the Left, and its repeated successes (which came to an abrupt halt on March 12, 1978). But we must also take into account certain changes in civil society which fostered the "renewal" of the Socialist party: notably, changes in attitude and behavior among sections of Catholic and women voters.[9]

The Ideological World and Practice of the Left Parties:

Few Changes

Let us begin with what seems to have been the most stunning paradox in the situation of Left parties during the course of the Fifth Republic.

Few political regimes have been so hostile to "ideologies" as the Fifth Republic. Few political regimes have criticized and ridiculed, as trenchantly and with such powerful means of communication, the traditional Left system of political representation, "republican" terminology, "leftist" rhetoric, the practices of Left parties,[10] and Marxism in its different forms. This critique was further reiterated, at least until 1968, by several "modernist" streams of thought which were situated on the perimeters of Gaullism. Until the crisis of May 1968, the political literature which was favored by editors, reviews, and the "intellectual" press, was ruthless in its attitude towards the "archaism" of traditional Left ideology and practice; the Left was rudely told to bring itself up-to-date, to adopt its Bad-Godesberg program, to modernize seriously, to abolish the Amiens Charter, to cast off its old habits and prejudices, and to bid farewell to Marx and Jaurés.

Despite momentary temptations between 1960 and 1965, and especially after May 1968, the ideological and rhetorical world of the pre-1958 Left was not only resilient but was reinforced considerably and the essence of its traditional political practice was maintained. Even the ideological concept which would seem to be most innovatory—*autogestion*—was new only in relation to the political world of 1920–58: in fact, it was an extension of "ultra-left" themes of the years 1909–20, which had functioned underground until 1968 when they reemerged simultaneously in Germany, Italy, the Netherlands, and France.

The major signs of resistance, if not reinforcement, in the Left parties' ideological and rhetorical world can be described only very cursorily here.

First was the extraordinary revival of Marxism—or at least what remains of it in the discourse of political organizations. They were not concerned with theoretical Marxism in the academic and intellectual sense, but rather with the applicability of its concepts, arguments, and terminology to the *political* arena. This more or less crude Marxism was no longer the exclusive perogative of the Communist party, the PSU, or the various Trotskyite or "Marxist-Leninist" organizations, but had become the most commonly used language (and was considered to be the only informed language) in the Socialist party (and not only in its CERES faction). By the time Mitterrand declared, "I am not a Marxist," his entire party claimed not to have heard this blasphemy.

A series of well-known thought and word associations resulted: capitalism, labor movement, class struggle, mode of production, working class, class alliance, class front, collective appropriation of the means of production and exchange, nationalization, transition to socialism, articulation of parties, unions and masses, and popular struggle.

108

To avoid caricaturization, it is fair to add that Marxism was not resuscitated within the Socialist party, or even in the Communist party, without undergoing refinements and additions. But such elaborations were limited in two ways. First, they barely circulated beyond the party circles of "intellectual" specialists, study commissions, and journals of restricted circulation for the PS, they were *Faire, Repères, La Nouvelle revue socialiste*; and for the PC, *France nouvelle, La Nouvelle critique*, and *La Pensée*). Second, the Marxist revival was characterized by an often superficial borrowing of the thought of Gramsci, Louis Althusser and their acolytes. Finally, frequently, the parties' theoretical output was a simple, incoherent combination of more or less orthodox Marxism with anti-statist and *autogestionnaire* themes.

Other signs of ideological and rhetorical continuity were the references to historical dates and symbolic events. "Repeat 1905," said Mollet at the beginning of the sixties, when invoking the necessity for the SFIO to win back all the socialists who had left the "old party." "The socialists were not wrong at the Tours Congress," said Mitterrand in order to justify perpetuating the link between Léon Blum and the Socialist party into the seventies. The Communist party always celebrates the same anniversaries in its liturgical year.

The Paris Commune, the Tours Congress, 12 February 1934, the Popular Front, the Spanish Civil War: all these references have remained fresh. Any works published during these twenty years on these events, on Blum, on Marceau Pivert himself, were guaranteed success. The respective "liberations" of Portugal and Spain were hailed as victories over fascism.

"Republican" ideology and rhetoric formed the basis of Mitterrand's campaign in 1965 and of the FGDS in 1967 (the journal that supported Mitterrand was called *Le Combat républicain*).

The reasons for this reinforcement of continuity are countless. From the moment the Left parties recreated the Union of the left and signed a common program—given both the socialist heritage and the specific role of the Communist party in the alliance—it was inevitable that they would recycle that ideological and rhetorical fuel which could be used most readily as a source of energy for this new Popular Front: Marxism and the entire mythology and symbolism of the great "working-class" revolutions.

Nor can we overlook the impact of the May 1968 crisis. Despite its strongly anti-communist tone, it was a powerful force in the revival of the various Marxist, and other, revolutionary ideologies. The Socialist and Communist parties and the PSU, having "retrieved" a great deal from the actors and ideas of May 1968, took what they could absorb and use (leaving the rest to the peripheral movements and to the curio shops). Ideologically, they "retrieved" from May '68 the only vaguely new departure from the traditional ideological heritage:

an awareness of and greater attention to problems of the articulation of socialism and "daily life" (sexuality, family, culture, delinquency, status of women, relationship to work, quality of life, ecology). This innovation was circulated first among the extreme-left, then through the Socialist party, and was accepted finally—after much resistance—by the Communist party after 1975.

This reemphasis on continuity was accelerated clearly by disillusioning economic growth after 1970 and by the economic crisis. The smug optimism of the sixties, the weakness of the "end of ideology" theories, the self-satisfied discourse on "modernization," and the "new society" lost authority and credibility. "You can't fall in love with a growth rate," read a slogan on the walls of the Sorbonne in May 1968; it made even more sense when growth rates actually stagnated. Ideological space, then, was given to revolution and to leftist ideology, and with greater reason when—after May 1968, especially—de Gaulle, and particularly Pompidou and Giscard d'Estaing, could no longer "inspire" people on the Left (even though de Gaulle's speech on Pnom Penh and his triumphant visit to Latin America succeeded partially in doing so).

The above remarks on the ideological world of the Left parties can be extended to some of their political practices. This area is so broad and incorporates so much that, clearly, we must concentrate on the essentials. Accordingly, before tackling the most significant practices, I shall limit the focus to continuities in election-related practices.

Leaving aside the PSU, the Left parties—despite their claims that militant action cannot be confined to electoral participation—always have treated elections as major occasions for action and summoned all their forces to the fray. This has been so throughout the Fifth Republic and the very frequency of elections under this regime has reinforced this tendency. During the twenty years—if we exclude the contests of 1958, which left it stunned—the Left showed that it could put up a good fight in the elections, that, at such times, it could draw on its reserves, gather its energies, and often (except for the 1969 presidential election and, to a lesser degree, March 1978) override its divisions, and bring Left discipline to bear against its opponents.

During the Gaullist period, the approach of election day almost always promoted reconciliation on the Left (in October 1962, at the end of 1965, in 1967, and before the municipal elections of 1971, 1973 and 1974).[11]

The other side of the coin is that this attention to elections also has helped considerably to suppress and conceal their difficulties and embarrassing problems: the policy of "closed doors." This was much more prevalent in the Socialist party and the Movement of Left Radicals than in the Communist party; however, the PCF has not been totally beyond the practice (thus, for example, the leadership did not make public the report by Georges Marchais to the Central Committee of 29 June 1972, expressing reservations about the attitude of the Socialist party; and in the interests of unity, it silenced the anxieties of its

110

militants over the signing of the Common Program until the 21st Congress in October 1974). Between 1972 and 1977, the Socialist party, too, often preferred silence and ambiguity regarding the consequences and specific ramifications of the Common Program, its commitments to its alliance partners, and the composition of a possible United Left government, because it was paralyzed by the importance of the election.

In true French tradition, the parties of the Left—with the exception of the Radical party—have chosen to remain what their terminology calls appropriately "mass parties." The precise meaning of this term has never been very clear and has been used in rather different senses by the Socialists and the Communists. It means, generally, parties for whom the recruitment of members (within a formalized system of membership) is a major objective, in which militancy is the extolled value and the privileged mode of action, in which grassroots organizations (sections and cells) constitute the source of power and the basis of the leadership, and in which each member, from party head to the most lowly adherent, is only another militant.[12] Mass parties are distinguished by their capacity to intervene, alongside the masses, in demonstrations, strikes, popular struggles, and by other means: speeches, marches (in which their presence must be indicated by the sign *par excellence*: the banner), distribution of tracts, and also by their press. Mass parties believe sincerely that political action must always be preceded and prolonged by the education of the masses and, after each defeat, they always draw the conclusion that victory was lost because the education of the masses had not been sufficiently advanced. This concern explains the lengths these parties are willing to go to develop or maintain their own press. Since education clearly begins with the militants, it entails training sessions, party schools, study days, publication of instructional manuals, etc.

All these practices not only have been kept intact during the Gaullist years (despite the overt recognition in the PC of a decline and reduction in militant practices) but they have been developed and reinforced. The PS, since the Epinay Congress, has restored these practices to a position of honor.

Since 1906 and 1920–22, relations between unions and the Left parties in France have followed a model without equivalent in any other country: the unions proclaim their total independence from political parties and their receptivity to adherents of all political tendencies (a legacy of the Amiens Charter); yet, at the same time, the Communist party exercises strict political control over the leadership and action of the most important union, the CGT. This situation has not altered during the Fifth Republic. Similarly, the relative strength of the unions has not changed substantially in twenty years (although the French society and economy have changed profoundly): the CGT remains the leading working-class union, followed at a distance by the CFDT, and further back still, by the CGT-FO; the FEN maintains a quasi-monopoly over the teachers' unions.

Since 1948, relations between the CGT and the PCF have been constant in the complete subordination of the first to the second. However, just as in the past, their relations have been the object of scathing criticism: from governmental authorities, from the CGT's rivals (CGT-FO, CFDT, FEN), from the Socialist party, and even from a minority within the CGT, when polemical conflict broke out between the PCF and the PS in the fall of 1977. But this has not bothered the Communist leadership of the CGT. On the contrary, after the 21st Congress, and above all after 1975, it helped reinforce the Communist party's control over the CGT using methods similar to those employed by the PCF towards the CGTU fifty years ago (in its "Bolshevization" phase).[13] The reason for such peremptory resumption of control lay clearly in the PCF's desire to show its socialist rival—which was overtaking it in the electoral field—that it still retained absolute supremacy in the world of labor.

Herein lies the relative weaknss of the PS, as well as its distinctiveness among European socialist parties (with the exception of the PSI). In fact, the socialist parties in Belgium, Germany, Austria, and the Scandinavian countries owe their present political importance to their long-standing and tight links—not always formalized—with labor union organizations. French socialism has never held this trump-card.

In spite of several attempts, proposed periodically during the course of the Fifth Republic, to promote structured links between the PS and the CFDT or the FEN, the PS continues to enjoy clearly the tacit sympathies of the FEN, the CGT-FO, and the CFDT and has militants in positions (most often at low levels) in these various union organizations, but has no real political ties with them. As a result, the PS, unlike the PCF, has almost no chance of recruiting activists or officials from among those who hold, or have held, union positions. Therefore, like the old SFIO, the PS is still a party in which the majority of office-holders and leaders are basically unrepresentative of the lower-level wage earners and workers. Some progress has been made, particularly between 1974 and 1978, but the situation has not really changed and the efforts (carried out in September 1974) of the "*Assises du socialisme*" group obviously brought the Socialist party only a very small number of experienced CFDT militants committed to exercising real political responsibilities inside the party organization.[14]

Two major consequences have ensued: the first is that it justifies—or is seen to justify—the Communist party's theory of a *natural* division of labor between itself and the PS. The PS is said to represent the middle classes and the *petite bourgeoisie* who unconscious of their exploitation and the PCF the working class and those organized wage earners who acknowledge the existence of class struggle and accordingly feel the need for a revolutionary party. This theory perpetuates indefinitely—in a totally static way—a functional hierarchy conforming to the PCF's opinions of its rival-ally.

The second consequence is the ambiguity surrounding the respective roles of the two parties in an eventual United Left government. The Socialist party will have major political responsibilities in a coalition government, but will never be able to rely on the CGT's cooperation; meanwhile, it will no more be assured of the support of the non-communist unions. The PCF will be in an entirely different situation: *present within* the government, it will at the same time be *outside* it, in that the CGT is only another aspect of itself. If the PCF wants to increase its political influence over a socialist-led government, it always will be able to use the CGT to pressure the government (but the CGT's powerful lobbying pressure would place the other unions in an embarrassing position: they would risk losing influence by not following the CGT, but, by following it, they would favor the PCF to the detriment of the government and the PS).

This has been the situation since 1938. But, in 1977–78, it actually helped to reduce the chances for electoral victory by the Union of the Left. Since the SFIO was founded in 1905—and even more so since the PC was founded—French political life has been marked by an unwritten rule to which there have been no *real* exceptions: viz., the Left has never *governed* and all elections since 1905 seem to indicate that the French electorate refuses to entrust it with real power to lead the country and to perform major governmental roles.

The following cases only seem to be exceptions:

1)The governments of national union, 1944–46, occurred within an exceptional context; once the situation had stabilized, the Ramadier government, which tried to unite Communists and Socialists, worked only because it also included the MRP and the Radicals.

2)From 1905 to 1936, the SFIO happened to support governments of the Center Left, but that can be explained by the power of the Radical party and by the absence of the SFIO from the government. The socialist-led Popular Front government, correctly regarded by the French public as an exceptional political occurrence, probably would not have come to pass without the strong presence of the Radical party, or if Blum and Daladier had announced in advance that their government would include Communists.

3)The narrow victory of the Republican Front in 1956 enabled Mollet (at a time when opinion was predicting a Mendès-France government) to become President of the Council in a government based on strong socialist participation. But this was possible only because the coalition included Gaullists, and because of a total split between the SFIO and the PCF. In any case, in no sense was this socialist-led government the clear choice of the electorate.

Whenever the electorate express its choice clearly—and we must recognize that such choices could be expressed much more clearly in the Fifth Republic than in the Third and the Fourth—the Left has been denied, often at the last moment, major political responsibility.

If we disregard the 1962 legislative elections and the 1969 presidential election, which took place when relations between the Left parties were very confused, and instead consider only the five elections of 1967, 1968, 1973, 1974 and 1978, which offered a very clear choice between maintaining the government or replacing it with a socialist-led Left coalition, we can see that this coalition lost *every time*. At the same time. the Left parties were able to achieve better results than the majority parties in by-elections, in the 1971 and 1977 municipal elections, and even in the 1976 cantonal election. Before the elections of 1973, 1974, and 1978, most of the pre-election polls predicted voting percentages for the Left as a whole which invariably were higher than those they actually received. Can the Left parties be a majority only when the issue *is not* leadership of the State and the Nation? Or only when those 4–5% of voters who hold the balance are persuaded, on the few days of real choice open to them, that the country would not run a great risk by "giving them a chance"?

If the elections of 1967, 1968, 1973, 1974 and 1978 were not isolated events, but a *series* stretching over eleven years, the resemblances that they offer is striking—the specific characteristics of each nowithstanding. In all of those elections, a victory of the Left seemed possible in the weeks immediately preceding the ballot, but the first round results were always lower than predicted (more or less definitively depending on the election in question). In every instance, the parties of the majority succeeded in the last week before the ballot in recovering part of the ground they had lost in the months before, and did even better in the second ballot. In every instance, the ultimate defeat of the Left was due primarily to the unwillingness of a certain fraction of Center-Left voters to vote for the Communist candidate on the second ballot (particularly if the latter had any real chance of success). In every instance, the prospect of a possible victory by the Left encouraged very broad electoral participation which, especially on the second ballot, seemed to favor the majority candidates more than those of the Left. These similiarities—when so many aspects of the political context differed among the elections—convincingly explains a common phenomenon: a *reaction* against a government *of* the Left.

One can argue that the Communist party alone provokes this reaction and fear on the part of potential voters whose support the Left ought to be capturing or consolidating,[15] and that the Socialist party, on the contrary, arouses no such reactions.

If this means that the Socialist party is the party which inspires least "negative" reactions among the electorate and has the most "potential" voters,[16] and that this distinguishes it from the Communist party, it is clearly true. But that is not the real problem. The real problem concerns the full exercise of highest governmental responsibilities. While the Socialist party benefits from a nebulous image which undoubtedly places it ahead of the Communist party but behind the Center parties (and at one time behind the Radical party) and the parties which have constituted the majority under the Fifth Republic, it is still not really permitted to occupy these roles.

This is not only because of its alliance with the Communist party since 1967. In French political history, the PS has governed (rarely and belatedly) only when it was *associated* with parties which had long enjoyed legitimacy as "government parties" and only then (1936, 1947, 1956), because it was given credit for its categorical refusal to compromise with the PC. Again, this role of governmental leadership was granted with certain reservations and only during periods which followed long conservative rule or when economic crisis weighed heavily on the wage earners and popular classes. The 1974 presidential election and 1978 legislative elections showed that the alliance between the Socialist and Communist parties revitalized opposition from a part of the electorate when it confronted the importance of the issue.

The twenty years of Gaullism have confirmed and reinforced a division of labor between Right and Left which the electorate seems to have established definitively: the Right governs, the Left checks, protects, and protests.

After 1974, when it looked as if the PS might come to occupy the presidency of the Republic and lead a United Left government, this party found itself in a dilemma: it was expected to become the normal and legitimate successor of Gaullism as governmental head, but not to renounce its traditional political function as the representative of those who had no enduring faith in the benefits of power. This dilemma has been one source of its disagreement with the PCF since the fall of 1974.

The latter, in fact, does not experience the same frictions as the Socialist party. Powerfully entrenched, since 1936, in positions where it has never been very seriously threatened, and knowing itself to be condemned—by the inevitable rejection of a large majority of the electorate—to assuming national political responsibility only under strict surveillance and with tenuous control, it has opted for a form of political action which is no more than a sort of super-unionism directed at the discontented and the weak. Its speciality is to be the "tribune of the people."

The Fifth Republic has reinforced this division of labor. The parties of the Left have not been able, or else have not wanted, to disturb it.

NOTES

1. The 1975 population census, for those aged 18 and over, show that the percentage of those who attained "political maturity" (i.e., approximately 18 years of age) only under the Fifth Republic is 36.5.

2.   For example, René Pleven, Edgar Faure, Georges Gorse, Léo Hamon, Arthur Comte, Emmanuel d'Astier de la Vigerie, and Pierre Lebrun.

3.   Cf. Janine Mossuz, *Les Clubs politiques*(Paris: Armand Colin, 1079. Collection U2). Also, see my article, "Les clubs devant l'action politique," *Revue francais de science politique*, XV, 3 (June 1965), pp. 555–569.

4.   Cf. Jean-Luc Parodi, "L'Union et la différence: les perceptions de la gauche après la crise de septembre 1977," in SOFRES, *L'Opinion francaise en 1977* (Paris: Presses de la FNSP, 1978), pp. 69–86. Also, see Georges Lavau, "Les Voies du PCF," *Etudes* (March 1977), and Georges Lavau and Janine Mossuz-Lavau, "The Union of the Left's Defeat: Suicide and Congenital Weakness," in Howard Penniman, *ed.*, *France at the Polls: The Legislative Election of 1978* (forthcoming, 1980).

5.   Cf. Denis Lindon, "L'Evolution des indicateurs du climat politique, de l'automne 1976 àl'automne 1977," in SOFRES, *L'Opinion francais en 1977*, pp. 11–27.

6.   Cf. Jean-Luc Parodi, *op. cit.*

7.   See especially the articles on the Socialist party in the Special Number of *Revue francaise de science politique*, xxviii, 2 (April 1978).

8.   Cf. Jean-Luc Parodi, *op.cit.*, and Roland Cayrol, "Les Attitudes des électorats de gauche," *op.cit.*, pp. 67 and 68.

9.   Cf. especially Janine Mossuz-Lavau and Mariette Sineau, "Les Femmes et la politique," *Revue francais de science politique*, XXVI, 5 (October 1976), pp. 929–956. The few detailed studies of the changes in the political and electoral behavior of Catholics seem to indicate that, in the regions of old Catholic tradition (and, more precisely, of Christian Democratic strongholds, e.g. in Brittany), these changes continue to affect non-practicing Catholics much more than practicing Catholics. The continuity of this phenomenon is masked by another which seems incomparably more widespread: viz., falling rates in religious practice, the rapid decline in careers in the priesthood, and the less and less confessional character of "Catholic" schools. On this point, see the article by Philippe Braud, "Les élections législatives de mars 1978 en Bretagne," *Revue francais de science politique*, XXVIII, 6 (December 1978).

10.   Let us not forget how de Gaulle ridiculed, among other things, *"les comités Théodore et les comités Théodule."*

11.   It is also one reason why Mitterrand, undoubtedly to maintain the cohesiveness of his party after the March 1978 defeat, was quick to mobilize in preparation for the next time around: the presidential election of 1981.

12.   In fact, apart from Mollet, none of the old leaders of the SFIO or the PS was trained by the party or worked his way up through the ranks. Jaurés was a "republican" deputy before becoming a socialist, and Blum came from Dreyfusard intellectual circles. Mitterrand came from the UDSR and had already served twenty-seven years in public life when he became a socialist.

13.   On all these questions, see my article, "Les Voies du PCF," *Etudes* (March 1977).

14.   On the relations between unions and left parties from 1968 to 1978, see my article, "Changing Relations between Trade Unions and Working Class Parties," *Government and Opposition*, XIII, 4 (December 1978).

15.   For the concepts of "distant," "captive," "potential," and "swing," see Denis Lindon and Pierre Weill, *Le Choix d'un député* (Paris: Editions de Minuit, 1974), pp. 104 ff.

16.   According to SOFRES opinion polls, before the elections of 1973, the PS had 30 percent of "potential" voters (the PC, 15 percent and the government, 13 percent). Again in November 1977, approximately a third of CDS, Giscardiens, or RPR voters did not dismiss the possibility of voting for a socialist candidate "if there were no other candidate in [their] district who conformed to [their] political ideas," SOFRES opinion poll, published in *Sud-Ouest* (16–19 November 1977).

The French Economy Under
The Fifth Republic, 1958–1978[1]

Bela Balassa

THE CHANGING ROLE OF PLANNING IN FRANCE

Planning in a Closed Economy

The first Plan for Modernization and Equipment (1949–53) concentrated on rebuilding and developing infrastructure (transport and electricity) and basic industries (coal and steel) after the destruction and dislocation of World War II. In the Second Plan (1953–57), the continuation of these efforts was accompanied by an attempt to plan production and investment on an industry-by-industry basis. Industry-level planning was to develop further during the Third Plan period (1958–63), with the use of input–output tables to ensure consistency on the national economy level.

Under the approach of "*économie concertée*" applied in the plans, the *Commissariat du Plan* reached an agreement with industrial firms on production and investment targets. Business accepted this approach as, in exchange for the commitment entered into, it enjoyed assured markets as a result of protection from foreign competition and subsidies to exports. And, to the extent that there were conflicts between various business groups, the *Commissariat du Plan* acted as their arbiter.[2]

The approach of "*économie concertée*" conformed to the French tradition of government intervention to business affairs and the distrust of domestic and foreign competition. As regards the latter, the aim was to import goods that were unavailable, or were not available in sufficient quantities, in France, or rather, in the Franc area. Indeed, trade within the Franc area could be viewed as

The French translation of this chapter was awarded the Prix Rossi of the Academie des Sciences Morales et Politiques of the Institut de France—Ed. note.

117

internal trade, since the associated overseas countries and territories provided a captive market for French industry and received preferential treatment in the French market.[3] In turn, exports outside the Franc area were designed to pay for the necessary imports.

This conception of the role of foreign trade was expressed in the statement that "the originality of the projection of French foreign trade in the Third Plan lies in taking imports as a constraint and deriving exports as a result of this constraint."[4] It contrasts with other European countries[5] which did not exclude foreign competition and aimed at exploiting the benefits of their comparative advantage in international trade. For one thing, whereas quantitative import restrictions were continued in France, they were well-nigh abolished elsewhere in Europe; for another, tariffs were substantially higher in France than in other European countries, Italy excepted.

The contrast is apparent from data on the relative importance of foreign trade in the national economy. The data of Table 1 show the ratio of exports and imports to value added in the production of traded goods (i.e. excluding construction and public as well as private services), which can be taken to express the "openness" of the individual national economies.

Excluding trade with the associated overseas countries and territories, the ratios of exports and imports to value added in the production of traded goods, respectively, were 12.0 and 15.2 percent in France in 1958, 30.2 and 25.2 percent in Germany, 20.7 and 25.8 percent in Italy, and 37.1 and 43.8 percent in the United Kingdom. The differences are even larger if comparisons are made with the smaller European countries and the share of exports in France was less than one-half that in Japan and hardly higher than in the United States. At the same time, the share of exports in manufacturing output and that of imports in the domestic utilization of manufactured goods, again excluding trade with the associated overseas countries and territories, hardly exceeded 10 percent in 1968 (Table 2).

Effects of Participation in the Common Market

The Third Plan did not envisage a change in this situation; rather, it aimed at a reduction in the share of imports. Thus, notwithstanding the projected growth of GNP by nearly one-third, imports from outside the Franc area were to remain at the base year (1956) level. During the same period, exports were supposed to rise by 33 percent.

The plan projections implied maintenance of the closed character of the French economy and "the consequences of the establishment of the common market were not taken into account."[6] In fact, imports from outside the Franc area rose by 25 percent between 1956 and 1961. At the same time, aided by two devaluations, exports increased 71 percent.[7]

These changes reflect the implications for planning of opening the French economy through participation in the Common Market. As the author noted elsewhere, "while information on interindustry relationships can be utilized to derive a feasible pattern of production associated with a growth target in a closed economy, disappointed expectations in regard to exports and unforeseen changes in imports will give rise to discrepancies between plans and realization if the foreign trade sector is of importance."[8] As a result, realization deviated substantially from plans in regard to production, exports, and imports for individual industries during the Third Plan.[9]

At the same time, the French planners had to forego instruments of import protection and export subsidization in the Common Market. The provisions of the Rome Treaty excluded the use of quantitative import restrictions and export subsidies; tariffs on intra-area imports were to be eliminated over a ten-year period; and the establishment of the common external tariff entailed reducing French tariffs on extra-area imports.[10]

The loss of trade policy instruments compromised the possibilities of industry-level planning in France. A detailed study showed that, "the utility of planning physical coherence of inputs and outputs declined very sharply—virtually to the vanishing point."[11] Because the government authorities could not ensure the fulfillment of plan targets, firms had little to gain from accepting commitments for production and investment. At any rate, business decisions had to be made in the Common Market rather than in national framework, taking account of competition in domestic as well as foreign markets. This increasingly led French business to assert its independence from government tutelage. Thus, the Patronat attacked the "illusion of a systematic dirigisme" and the "myth of the Plan," suggesting that it be limited to non-binding forecasts.[12]

With the practical impossibility of continued industry-level planning in France, suggestions were made for transferring it to the Common Market level. For reasons discussed elsewhere,[13] this had not happened. Correspondingly, planning targets on the industry level had no further role to play in France and were abandoned in the Fourth and Fifth Plans that covered the period 1963–1973, i.e., the decade preceding the oil crisis and the world recession.

French Planning and Policy Making after the
Common Market's Establishment

Alain Cotta distinguishes between horizontal (general) and selective policy measures, the former being available to all firms while the latter benefit particular sectors, firms, or projects.[14] After the selective policies applied during the period preceding the establishment of the Common Market, with the exceptions considered in Section III below, general policy actions were employed in the next fifteen years. They comprise tax provisions and accelerated depreciation favoring investment; measures aimed at encouraging research and product development; credits, guarantees, insurance against price and exchange rate changes, and technical assistance to exporters; various forms of regional aids; and fiscal and credit measures favoring concentration.[15]

The measures encouraged industrial investment in France. They also benefited technological change and the expansion of exports. At the same time, regional aids were nondiscriminatory in their effects on individual industries. The policy of industrial concentration will be discussed in greater detail below.

The principal instruments for encouraging concentration were tax exemptions for the capital gains of firms in the case of mergers and medium- and long-term credits for purposes of mergers. These measures, together with the pressure of competition in the Common Market, contributed to industrial concentration. Thus, while the number of mergers was relatively small and practically unchanged during the postwar period until 1958, considerable increases occurred in subsequent years. This was the case in particular during the period of the Fourth and Fifth Plans, whose principal aim was to restructure manufacturing industry through concentration.

In fact, the average number of mergers more than doubled between the 1950s and the second half of the 1960s. Moreover, in the case of corporations for which the relevant data are available, the value of the assets of the absorbed companies rose from an annual average of 85 million francs during the 1950s to 1 billion francs in 1965 and 5 billion francs in 1970.[16]

Industrial concentration resulted in increases in firm size. Between the 1962 and 1970 Industrial Censuses, firms with more than 1000 workers increased their share among firms employing more than 10 workers by about one-fifth while the total number of firms employing more than 10 workers declined.[17]

Increases in the size of firms were accompanied by increased plant size. Thus, between 1962 and 1968, the average number of workers per plant employing more than 50 workers rose from 215 to 250. Also, the share of plants with 50 to 100 workers declined and that of plants employing more than 500 workers in total employment increased.[18]

Concentration occurred in all industries, particularly those producing intermediate products, machinery, and transport equipment. Examples are Imétal in the non-ferrous metal, Elf and Rhône-Poulenc in the chemical and petrochemical, C.G.E. and Thomson-Brandt in the electrical equipment, and Peugeot and Citröen in the automobile industry.

FRENCH ECONOMIC PERFORMANCE UNTIL 1973

Business Attitudes toward the Common Market[19]

The mistrust of domestic and foreign competition, prevalent in earlier periods, extended to the government as well as to business in France. During the 1950s, changes occurred in governmental attitudes, first for political and subsequently for economic reasons. The political idea of a united Europe, aimed at preventing the re-emergence of Germany as a military power and, subsequently, at increasing the weight of European countries between the two superpowers,[20] carried with it the acceptance of increased competition from other European countries. But, subsequently, the economic side of integration acquired a life of its own, as it came to be considered desirable to expose French industry to foreign competition in order to effect the transformation necessary for increasing productivity.[21]

French business, however, remained *méfiant* toward international competition. According to Georges Villiers, the President of the Patronat, "insofar as excessive charges weigh on French production costs, it will be impossible for French firms to bear up under international competition."[22] Subsequently, in *L'Usine Nouvelle*, representing steel, engineering electrical, and automobile industries that were most fearful of trade liberalization, were warnings of "the catastrophic consequences and the eventual defeat of French industry unless all kinds of disparities are eliminated before the removal of trade barriers"[23] in the Common Market.

As the establishment of the Common Market became increasingly likely, the Patronat concentrated on putting forward demands for "shock absorbers" and "safeguard measures" as preconditions for French participation. The first heading included harmonizing social charges, equalizing social benefits (in particular the so-called "*trois vaches sacrés*": the lengths of vacations, male and female wages, and the length of the work week), extending the transition period into the EEC, making passage to subsequent stages subject to unanimous rather than majority vote, increasing the height of the common external tariff, and avoiding limitations on cartels. Further demands were made for each country to have unilateral recourse to safeguard measures as well as the right to set import taxes and export subsidies in case of balance-of-payments difficulties.[24]

While some changes were made in the proposal for the Rome Treaty toward harmonizing social benefits, the Patronat's demands were far from met. Correspondingly, interest attaches to the performance of French industry after the Common Market was established. The following will examine this and give further attention to the factors effecting economic performance.

121

The Impact of the Fifth Republic on France

Economic Developments in France, 1958–73

In the period following the establishment of the European Common Market economic growth accelerated in France. Between 1958 and 1973, the annual average rate of growth of GNP averaged 5.5 percent, compared to 4.8 percent between 1953 and 1958 (Table 3). France showed the best economic performance among the EEC countries, where GNP growth rates in the period 1958–73 averaged 4.9 percent in Belgium, 5.0 percent in Germany, 5.3 percent in Italy, and 4.2 percent in the Netherlands. The comparisons are even more favorable with Norway (4.2 percent), Sweden (4.1 percent), the United States (4.1 percent), and the United Kingdom (3.2 percent) although France fell behind Japan (10.4 percent).

Rates of economic growth in France exceeded those in Germany during each five-year subperiod while the opposite was the case during the five-years preceding the Common Market's establishment. France also surpassed Germany in rate of growth of industrial production. For the period as a whole, industrial production increased at an annual average rate of 5.5 percent in France and 5.2 percent in Germany.[25]

These changes occurred in an increasingly open economy as the relative importance of foreign trade increased greatly between 1958 and 1973. As noted earlier, in trade with countries outside the Franc area, exports and imports, respectively, accounted for 12.0 and 15.2 percent of value added in the production of traded goods in 1958, these proportions rose to 17.5 and 19.3 percent in 1963, 21.3 and 23.1 percent in 1968, and 31.0 and 33.1 percent in 1973. As a result, France greatly reduced the distance that separated it from Germany and Italy, and far surpassed Japan, in regard to the openness of the national economy (Table 1).

Changes in the national economy reflect, to a large extent, the increased openness of manufacturing industries in France. Non-Franc-zone export and import shares in manufacturing production and utilization, respectively, increased from 11.0 and 12.6 percent in 1958 to 22.3 and 20.8 percent in 1973. All major industrial groups for which comparable time-series data are available showed similar changes (Table 2).

Increases in export *and* import shares are explained by the growing importance of intra-industry specialization. Thus, rather than the demise of particular industries that had been feared prior to the Common Market's establishment, the exchange of intermediate products, consumer goods, and investment goods increased within individual industries. Intra-industry specialization in narrower ranges of products, in turn, permitted longer production runs and the use of specialized machinery, with consequent gains in productivity.[26]

At the same time, the structure of French manufactured exports underwent substantial transformation, with a shift from intermediate products and consumer nondurables toward producer and consumer durables. Between 1960

122

and 1971, the share of durables increased from 36.3 to 49.0 percent while intermediate products declined from 38.9 to 33.1 percent and nondurable consumer goods fell from 24.8 to 17.7 percent.[27]

Changes were particularly noteworthy in the French export structure relative to that of the other Common Market countries. This is indicated by the "indices of specialization," calculated as the ratio of the percentage shares of individual product groups in the total exports of France to the percentage share of the same product groups in the combined exports of the Common Market countries. That index for France rose from 72 in 1960 to 92 in 1971 for durable goods, declined from 104 to 99 for intermediate products and from 129 to 99 for nondurable consumer goods.[28]

Furthermore, the competitive position of French industry improved considerably following the Common Market's establishment. This is reflected in the increase in the export/import ratio in trade in manufactured goods outside the Franc area from .86 in 1958 to 1.10 in 1973. Among major product groups, this ratio rose in machinery and equipment, chemical industries, and textiles, clothing, and shoes while declines occurred in building materials and glass and in wood, paper, and related industries where the availability of domestic materials was a limiting factor (Table 2).

Table 4 provides information on export-import ratios in greater industry detail for 1973. Particular interest attaches to the large export surplus of the automobile industry (an export/import ratio of 1.98), the chemical and pharmaceutical industries (2.00), and shipbuilding, aircraft and armament (1.49); within the latter group, aircraft sales are dominant. Apart from natural resource-based industries, the export/import ratio exceed .95 in all cases other than household equipment. (.51).[29]

Aside from household equipment (chiefly refrigerators imported from Italy), then, no French manufacturing industry was adversely affected by the Common Market's establishment. Rather, the competitive position of non-resource-based industries improved, leading to higher export-import ratios and an export surplus. These developments, together with the more-than-doubling of industrial production in a period of fifteen years and the shift in exports from intermediate products and consumer nondurables toward producer and consumer durables, show that France established itself as a major industrial power.

Factors Affecting the Performance of French
Industry in the European Common Market

Several factors explain the favorable performance of French industry in the EEC. First, the period following the Common Market's establishment saw the modernization and restructuring of French industry. In fact, "the industrial structure underwent greater transformation in ten years than during the preceding half century."[30]

This transformation was, in part, related to the concentration of French industry, described above, that occurred in response to governmental measures and the pressure of competition. Concentration made French industry more competitive in the Common Market as the merged firms benefited from economies of scale in production, research, and marketing, as well as access to finance.

But, data on concentration do not indicate adequately the transformation of the industrial landscape. Thus, concentration was accompanied by the development of subcontracting relationships between small and medium-size firms on the one hand, and large firms on the other. Subcontracting in turn, led to higher productivity through increased industrial specialization. More generally, small and medium-size firms responded to foreign competition by disappearing, merging, or specializing and modernizing.

Another factor contributing to the improved performance of French industry was the monetary and economic stability made possible by political stability under the Fifth Republic. This contrasts with the situation of the last years of the Fourth Republic when political instability contributed to financial instability and to recurrent foreign exchange crises.[31]

Monetary and economic stability were established through the Pinay-Rueff Plan that was "the most far-reaching reform of the French economy since the Liberation, affecting at the same time the monetary system, the budget, the foreign exchange regime, foreign trade, and minimum wages."[32]

The application of the Pinay-Rueff Plan greatly improved the economic climate and reduced uncertainty that had adversely affected business decision-making on investments and exports previously. Thus, it conformed to the demands of the Patronat for monetary and economic stability, which were put forward as the November 1956 Brussels Conference and the January 1957 National Assembly debate made clear that most of its earlier demands for "shock absorbers" and "safeguards" were not met.[33]

Reducing the budgetary deficit took the form of raising taxes and decreasing government spending. This permitted a shift in the use of resources from domestic expenditures to exports. These changes, together with the 20 percent devaluation of the franc, re-established equilibrium in the French balance of payments, notwithstanding the increase in imports resulting from the liberalization of quota restrictions and reductions in tariffs in the EEC.

The budgetary measures, together with the elimination of wage indexing, permitted lowering inflation rates considerably. Nevertheless, the inflation rate did not decline to that of other industrial countries. While manufactured prices rose at an average annual rate of 2.7 percent in France during the decade following the Common Market's establishment, increases were in the 1.5 to 2.0 percent range in the other EEC countries, for an average cumulated price differential of 10 percent between 1958 and 1968.[34]

Nevertheless, France could avoid a further depreciation of the franc until after the May 1968 events because it "overdevalued" its currency in 1958, i.e., the extent of the devaluation exceeded that necessary to re-establish balance-of payments equilibrium. Apart from leading to a tenfold increase of foreign exchange reserves between 1957 and 1967, the over-devaluation also gave a "*coup de pouce*" to manufactured exports by raising the domestic equivalent of foreign exchange earnings and increasing profits.[35]

Higher profits, in turn, provided funds for investments that were encouraged by access to wider markets. The moderate inflation in France also contributed to the growth of investment by favoring profits, without giving rise to the distortions that accompany high rates of inflation.[36] Last but not least, investments were promoted through tax concessions and accelerated depreciation provisions. As a result, the share of gross fixed investment in the gross national product rose from 17.9 percent in 1953-58 to 19.9 percent in 1958-63, 22.3 percent in 1963-68, and 23.8 percent in 1968-73, thus favoring economic growth.[37]

Thus, the policies applied during 1958-73 contributed to the favorable performance of French industry and of the national economy as a whole. They permitted industry to exploit the benefits offered by the large markets of the EEC. At the same time, the intra-industry specialization minimized the cost of dislocation.

In conjunction with these developments, the attitude of French industrialists toward the Common Market changed. Recognizing the advantages of the EEC and the costs France's exclusion from it would entail, in the second half of the 1960s they came to oppose plans attributed to de Gaulle for France to "go it alone."

THE FRENCH ECONOMY AFTER THE OIL CRISIS

"Virtuous" and "Vicious" Circles

The events of May 1968, the shift from fixed to flexible exchange rates in 1971, and the rise of material prices in 1972 created disturbances in the French economy. But, although the rate of increase of manufactured goods prices rose from 2-3 percent to 5-6 percent a year, France maintained a high rate of investment and economic growth.[38]

In turn, with two-thirds of French energy needs supplied by oil imports, the oil crisis gave a substantial shock to the French economy. The quadrupling of oil prices was equivalent to a "tax" of about 3 percent on domestic incomes and expenditure in France, entailing an income transfer to the oil producing countries. The situation was aggravated by the world recession of 1974-75 that reduced demand for French exports.

In examining the situation during the years following the oil crisis, pessimistic conclusions were reached by two authors, Alain Cotta and Christian Stoffaes, whose books have been widely cited in France.[39] In the following, their views will be subjected to scrutiny. Subsequently, an alternative explanation of French economic performance in the 1973–78 period will be offered and the policy implications of the findings will be examined.

Christian Stoffaes claims that the "virtuous circle" in Germany and Japan contrasts with the "vicious circle" in France and in the United Kingdom. In his view, the former two countries have an export orientation, resulting in a favorable export structure oriented toward goods for which world demand is rising rapidly, that has created a virtuous circle of expanding exports and GNP. Conversely, the lesser attention given to foreign trade in the latter group of countries resulted in a less favorable export structure, with the actions taken to support weak industries having led to the vicious circle of lower growth rates and balance-of-payments difficulties.[40]

In particular, Stoffaes sees the prospects for economic growth as adversely affected by the unfavorable export composition and the high income elasticity of demand for imports in France as compared to Germany and Japan. Thus, "Only the braking of the economy will reduce the foreign trade deficit; every expansion increases it again. The unavoidable need to equilibrate the balance of payments risks eventually a durable reduction of the rate of economic growth on the pattern of what has been happening in the United Kingdom for years."[41]

Alain Cotta, too, speaks of a vicious circle in France, and submits that the French balance-of-payments is in equilibrium only if the rate of economic growth is nil.[42] According to Cotta, "since 1973 the elasticity of our imports in relation to the national product is systematically greater (and by much) than that of exports," further adding that "in 1976, a growth rate of about 4 to 5 percent was accompanied by an increase in import volume about four times greater than that of GNP while exports rose only twice as much."[43]

Correspondingly, Cotta claims, the balance-of-payments constraint limits the possibilities for economic growth. Like Stoffaes, Cotta expresses pessimism on the prospects for economic growth in France without a change in the composition of exports to conform better to world demand. In particular, Germany and Japan are said to have acquired superiority in capital goods industries.[44] Yet, as Stoffaes also suggests, these products have the best export possibilities for developed countries, given the continuing improvements in the competitive power of the developing countries in textiles, clothing, and shoes.[45]

French Economic Growth: A Reconsideration

A study by the author for 1962–71 does not confirm the fears of Cotta and Stoffaes as regards the product composition of French exports; nor does it show that favorable export composition was the dominant factor determining export performance. Thus, the average annual rate of growth of world demand for the manufactured goods exported by France (12.2 percent) was only slightly below that of Germany (13.3 percent) and Japan (12.4 percent) and exceeded the latter two in machinery and equipment (11.4 percent, 11.1 percent, and 10.4 percent, respectively). At the same time, while world demand increased relatively rapidly for manufactured goods exported by the United States (12.9 percent) and the United Kingdom (12.5 percent), their export growth rates were the slowest in the industrial world.[46]

The latter result indicates the importance of changes in the competitive position of individual countries, represented by changes in market shares, as a determinant of export growth. In this connection, in the period 1970 to 1974, the evolution of the competitive position of France matched that of Germany.[47] Following the oil crisis, the French competitive position has been superior: between 1973 and 1978, French exports of manufactured goods rose three-quarters of a percentage point more than the average growth rate of their markets while Germany just maintained its average market share unchanged.[48]

At the same time, as noted above, France came to specialize increasingly in durable goods during the 15 years following the Common Market's establishment. This trend continued after 1973 for producer durables, for which world demand is expected to rise the most rapidly. Thus, between 1973 and 1976, the export/import ratio in France increased from .95 to 1.23 for mechanical engineering products, from 1.01 to 1.18 for electrical engineering and electronic products, and from 1.49 to 2.20 for shipbuilding, aircraft, and armament. Notwithstanding the increased importation of textiles, clothing, and shoes from developing countries, these changes resulted in an increase of the export/import ratio in manufacturing from 1.14 in 1973 to 1.18 in 1976 (Table 4).

Finally, the extent of export orientation of the French economy is much greater than that of Japan and comparable to that of Germany. In 1976, the ratio of exports to value added in the production of traded goods in France was 47.0 percent including, and 44.3 percent excluding, trade with the Franc area as compared to 50.4 percent in Germany and 32.0 percent in Japan (Table 1).

The next question concerns the income elasticity of demand for imports, measured as the ratio of the percentage change in the volume of imports to that of GNP. In the historical context, the elasticity of 4.5 for 1976 is an aberrant result. Thus, the 21 percent increase in import volume in 1976 compensated in part for the 7 percent decline the previous year; the elasticity fell to .3 in 1977; according to OECD estimates, it was 1.6 in 1978. In turn, the income elasticity of import demand in Germany was 2.8 in 1976, 1.4 in 1977, and 2.3 in 1978. Finally, for 1973-78, taken as a whole, this elasticity averaged 2.3 in Germany and 1.6 in France.[49]

Thus, France does not suffer in comparison with Germany and Japan in rate of growth of world demand for its exports, the export orientation of its economy, and the income elasticity of demand for its imports. The sources for its unfavorable balance-of-payments situation, 1973 to 1977, must be found elsewhere.

Policy Reactions to the Oil Crisis

As noted above, the quadrupling of oil prices was a "tax" amounting to about 3 percent of domestic incomes and expenditure in France. Apart from the United States, where oil imports were a relatively small proportion of total energy consumption, increases in oil prices had similar effects in the other industrial countries. At the same time, as Cotta shows, policy reactions to the oil price increase by the industrial countries were far from uniform.[50]

For a given output, the tax or transfer resulting from higher oil prices has to be "financed" by reducing domestic incomes and expenditures. The transfer was financed relatively rapidly in Germany and Japan which accepted an absolute decline in real incomes in 1974-75. However in France, the government accepted a *fuite en avant* of continued economic growth for electoral reasons and possibly in the hope that the higher oil bill would be paid from the increment of output and exports. This did not happen, in part because wage earners demanded continuing increases in real incomes in disregard of the rise of oil prices and in part because low economic growth in France's major markets did not permit a rapid expansion of exports. Correspondingly, the French balance-of-payments deteriorated to a considerable extent and inflation accelerated.

To remedy the situation, deflationary measures were applied under the first Plan Fourcade from late 1974 to late 1975. Then, expansionary measures under the second Plan Fourcade were applied between late 1975 and late 1976 at the behest of Prime Minister Jacques Chirac. This, in turn, gave place to the anti-inflationary Plan Barre announced in October 1976. The latter permitted avoiding an acceleration of price increases following the rise of public utility rates and the abolition of price control, while the rate of economic growth was maintained at 3 percent a year and the trade deficit became a surplus.

In making a comparison with the early financing of the transfer implicit in the quadrupling of oil prices in Germany, Cotta criticizes the policies applied in France that in his view have led to the "vicious circle of non-transfer."[51] A different picture emerges if the rate of economic growth in the two countries is compared. French growth performance has been superior, with a 2.8 percent average annual rate of GNP growth between 1973 and 1978 as against 1.9 percent in Germany (Table 3). Thus, over five years, the cumulated difference in GNP was nearly 5 percent.

Differences in growth rates, in turn, largely explain differences in the balance of payments of the two countries. If exports were unaffected by GNP growth rates and income elasticity of import demand were to be calculated as 2.3, the average for the period 1973 to 1978, German imports in 1978 would have been 10.3 percent higher if Germany had matched the French growth performance between 1973 and 1978. Correspondingly, the 1978 German trade surplus of $25.2 billion would have declined to $13.5 billion. Assuming an unchanged service balance and private and official transfers, this decline in the trade surplus would have transformed the 1978 German current account surplus of $8.8 billion into a deficit of $2.8 billion.[52] This estimate is on the conservative side to the extent that more rapid growth of domestic demand would have led to the absorption of goods which were sold abroad.

In turn, lower growth rates in France and higher rates of economic growth in Germany, her main export market, would have improved her balance of payments. If the rate of economic growth in France had equalled that of Germany between 1973 and 1978 and if the income elasticity of import demand is calculated at 1.6, the average figure for 1973 to 1978, imports into France would have been $4.7 billion lower in 1978, raising the trade surplus of $1.6 billion to $6.3 billion and resulting in a current account surplus of $8.7 billion. The results would have been even more favorable if allowance were made for the fact that the slower expansion of domestic demand and higher rate of economic growth in Germany would have led to higher French exports. At any rate, the current account balance of France has been improving rapidly; the deficit was $5.9 billion in 1976; it fell to $3.3 billion in 1977; and a surplus of $4.0 billion was attained in 1978.[53]

After several years of deficits then, France has been able to attain equilibrium in its balance of payments, notwithstanding a rate of economic growth exceeding that of Germany. And while low growth rates have reduced the rate of inflation and accumulating surpluses in Germany, they have affected adversely exports and output in other countries, including France. Considering further the deflationary effects of the appreciation of the German mark, Germany's interests as well as those of other countries require that she follow expansionary policies. Similar conclusions apply to Japan.[54]

Policy Implications for France

Thus, rather than a structural disequilibrium, the different experience of France and Germany in recent years may be explained by differences in their countercyclical policies. In France, exports suffered as a result of the relatively slow growth of the German economy and the pressure of domestic demand that also led to higher imports. By contrast, German exports benefited from more rapid growth in France and low rate of expansion of the domestic economy that also limited the growth of imports. Nevertheless, as we have seen, the French balance-of-payments situation had improved greatly by 1978.

This is not to say that the countercyclical policies followed after the oil crisis in France are immune to criticism. In particular, a less expansionary policy followed in 1974 would have avoided, or at least moderated, the stop-and-go policies of subsequent years. More generally, with a lower rate of increase in the money supply, France could have attained the same rate of economic growth with less inflation and a smaller loss in net foreign exchange reserves.

The next question concerns the structural policies to be followed. Both Cotta and Stoffaes contend that the general—or horizontal—policies applied after 1958 should be supplemented by selective policies. In Cotta's view, measures should be taken to reduce imports of energy, mechanical engineering products, and household equipment; to increase exports of processed food, petrochemicals, computer-related products, and electrical goods; to assist sectors, such as glass, automobiles, construction, public works, transportation, and telecommunications, which contribute to employment and to other national objectives; and to restructure the textiles, clothing, shipbuilding, and coal industries.

> Within these industries, one should
> "—identify the subsectors and, more exactly, the groups of products, for which favorable results can be obtained at least cost;
> —select carefully the firms that are best able to reach these objectives;
> —and even more precisely, choose with care what we call nodal actions, i.e., those that would bear on several sectors simultaneously and, as a result, would have multiplicative effects."[55]

The idea of selecting firms within particular industries for special treatment originated with Lionel Stoléru, a Secretary of State in the French government, who called for providing assistance to a single firm within each industry.[56] Stoffaes claims that changes in this direction have been made in recent years, in particular through diversification of state-owned enterprises, such as Renault, Charbonnages de France, and Elf Aquitaine,[57] and recommends that this policy be generalized and strengthened by identifying industrial sectors that correspond to certain criteria and selecting a firm in each sector to receive assistance.[58]

The Cotta and Stoffaes recommendations are subject to criticism on several grounds. First, while both Cotta and Stoffaes decry the use of protectionist measures,[59] granting special assistance to particular sectors will have protectionist effects, directly or indirectly. Also, assistance to weak industries may lengthen their lives as happened in shipbuilding, while the choice of sectors with the greatest multiplicative effects neglects the gains to be obtained through foreign trade.

Also, one may doubt that the same government could appropriately select particular sectors on the basis of a series of criteria or identify the subsectors with the highest benefit-cost ratio. Assistance given to selected sectors in the past brought limited benefits and entailed a considerable cost to the French economy. The Concorde which, apart from requiring substantial investment by the French as well as the British governments, cannot cover the cost of its operations. Also, granting government subsidies to research and development and ensuring markets at home and in socialist and developing countries did not ensure the success of the Plan Calcul. A careful study of the French electronics industry showed that, "state support appears to have reduced the pressure on firms under its tutelage to adopt structures more suited to their technological and market problems."[60] And, "the technological goals of the state weakened the competitive position of the firms ..."[61] so that eventually France had to increase foreign, in practice American, participation in her computer industry. Finally, government intervention in the steel industry induced firms to retain outdated capacity and encouraged them to create new capacity from borrowed funds, resulting in increased indebtedness and eventually necessitating the restructuring of the industry with substantial reductions in capacity.

Moreover, the distinction between a policy of "projects" followed in the past and that of "firms" is not so clearcut as Cotta and Stoffaes claim.[62] Thus, the former, too, provided benefits to particular firms. And while both authors suggest that, to avoid repeating the failure of the project approach, government aid should be granted with a view to increasing competitiveness in world markets, in fact this may not occur. In particular, the contractual approach proposed by Stoffaes[63] may well lead to subsidizing exports at high cost to the government budget as happened in the case of computers. More generally, in the face of uncertainty in foreign markets, the firm needs to take the risks and reap the rewards of its own actions. An example is Dassault, which has been successful by following a strategy oriented toward export markets.

A further problem is that assistance to a particular firm in a certain sector or subsector entails discrimination against other firms in the same sector (subsector). Apart from the legal aspects noted by Stoffaes,[64] this raises questions of economic efficiency. A case in point is the diversification of state-owned enterprises. From the efficiency point of view, Peugeot's decision to absorb first Citroen and, subsequently, the European operations of Chrysler, is superior to Renault absorbing small, often high-cost firms in a variety of unrelated sectors. Similar comments apply to the acquisitions by Charbonnages de France.

These considerations point to the conclusion that the application of selective measures should be minimized. Such measures might find justification on a temporary basis when the "infant industry" argument applies. This might be the case in some sectors where social benefits due to advanced technological improvements exceed the private benefits. However, these sectors should be exposed to competition from other European firms in the domestic market as well as in world markets.

Furthermore, for declining industries, the measures applied should aim at easing the transition rather than perpetuating their lives. Changes in this direction since the 1978 elections are indicated by official pronouncements[65] as well as by actions to abolish price controls and phase out subsidies to unprofitable firms. The new policy direction has been reconfirmed in the orientation of the VIIIth Plan, made public in April 1979.

Instead of selective intervention, emphasis should be given to general—or horizontal—policy measures, aimed at promoting productive investment and technological change. To begin with, on the example of Germany, tax incentives for investment should be increased and transfers of tax deductions for losses within groups of companies should be permitted.[67] Also, discrimination against manufacturing industries in favor of construction in allocating credits should be eliminated and facilities for the financing of new enterprises should be provided.[68] Other general measures might aim at accelerating technological change by increasing tax incentives for research and development and furthering technical education. Finally, as Stoffaes notes, the cost of social legislation should be lowered for industrial firms by changing the mode of financial social charges and easing legislative provisions that limit reductions in the work force.[69]

These measures would contribute to the continuing transformation of the French economy while relying on market forces for the choice of products. Also, they might permit attaining a rate of economic growth exceeding the 3 percent a year that Cotta calls an upper limit and even the 3 to 4 percent assumed by Stoffaes.[70]

Concluding Remarks

This chapter has reviewed developments in the French economy since the Establishment of the Fifth Republic and the creation of the European Economic Community in 1958. It has shown that this period saw a reorientation of planning and policy-making from selective interventions to general policy measures aimed at encouraging investment, technological change, and exports, and promoting industrial concentration. These measures, together with the success of the Pinay-Rueff Plan, the overdevaluation of the franc in 1958, and a moderate rate of inflation, contributed to the rapid expansion of manufacturing production and exports and the transformation of the industrial structure during the fifteen years preceding the oil crisis. Thus, while entrepreneurs had feared the adverse effects of participation in the Common Market, France enjoyed the highest rate of economic growth among the EEC countries and became a major industrial power.

The policies followed after the oil crisis maintained the relative advantage of the French economy vis-à-vis Germany in terms of economic growth rates at the expense of a higher rate of inflation and loss of foreign exchange reserves.

Nevertheless, by 1978 France has transformed its balance-of-payments deficit into a surplus.

For the future, encouraging productive investment and technological change appears to have highest priority. Exceptions apart, selective measures for assisting particular sectors, subsectors, and enterprises do not seem appropriate for this pupose. Rather, general measures should be used to promote the continuing transformation of the economy.

NOTES

1. The author is indebted to Henri Bourgignat, Pierre-Henri Cassou, Alain Cotta, Patrick Guillaumont, Edmond Malinvaud, Paul Mentre de Loye, and Christian Stoffaes for helpful comments and discussions on issues raised in the paper. The author alone is responsible, however, for the opinions expressed therein.

2. For example, in the case of differences of opinion between the cotton yarn and garment industries, "it is actually arbitration by the supreme agencies of the Plan that will establish cotton yarn imports within the framework of Plan forecasts, both for the industry that weaves these yarns and for the ready-to-wear garment industry that uses them." CEPES, *French and Other National Economic Plans for Growth* (New York: Committee for Economic Development, 1963) p. 68.

3. While some of the associated overseas countries and territories subsequently left the Franc area, the two expressions will be used interchangeably.

4. J. Bénard, C. Roux, and C. Girardeau, *L'execution du IIIe Plan francais: Essai de Mesure et d'analyse,"* Bulletin de CEPREL, July 1964, p. 117.

5. The expression "European countries" will be used throughout to refer to the countries of Western Europe excluding the less developed countries of Southern Europe; also, Western Germany will be referred to as "Germany."

6. Commissariat Général du Plan et Services des Etudes Economiques et Financiéres, "L'équilibre économique en 1961," July 1957, p. 112.

7. J. Bénard, C. Roux and C. Girardeau, *op. cit.*, pp. 117-20.

8. Bela Balassa, "Planning in an Open Economy," *Kyklos*, 1966 (3), p. 385.

9. Ibid., Table I.

10. "No special measure is available anymore that would permit the regulation of imports, there is no mechanism that would guarantee that export objectives would be regarded with confidence. Everything depends on international competition." Commissariat Général du Plan et Services des Etudes Economiques et Financiéres, "Projet de Rapport du Groupe d'Equilibre de la Commission de l'Economie Générale du Financement du Plan," June 1961, p. 57.

11. J.H. McArthur and B.R. Scott, *Industrial Planning in France*, Cambridge, Mass., Graduate School of Business Administration of Harvard University 1968, p. 475.

12. "De la forme et des méthodes d'un plan national dans un systéme d'économie de marché," Déclaration du Conseil National du Patronat Francais, January 1965. For a discussion of changes in business attitudes towards planning, cf. Bela Balassa, "Whither French Planning?" *Quarterly Journal of Economics*, November 1965, pp. 537-54.

13. Bela Balassa, "Planning and Programming in the European Common Market," European Economic Review, October, 1973, pp. 217-33.

14. Alain Cotta, "Réflexion sur la politique industrielle de la France," *Le redéploiement industriel*, Etudes de politique industrielle, No. 17, Ministére de l'Industrie, 1977. pp. 75-76.

15. For a detailed discussion, see Pierre-Henri Cassou, *Les aides financiéres aux entreprises*, Paris, Librairies Techniques, 1977.

16. Bernard Guibert et al., "Le mutation industrielle de la France," *Les Collections de L'INSEE*, Serie E No. 31–32, Vol. I., November 1975, p. 95.

17. Ibid., p. 132.

18. Ibid., pp. 114, 123.

19. The discussion draws extensively on Carol Balassa, "Organized Industry in France and the European Common Market: Interest Group Attitudes and Behavior," Ph.D. dissertation on International Relations at the Johns Hopkins University, Baltimore, Md., September 1978.

20. See two declarations by Guy Mollet, the French Prime Minister at the time when the Rome Treaty was negotiated, "it is only by integrating Germany in a European grouping superior to her [that there] will be a durable solution to the German problem" ("Débats Parlementaires de l'Assemblée Nationale", *Journal Officiel* 11 July 1956, pp. 3382–85) and "How many times have we deplored the absence of a European view independent of the two blocs? We do not have the right to permit the opportunity offered to us to escape" (*Débats parlementaires* 22 January 1957, p. 70).

21. In the debates on the Rome Treaty at the National Assembly, the Minister of External Affairs, Maurice Faure, emphasized the hoped-for economic effects of the EEC—the modernization and restructuring of French industry (*Le Monde*, 9 July 1957).

22. *Bulletin du Conseil National du Patronat Francais*, No. 124, September 1954.

23. 31 May 1956.

24. "Le Projet du Marché Commun European," *Bulletin du CNPF*, No. 156, November 1956.

25. Organization for Economic Co-operation and Development, *Main Economic Indicators*, various issues.

26. Cf. Bela Balassa, "Tariff Reductions and Trade in Manufactures among the Industrial Countries" *American Economic Review*, June 1966, pp. 466–473, and Bela Balassa, et al., *European Economic Integration*, Amsterdam. Elsevier-North Holland, 1975, Ch. 3.

27. Institut national de la Statistique et des Etudes Economiques, "Performances économiques nationales et compéitivité, Un essai de comparaison entre trois pays du Marché Commun: France-République Féderale d'Allemagne-Royaume Uni" Paris, may 1978, p. 237.

28. "Fresque historique du système productif," *Collections de l'INSEE*, Série E, No. 27 October, 1974, p. 207. The results for 1971 are biased downward by reason of the rapid expansion of French food exports to other Common Market countries, which led to an increase in the index of specialization for agriculture from 133 to 174 and for food processing from 119 to 141.

29. The data include trade with countries of the Franc zone as well. This is warranted, since, by the late sixties, the other countries of the Common Market had equal access to these markets.

30. Bernard Guibert et a., "La mutation industrielle de la France," *op. cit.*, Vol. II, p. 205.

31. A knowledgeable observer described the situation in Winter 1958: "France does not have any more foreign exchange reserves. Its gold holdings are hardly sufficient to provide a guarantee for its loans. Quantitative restrictions, which France eliminated less rapidly and less completely than its OEEC partners in the framework of import liberalization, were in their entirety reestablished. At the same time, the financing of imports that are indispensable for its industry depend on the availability of new foreign loans" (Guy de Carmoy, "L'adaptation de l'économie francais au marché commun," *Revue d'Economie Politique*, January-February, 1958, p. 153.

32. Drouin, *op. cit.*, p. 41.

33. Cf. the Georges Villiers speech reported in *Le Bulletin du CNPF*, No. 158, February 1957. A detailed discussion of the changing attitudes is in Carol Balassa, "Organized Industry in France and the European Common Market: Interest Group Attitudes and Behavior."

34. OECD, *National Accounts*, various issues.

35. Average profit rates, defined as own rates of return to capital in the business sector, increased from 5.6 percent in the second half of the 1950s to 8.3 percent in the second half of the 1960s (L.R. Christensen, D. Cummings, and D.W. Jorgensen "Economic Growth 1947-73: An International Comparison," in J.W. Kendrick and B. Vaccara (eds.), *New Developments in Productivity Measurement*, New York, Columbia University Press, 1978.

36. Alain Cotta, *Inflation et crossance en France depuis 1962*, Paris, Presses Universitaries de France, 1974.

37. OECD, *National Accounts*, various issues.

38. Ibid.

39. Cf. e.g., the interview with Jean-Francois Deniau, Minister for Foreign Trade, in *Le Nouvel Observateur*, No. 718, 12-18 August 1978—The following summary cannot do justice to the richness of the argumentation of the two authors that also extends to social and political factors.

40. Christian Stoffaes, *La grande menace industrielle*, Paris, Calmann-Levy, 1978, Part II, Ch. 1.

41. Ibid., p. 102.

42. Alain Cotta, *La France et l'impératif mondial*, Paris, Presses Universitaires de France, 1978, p. 151.

43. Ibid., pp. 153-4.

44. Ibid., pp. 170-71.

45. *La grande menace industrielle*, p. 79.

46. Bela Balassa, "U.S. Export Performance: A Trade Share Analysis," Baltimore, Maryland, November 1976.

47. "Performances économiques nationales et compétitivité," *op. cit.*

48. OECD, *Economic Outlook*, December 1978.

49. IMF *International Financial Statistics*, June 1979—Due to the substantial stockpiling of imported materials in 1973, comparable figures could not be derived for Japan.

50. *La France et l'impératif mondial*, Part I, Ch. 2 and Part II, Ch. 2.

51. *Op. cit.*, p. 149.

52. The author's estimates based on IMF, *International Financial Statistics*, June 1979.

53. Ibid.

54. For a detailed discussion, see Bela Balassa, "Resolving Policy Conflicts among the Industrial Countries for a Rapid Growth of the World Economy," *Banca Nazionale del Lavoro Quarterly Review*, September 1978, pp. 271-281.

55. *La France et l'impératif mondial*, pp. 131-192/

56. *L'impératif industriel*, Paris, Edictions Seuil, 1963, p. 218.

57. *La Grande menace industrielle*, p. 256.

58. Ibid., Part III, Ch. III.

59. *La France et l'impératif mondial*, p. 225 and *La grande menace industrielle*, p. 199—This contrast with the view in Jean-marcel Jeanneney, *Pour un nouveau protectionnism*, Paris, Seuil, 1978.

60. John Zysman, *Political Strategies for Industrial Order State, Market and Industry in France*, Berkeley, University of California Press, 1973, p. 88.

61. Ibid., p. 207.

62. *La France et l'impératif mondial*, p. 195 and *La grande menace industrielle*, p. 256.

63. *La grande menace industrielle*, Part III, Ch. IV.

64. Ibid., p. 431.

65. Cf. e.g., the statements of M. Giscard d'Estaing, *Le Monde*, 18 October 1978.

67. On this point, see the article by Michel Debré in *Le Monde*, 14 August 1978.

68. Cf. *La grande menace industrielle*, pp. 259-60.

69. Ibid., pp. 257-61—Another important measure recommended by Stoffaes, the abolition of price control, occurred in May 1978.

70. *La France et l'impératif mondial*, p. 203 and *La grande menace industrielle*, pp. 199 and 223.

TABLE 1

THE RATIO OF FOREIGN TRADE TO VALUE ADDED
IN THE PRODUCTION OF TRADED GOODS

	1958		1963		1968		1973		1976	
	Export Ratio	Import Ratio	Export Ratio	Import Ratio	Export Ratio	Import Ratio	Export Ratio	Import Ratio	Export Ratio	Import Ratio
Belgium	83.6	85.6	100.5	100.7	108.9	111.9	140.4	138.2	152.6	165.1
France[a]	12.0	15.2	17.5	19.3	21.3	23.1	31.0	33.1	44.3	51.9
France[b]	17.8	19.5	21.8	23.5	24.4	25.9	32.9	34.3	47.0	53.6
Germany	30.2	25.2	30.8	27.5	39.0	31.8	42.6	34.8	50.4	43.6
Italy	20.7	25.8	26.1	38.9	38.8	39.2	39.1	49.0	55.2	64.4
Netherlands	87.5	98.5	92.7	111.5	97.6	108.8	118.5	120.4	131.0	132.1
Norway	52.5	92.5	58.7	99.6	67.9	94.8	86.1	114.5	84.9	118.6
Sweden	49.1	55.7	51.5	54.5	58.6	61.4	76.5	66.7	70.9	74.2
United Kingdom	37.1	43.8	37.8	44.9	46.6	57.2	55.3	70.1	70.2	85.2
United States	11.5	9.4	11.7	9.5	12.1	12.5	12.8	18.5	23.2	26.3
Japan	26.7	28.1	24.6	30.4	21.2	21.2	22.0	22.8	32.0	32.9

NOTES: a = Excluding associated overseas countries and territories; b = Including associated overseas countries and territories.

SOURCES: Value Added; O.E.C.D., *National Accounts*, various issues.

Foreign Trade: Exports and f.o.b. prices, imports at c.i.f prices. I.M.F., *International Financial Statistics*, May and August 1978

TABLE 2
THE SHARE OF FOREIGN TRADE IN MANUFACTURING INDUSTRIES IN FRANCE, 1953-1976

	Manufacturing Industries (06), (09), to (12)		Building Materials and Glass (06)		Machinery and Transport Equipment (09)		Chemical Industries (10)		Textiles, Clothing, Leather (11)		Wood, Paper and Related Industries (12)	
	a	b	a	b	a	b	a	b	a	b	a	b
1953 A	21.8	11.0	14.2	6.2	20.5	10.2	21.1	12.0	30.4	14.8	15.6	8.2
B	14.8	12.6	6.6	4.1	11.1	9.1	18.3	14.3	24.9	23.0	10.1	8.0
C	1.60	.86	2.34	1.54	2.06	1.13	1.19	.82	1.32	.58	1.65	1.03
1958 A	n.a	11.2	n.a	5.7	n.a.	12.2	n.a.	12.6	n.a.	13.1	n.a.	7.2
B	n.a.	12.1	n.a.	4.7	n.a.	11.1	n.a.	15.6	n.a.	17.0	n.a.	9.0
C	n.a.	.92	n.a.	1.23	n.a.	1.11	n.a.	.78	n.a.	.74	n.a.	.78
1963 A	22.2	17.8	12.3	10.3	24.5	19.9	25.2	20.7	26.0	20.2	17.1	10.4
B	18.4	17.7	8.1	8.1	18.5	18.5	23.3	21.8	21.5	20.4	14.3	12.3
C	1.28	1.01	1.59	1.30	1.43	1.09	1.11	.94	1.28	.99	.90	.83
1968 A	20.8	17.8	9.9	8.7	22.9	19.8	29.9	25.6	23.0	19.8	8.1	6.5
B	19.3	18.3	9.7	9.5	19.8	19.1	28.6	26.5	19.4	18.0	14.5	13.0
C	1.10	.97	1.02	.91	1.20	1.05	1.07	.95	1.24	1.12	.52	.67
1973 A	23.5	22.3	12.9	12.1	29.2	27.7	26.2	24.7	22.1	21.1	10.9	10.0
B	21.1	20.8	13.8	13.1	25.5	25.1	23.6	23.2	16.0	15.7	15.3	15.0
C	1.14	1.09	.93	.91	1.20	1.14	1.15	1.09	1.49	1.43	.68	.63
1976 A	27.9	26.2	13.5	12.6	36.8	34.8	28.9	27.2	21.4	20.3	11.8	10.8
B	24.7	24.3	15.5	14.7	29.3	28.7	26.1	25.6	21.7	21.3	18.1	17.8
C	1.18	1.10	.85	.84	1.41	1.33	1.15	1.09	.98	.94	.61	.56

n.a. = not available

NOTES: A = Exports as a percentage of production; B = imports as a percentage of utilization; C = export/import ratios.
a = including associated countries and territories; b = excluding associated countries and territories.
SOURCES: INSEE, *Rapport sur les Comptes de la Nation* and *Etudes et Conjoncture*, various issues.

TABLE 3

GROWTH RATES OF THE GROSS NATIONAL PRODUCT, 1953–1978

	1953–58	1958–63	1958–73	1963–68	1968–73	1973–78
Belgium	2.7	4.6	5.9	4.3	4.9	2.4
France	4.8	6.0	5.2	5.3	5.5	2.8
Germany	6.9	5.5	5.1	4.2	5.0	1.9
Italy	n.a.	6.4	4.4	5.0	5.3	4.0
Netherlands	n.a.	1.5	5.6	5.6	4.2	2.2
Norway	2.9	4.8	7.4	2.0	4.7	4.6
Sweden	3.5	4.7	3.4	4.1	4.1	1.3
United Kindom	2.3	3.4	3.1	3.1	3.2	0.9
United States	1.8	4.1	3.3	4.8	4.1	2.3
Japan	7.0	10.8	9.6	10.8	10.4	3.6

n.a. = not available
SOURCES: O.E.C.D., *National Accounts* and *Economic Outlook*, various issues.
I.M.F., *International Financial Statistics*, various issues.

TABLE 4

EXPORT-IMPORT RATIOS IN FRENCH MANUFACTURING,
1973 and 1976

	1973	1976
Construction Materials	.67	.61
Glass Products	1.71	1.56
Chemicals and Synthetic Fibers	.96	1.01
Pharmaceuticals	2.00	1.68
Foundry Products	.98	1.23
Mechanical Engineering Products	.95	1.23
Electrical Engineering and Electronics Products	1.01	1.18
Household Consumer Durables	.51	.46
Automobiles, and Related Products	1.98	1.91
Shipbuilding, Aircraft, and Armament	1.49	2.20
Textiles and Clothing	1.48	1.01
Shoes and Leather Products	1.57	.83
Furniture and Other Wood Products	.76	.63
Paper and Cardboard Products	.50	.45
Printing and Publishing	.89	1.01
Plastic Products	1.26	1.20
ALL MANUFACTURING	1.14	1.18

SOURCE: INSEE, Rapport sur les Comptes de la Nation de l'année 1977, *Les Collections de L'INSEE, Série C,* 662-63 / 1978.

The Corporatist Dynamic of Agricultural Modernization in the Fifth Republic

John T.S. Keeler

At the dawn of the Fifth Republic one could feel relatively safe in making at least two key assumptions about the future of French agriculture.[1] First, in one form or another, the modernization process which had been accelerating since the time of the Liberation would continue. Second, proposals for increased state intervention to guide this process and hasten the exodus from the land would continue to be resisted staunchly by organized agriculture and especially by the farmers' principal spokesman, the FNSEA (*Fédération Nationale des Syndicats d'Exploitants Agricoles*). Some members of the 'New Generation' of French farmers were beginning to question the prudence of that purely defensive posture; but they were a small and powerless minority. At this point it was nearly as difficult as during the Liberation period to imagine that, 'the French peasant milieu could respond to this natural pressure other than by a passive resistance and sporadic agitations.'[2]

After twenty years of the Fifth Republic, the first assumption remains valid—but not the second. One of the most remarkable political developments of the past two decades has been the fundamental transformation of the FNSEA's stance on agricultural modernization. Since the early 1960s the FNSEA has actively encouraged a reform policy to increase agricultural efficiency and productivity at the expense of a tremendous decrease in the number of farms and farmers. The modernization process has been furthered through a corporatist dynamic, i.e., through the development of an intimate, symbiotic relationship between the state and the FNSEA. Largely because the FNSEA has played the role of an 'official union' or corporatist client, the drama of the modernization process has unfolded without creating the sort of widespread 'climate of disintegration' which many observers expected and feared twenty years ago.[3]

While the modernization process has proceeded in this surprisingly tranquil manner, it has not failed to generate problems for the farmers, the FNSEA and the state. The hopes of a great many farmers have been dashed by the harsh realities entailed in the reform policies sponsored or supported by the FNSEA. Opposition to these policies and to the FNSEA's intimate *concertation* with the state has led to the emergence of rival unions and to unprecedented tension within the FNSEA itself. In the face of increasingly stiff sectoral opposition, the FNSEA has maintained its hegemonic status largely because of tangible and intangible benefits it receives from the state in exchange for performing the official union role. By reinforcing FNSEA hegemony, the state has pushed forward the modernization process while maintaining at least a semblance of social peace. But it has also been forced to ignore if not sanction the misuse of public funds and semi-public agencies and to stifle legitimate expressions of pluralism in agriculture.

The first section of this chapter will provide a brief account of how and why the FNSEA was moved to support agricultural modernization shortly after the inception of the Fifth Republic. Section two will discuss the nature and the consequences of the reform policy and *concertation* strategy which the FNSEA has pursued since the early 1960s. The third section will discuss how the corporatist dynamic of the modernization process has reinforced the hegemony of the FNSEA—at some expense to sectoral and national interest.

THE NEW GENERATION AND THE FNSEA'S SUPPORT OF REFORM

Throughout the 1950s the FNSEA pursued a prices-first policy, arguing that the essential interests of all farmers could be satisfied only through united struggle to obtain a level of prices that would yield income 'parity' with the industrial sector. The concentration on prices made it possible to maintain syndical unity by linking the foremost demands of small family farmers in France's polycultural regions to those of large-scale farmers in the regions of modernized and specialized commercial agriculture. Policies which would acknowledge disparity in the needs of agricultural subgroups and aid certain segments of agriculture selectively to the exclusion of or at the expense of others were avoided assiduously. The FNSEA stated repeatedly that such measures were unnecessary, as state price supports could be sufficient to ensure the technical advancement and continued prosperity of even the smallest farmers. In the words of one FNSEA president of the 1950s, if prices 'were normal, there would be no marginal farms'.[4]

A logical conclusion from the FNSEA's theory of 'normal prices' was that the agricultural profession bore no responsibility for the problems of the sector. These could be attributed wholly to a state which failed to assure the 'just' or 'proper' functioning of the agricultural economy and forced the farmers to sub-

140

mit to officious harassment by 'statist technocrats.' With the state portrayed as the 'permanent enemy' of agriculture, the FNSEA fought for high prices through a strategy of *contestation*—the application of pressure through appeals to sympathetic groups in parliament and periodic mass demonstrations.[5]

Dominated by relatively old and conservative men, the FNSEA continued to pursue its prices-first policy by *contestation* throughout the 1950s. Near the end of the decade, however, that policy began to be challenged—first in the Federation's youth branch, the CNJA (*Centre National des Jeunes Agriculteurs*), and then in the FNSEA itself—by a New Generation of young reformers from the underdeveloped areas of France. Led by Michel Debatisse, the reformers attacked the prices-first policy and called for a more constructive and imaginative response to the agricultural modernization process. To fight the battle for high prices in the guise of defending small farmers was, the reformers claimed, deceitful and demagogic. A price rise of as much as 20–30 percent would do little to alleviate the plight of the small, inefficient producers. Continuation of the emphasis on prices would simply ensure that thousands of small farmers would be forced to abandon their properties, '*chassés par la misère.*'[6]

To defend truly the interests of the small and medium-sized farmers, argued the reformers, economic realities would have to be recognized and realistic policies to accommodate them developed. High prices alone were not the solution. Increased productivity would also be necessary, and this would entail FNSEA support for structural reforms to facilitate the enlargement of inefficiently small agricultural 'enterprises.' Moreover, some measure of economic concentration and a concomitant diminution in the number of farmers were ineluctable. French agriculture could not fight for the survival of all family farms. Instead, the process of concentration and rural exodus could proceed either in an 'anarchic' fashion or with guidance to 'humanize' it to save the largest possible number of family farms and minimize the attendant human sacrifices.

The advent of the Fifth Republic proved to be a godsend for the young reformers and their proposals. Establishing influence within the Fourth Republic, where parliament was supreme and the govermental ties of the traditional FNSEA leaders were powerful, would have been difficult on into the 1960s. The new regime, however, had completely different rules of the game. Old-style lobbying 'could produce little more than noisy reverberations,' and it was 'now better to know two well-placed civil servants than twenty deputies.' Moreover, many well-placed civil servants were eager to know the young proponents of agricultural reform. Many young technocrats of the new regime—in the Planning Commission and the offices of the president and the prime minister—hoped to initiate an innovative, coherent agricultural policy and were impressed by the fresh ideas and the dynamism of the New Generation. Consultations between these officials and CNJA leaders became frequent in the early months of the Fifth Republic, and in 1959 the leaders of the CNJA were 'elevated to the dignified status of privileged interlocutors of the regime.'[8]

Complementary policy goals led to increased CNJA cooperation with the Gaullist government in the early 1960s. On the one hand, the young reformers felt that 'the *rôle moteur* of the state' had to be exploited to produce a comprehensive reform program that would allow the farmers to 'take charge of their economic destiny.' Their structural reforms could not be achieved through *contestation* and *revendication*'but only through 'active solidarity' with the state. On the other hand, the Gaullist government intended—in the words of one of Michael Debré's advisers—'to make the maximum effort to enable agriculture to modernize and become competitive internationally,' and believed that 'these results can only be obtained by the implementation of profound reforms which necessitate the active cooperation of the farmers.'[9]

The FNSEA was slow to cooperate. Thus, the CNJA played a major role in shaping the crucial government policies of the early 1960s. Michel Debré's Orientation Law of 1960 and Edgard Pisani's Complementary Law of 1962 were formulated with minimal input from the FNSEA and adopted many of the CNJA's central proposals. Most importantly, these legislative packages included provisions for: a network of regional agencies, the SAFER†, which 'would be authorized to buy land as it came onto the market, to carry out necessary improvements (including the consolidation of microfundia into viable farms), and to sell or lease this land to qualified family farmers'; and a Social Action Fund for the Amelioration of Agricultural Structures (FASASA), empowered to grant a special subsidy—an IVD**—to those peasants who would agree to retire early and render their land available for redistribution as well as other types of subsidies to 'humanize' the rural exodus.[10]

The government's adoption of CNJA-sponsored reforms increased greatly the immediate influence and apparent autonomy of the FNSEA's youth branch. From 1959 until roughly 1964, the CNJA appeared to be carving out an independent niche for itself among agricultural organizations and even to be 'on the verge of . . . becoming predominant over its parent organization, the FNSEA.' The more important, long-term effect proved to be what a *Le Monde* reporter has termed the 'absorption' of the CNJA by the FNSEA. Ironically, the CNJA declined in infuence precisely because of its success; from 1961 onward its first-generation leaders moved into positions of power within the FNSEA and forced the incorporation of reformist ideas into the FNSEA's program. This renewal of the FNSEA elite and the alteration of FNSEA policy attenuated the celebrated 'struggle of the generations' which gave way to a recrudescence of more traditional agricultural conflicts along partisan, regional and other lines.[11]

THE REFORMIST FNSEA, THE FARMERS AND THE STATE: 1962-1978

Since its initial incorporation of reformist demands in the early 1960s, the basic program of the FNSEA has changed only in nuance. The policy component of this program has included acceptance of a continued decline in the agricultural population and encouragement of structural reform through selective policies geared to the disparate needs of the various segments of the agricultural sector. The strategy for articulating these policy positions has been *concertation* with the state, i.e., extensive FNSEA participation in formulating and implementating the state's agricultural policy.

FNSEA Policy

The reform policy of the FNSEA has been guided by a vision of a modernized agricultural structure, composed of farms that are neither the tiny, inefficient units predominant in the past nor the giant, agro-business concerns found in the United States, but rather a compromise between these two extremes: medium-sized family farms which are 'socially and humanly viable.' To 'prepare the future' in this manner while attempting to assure equitable agricultural incomes in the short run, the FNSEA has developed a complex package of policy positions based on the premise that the agricultural sector is composed of the following 'three agricultures.'

1) *A competitive agriculture* possessing sufficient land 'to assure the full employment of labor and material' and utilizing the most advanced techniques. Farmers in this category, capable of producing at a cost below the level of fixed prices, can prosper merely through the continuance of governmental market supports.

2) *An intermediate agriculture* which 'is not yet perfectly competitive, but which has already largely commenced its evolution and which can win or lose the game depending on the agricultural policy followed.' The farmers in this category are relatively young, predominantly engaged in livestock production (the sort which is most efficient for a medium-sized farm) and 'animated by a desire for growth.' Lacking the land, capital and technical education necessary for such growth, these farmers need state aid to improve and expand their enterprises sufficiently to move from category 2 to category 1.

3) An *agriculture victimized by change*, composed of aged farmers living on excessively small farms and of young farmers unable—because they lack land, capital and/or education—to advance into category 1. The departure of these farmers is accepted as an inevitable preconditon for ameliorating the structures and improving the incomes of those who stay. These farmers need 'personalized subsidies' such as the IVD or occupational training subsidies.[12]

This diversified, coherent 'three agricultures' program seems well suited to the needs of an era featuring rapid socio-economic and technological change. From 1962 onward, however, it has gradually become evident that such a program—however 'reasonable'—is suited poorly to the organizational needs of the FNSEA. New Generation reformers argued in the early 1960s that their program would reinforce the unity of the FNSEA by responding better to the particular needs of each category of farmers than could the prices-first policy. This optimistic prediction proved to rest on two rather unrealistic assumptions: a) that all farmers would fit comfortably into those abstract 'categories,' and b) that the state would support FNSEA–sponsored reforms sufficiently to ensure their popularity. Unfortunately, these assumptions were invalid.

In retrospect, it is clear that tensions within the profession were virtually intrinsic to the structural reform program. In the abstract, the logic of the program was seductive. A 'humanized exodus' from the land would have allowed 'the maximum' possible number of farmers to remain on the land working viable farms. As long as reform policy remained theoretical, each relatively young farmer could imagine that *he* would stay in agriculture and benefit from structural improvements. Once the policy began to be implemented, however, inevitably many farmers were disappointed. Its popularity was bound to decline when it became clear that 'many are called, but few are chosen.'[13]

The reform program was certain to meet opposition not only from those 'not chosen,' but also from some members of category 1. These relativeyly prosperous farmers were assumed to be content with their large, modernized farms. In reality, however, many were eager to enlarge and improve their farms. These 'liberals' resented even the modest activities of the SAFER, for example, and fought to maintain a free market in land. Conflicts between pro-SAFER and anti-SAFER forces have generated considerable tension in regions such as Nord-Picardie, where implmentation of the regional SAFER was blocked until the mid-1970s and many of the more 'savage liberals' defected from the FNSEA to a conservative rival, the FFA (French Federation of Agriculture).[14]

Although opposition to the 'discriminatory' reform program was inevitable, sectoral tensions have been exacerbated greatly by the half-hearted manner of successive governments in keeping the promises of the early 1960s. The appeal of the reformers during that 'heroic era' rested on the assumption that 'humanized modernization' would impede 'capitalist concentration' of land, save 'the maximum' of family farms (a 1962 estimate was that only 15–20 percent of farms were 'unviable'),[15] decrease the disparities of income within agriculture and allow farmers to achieve income parity with the industrial sector. None of these goals has even been approached to the degree expected by reformers.

First, largely due to the underfunding and legal restriction of SAFER activity, the concentration process has scarcely altered its 'capitalist' character. As Table 1 shows, a dramatic decline in the number of small farms since 1955 has led to a relatively modest increase in medium-sized farms, but a striking increase in large farms.

Table I

Distribution of Farm Land by Size of Farm

	Small Farms (< 35 hectares)	Medium Farms (35–70 hectares)	Large Farms (> 70 hectares)
1955	64 %	21 %	15 %
1970	50 %	26 %	24 %
1980	36 %	31 %	33 %
1985	31 %	31 %	38 %

Moreover, the projections for 1985 are even bleaker: no increase in medium-sized farms is expected from 1980 to 1985, while large farms will become predominant for the first time.[16]

Secondly, to 'save' family farms while encouraging modernization has been much more difficult than anticipated. From 1963 to 1975, the number of farms declined by more than 27 percent; moreover, the decline from 1963 to 1985 is projected to exceed 40 percent. The first twenty years of the Fifth Republic have led to approximately a 50 percent decrease in the percentage of the labor force engaged in agriculture—and the decline has held steady during the past few years despite high unemployment in industry.[17]

Third, the disparities of income within agriculture, region by region, increased between 1963 and 1970. In fact, in 1972 the regional disparities of agricultural income in France were the greatest in the European Community by far. The disparity in France was about one to five, but one to three in the other states; moreover, when calculated by department rather than region, the disparity in France was about one to ten.[18]

Fourth, very few farmers have achieved income 'parity' with the industrial sector. True, as President Giscard d'Estaing proudly proclaimed in 1977 at Vassy, agriculture has obtained global parity of income. But the President failed to mention the fundamental problem of 'shocking inequalities which it is impossible to ignore.'[19] In 1972, according to the Ministry of Agriculture, only 12 percent of the farmers had an income superior to parity, and this 12 percent accounted for 45 percent of agricultural income. Moreover, agricultural income has become increasingly vulnerable because of the indebtedness entailed in the modernization effort. Indebtedness has increased dramatically since the launching of the Orientation Law, from 30 percent of added value in 1960 to 147 percent in 1977. Furthermore, the increase has been greatest in such small farming sectors as livestock raising (*élevage*) and wine grape production.[20]

In the 1950s, such a negative balance sheet on agricultural policy might have led farmers to question the efficacy of the FNSEA as a mechanism to defend agricultural interests. However, it would have posed at most a limited threat to the Federation. For in the 1950s the union could have disowned convincingly responsibility for state policy and pointed to its strategy of *contestation* to prove its perennial dissatisfaction. Since then, however, the failures of state policy have posed a much greater organizational problem for the Federation. Having assumed an important role in the formulation and implementation of agricultural policy, the FNSEA has been held accountable by many farmers for its failures.

FNSEA STRATEGY

Except for a brief period in 1964 and 1965, the FNSEA has consistently pursued a strategy of *concertation* with the state sine the emergence of the New Generation reformers in the early 1960s. Originally, *concertation* was defended as essential primarily to obtain beneficial structural reforms. However, given its disappointing results, the FNSEA elite has been forced to develop an extensive rationale for its retention—a rationale which could hardly satisfy a significant portion of the farmers and leaves unstated some principal reasons to retain *concertation*.

FNSEA leaders argue that the *concertation* strategy represents a realistic adaptation to changes in the political and economic environment of the Federation. The use of pressure through parliament has become outmoded, as the Fifth Republic's powerful presidency and stable governmental majority 'pose in new terms the possibilities of action *vis-à-vis* the state.' Moreover, the European Community and the Common Agricultural Policy necessitated a reevaluation of the traditional relationship between the FNSEA and the state. With 'agricultural decisions being made at Brussels, it is important to make an ally of the minister who represents us.'[21]

Concertation has been called necessary not only because of changes in political structure, but also due to the dramatic increase in state intervention into the agricultural economy under the Fifth Republic. The FNSEA's engagement in *concertation*, it is argued, results from the uniqueness of the agricultural context. 'In effect, the intervention of the state is permanent in the elaboration and application of agricultural policy.'Therefore, the FNSEA is compelled to negotiate or dialogue with any government, whatever its composition. 'Every day' the FNSEA is compelled to contact the government or the administration in defense of agricultural interests. Since 'this defense is no longer possible' when relations between the FNSEA and the state are severed, a rupture of relations can only be considered in the most 'grave cases.'[22]

The logic of the FNSEA strategy of *concertation* is by no means without substance. State intervention in agriculture has increased enormously in the Fifth Republic; between 1960 and 1976, the budget of the Ministry of Agriculture increased by almost 90 percent and state spending on agriculture swelled from 5.4 percent to 13.5 percent of the total state budget. Dialogue with the state has doubtless been necessary to guide this intervention and in the 'daily defense' of agricultural interests. Especially with the complications entailed in the shift of decision-making power to Brussels, the FNSEA elite is understandably concerned with maintaining the French agricultural minister as an 'ally' and with employing 'forms of action' which are 'seriously deliberated and then applied with determination under the control of those who have responsibility for them.'[23]

While this rationale for permanent *concertation* may seem reasonable to the FNSEA elite, it has proven to be less than cogent for many farmers at the *base*. When a 1973 opinion poll asked for 'the most effective type of action' for a farmers' union, only 46 percent of the farmers responded: 'permanent *concertation* with the government and state administration.' Responses to another question showed, moreover, that even some farmers who favored *concertation* questioned the tenacity with which the FNSEA defended their interests. Fully 55 percent of the respondents felt that the FNSEA and CNJA 'allow themselves to be influenced by the government,' while only 38 percent felt that the officially recognized interlocutors of the state were 'really independent.' Finally, only 47 percent believed that the FNSEA should be allowed to remain the sole farmers' union recognized by the state as an official interlocutor. The FNSEA's present status was favored by 66 percent* of the farmers with 50 or more hectares of land, 65 percent of those specializing in wheat and other grains, and 66 percent of those politically aligned with the present majority; in contrast, the FNSEA's privileged position was supported by only 45–47 percent of the farmers with less than 50 hectares of land, 41–47 percent of the livestock raisers and 22 percent of those politically aligned with parties of the Left.[24]

The retention of the *concertation* strategy in the face of widespread dissatisfaction with the modernization policy has eroded the FNSEA's 1950s image as the 'independent' defender of the agricultural sector. Since 1962, *concertation* has been abandoned on only two occasions—or rather, *concertation* was not so much abandoned as rendered impossible by the government's refusal to negotiate. Not once since 1965 has the FNSEA severed relations with the government and engaged in *contestation* even in times of acute agricultural crisis. The FNSEA's response to some major agricultural crises since 1962 demonstrates why, to many farmers, *concertation* has begun to 'convey the impression of the complicity of the Federation in the orientations taken [by the government]'[25]

147

1964-1965: Forced Contestation. In 1964, three months of negotiation with the government failure to bring about any compromise measures to alleviate the effects on the agricultural sector of the government's austerity program. The majority of the FNSEA elite rejected minority demands for an appeal to parliament for a censure motion or for national mass demonstrations; instead it launched a nation-wide strike of all milk home deliveries. Though the strike was a technical success, the government did not respond. It placed the proponents of *concertation* in a difficult position by refusing to talk with the striking farmers or to convoke the *'commission des sages'* suggested by some FNSEA leaders. Only after the government had prevented the continuance of the *concertation* strategy did the FNSEA adopt *contestation* measures. In October 1964, the FNSEA broke off relations with the government and appealed to parliament for a motion of censure; the motion was proposed, and, though not adopted, received 209 votes.

Still resentful over its treatment in 1964, the FNSEA engaged in *contestation* again in 1965. At a time when agricultural income was declining, the Gaullist government halted (on June 30) negotiations in Brussels, at least ostensibly over the issue of the financial regulation of agriculture. While this action disappointed the FNSEA, which had been promised much by the government from the establishment of the CAP (Common Agricultural Policy), its initial response was cautious. However, the FNSEA rapidly became convinced that the fault lay primarily with the government, which seemed to have little interest in *concertation* with the FNSEA. In August, prime minister Pompidou dismissed brusquely an FNSEA letter encouraging a reopening of the Brussels negotiations. In September, president de Gaulle's press conference made clear that the June 30 rupture had been motivated more by his political concerns about supranationality in the E.E.C. than by solicitude for agriculture. As a result the FNSEA engaged in its last major expression of *contestation*; over the objections of reformers hesitant to condemn a government which had launched the structural reform policy, the FNSEA urged its members to oppose de Gaulle in the 1965 presidential election. That tactic produced impressive results. Many electoral analysts attributed de Gaulle's failure to win the election on the first ballot primarily to a decline in his support from the farm sector, and the government's attitude in early 1966 indicated that it agreed with these assessments. A major political figure, Edgar Faure, was appointed Minister of Agriculture and the government rapidly granted most of the policy compromises which the FNSEA had been demanding for three years.

That success indicated that *contestation* could be effective and seemed to assure its future use. Instead, however, it eliminated the major factor which had prompted its employment: governmental intransigence. Since the appointment of Faure and his institution of 'operation charm,' the government has never failed to negotiate with the FNSEA in times of crisis and the FNSEA has never opposed the government overtly.[26]

1965-1974: Crises and Concertation. Since 1965 the FNSEA has attempted to accomplish two mutually exclusive goals. On the one hand, it has attempted to moderate its demands sufficiently to remain the privileged agricultural interlocutor of the state. On the other hand, it has tried to articulate those demands with sufficient vigor to maintain legitimacy and authority in the eyes of all farmers. A brief examination of agricultural crises in 1967, 1969 and 1974 will show that the second goal has been sacrificed more often.

1) *1967* was marked by locally organized demonstrations in the regions dominated by small livestock farmers: the West, Normandy, Burgundy and the Franche-Comté. Their essential demand was revision of the 'liberal orientation of French and Common Market agriculture' to afford increased benefits for the disadvantaged regions and product specializations (e.g., livestock raising). While the FNSEA claimed to support such measures, many small farmers remained unconvinced. For most of the summer, FNSEA dissidents condemned *concertation* and called for national demonstrations to manifest the rejection of government policy. Meanwhile, similar demands were made by MODEF and the *Comité de Guéret,*** the two organizations largely responsible for demonstrations in the Massif-Central. Only after MODEF and the Guéret Committee had called for national demonstrations did the FNSEA issue such a call; when 'constrained' to act on a national scale, the FNSEA urged moderation and the use of the demonstrations primarily to assist the national elite in presenting its demands through *concertation*. Despite the FNSEA appeal, the demonstrations were 'tragically violent,' especially in the West. Thus, they seemed to signify a waning of FNSEA authority. The FNSEA had begun to appear 'emprisoned in the threads of its *concertation* policy,' 'deprived of a good part of its freedom to maneuver.' Forced to introduce '*le sérieux*' into its demands and 'to defend only that which is economically defensible,' the Federation had gradually 'ceased to support the small farmers in acts, and even in words.' As a result, the FNSEA left an 'open field' for rival unions willing—perhaps demagogically—to employ the themes which the FNSEA had used successfully in the 1950s (the defense of all farms, etc.).[27]

2) *1969.* Another, even more significant, challenge to FNSEA authority arose in 1969 following a recrudescence of mass dissatisfaction with the government's agricultural policy. In August and September, a devaluation of the franc and related governmental actions placed a pall over a relatively good year for agriculture. These measures raised hourly wages by more than 11 percent but agricultural income by only 4.3 percent; indeed, real agricultural income actually declined by more than 2 percent. Furthermore, the long-term outlook for agriculture appeared even bleaker with the publication of the 'Vedel Report' by a government commission; this report suggested, among other things, that a rational agricultural policy for France would entail the exodus of 5/6 of the farm population by 1985.

While mass demonstrations took place under FDSEA (i.e., departmental) or rival-union direction in a number of localities (especially in the livestock regions) during August and September, the FNSEA hesitated to coordinate a national demonstration and urged moderation on its departmental affiliates. No national action was organized until October, and even then the FNSEA encouraged a moderate approach symbolized by a photo in the union journal: an FDSEA president engaging in a 'courteous, but animated' conversation with a prefect.

Even more than in 1967, the FNSEA's moderation and *concertation* in time of crisis engendered widespread discontent at the *base*; farmers joined in demonstrations organized by rival union movements, while many FDSEA leaders, especially in the more disadvantaged regions, severely criticized FNSEA policy. Despite repeated pleas for syndical unity, the challenges to the FNSEA continued and, in fact, increased dramatically after October. Tensions within the FNSEA climaxed in late November with a tremendous show of rank-and-file opposition to the national elite's persistent moderation. An estimated 30,000 farmers participated in a national demonstration which called for staunch opposition to governmental policy and rejection of *concertation*. In early December, the FDSEA leaders in Indre-et-Loire (which had seceded from the FNSEA in October) announced the formation of a new rival union—FFA—with the ambition of recruiting all farmers opposed to the official union.

Faced with these signs of unprecedented tensions within the FNSEA, the Federation's national elite was forced to call the organization's first *Congrès Extraordinaire*. As President Caffarelli admitted in his opening speech, the challenges had generated a most severe organizational crisis: 'It is necessary to establish contact with that which constitutes the *base* of the FNSEA . . . . There is no way that those who defend the farmers will be heard by the government if they themselves are the object of permanent criticism.' Caffarelli was forced to defend the strategy and the policy of the Federation. He noted that many farmers had cricitized the FNSEA's relationship with the state as 'excessively intimate.' However, he contended, *concertation* must continue and would not compromise the independence of the FNSEA. Also, Caffarelli asserted that FNSEA policies were designed to defend the farmers as well as possible within realistic bounds. 'Poujadist slogans,' he said, could not lead to meaningful results. The farmers would have to recognize that, like artisans and small-shopkeepers, they were faced with an ineluctable modernization process 'without precedent.' Rather than ignore this evolution, it was better to 'look it in the face and put in place mechanisms which would render it socially and humanly acceptable.'[28]

While the *Congrès Extraordinaire* allowed for the release of some of the tension which had built up within the FNSEA, it hardly eliminated its causes.

Limited to moderate reform by the conflicting demands of its disparate membership and constrained (by various forces) to pursue *concertation* even during crises, the FNSEA simply could not rally the farmers for whom the inevitable economic evolution could not be made 'acceptable.'

3. *1974.* Serious challenges to the FNSEA arose once again during the summer of 1974. Primarily as a result of the oil crisis, inflation in the price of materials necessary for farming reached enormous levels by July: the price of fuel had risen approximately 80 percent since 1973, while the price of fertilizer had increased 40 percent and the prices of other necessities had increased by lesser, but still impressive, amounts. This inflation, combined with the government's austerity program designed to counter it, produced a staggering impact on agriculture. Agricultural income in 1974 declined 15.9 percent from 1973—the greatest yearly decline in the income of any French economic sector since the Liberation.

Throughout the summer, sometimes-violent demonstrations appeared in virtually every region of France in reaction to the crisis; some were organized by FDSEA, many were organized by rival unions and many others were relatively spontaneous actions of the *base* without apparent organizational sponsorship. However, the FNSEA made no effort to canalize the greatest agricultural unrest since 1961 and use it to force concessions from the government. The FNSEA reacted to the continuing demonstrations much as it had in 1967 and 1969. FNSEA president Debatisse announced that the FNSEA planned no nationally coordinated demonstrations until September when it would join with other European agricultural organizations in a Community-wide demonstration to influence the fall meeting of the Council of European Ministers. Before September, Debatisse announced, the FDSEA would organize demonstrations only if they were 'strictly controlled' so as to 'avoid shocking public opinion.' Despite this 'order,' mass demonstrations entailing violence reminiscent of 1961 continued for more than a month.

The 'disobedience' of some FDSEA, especially in the West, Centre and Southwest, was serious enough to place the topic of the proper use of *manifestations* on the agenda for the FNSEA's March 1975 Congress. In one of the Congress' major reports, several strongly-worded pages reminded Federation members that 'direct action is not an end in itself' but rather a means of 'reinforcing the position of the union during the course or at the approach of a negotiation'; that all demonstrations, even those at the department level, were to be approved by the FNSEA; and that excessively long or violent demonstrations would 'demobilize the farmers' and alienate public opinion. FNSEA Secretary General Cormorèche acknowledged that the Federation's national elite had been 'frequently' reproached for the 'style of our relations with the *pouvoirs publics.*' Cormorèche proclaimed: 'As if the great majority of unionized farmers wanted the FNSEA to become a machine of war in the service of profound political change! The farmers' union could not become such a machine—its members would desert it.' 'What would be grave for all,' he continued, 'is if the groups in disaccord decided to constitute (separate) unions. We will not cease repeating that the coexistence of several agricultural unions will weaken the peasant world.'

The FNSEA was hesitant to admit that several rival unions had been constituted already and had used the spontaneous unrest of 1974—as the FNSEA had used unrest in the 1950s—to demonstrate the representativeness of their organizations and their concern for the plight of the small, disadvantaged farmers threatened by the government's policy. Blaming the government for the 1974 crisis may have been demagogic and continual demonstrations may have had less impact on policy formation than negotiations at the summit; but these words and actions clearly responded to the frustrations of many farmers and enabled the rival unions to demonstrate that the FNSEA was not the only union of significance. Because the FNSEA failed to engage in nation-wide *contestation*, MODEF, FFA, and the *Paysans-Travailleurs*[+] were able to show that the farmers would would obey 'orders' from other sources.

Moreover, their absence from negotiating sessions with the government began to seem somewhat counterproductive to the representatives of the state. Clearly, the authority of the FNSEA had been attenuated. Though the government did not recognize rival unions during the 1974 crisis, it did take a step in this direction. In August, the Minister of Agriculture granted an audience to the leaders of FFA in his home department. This was guaranteed to trouble the FNSEA as the first major contribution of the state to the destruction of 'the myth of syndical unity.'[29]

Motives for the Continuance of Concertation. The strategy of permanent *concertation* has produced so much organizational stress that one wonders why the FNSEA has not reasserted its independence more, at least during times of crisis. If its leaders wish to maintain the unity and authority of the FNSEA, why have they rejected *contestation* when it seems to have been widely supported?

One explanation is quite popular among leaders of rival unions. One MODEF leader has asserted: 'It is the result of political calculations; the reactionaries leading the FNSEA will do nothing to weaken the power of a right-wing government.' While this hypothesis is hardly plausible in its crudest form, it does seem to contain a good deal of truth. It may be,as the FNSEA elites argue, that the dependence of the 'plight of the farmers' on the *pouvoirs publics* leads the FNSEA to try 'not to oppose uselessly the political parties in power, whoever they may be.' But the FNSEA's maintenance of *concertation* during the tenure of a right-moderate governmental majority is hardly coincidental. A key FNSEA official has admitted as much with unusual candor. For one thing, 'the degree of convergence between (the Federation's) demands and the programs of the different political parties is not the same for all.' Furthermore, 'the political votes of (the Federation's) members are not sufficiently diversified for their union organization not to have a tendency to tilt toward a position which their votes direct.' According to opinion polls, he notes, 56 percent of the farmers voted for the majority in 1973 and 13 percent voted for the Reformers.[30]

The FNSEA has not admitted publicly that this membership-induced support for the present majority is compounded by an organizational factor: the FNSEA's national elite is even less politically 'diversified' than agriculture as a whole. Since the purge of Leftists in the early 1950s, control of the FNSEA has been virtually monopolized by non-Leftists. Some socialists and even a few communists have held seats on the national Administrative Council in the past two decades. However, 'no member of the National Bureau belongs to one of the parties of the Left.'

The bureau's non-Leftism has not always assured cordial relations with the political majority; conflicts among the right-moderate parties have posed some difficulty for *concertation* at times. For example, the anti-Gaullist sentiment of some ex-Vichy conservative notables contributed to the 1965 decision to oppose de Gaulle's reelection. Since 1966, however, the movement of most 'centrists' into the majority has lessened such conflict. Moreover, 'certain leaders who weakly supported the presidential regime' have been eliminated gradually from the FNSEA elite.[31]

Thus, the FNSEA has, indeed, had a political motive for maintaining intimate relations with the governments of the Fifth Republic. Nevertheless, its significance should not be exaggerated. Another—much more important—factor has motivated the FNSEA elite to refrain from disrupting its special relationship with the government.

CORPORATIST MODERNIZATION AND FNSEA HEGEMONY

The Orientation Law and the Complementary Law stipulated that the Gaullist modernization program was to be implemented with the 'collaboration of the professional agricultural organizations.' The significance of this phrase was not at all clear in the early 1960s. Today, however, it is apparent that *concertation* not only facilitated the process of agricultural modernization, but also reinforced the sectoral hegemony of the FNSEA through privileged access, devolved authority and monetary subsidies.[32]

*Privileged Access.*Even before the age of systematic *concertation*, the FNSEA was 'invited to send representatives to more than 200 communities, commissions and councils.' Since the early 1960s, however, such formal advisory bodies have increased dramatically in number and importance. At the *national level*, the FNSEA now can exert considerable influence in councils that formulate policy on such matters as state intervention into agricultural markets, development, and structural reform. Moreover, the FNSEA is also the most influential sectoral representative at the Annual Conference, a series of meetings between the leaders of the profession and the government that has symbolized *concertation* since 1971. A sure indication of the utility and prestige value of the FNSEA's exclusive⁺⁺ access to these many formal institutions is that it has been contested hotly by rival union movements, especially MODEF and the FFA.

At the *departmental level* each FNSEA enjoys exclusive access to a parallel network of councils or commissions that deal with everything from prices and tax policy to the administration of disaster relief. FDSEA leaders derive prestige and sometimes a great deal more from their seats on bodies such as the *commission des cumuls*, a commission established in 1962 to restrict the activities of so-called *cumulards*—non-agriculturalists who buy land, evict the established tenant and operate the farm with hired labor. An unfavorable judgment by such a commission can be of enormous consequence for a small farmer. The possibility of such a judgment is a powerful incentive to join or at least stay on good terms with the FDSEA.

Privileged *informal* access to the government and the administration also furnishes the FNSEA with valuable 'means to present and defend its dossiers' and increases its authority. At both the national and departmental levels, the administration is readily accessible to the FNSEA and assists it virtually every day in solving particular problems. Intermediation by FDSEA officials is almost a necessity for a small farmer who cannot understand the workings of the state machine and is hesitant to deal with its faceless and fearsome bureaucrats. In most departments, an FDSEA director can telephone the *prefecture*, speak with an official and—often immediately—resolve a farmer's problems. In contrast, the leaders of most rival unions have difficulty even obtaining a hearing from the administration. In many ways, therefore, the FNSEA's privileged access contributes to its prestigae and influence.[33]

Devolved Authority. Since the early 1960s, the FNSEA has had the means not only to *influence* policy through privileged access, but also to *implement* and even *formulate* policy at the sub-national level. Authority to administer many aspects of modernization policy has been devolved to a network of co-management (*co-gestion*) institutions directed by representatives of 'the profession' and, in most cases, dominated by the FNSEA. The most important are the SAFER, the ADASEA, the SUAD and the Chambers of Agriculture.

France has thirty-three *SAFER*, regional agencies which purchase and redistribute land, with a combined budget of roughly fifty million francs. The powers of the SAFER are exercised by administrative councils composed entirely of delegates selected by the FNSEA and other 'recognized' agricultural organizations. Though subject to the *tutelle* of the state for their most important decisions, the SAFER councils wield considerable power and provide small farmers with yet another incentive to remain on good terms with the official union.[34]

The *ADASEA (Associations Départementales pour l'Aménagement des Structures des Exploitations Agricoles)* were established in 1966 to 'furnish the cooperation of the agricultural profession in the implementation' of the various FASASA programs: the IVD, the subsidies for occupational conversion, etc. The ADASEA counselors in each department provide farmers with information on available subsidies and assist them in preparing necessary forms. Because they are hired and controlled by a council that is dominated by the FDSEA elite, however, the ADASEA personnel are often utilized for union purposes. In many departments, the ADASEA employees are virtually indistinguishable from those of the FDSEA and serve more or less as a state-financed adjunct to the staff of the official union.

Another source of very tangible benefits for the official union is the development program, administered in each department since the mid-1960s by the SUAD *(Services d'Utilité Agricole de Développement)*. The SUAD boards of directors, selected according to a formula that assures FDSEA predominance, are empowered to allocate millions of francs (roughly two million per department in 1976) to organizations which serve some sort of development function. Many organizations funded by the SUAD are more or less intimately related to the official union. While some organizations with no FNSEA connection also receive funding, few with overt ties to rival unions ever do.

The co-management institutions that make the greatest contribution to FNSEA power and influence are the *Chambers of Agriculture*. By controlling a majority of Chamber seats (through an electoral system that makes effective competition by rival unions extremely difficult) in virtually every department, the official union obtains an additional block of seats—and hence its monopoly of power—in all the advisory councils and other co-management institutions described above. Furthermore, control of the Chambers provides the FNSEA's departmental affiliates with a variety of 'disguised' subsidies from public funds. Nearly two-thirds of the FDSEA are housed in the same building as the local Chamber, and most of them employ freely the equipment and staff of the Chamber for syndical purposes. Not surprisingly, a 1971 report compiled by the *Inspection Générale des Finances* uncovered many 'abnormal' and 'contestable' aspects of this relationship. But despite protests by rival unions, the state administration did not publicize or pursue this evidence of mismanagement of public funds—evidence which could have been highly embarrassing to the 'official' representative of the sector.[34]

Monetary Subsidies. By far the least publicized benefit that the FNSEA derives from *concertation* is the receipt of financial grants from the state for a variety of organizational activities. Since the early 1960s, the FNSEA and its affiliates have received millions of francs per year through various national subsidy programs—none of which has granted even one centime to the rival, non-official unions. The two most important sources of Federation subsidies have been the development and *promotion sociale collective* programs.

155

Annual development subsidies have been granted for the past decade to the FNSEA itself, to the CNJA and to various other organizations more or less connected to the official union. In 1974, for example, the FNSEA received nearly 900,000F from ANDA (the Association Nationale pour le Développement Agricole). The CNJA, charged with implementing programs for the younger farmers, received just under 3,000,000F. In some years, state subsidies have provided fully 92 percent of the CNJA budget!

The FNSEA has also received subsidies from the *promotion sociale* program since it began, in 1959, with the goal of aiding recognized interest groups to educate activists for leadership roles and to become interlocutors of the state. The FNSEA says that the *promotion sociale* subsidies enable union leaders to become more competent not only in 'union techniques' but also in 'economic, legal, fiscal and social' matters, thus assuring that 'the union-administration dialogue can build on a base of common vocabulary.' The *promotion sociale* program has underwritten the cost of an enormous number—51,741 in 1973 alone—of FNSEA 'education and training' sessions. These sessions have served not only to educate and inform FNSEA *cadres*, but also to help the FNSEA elite maintain contact with the *base* (by subsidizing travel from Paris to the localities), to facilitate FDSEA efforts to elicit membership participation (by subsidizing travel expenses and free meals at meetings), and to assist in the *relance* efforts of weak FDSEA threatened by rival unions (by targeting funds toward departments faced with such power struggles).

The *promotion sociale* subsidies to the FNSEA and CNJA increased steadily throughout the 1960s. By 1970 each was receiving more than one million francs per year. By comparison, the 1970 operating budget of the FNSEA central office, comprised of the dues of all affiliated organizations, was slightly less than 3,000,000F. In short, these subsidies have contributed substantially to the organizational strength of the state's official interlocutor.[35]

CONCLUSION

Corporatist *concertation* may have facilitated an agricultural modernization process beneficial to the general economy, involved the profession to an unprecedented degree in determining its own socio-economic destiny, improved communication between the sector and the state and, at least in some cases, allowed for a more flexible and humane implementation of reform policy than could have been done by what many farmers perceive to be faceless and fearsome bureaucrats. Nevertheless, many characteristics of the corporatist system raise questions about its efficacy and legitimacy.

First, the corporatist system has not, in fact, involved 'the profession' in shaping its destiny. A significant percentage of farmers—those affiliated with or sympathetic to the rival unions—have been excluded systematically from such involvement. Second, the corporatist system has, thus, impaired com-

156

munication between the sector and the state in regions where opposition to the FNSEA is concentrated, and consequently had encouraged the outbreak of disruptive and sometimes violent demonstrations. With all channels of routinized access closed, FNSEA dissidents and rival union activists can express fundamental criticism of state policy only in the streets. Third, the corporatist system has virtually institutionaized the misuse of public funds and semi-public commissions, committees and agencies.

Will the corporatist system in agriculture remain intact for the immediate future? While such speculation is inevitably hazardous, efforts to change the system *from below* are unlikely to succeed. Though both 'savage liberals' and the 'victims of modernization' can be expected to keep challenging the system, their organizational efforts probably will remain inadequate in the face of the state-subsidized FNSEA machine. Changes in the corporatist system are more likely to be imposed *from above*. If the FNSEA cannot discipline its troops in another serious agricultural crisis, the state might modify the corporatist system for tactical reasons. Alternatively, a new governmental majority might change the system for political reasons. A government of the Left might inject some semblance of pluralism into the system by recognizing MODEF and other rival unions. François Mitterrand 'perhaps' favors an alteration in the structures of *concertation*.[36] But it is by no means certain that he would opt for the recognition of MODEF. For one thing, such a move would strengthen the Communist party in the countryside. Moreover, it would generate a political reaction by the FNSEA elite—and the Left might not be able to withstand such a reaction.

In short, some change in the corporatist system *may* be imposed before long. For the foreseeable future, however, the corporatist dynamic of modernization and the hegemony of the FNSEA probably will remain central features of agricultural politics in the Fifth Republic.

NOTES

†SAFER: *Sociétés d'Aménagement Foncier et d'Etablissement Rural.*
**IVD: *Indemnité Viagère de Départ.*
*The figures cited in this sentence are percentages of the farmers who responded.
**MODEF (*Mouvement de Défense des Exploitants Familiaux*) is a rival union movement organized shortly after the inception of the Fifth Republic by Leftist—primarily Communist—farmers; its appeal remains strongest in the Southern and Central regions dominated by small, Left-oriented farmers, but it has been somewhat successful recently in mobilizing farmers of the Center-Right who oppose the FNSEA reform policies. The *Comité de Guéret* is an informal organization of delegates from MODEF branches and the sometimes-dissident FDSEA in the Massif Central and the Vendée-Poitou regions.
†The *Paysans-Travailleurs* movement is composed primarily of young farmers on the extreme Left opposed to *concertation* and 'moderate' reform policies; the movement is fairly strong in Brittany but has limited importance elsewhere.

++Exclusive of other farmers' unions, though not of other professional organizations; representatives of the Chambers of Agriculture and the cooperative associations have seats along with the FNSEA and its youth branch, the CNJA.

1. This paper is derived from my Ph.D. dissertation, 'The Politics of Official Unionism in French Agriculture: A Study of the Corporatist Bases of FNSEA Hegemony' (Harvard University, Department of Government, 1978), henceforth referred to as 'Official Unionism.' The dissertation contains details on sources.

2. Michel Crozier, *La Société bloquée (Paris: Editions du Seuil, 1970), p. 136.*

3. *Crozier, p. 138.*

4. *Cited by Suzanne Berger, Peasants Against Politics* (Cambridge: Harvard University Press, 1972), p. 184.

5. Gordon Wright, *Rural Revolution in France* (Stanford: Stanford University Press, 1964), pp. 132-133; Louis Prugnaud, *Les Etapes du syndicalisme agricole en France* (Paris: Editions de l'Epi, 1963), pp. 178-181; Paul Houée, *Les Etapes du développement rural* (Paris: Les Editions Ouvrières, 1972), tome II, p. 71.

6. 'Official Unionism,' pp. 123-130.

7. Michel Debatisse, *La Revolution silencieuse* (Paris: Calmann-Levy, 1963), esp. pp. 235-242; 'Official Unionism,' pp. 130-134.

8. François-H. de Virieu, *La Fin d'une agriculture* (Paris: Calmann-Levy, 1967), pp. 200-202; Yves Tavernier, 'Le Syndicalisme paysan et la politique agricole du gouvernement,' *Revue française de science politique*, septembre 1962, esp. p. 621; Wright, pp. 162-163.

9. Tavernier, 'Le Syndicalisme,' pp. 621-622; 'Official Unionism,' pp. 136-140.

10. Wright, pp. 165-170; 'Official Unionism,' pp. 144-147.

11. Roy Pierce, *French Politics and Political Institutions* (New York: Harper and Row, 1968), p. 199; 'Official Unionism,' pp. 148-152.

12. Pierre Coulomb and Henri Nallet, 'Les Organisations agricoles à l'épreuve de l'unité,' in Yves Tavernier et al., *L'Univers politique des paysans dans la France contemporaine* (Paris: Armand Colin, 1972), pp. 399-402; 'Official Unionism,' pp. 154-157.

13. André Vial, 'Editorial,' *Paysans*, juin-juillet, 1970, pp. 7-8; Bernard Lambert, *Les Paysans dans les luttes des classes* (Paris: Editions du Seuil, 1970), p. 103.

14. See 'Official Unionism,' ch. V (a case study of Aisne).

15. *Jeunes agriculteurs*, mars 1962, p. 4.

16. *L'Information agricole* (henceforth cited as *IA*), no. 483, septembre 1977, p. II of the 'Connaissance de l'agriculture' insert.

17. *IA*, no. 483, septembre, 1977, p. IV of 'Connaissance de l'agriculture' insert.

18. Pierre Boulnois, 'Europe: Le Defi des jeunes agriculteurs,' report presented at the Journées d'études du CNJA, 3-4 juin 1975, Caen, p. 34.

19. *Le Monde*, 18-19, décembre 1977.

20. Boulnois, pp. 51, 55; *IA*, no. 492, juin 1978, p. 7.

21. 'Official Unionism,' pp. 166-168; a lengthy justification of the *concertation* strategy can be found in the report delivered by M. P. Cormorèche at the 1972 FNSEA Congress.

22. See the Cormorèche report as well as *30 ans de combat syndical* (a supplement to *IA*, mars 1976), esp. p. 30.

23. 'Official Unionism,' pp. 170-171.

24. Yves Tavernier, *Sociologie politique du monde rural et politique agricole* (Paris: Fondation Nationale des Sciences Politiques, 1973), fascicule III, pp 322-323, 358.

25. See the report delivered by dissident Antoine Richard to the 1970 CNJA Congress, 'Pour un syndicalisme de travailleurs.'

26. This account is primarily based on Yves Tavernier's 'Le Syndicalisme paysan et la cinquième republique: 1962-1965,' *Revue française de science politique*, octobre 1966, pp. 878-909; 'Official Unionism,' pp. 173-176.

27. Coulomb and Nallet, p. 402; *Le Monde*, 3-4 octobre 1967.

28. 'Official Unionism,' pp. 178-184.

29. 'Official Unionism,' pp. 184-189.

30. 'Official Unionism,' pp. 189-191; Françoise Clerc, 'Le Syndicalisme agricole: de l'unité agricole à l'unité syndicale,' *IA*, no 443, janvier 1974.

31. 'Official Unionism,' pp. 192-193; Tavernier, *Sociologie politique*, pp. 291, 295 and 407. As the final draft of this paper was being completed, Michel Debatisse announced that he was resigning as FNSEA president to become a candidate for the European parliament on the UDF (Giscardist) list—see *Le Point*, 16 avril 1979.

32. For a more extensive discussion of the corporatist bases of FNSEA hegemony, see John T.S. Keeler, 'Corporatism and Official Union Hegemony: The Case of French Agricultural Syndicalism,' in Suzanne Berger, ed., *Organized Interest in Western Europe* (New York: Cambridge University Press, 1980).

33. 'Official Unionism,' pp. 217-224; Prugnaud, pp. 219-238; Tavernier, *Sociologie politique*, pp. 216, 281.

34. 'Official Unionism,' pp. 224-247.

35. 'Official Unionism,' pp. 248-254.

36. See *IA*, juillet-août 1974, p. 17.

Lame Ducks and National Champions: Industrial Policy In The Fifth Republic

Suzanne Berger

Two centuries after the bourgeois revolution, has France at last accepted economic liberalism and the market?[1] Do the Barre government's professions of faith in the virtues of economic liberalism and the 1978 renunciation of price controls mark the beginning of a new relationship between state and economy in France? Have the French finally been shocked out of statism by the example of liberal West Germany's recovery from energy crisis and recession?

The history of the industrial policies of the Fifth Republic suggests that economic liberalism is not new in France. Rather, liberal and statist doctrines and practices have co-existed from the beginning of de Gaulle's Republic. The basic premise of French statism is that the state represents the collective interest of the nation against and above particular interests and, therefore, that the nation's economic objectives and the choice of the policies to realize them ought to be defined by the country's political representatives and not simply allowed to emerge from the actions and decisions of individual economic actors. As General de Gaulle expressed it in his last writings:

> While the country works, it is my task to give a national ambition to the mass of activities. It is my task to demand that the common interest rise above the routines and claims of particular social categories and to show that the object of our striving for prosperity is not so much to make life easier for certain Frenchmen but, rather, to build the security, the power, and the grandeur of France.[2]

Liberal economic doctrines, as expounded in France, start from the notion that it is fundamentally undesirable to have the state make economic choices that could be made by individual entrepreneurs. The American liberal view of why the state should play a very limited economic role—that the public interest is the sum of individual interests; that individuals know these interests better than the state; and that the common good is thus promoted by leaving in-

160

dividuals free to pursue their goals—is rarely advanced in France. Rather, French liberals remain silent on how the collective good is determined or even accept the notion that the state defines it. But they diverge from the statists in insisting that government is fundamentally incompetent to determine the choices individual firms ought to make in order to contribute to the common good. In the liberal vision this incompetence is both technical and political: technical, because bureaucrats lack the detailed knowledge of particular situations that is necessary for optimal economic decisions; political, because bureaucrats, having no direct stake in the enterprise, are basically irresponsible in the choices they make for any particular firm and hence likely to make bad decisions.

However incompatible in theory liberalism may be with statism, the ambiguous character of French liberalism and its instrumentalism allowed it to find practical expression even in the high moments of Fifth Republic *dirigisme*. Thus, during the early sixties, General de Gaulle considered making the Plan obligatory and not simply indicative, and in the same period launched the liberal Armand-Rueff Committee on the inquiry that led to proposals for a major liberalization of the economy.[3]

What is new since about 1974, then, is not the emergence of liberalism alongside *dirigisme*, nor even the growing scope of liberalism, a phenomenon which dates at least to the mid-sixties and to France's entry into the Common Market. Rather, the change is a reversal between those economic objectives which the government seeks to achieve through intervention and those which the government believes can be brought about best by allowing individual entrepreneurs the freedom to take their cues from market forces. To put it simply, in the past government intervention was directed primarily to the realization of the positive objectives of economic policy—higher growth, the creation of national champions, the development of industries based on advanced technologies, and so forth. The negative objectives of government policy were, on the other hand, left to the market. Shrinking the agricultural population, reducing the share of small commerce in distribution networks, eliminating inefficient industries—these were to be achieved by market pressures. When the state intervened to cushion the impact of the market on declining sectors it did so in the first fifteen years of the Fifth Republic on grounds that were explicitly social and political. In the first decade, these rescue interventions were relatively rare: in agriculture, commerce, and business, this is the period in which legislation sought to encourage the modern and larger firms and to strip away the protective cover under which inefficient producers had found shelter. After 1968, these interventions became more frequent and more significant economically, particularly with the *loi Royer* and a return to a more traditional agricultural policy; but they were still a minor part of the government's economic program.

161

Since 1974, the principal targets of government economic interventions have been industries that the government's own policies identify as *canards boiteux*, lame ducks that are candidates for demise, while government intervenes less and less often to bring about economic outcomes it deems desirable and leaves to the market those industries which the new industrial policy defines as the hope of the future. While the state nationalizes steel to save it from bankruptcy, bails out the largest textile manufacturer, and salvages hundreds of tottering small- and medium-sized enterprises, its role in the construction of a new economic structure has been defined in progressively narrower and less activist terms. Asked how the state intended to encourage the *redéploiement* and *restructuration* that Giscard has defined as the principal objective of French economic policy in the seventies, the *Commissaire au Plan* explained that it was up to individual industrialists: 'Redéploiez-vous!'[4]

Statism and liberalism, then, continue to coexist, but now state action mainly supports activities which by any reading of the government's policy statements are a drag on the economy whilee the market is supposed to stimulate and reward the creation of new economic activities to make France competitive in world markets, create jobs at home, and bring growth without excessive inflation. How this reversal in economic policy came about is the question this essay explores, by considering the progressive disillusionment with the results of state interventions, the growth of new political pressures to protect declining sectors, and the response to the economic crisis of the mid-seventies. What the political and economic consequences of this reversal are likely to be is the question the essay begs, for the policy changes that were the outcome of the transformations traced here have only begun to alter old relationships between state and industry.

CREEPING LIBERALISM?

Economic policy in the first decade of the Fifth Republic deployed state interventions less and less frequently to bring about the broad changes in economic infrastructure and basic industries that had been the principal objectives of the first three Plans; it focused increasingly on a limited number of *grands projets.* In terms of government commitment or the expenditure of new public resources, these projects constitute the principal Gaullist innovation in economic policy. But the decisions to intervene with vast sums to build the Concorde and Airbus, to develop a French technology for producing nuclear energy, or to maintain an independent French computer capability (*Plan Calcul*) were motivated only in minor part by concern over the economic consequences of allowing the most advanced technologies to be developed outside France. In large measure, the state's commitment to these projects was justified by strategic military or national prestige considerations.

State intervention to promote industrial concentration—the second of the new directions of industrial policy in the sixties—did, however, reflect primarily an economic analysis. The diagnosis of the weaknesses of French industry as it moved into the European Common Market identified two problems: one, in the incomplete character of French industrialization and the other, in the structures and behavior of French firms.[5] The most general argument focused on the resistance in French society and culture to acceptance of the values and structures of industrialism. The anti-industrialism of the culture, the lack of entrepreneurial drive for profit and expansion, and the unwillingness to accept risk and competition were blamed for the failure of French businesses to seize the opportunities for capturing foreign markets (or even, recapturing the domestic market). On this level, the government could do little beyond exhortation.

Economic policy was, rather, inspired by the second part of the argument, which identified specific obstacles to competition in the structures of French industry. Here the analysis focused on rates of investment lower than those in other advanced industrial economies and, above all, on the inadequate dimensions of French firms. As expressed in Lionel Stoléru's *L'Impératif industriel* (1969),[6] the case for promoting mergers in order to create a number of giant French firms—national champions—that could compete in world markets on a footing of equality with American multinationals rests on a double claim: that only the largest firms could develop and exploit the new technologies and that in critical sectors of the economy, the optimal firm size for efficiency, profitability, and competitiveness was much larger than that of the major French firms in those sectors.

The themes of this analysis were announced in the Vth and VIth Plans and in legislative projects of the late sixties and early seventies. A number of measures aimed at increasing the rate of investment, liberalizing and expanding the banking system (1966), directing state funds to research and development in the private sector, and providing tax incentives for investment.[7] In the same period, the fiscal regime was modified to reduce taxes on industrial mergers. In fact, the number of mergers increased substantially in the mid- to late-sixties and the magnitudes involved in these operations, which in most cases merged medium-large to large firms, went up even faster: in each of the years 1966–1969, the value of the merger operations was double or more the sum of the values in the entire period 1950–1960.[8] The rate of investment increased from 22 percent to 28 percent over the first decade of the Fifth Republic.

It is impossible to determine the part played in these transformations by the new industrial policy orientations of the state, the changes in the rules of banking and fiscal systems, or specific investment incentives. One study concluded that tax advantages mattered less than the state's general orientation toward larger firms in influencing industrialists' decisions on mergers.[9] But the persuasive powers of the state may have had little scope except in those firms (the computer industry, for example) where massive state aid was needed to keep companies afloat or in those heavily dependent on government contracts. These cases were the minority.[10] In the others, the state probably had rather little influence on merger decisions. For example, in the Saint-Gobain-Pont à Mousson merger, according to one of its top managers, the state offered no particular encouragement, indeed played no role at all.[11] After the deal was concluded, the presidents of the new company paid a courtesy call on Pompidou to inform him. This manager concluded: 'Industrial policy exists only at the level of speeches; in reality, there is none. The government lacks leverage.' While changes in the fiscal system undoubtedly contributed to increasing the rate of investment, still, firm decisions basically reflected new market opportunities, as economist Alain Cotta argues: 'Private companies were bound to rush into all the new points opened to their market by the pursuit and acceleration of growth. How could they have failed to go along with an *impératif industriel* that guaranteed them a more intense development than they could have dreamed?'[12]

It is debatable whether the state's industrial policies had much impact in bringing about a transformation of firm behavior other than that which would have occurred anyway, because of the stimulation provided by larger markets and the accumulated advantages of past growth and because of the wide circulation and general acceptance in the mid-sixties of certain ideas about the relationship of firm size to profits. Similarly, unambiguous conclusions about the effectiveness of *dirigisme* in implementing the general will, as expressed at least in the Plan, are difficult to draw from the actual allocations of state funds. If one compares the priorities set in the Vth and VIth Plans with the actual expenditures, the disparities are striking. For example, in the VIth Plan, the mechanical, chemical, food processing industries and the complex of information-electronics-telecommunications industries were designated as priorities. But when the taxes these industries paid are subtracted from the sums the state transferred to them the net transfers are negative.[13] In the same period, the steel industry and the shipbuilding and armaments industries—neither of which were Plan priorities—received positive transfers of 3 billion francs out of a total of 42 billions transferred by state to industry. The transfers to the public sector enterprises in transportation and energy—also non-priority items in the Plan were even more important.[14]

The real issue raised by this consideration of the effectiveness of state intervention in the Fifth Republic is whether they reflect a decline in statism. Can the liberalism of the mid-seventies be traced to a withering away of the state in the economy during the first decade of the Fifth Republic? The rhetoric of economic policy at the end of the sixties—despite its growing concern with the competitiveness and profitability of French firms in an open economy—hardly makes a case for economic liberalism. Stoleru, for example, concludes his sector-by-sector analysis of the state's economic interventions with the observation that nonintervention has no meaning in an economy when governmental action in any domain has a myriad of influences on industry. Rather, nonintervention means leaving industry subject to *ad hoc* and uncoordinated decisions. For this reason, 'the sectors in the greatest difficulty are often those where the deliberate intervention of the state had been delayed the most.'[15] 'The daily decisions of public authorities end up affecting one or another industrial sector in a manner which is the more harmful for its involuntary or blind character... Rather than a false liberalism which is translated into the confusion of *ad hoc*, contradictory measures it would be better for the State to analyze sectoral problems and clearly define a strategy to facilitate the search for competitiveness.'[16] Even Pompidou, who argued that in normal times, the state should 'reduce its role to a minimum, which is already considerable... and refrain from interfering for the sake of interfering' defined this minimum very broadly.[17] The arguments for the new industrialization policies of the late sixties and early seventies, though they stress profits and competition in ways that de Gaulle did not, still do not call for any reduction in the state's role in the economy.

Evidence for creeping liberalism can be found, not in the rhetoric but in the institutional development and practice of the Fifth Republic after the midsixties. This is the period of the progressive weakening of the *Commissariat du Plan* and the recuperation by the Ministry of Finance of virtual sovereignty over economic decision-making. The Ministry of Finance, relying almost exclusively on price control and fiscal policy as instruments of its economic policy, in fact had less and less leverage on the economy. As Cotta has argued, 'The more French growth proceded, the less sensitive public intervention was to it. In this sense, the economy became more 'liberal' than it had ever been before.'[18] Also, the magnitude of state intervention shrank in this period. From 1959 to 1969, the public sector's share in national production decreased.[19] Direct support of private industry by the state stagnated. Loans granted by the *Fonds de Développement Economique et Social* (FDES) fell from 2.3 billion in 1962 to 1.6 billion in 1972.[20]

The weakening leverage of the state on industry—this liberalism in effect when not yet in intent—had its origins, then, quite early in the Fifth Republic and preceded any significant change of the policymakers' views on the proper role of the state in the economy. To bring about that change in views now expressed in the 'neo-liberal' doctrines of Barre and Giscard, three other changes intervened: disillusionment with the *grands projets*; increasing political pressure to protect declining industries; and economic crisis.

ASSESSING THE RESULTS OF STATE INTERVENTION

The growing skepticism about the use of state power to accomplish economic projects that private firms would not undertake on their own initiative and with their own resources was fed not so much by failure to achieve the original purposes as by the high costs and low rewards of success. This was the case, not only with projects conceived to demonstrate technological prowess and to enhance French prestige and influence abroad, like the Concorde, whose costs escalated far beyond original estimates. It was true as well for projects which had had more specifically economic objectives: interventions to restructure certain industrial sectors and to promote 'national champions.' The failure of the state's sectoral interventions was demonstrated nowhere more clearly than in the case of steel. In this dispersed and uncompetitive industry, the state had contracted with the industrialists (the *Plan professionnel* of 1966) to lend large sums for investment on condition that a major restructuring and concentration take place. The five largest firms merged into two groups; the number of firms and plants was reduced somewhat; existing installations were modernized substantially and a new steel complex at Fos was constructed; and production and productivity increased. J.E.S. Hayward was able to conclude in 1973: 'The success of the 1966 agreement in achieving its objectives demonstrated how the French government, thanks to generous financial aid, was able to secure the concentration and modernization of the industry without public ownership because it was assisted by a powerful trade association.'[21]

But only five years later, the indebtedness of French steel was so great that it threatened to sink the industry.[22] Production had been falling since 1974, contrary to the VIIth Plan's forecasts. Productivity remained significantly lower than in any of France's main competitors.[23] To rescue the industry from collapse, the government decided to transform part of its debt into shares to be held by the state and the banks, thus effectively nationalizing the industry; to declare a moratorium on the short and medium term bank loans to the industry; and to have the Trésor assume the financial obligations contracted to the public by the Groupement de l'industrie sidérurgique.[24] At the same time, massive lay-offs in the steel industry were pronounced the indispensable condition of restoring its competitiveness. More than twenty thousand jobs were to be eliminated over two years.

Whose fault was it? In response to criticism of the management of the industry and to the government's pointed announcement that the top managers in the industry would be changed, the steel *patronat* pointed out that the state had collaborated in or instigated directly, every important decision in the sector.[25] The state had actively encouraged the industry to make massive investments. At the same time, the government had controlled steel prices at a low level, thus preventing the industry from financing its own expansion. Ac-

166

cording to the *patronat*, the government bore major responsibility for low productivity also, because for political reasons, it refused to allow the industry to lay off workers at the same rate as steel plants in other countries. The industrialists cited a study purporting to show that state aid to the steel industry (via lower interest rates) amounted to only one-third of the cost of state control in price constraints and restrictions on firing.[26] One observer noted in *Le Monde* that steel represents 'the failure of a twenty-year old *dirigiste* policy that seeks to preserve capitalism while tying its hands.'[27]

The lesson many drew from steel and, earlier, from the state's other sectoral projects was that state intervention not only was unable to remedy the weaknesses of private initiative, but generated its own irrationalities systematically. While the market punishes the failures of private enterprise, the political mechanisms which ought to work to hold officials accountable for the mistakes of *dirigisme* are, in fact, inoperative in the absence of an opposition that represents a plausible alternative government. Thus, the disappointment with the results of state sectoral interventions was translated not into an argument for new economic instruments and policies but into a case that the government was fundamentally incompetent to reorganize industrial sectors, that is, into a liberal assault on *dirigisme*.

Along with the projects undertaken for international prestige and the sectoral policies, the programs to develop national champions were a third source of disillusionment. By 1975–76, it was already becoming clear to the policymakers that the mergers and concentrations that they had encouraged with their energies and the state's resources were a mixed blessing. First, economic advantages in increased productivity and competitiveness were rarely attained in large measure because the mergers did not rationalize the structures of the enterprises they joined, but simply 'confederated' firms in such a way as to maintain intact the authority prerogatives and hierarchies of the old enterprises.

The second disappointed hope was that of creating champions large enough to compete as equals with American multinationals. In fact, the champions that took the field were too small to be global contenders. They were too little for international competition, but in many ways too big for France. They were too large to be run efficiently with the largely unreformed techniques of management they employed. Wages in the merged firms climbed to the levels of those parts of the enterprise where unions were strongest. Most important, the new firms were so big that they immediately became the targets of the Left's proposals to transform the economy by nationalizations. A top manager of one firm that had grown through mergers in the sixties and now figures on the *Programme Commun* list of industries to be nationalized argued that if the firm had the merger to do over again, it likely would not repeat it.[28] Because of its size, even small decisions by the firm now have widespread political repercussions, and these are eroding the firm's freedom of action. By the seventies, policymakers were announcing that the concentration policy was over—alternatively because it had achieved its objectives, or, as officials explained privately, because its results were politically and socially destabilizing and economically too far short of the optimistic predictions of the sixties.[29]

Nothing underscores more the discredit into which the national champions policy has now fallen than the rediscovery of the importance of small and medium firms.[30] François de Combret in a presentation of the government's new industrial policy ranked support for small and medium firms as one of the three principles of the new focus, which 'no longer takes large size as an absolute strategic objective.'[31] The advantages of smaller and medium-sized enterprises are, according to de Combret, that they are easier to manage, more responsive to the market, have lower overhead, and create more jobs because they are less capital-intensive and grow faster. Moreover, work in these firms is less alienating. This description of small and medium firms hardly matches the economic reality of this sector in France, as an official in the Ministry of Industry confessed: 'If we had to rely on technical arguments, we'd never have a *pmi* (*petites et moyennes industries*: small and medium industries) policy. The real reasons are political.'[32] To the extent that the new enthusiasm for the *pmi* has an economic content, it is disillusionment over the offspring of the policies of the sixties, the national champions, and not the discovery of a universe of well-managed, competitive, fast-growing small and medium firms, with satisfied and expanding labor forces.

POLITICS OF DECLINING SECTORS

The second major push toward a reversal in the objectives of the liberal and *dirigiste* strategies of industrial policy came from mounting demands for state intervention to protect declining classes and industries. These pressures became very strong at the end of the sixties; that is, they antedated the economic crisis and were not its consequence. There were two principal sources: the growing unrest and mobilization of the traditional middle classes and the political parties.[33]

The first major resistance of declining economic groups to the modernization and liberalization of the economy in the Fifth Republic was the shopkeepers' movement organized by Gérard Nicoud at the end of the sixties. The CID-UNATI attacked tax offices, kidnapped tax collectors, and staged mass demonstrations. By the early seventies, its lists controlled the *chambres de métiers* and the *chambres de commerce* in much of France. As the shopkeepers' movement, mollified by the passage of legislation that restricted supermarket expansion, subsided as a threat to political stability, new groups relayed them. In the fall of 1974, the Confédération générale des petites et moyennes entreprises (C.G.P.M.E.) organized a rally of four thousand businessmen in Paris to protest government credit and tax policies. In its wake, Léon Gingembre, president of the C.G.P.M.E., founded a new organization, Union des chefs et responsables d'enterprise (U.N.I.C.E.R.) as a political movement to express the demands of small businesses. The organization quickly enrolled twenty-five thousand members and five times as many approving letters poured in. In March 1977, the presidents of the peak organizations of the farmers, artisans, *cadres*, doctors, and the C.G.P.M.E. announced a new movement, Groupes Initiative et Responsabilité, to defend the common interests of the middle classes. These new organizations reflected a rising tide of anger into which two streams fed: the protest of groups whose fortunes were declining because of modernization of the economy; and protest from modern sectors of the economy that were hurt badly in the recession and saw government policies as increasingly hostile to their interests. The proposed profits tax, the plan for workers' participation in the enterprise, the more frequent legal prosecution of industrialists for accidents in their plants, the obstacles raised by the *inspecteurs du travail* to firing workers were cited as examples of Giscard's betrayal of his electorate. An official of the Chambre de Commerce et de l'Industrie reported in 1976 that he had never seen businessmen so angry at government: 'It's a political regression to 1936!'[34]

In the wake of the events of May-June 1968, this kind of protest was bound to preoccupy the government. Its importance was greatly magnified by its convergence with major political shifts in the regime, as the Left gained strength and competition intensified within the Center-Right majority. Both factors contributed to the growing weight of the independent middle classes within the majority. Not fear of losing these voters to the Left, but increased dependence on their votes and on their extra-electoral opposition to the Left led the Center-Right to respond to the Left's inroads on working class and white collar constituencies with an increased solicitude for the traditional electorate. At the same time, the struggle between the Republicans and the U.D.R. (later, the U.D.F. and the R.P.R.) set up a competitive bidding for the votes of small independent property. Thus even the most ardent proponents of the new economic liberalism would trim their sails when the question came up of protective legislation that sheltered small commerce, agriculture, and business from the winds of free competition.[35]

The response to the mobilization of the business sector and to the Center-Right's growing dependence on its electorate in the declining sectors was a flood of rhetoric about small and medium enterprises, 'the basic cells in the social and economic fabric' of the country, and a series of governmental measures that extended preferential treatment to these firms. The most important measures were the 'Royer law' on commercial development (*loi d'orientation pour le commerce et l'artisanat*) and the new professional tax. The Royer law (1973) requires approvals for new supermarket constructions by a departmental commission in which representatives of shopkeepers and artisans sit together with elected officials. The number of new supermarket openings dropped precipitously.[36] The professional tax that replaced the *patente* in 1975 favored small business. The result was that small firms paid, on the average, two-thirds less with the new tax than they had with the old.[37] Larger firms and stores, which had paid 80 percent of the *patente*, paid 93 percent of the professional tax.

The other consequence was to involve government more and more deeply in the tutelage of the interests of these segments of the business and commercial world. In 1969 a state secretary for medium-sized and small industry (*secrétaire d'état à la moyenne et petite industrie et à l'artisanat*) was named and a set of programs established that involved regular meetings between bureaucrats and groups of industrialists organized by region, *Groupe d'échange et de coordination*.[38] By designating the ministry as one for medium-sized and small industry—as opposed to small- and medium-sized enterprises, which would have corresponded to the mix of commercial and business categories represented by the C.G.P.M.E., by fostering the discussions and 'experiments' of the G.E.C., the government announced its intention of working with modern, innovative small- and medium-sized firms and not simply tending old political clienteles. This focus had very limited appeal. By 1976, the government came up with a new bureaucracy (*un délégué à la petite et moyenne industrie*) and a new program to facilitate the creation of firms, help existing ones to expand, and provide management consulting.[39] But despite the emphasis in these policies and in government declarations on the dynamic modern small- and medium-sized firms, the candidates for these programs were predictably few. The real demand was for the other kinds of assistance the state was providing to industry, namely rescue from bankruptcy.

DIRIGISME IN THE SEVENTIES

The government's commitment to interventions to salvage enterprises in economic difficulties was shaped in 1968 in the policies for declining sectors; it emerged full-blown in the response to the economic crisis of the mid-seventies. The *dirigisme* of the seventies would commit the state far more extensively than ever before in the Fifth Republic to the survival of particular enterprises and of particular jobs.[40]

In the wake of the 1973 hike in oil prices, rising rates of inflation and unemployment, and a recession, the depth of which became clear only after the abortive recovery of fall 1975–fall 1976, the government with many hesitations and detours finally fixed upon a strategy for dealing with France's new economic troubles.[41] Its primary objective was to restore a favorable balance of payments by improving the competitiveness of French industry, thereby increasing exports.[42] Once this goal was attained, it was argued, the resulting economic growth would create new jobs and resolve the second major economic problem of the seventies, unemployment.

Aside from the various difficulties this approach raised and left unresolved about how French industry might be restructured for exports and growth, the more pressing problem was that losses of jobs were immediate, whereas the effects of increased competitiveness, exports, and growth on the creation of new employment would be only long-term and indirect, at best. Even though the French had proved to have a higher tolerance for unemployment than anyone had predicted before the crisis, that is, even though the destabilizing effects of the reactions to unemployment by the Left, the unions, and the unemployed themselves had not posed serious problems for the government, still, politically it remained unacceptable to allow as much unemployment as would ensue if entrepreneurs were free to lay off workers at will. The dilemma lay in the fact that though, politically, the government needed to maintain unemployment rates below a certain level, to realize its economic program it needed to reintroduce more flexibility in the use of labor so that industrialists could use layoffs to keep prices competitive and make profits. Indeed, by the mid-seventies, it had become clear that unless industrialists were freer to fire, the chances of substantial new hiring in times of expansion were slim.

Two principal concerns militated for an active state role in restraining industrialists from laying off workers. First, reasons of political conjuncture led the government to apply as much pressure as it could to avoid increases in the unemployment rate in pre-electoral periods. The period 1974–1978 was one long electoral campaign, marked by various polls in which the sides measured their forces. Only after March 1978 did the government feel safe enough to allow industrialists more leeway in the labor market. The second major consideration was regional. In those regions where the firm on the verge of collapse was the sole employer of any importance or where industrialization was recent and frail, the government deployed its maximum effort to avoid lay-offs, because workers could not find other jobs. The textile, shoe, and steel industries were examples of the first, since they were located in zones with few other sources of employment. The areas of recent industrialization were an even more serious problem, for they were harder hit by the recession than the rest of the country: the unemployment rate in March 1978 in the West and the South was 9.5 percent, as contrasted with 5.1 percent in the rest of France.[43]

The concern over maintaining employment in peripheral regions was hardly new. By wielding the carrot of subsidies and loans and the stick of refusals of new construction permits in the Paris region the *Délégation à l'aménagement du territoire* had some success in getting firms to locate new plants outside the already industrialized zones of the country.[44] Other state agencies also enforced regional priorities in dispensing support to industry: in the massive state loan to industry after the May-June 1968 events, for example, the regional location of a firm counted more than other factors in whether it received a loan.[45] But by the mid-seventies, the government's most effective regional policy was to save jobs in regions where those laid off would not be able to find other work.

The many instruments of this policy were wielded, first, to put pressure on industrialists to keep workers or to find them other jobs; secondly, to use state resources to rescue enterprises that would go out of business otherwise. On the first front, after 1974 the jaw-boning sort of pressures were backed up by the power to refuse lay-offs. The 1975 law on collective lay-offs (that restated the terms of a 1974 agreement between the *patronat* and the unions) requires employers to obtain permission from the *inspection du travail* to fire workers and to justify this request by providing information on the financial state of the firm. Though accounts vary on how important the refusals by the *inspecteurs du travail* have been in forcing industrialists to keep workers, at the very least the delays in obtaining authorizations and the uncertainties about the outcomes get many industrialists to agree to solutions short of all-out unemployment. They reduce overtime and, even more important, put workers on a part-time status (*chomage partiel*) that is jointly financed by the firm and the state. In other cases, firms negotiate lay-offs by finding other jobs for their workers, sometimes even financing the establishment of new companies in the region.[46]

The unions may well be as important as the bureaucracy in influencing the entrepreneur's calculations about the cost of lay-offs.[47] For example, an industrialist with one plant in a communist-run suburb of Paris and another in Normandy who wished to close the former and concentrate operations in the latter expected to receive authorization to do so, since the town was lost to the majority in any event. But he realized that the unions would occupy the plant he shut, and the troubles might well spread to the plant in Normandy. So, despite the financial precariousness of his firm he kept both plants open.[48] An official of one of France's largest companies argued that the basic constraint on their personnel reductions was not the state but the C.G.T., with whom management has a complex, unwritten set of understandings: 'We only do what the unions, at the limit, will accept.'[49]

To save jobs, the state had to save enterprises with increasing frequency. The interventions to salvage the lame ducks of industry multiplied after 1974, when two new institutions were established to examine the dossiers of firms in economic difficulties. On the departmental level were established the so-called *Comités Fourcade* or *infirmeries de campagne*, made up of the *trésorier-payeur général*, the head of the Banque de France, the departmental tax director, and the head of the departmental price office. These departmental committees considered ways to aid 'dynamic firms' that were in 'temporary' trouble because of credit restrictions. The committees could grant delays in tax and social security payments, accelerate compensation for work performed on government contracts, and exert substantial pressure on local bankers to extend loans. Five months after its June 1974 creation, the *infirmeries de campagne* already had treated over three thousand cases, helping 80 percent of them.[50]

Cases involving larger firms and larger sums were referred to the second new institution, the *Comité interministériel pour l'aménagement des structures industrielles* (CIASI), set up in November 1974, and composed of Jérôme Monod, the head of DATAR, as chairman; the *commissaire au Plan*; the director of the Trésor; the director of construction and public works; the director-general of the Ministry of Labor; the director-general of credit of the Banque de France; and a representative of the Prime Minister.[51] These officials sat personally for the committee's deliberations.

The first operating principle of the CIASI has been to act only in those cases in which a solution can be found which leaves the firm in private ownership and management. These solutions are usually worked out through negotiations by the Ministry of Industry or the DATAR with bankers, the current owners, the unions, the *syndic* and the *tribunal de commerce*, and potential new shareholders or managers. Unlike the Italian government agency, *Gestione Partecipazioni Industriali* (GEPI), which takes over collapsing firms, runs them with managers it selects, uses its own funds to pay off creditors and to relaunch operations, and has found new owners for only some of its lame ducks, the CIASI will not intervene until bankers and industrialists propose reorganization that leaves the firm in the private sector. The CIASI, then, neither owns, manages, nor exercises any control over the firms it treats. Moreover, the resources the CIASI levers are largely private funds. The CIASI puts pressure on banks to make loans to the firms they indicate and, on the average, only 15 to 20 percent of the funds utilized are from the public treasury (via the F.D.E.S.). Even after the CIASI has decided on a package of assistance to a firm, the banks (often the Crédit National or the Crédit Hôtelier) still use their own loan procedures.

By Fall 1978, the CIASI had handled some six hundred cases, granted one billion francs in F.D.E.S. loans, and mobilized eight billion francs in private funds.[52] In disproportionate numbers, the firms helped have been located in peripheral regions with few possibilities of alternative employment. Many of the firms the CIASI has assisted are medium-sized enterprises, with fewer than 200 workers. In a few cases, the CIASI has attempted to deal with whole sectors—printing, shoes, mechanical industries—but its usual procedure remains a case-by-case examination of individual enterprises. In Fall 1978, with unemployment rising, the government proposed to increase the powers and scope of the CIASI.[53]

At the same time that the government was saving employment by rescuing firms, it was searching for ways to increase mobility in the labor market, that is, to reduce the legal and political constraints on lay-offs which by the seventies had led workers in large firms to expect lifetime security in the same job. 'We're caught in a system of terrible rigidity,' said Jose Bidegain, one of the C.N.P.F. leaders most open to cooperation with the unions.[54] Unable to fire workers in the recession, employers tried at all costs to avoid new hiring when demand picked up. They made more and more use of temporary employment agencies; they tried to subcontract out work; and they pushed up overtime. When industrial production rose 3 percent in the last trimester of 1975, employment fell by 1 percent.[55]

Lacking leverage on the other factors that were contributing to the steady rise in unemployment—the arrival on the labor market of the larger postwar generations and of more women and the job-economizing consequences of technological innovation—the government tried to deal with the businessmen's reluctance to hire. The government launched major campaigns to encourage the hiring of young workers looking for first jobs, paid part of their salaries, and allowed the firms that hired them a 'trial period'longer than the legal minimum to decide whether to offer a regular job. By late 1978, the government was proposing a new system of work contracts with limited terms and a reform of the legislation regulating temporary work agencies. Perhaps most important, Barre announced that 'more flexibility' had to be introduced into the social security system, so that firms of different sizes would not be subject to the same constraints and costs.[56] Gradually the government edged toward an 'Italian solution' to the crisis: allowing, even facilitating the development of small- and medium-sized firms which would adopt more labor-intensive technologies since their labor costs would be lower than in larger firms making the same products and since they would have more freedom to hire and fire than the highly politicized and unionized large companies.[57]

REDEPLOIEMENT FOR WHAT?

Neither economic liberalism nor the new industrial policy of redéploiement which Giscard d'Estaing announced at the end of 1973 provide any defense of the measures to save jobs and enterprises which the government adopted in the seventies. As Christian Stoffaes argues in La Grande menace industrielle, the book which, like Stoléru's L'Impératif industriel a decade earlier, sets out quasi-officially the new economic orthodoxy, such rescue operations fail to promote a specialization in product lines where the French have a comparative advantage that could allow them to capture créneaux in world markets.[58] Stoffaes declares: 'Making full employment at a national and regional level the priority in industrial policy is the best way to lead industry down the road to underdevelopment.'[59] As for the interventions to maintain critical industries in

France, 'One must accept the ultimate consequences of the international division of labor, that is, a certain degree of industrial specialization in some branches and, in exchange, the abandonment of other branches. . .[A] country that
does not know how to give up wanting to produce everything condemns itself
to never becoming competitive on the world market.'[60]

Politicians not only recoiled from implementing these doctrines; they bent
ideas to fit their practices. Giscard d'Estaing denied that competition from
developing countries would put one-third of French industry 'up for auction'
(as Stoffaes had charged in his book).[61] The Minister of Industry, André
Giraud, specified that in the struggle to become competitive 'there are no condemned sectors.'[62] And Stoffaes himself concluded that while liberalism and
aggressive *redéploiement* seem to require no more of the state than 'to open
the frontiers, give the laws of the market free rein, and let the best man win,' in
France the 'pragmatic realities' require that the state continue to play an active
role in the economy.[63]

But what the state should do to bring about changes in the economy and in
firms beyond those that would be achieved by a simple laissez-faire laisser-
passer policy remains unclear. In part, the ambiguities lie in the new doctrines,
which provide few guidelines for discovering which firms and sectors ought to
be encouraged. That the fate of enterprises depends on their capacity to export;
that to export they must be competitive; that they can be competitive only if
they find a segment of the market in which neither Third World countries nor
the more advanced capitalist economies have a comparative advantage—these
dicta when applied to French industries suggest rather few promising candidates for government support. *La France n'a pas l'industrie de sa politique.*
Or, rather, the vagueness of the propositions for a new industrial policy and the
scant traces of state activism in the spheres in which new activities are to be promoted and firms with potential encouraged suggests that France lacks a strategy
for moving from the firms it does have toward the more competitive economy it
seeks.[64]

This is hardly surprising. How, indeed, could the state identify individual
enterprises? Even if it were to do so, how could it weather the political storm
that would be stirred up by discrimination in favor of some firms and, inevitably, against others? In fact, none of the countries that France seeks to
emulate—West Germany, Japan, the United States—produce the results that
French policymakers envy through the kinds of policies the French advocate.

In coming decades, governments everywhere may find it difficult to win
much political capital in the economy. Increasingly they are likely to try to
disavow political responsibility for economic outcomes. Various forms of
'neo-liberalism' may well serve this end. But what is striking in the French case
is that government is retreating from the sectors and activities that are likely to

grow, while increasing its involvement in declining sectors. That it calls the former economic liberalism and the latter social intervention may matter little for the political result. What kinds of successes can the government hope for with no more direct strategy for defending employment than industrial rescue operations and with little visible commitment to new industrial development? What kind of successes can government survive, when it engages its resources and prestige to prop up industries whose preservation may be as problematic as their demise?

NOTES

1. I am grateful to Henri Aujac and Peter Gourevitch for detailed comments on a draft of this essay.
2. Charles de Gaulle, *Mémoires d'espoir* (Paris: Plon, 1970), p. 168.
3. See Alain Prate, *Les Batailles économiques du Général de Gaulle*, (Paris: Plon, 1978), p. 83.
4. Michel Albert, *commissaire au plan*, talk at Center for European Studies, Harvard University, 7 December 1978.
5. See the development of these themes in Commissariat général du plan d'équipement et de la productivité, *Le Développement industriel*. Rapport du groupe d'experts. Comité de développement industriel. 23 avril 1968 (Paris).
6. Lionel Stoléru, *L'Impératif industriel* (Paris: Seuil, 1969).
7. An analysis of the various incentives the government used to further its industrial policy and of the impact of these measures can be found in Jean-Jacques Bonnaud, 'Les instruments d'exécution du Plan utilisés par l'Etat à l'égard des entreprises,' *Revue économique*, no. 4 (July, 1970).
8. Statistics from *Direction*, February, 1970, reproduced in Ezra Suleiman, 'Industrial Policy in France,' in Steven J. Warnecke and Ezra N. Suleiman, eds., *Industrial Policies in Western Europe* (New York: Praeger, 1975), p. 27.
9. Cited in Bonnaud, *op. cit.*, p. 589.
10. Government contracts are highly concentrated in a few sectors: building and civil engineering, aerospace, electronics. For a group of industries responsible for 10 percent of industrial production, government contracts account for 25 percent of sales. Bonnaud, *op. cit.*, p. 565.
11. Interview, April, 1976.
12. Alain Cotta, *La France et l'impératif mondial* (Paris: Presses universitaires de France, 1978), p. 157.
13. Schéma général d'aménagement de la France, *Restructuration de l'appareil productif français*, no. 65 (Paris: Documentation française, 1976), p. 62.
14. Ibid., p. 67.
15. Stoléru, *op. cit.*, p. 148.
16. Ibid., p. 149.
17. Georges Pompidou, *Le noeud gordien* (Paris: Plon, 1974), p. 134.
18. Cotta, *op. cit.*, p. 130.
19. *Restructuration*, op. cit., p. 71.
20. Ibid., p. 78.
21. J.E.S. Hayward, 'Steel,' in Raymond Vernon, ed., *Big Business and the State* (Cambridge, Mass.: Harvard University Press, 1974), p. 269.
22. In 1977, the indebtedness of the French steel industry equalled 111 percent of turnover (*chiffre d'affaires*); in West Germany in 1976, the comparable figure was 22 percent; in the U.S., 21 percent; in Italy, 104 percent. *Le Monde*, 27 September 1978.

23. *Le Monde*, 27 September 1978, p. 36, estimates that in 1977 in France 149 tons of steel were produced per worker, as contrasted with 190 in West Germany, 175 for the Common Market as a whole, 249 in the United States, and 325 in Japan.

24. *Le Monde*, 16 September 1978.

25. *Le Monde*, 19 September 1978.

26. Research published by Association de recherche et d'information socio-économique de l'université de Paris-Dauphine, cited in *Le Monde*, 19 September 1978, p. 44.

27. François Renard, *Le Monde*, 16 September 1978.

28. Interview, April, 1976.

29. François de Combret, 'Le redéploiement industriel,' *Le Monde*, 31 March 1978, 1 and 2-3 April 1978. De Combret was *conseiller technique au secrétariat général de la présidence de la Republique*. Also, persons interviewed in the Ministry of Industry, Spring 1976, made the same points.

30. As an article in the *Nouvel économiste*, 26 January 1976, announced, the Ministry of Industry has come up with a new idea: 'the industrial fabric of promising sectors—ones worthy of being encouraged and which moreover do not involve technologies on the cutting edge of progress—is composed essentially of medium and small firms. The era of *redéploiement* and of the post-crisis should belong to small- and medium-sized firms.'

31. De Combret, ibid., 31 March 1978.

32. Interview in Ministry of Industry, Spring 1976. A SOFRES survey of industrialists with firms employing fewer than 500 workers is revealing: 60 percent would reject an increase in their capital that gave a bank or a state agency some share in their firm; on management, 78 percent of them use no market studies; 31 percent never market test a new product; 67 percent have no syndical organizations in the plant. Cited in *Le Monde, Dossiers et Documents: Les Petites et Moyennes Industries*, no. 30 (April 1976).

33. I have discussed these two political movements in 'D'une boutique à l'autre: Changes in the Organization of the Traditional Middle Classes from the Fourth to Fifth Republics,' *Comparative Politics* (October, 1977) and 'The Traditional Sector in France and Italy,' in S. Berger and M. Piore, *Dualism and Discontinuity in Industrial Societies* (Cambridge University Press, 1980).

34. Interview, March, 1976.

35. There is no better example than the vying between government and the R.P.R. over who is the best guardian of the Royer law. Before an audience of industrialists and shopkeepers in 1977, René Monory, the standard-bearer for the new liberalism and then Minister of Industry, announced his determination to keep on refusing new supermarket authorizations. *Le Monde*, 2 May 1977. On another occasion, queried about restrictions on textile imports, the liberal Monory pointed out that 'the reconversion of certain specially menaced sectors requires a certain protectionism, which must, I insist, be temporary.' *Le Monde*, 3 December 1977. And the Gaullists, originally rather tepid about the Royer law, have become its great supporters, Chirac announcing that the R.P.R. would beat back 'any threat to the *loi Royer*,' *Le Monde*, 17 November 1978.

36. There were 30 percent fewer supermarket openings in 1974 than in the preceding year. *Le Monde*, 3 January 1975.

37. *Le Monde*, 20 November 1976.

38. I am grateful to MM. Duverger and Amouyel in the Ministry of Industry and Bernard Long and Jacques Delahousse for long discussions of the G.E.C. The interest of this attempt to develop new kinds of relationships between bureaucrats and industrialists merits much longer treatment.

39. *Le Monde*, 13 March 1976.

40. The most comprehensive treatment of interventions to rescue industries in trouble in the Fifth Republic is Enzo Pontarollo, *Il salvataggio industriale nell'Europa della crisi*, (Bologna: Il Mulino, 1976), Chapter III.

41. The best treatment of economic policy in the wake of the energy crisis is Cotta, *op cit.*, Part II, ch. 1, 'L'économie française depuis 1973.'

42. This strategy is spelled out in the *Rapport sur l'adaptation du VII⁰ plan* (Paris: Documentation française, September 1978). See Michel Rocard's criticism of these 'théorèmes d'Albert,' so-called after Michel Albert, *commissaire au plan* and author of the *Rapport*, in the Assembly debate, *Le Monde*, 1 December 1978.

43. *Le Monde*, 17 October 1978.
44. See the balance sheet drawn in Pierre Durand, *Industrie et régions* (Paris: Documentation française, 1974: Second edition).
45. Direction générale de la politique industrielle, 'Quelques éléments d'appreciation de critères de choix économique à partir de l'échantillon des entreprises ayant sollicité un prêt du F.D.E.S.' (Mimeo., May, 1969).
46. See for example the cases related by François de Witt, 'Comment réparer les colosses,' *L'Expansion*, November 1978.
47. Unions also play a role in influencing the decisions of the *inspecteurs du travail*, who are regarded by many *patrons* and also by some officials in their own corps as especially pro-labor.
48. Interview, April 1976.
49. Interview, April 1976.
50. *Le Monde*, 1 November 1974.
51. The account here draws on interviews with three members of the CIASI in the spring of 1976.
52. *Le Monde*, 19 October 1978.
53. Council of Ministers, 18 October 1978, reported in *Le Monde*, 19 October 1978.
54. Interview, 7 April 1976.
55. Cotta, *Op. cit.*, p. 145.
56. *Le Monde*, 16 December 1978.
57. On the decentralization of work from large to small firms in the recession in Italy and the development of segmented labor markets, see Suzanne Berger, 'The Uses of the Traditional Sector in Italy: Why Declining Classes Survive,' in Frank Bechhofer and Brian Elliott ed., *The Petite Bourgeoisie in West Europe* (Macmillan, forthcoming).
58. Christian Stoffaes, *La Grande menace industrielle* (Paris: Calmann-Lévy, 1978). The first full presentation of the *redéploiement* thesis was worked out in the Ministry of Industry by the Groupe de réflexion sur les stratégies industrielles (GRESI) and presented in *Problématique d'une stratégie industrielle* (Paris: Documentation française, 1974).
59. Stoffaes, *op. cit.*, p. 146.
60. Ibid., p. 147.
61. On the television program *Questionnaire*, 16 October 1978. *Le Monde*, 18 October 1978.
62. *Le Monde*, 15 September 1978.
63. Stoffaes, *op. cit.*, pp. 236–7.
64. See Pierre Uri, 'Le VIIe Plan: adaptation ou répudiation?' *Le Monde*, 28 and 29 November 1978.

Energy Policies of the Fifth Republic: Autonomy Versus Constraint

Robert J. Lieber

INTRODUCTION

French political and economic life exhibits both change and continuity under the impact of the Fifth Republic. Energy policy has particularly reflected this combination. Indeed, its roots lie more than a half-century deep. The transition from the Fourth to the Fifth Republic does not in itself mark a Watershed in energy policy. The major configurations of this policy were shaped by France's scarcity of indigenous energy resources, by a general pattern of movement from a coal-based to a modern export-oriented economy based on imported oil, by the profound impact of interdependence within a relatively open international economy and by the enduring constraints of the post-1973 oil crisis.

A decade or more ago, the subject of energy policy would have been largely ignored in a book such as this. Yet, the impact of energy problems and policies on French life has become significant and pervasive. General recognition of energy-related effects upon political, economic and even social concerns has come about only following the 1973-74 energy crisis.[1] The post-1973 rise of 500 percent in crude oil prices, the sudden awareness of France's extraordinary dependence on imported oil and resultant vulnerability, and the effects of energy costs and balance of payments problems upon economic performance in France and throughout the industrialized world explain, in part, why energy policy has become so much more central in recent years. Nonetheless, the energy problem did not come into being instantly with the movement of Egyptian troops across the Suez Canal on the morning of 6 October 1973. In fact, French energy policies have been shaped consciously by successive governments over a half-century.

Energy policy decisions within the Fifth Republic stemmed from a series of explicit governmental choices. They reflected a coherent strategy by de Gaulle to modernize France and its economy in order to increase the country's independence in foreign affairs, especially *vis-à-vis* the United States.[2] Yet, the enduring constraints de Gaulle encountered in his efforts to increase France's autonomy in economics, technology, politics and defense appeared in the energy sphere also. Indeed, at times energy policies followed by the Fifth Republic had the ultimate effect of narrowing its choices, despite Gaullist aspirations to the contrary. These policies, and the domestic and international energy difficulties, have left French governments significantly constrained in their ability to take domestic and foreign policy inititatives.

The area of energy policy embodies a number of themes found elsewhere in contemporary France: the intimate linkages between domestic and international affairs, between politics and economics, and between the aspirations for enhanced autonomy and the constraints imposed by interdependence.[3] This essay describes the major energy policy choices of successive administrations; explores the reasons for and subsequent effects of those decisions; treats the impact of the energy crisis and its aftermath in reshaping energy policy; notes government efforts to lessen *dirigisme* and move toward liberalism; and concludes with an analysis of the pervasive effects of transnationalism and interdependence upon French energy policy.

FRENCH ENERGY POLICY: FROM THE THIRD TO THE FIFTH REPUBLIC

The institutional framework for contemporary French energy policy had its origins in the years from 1926 to 1929. During that period, there were major governmental efforts to increase control over the domestic market and acquire an important foothold for French companies in the control of international oil.[4] Legislation, particularly the 1928 *lois Poincaré*, established a governmental monopoly on oil imports and enacted tariff policies to favor French refineries and the export of refined oil products. During the 1920s, the government encouraged the formation of *Compagnie française des pétroles* (CFP), a partly state-owned oil company. Thus, it established a *dirigiste*, mercantilist and nationalist energy policy, in the sense of using state power to intervene or structure market arrangements to serve national goals and priorities. In effect, the treatment of energy fit within a tradition of French economic policy reaching back three centuries to Colbert.

Under the French Republic, until the mid-1950s, the French energy economy was predominantly national, in the sense of an essentially national market and supply pattern, based on close, privileged relations between French energy enterprises and the state. Relying on natural resources in France, particularly coal, this provided expensive energy in somewhat limited quantities.[5] However, the options available to France were relatively narrow. Apart from coal (much of it difficult to mine), limited quantities of natural gas in the Lacq field, and modest amounts of hydroelectric power, France depended on imports for petroleum, natural gas, and even some coal. The extensive discoveries and production of cheap Middle Eastern oil in the 1950s, coupled with the opening of the French economy to European and world competition in 1959, created incentives for the new Gaullist regime to adopt a policy of reliance upon inexpensive imported energy to aid French industry to achieve competitiveness, particularly within the new European Economic Community.[6]

Gaullist administrations, beginning in 1958, encouraged vast increases in the consumption of imported oil in their pursuit of this cheap energy policy. To aid the development of French industry, they resisted tax increases on industrial fuels. Although gasoline—which had no readily available substituted for use in automobiles—was taxed substantially, no excise tax was charged on fuel oil[7]—which competed directly with coal and natural gas. By contrast, important international competitors, such as Britain and the German Federal Republic, imposed fuel use taxes, thus at least partly cushioning the competitive damage to their domestic coal production. Hence, by 1969 the effective price of heavy fuel oil to French consumers (principally industries and power plants) was the lowest in the European community.[8] French, as well as British and American, oil companies sought to maximize their sales in France, particularly from 1966 onward. And, as a result of a 'veritable gluttony for fuel oil,' amidst a world 'euphoria' over petroleum supplies, oil consumption in Fifth Republic France increased an almost incredible ten-fold between 1959 and 1972.[9]

These events had a devastating impact upon the French coal industry. Domestic coal deposits were already difficult to exploit economically and mines had been starved of necessary investment funds for modernization. Falling prices for oil and aggressive oil company marketing policies, competition from imported American coal, pressure from industries seeking cheaper energy supplies, and governmental interest in decreasing the number and power of coal miners, all contributed to an official policy of running-down the French coal industry[10] more rapidly than in Germany or Britain.

In effect, between 1950 and 1973 (particularly after the Fifth Republic was founded in 1958) France converted from an energy economy based on domestic coal to one centered on imported petroleum. In 1950 coal accounted for 77 percent of French energy consumption and petroleum for 20 percent; by 1973 their relative positions had become virtually reversed, with coal providing 16 percent and oil 72 percent of total consumption. In the Federal Republic, where coal resources were somewhat more extensive, the movement from coal to oil had been slightly less drastic, and coal accounted for 30 percent of West German energy consumption in 1973, as against 58 percent for oil.[11]

The implications of this shift did not go entirely without notice. Unlike other Western governments, the French government directly or indirectly exercised

181

supervision over most facets of their national energy industry.[12] Through CFP and ELF-Erap, it sought to maintain control of an amount of oil production at least as great as total French consumption, to diversify sources of supply, and to limit foreign oil companies' share of the domestic oil market to less than half.[13] For a time, these policies seemed to work. Thus, at state-direction, ELF-Erap negotiated important oil-trade relationships with a newly independent Algeria.[14] Together with French-contracted production in Iraq, these two countries accounted for more than half of French oil imports.[15] However, French control was eliminated by nationalization of the Algerian oil industry in 1971. With continuing huge growth in oil consumption, this left France increasingly dependent on Middle Eastern oil imports.

Table I

Energy Sources
Percentages (in terms of metric tons of coal equivalent), 1975

DOMESTIC

	Total Domestic	Coal	Natural Gas	Crude Oil	Hydro & Nuclear
France	24.9	9.4	3.8	1.1	10.6
W. Germany	49.1	37.2	6.0	2.4	3.5
UK	59.9	39.9	15.3	.5	4.2

IMPORTED

Total Imported	Coal	Arab Oil	Non-Arab Oil	Other
75.1	6.3	47.7	15.1	6.0
50.9	-7.1	24.2	24.6	9.2
40.1	-4.2	24.3	19.6	.4

Source: International Economic Report of the President,
Transmitted to the Congress, January 1977, p.173

In early 1971, the French Council of Ministers proposed measures to dilute France's growing dependence; these included increased oil exploration offshore and in the franc-zone countries of sub-Saharan Africa (to lessen the foreign exchange burden of petroleum imports), greater diversification of supply, increased oil stockpiles, longer term contracts with producers, and a greater role for France in petroleum transportation. Ultimately, the Ministry of Finance prevailed in opposing these measures as too costly. Despite its traditions of *dirigisme*, France was deeply enmeshed in an international petroleum economy which it could not control and whose domestic impact it could influence only partly. France's absence of indigenous oil supplies, inability to retain control in Algeria, need to encourage economic growth, and lack of sufficient economic muscle to play off producer companies and governments[16] reflected the limitations of a middle-sized power in an increasingly interdependent international political economy.

The preponderant consideration shaping energy policy was de Gaulle's desire to modernize the economy to compete with France's major European partners and the United States., and thereby to enable France to play a larger world role. In addition, during the mid-1960s, Gaullist international monetary policies aimed at maintaining a strong domestic currency and weakening the international role of the dollar to lessen American economic and monetary hegemony. Thus, in the mid to late 1960s de Gaulle preferred to adopt deflationary policies and, after the events of May 1968, refused to devalue the franc because of his international priorities.[17] In some measure, short-term economic and monetary policies ran counter to long term growth objectives. Hence, the reliance (even over-reliance) upon low energy prices, cheap imported oil and a run down of the coal industry inasmuch as these provided important benefits to French industry. Ironically, the increased dependence on external energy ultimately brought a further loss of autonomy *vis-à-vis* both OPEC and France's Western partners.

In the interim, however, Gaullist policies substantially succeeded in the areas of modernization and rapid economic growth. Indeed, the country's gross domestic product grew faster from 1961 to 1972 than that of any other Western European state.[18] Given the importance and priority of this transition, particularly during the first decade of the Fifth Republic, it is not surprising that miscalculations in the energy sector occurred. Not only was it impossible to maintain political or economic control over the external sources of France's petroleum, but the neo-mercantilist stress on domestic refining capability and the maintenance of French oil company control over more than half the domestic market was entirely inadequate to shield France from vulnerabilities of supply and price. The tradeoffs between minimum cost and secure supply were resolved by overestimating the regulatory and balancing role of international market competition and underestimating the strategic positions of the Anglo-American oil companies and of the petroleum producing countries.[19] Despite Gaullist priorities, French energy policy makers shared with other Europeans a failure to understand the relationship between higher energy prices and greater political-economic security. While the advantages of cheap energy for economic growth were obvious, the political consequences of concentrated dependence on Middle Eastern oil were not appreciated fully until the autumn of 1973, when the escalation of prices and temporary reduction in oil supply revealed that oil could have a major impact in international politics.[20]

183

Before this, however, the Fifth Republic, under President de Gaulle, had made one significant policy change. Following the June 1967 Middle East War, de Gaulle shifted abruptly from a pro-Israeli to a pro-Arab foreign policy orientation. Although a series of personal and geo-political factors contributed to this action (not least the opportunities for extensive arms sales), the factor of dependence on imported oil was probably paramount. Indeed, Guy de Carmoy has argued that the shift to a pro-Arab policy constitutes the principal energy policy-related change.

THE FIFTH REPUBLIC IN THE ENERGY CRISIS

By the October 1973 Middle East War and ensuing energy crisis, France depended on oil (virtually all of it imported) for approximately 67 percent of her primary energy supply.[21] Among the major countries of the European Community only Italy had a higher rate of oil dependence. Thus, the immediate concern for France was to ensure adequate supplies of oil, particularly after the October 17 announcement of an oil embargo by the Organization of Arab Petroleum Exporting Countries (OAPEC). During subsequent months, French policies aimed at warding off the direct effects of the crisis through specific political and economic strategies.

Politically, President Pompidou and the French government followed a deliberately pro-Arab approach. While this reflected a continuation and elaboration of previous French policies, it further distinguished France from the United States and, more importantly, caused OAPEC to place France in a favored category of states to receive normal supplies of oil rather than face phased reductions or a complete embargo. During this stage of the crisis, France also sought to steer the European Community (whose nine members had been separated into three different categories by OAPEC) toward a Middle East policy consistent with her own. However, this became the source of abrasive Community division, particularly over France's initial unwillingness to support the Netherlands, which had become the target of an Arab oil boycott.[22]

Economically, French policies of *dirigisme* were also used in an attempt to blunt the impact of the crisis. ELF-Erap and CFP were pressured (the former successfully, the latter less so) to maintain their oil deliveries to France, at the expense of other supply commitments, to offset the actions of the major multinational oil firms which had responded to the crisis by allocating reduced world supplies largely on a pro rata basis. In addition, the companies were used as vehicles to negotiate bilateral national arrangements to assure long-term supplies of foreign oil in exchange for massive exports of French manufactured goods, technology, arms, and investments.

The supply phase of the energy crisis tested the ability of France to follow explicitly national priorities through more or less autonomous political and economic means. French policy failed to achieve its major aims. Oil supply reductions were nearly comparable to those elsewhere in Europe.[23] In addition, many of the ambitious bilateral negotiations with oil producing countries failed. Also, despite initial success at wooing the EC toward the mid-East policies, her European partners pulled in the opposite direction through their political, economic and even military linkages with the US and Germany, as well as by their own priorities. Most damaging of all, Gaullist energy policies completely failed to isolate France from the operation of the international petroleum economy and the sudden four-fold rise in crude oil prices.

The limitations on French policy were particularly evident in the second phase of the energy crisis as initial concerns over the availability of oil supplies gave way to serious worries over the staggering impact of oil price increases. The shift in focus from supply to price brought a propensity to move from national to multinational levels in dealing with the energy problem. While certain kinds of supply arrangements might be negotiated on a state-to-state basis, the impact of price increases necessitated attention to international monetary arrangements, recycling of petrodollars, balance of payments problems, inflation, and other concerns, most of which demanded multilateral responses by the advanced industrial democracies through such agencies as the OECD, IMF and the American-inspired International Energy Agency. France's hostility to the establishment of a consumer group failed to prevent her EC partners from joining the IEA in early 1974, and ultimately the French were forced to be less hostile toward the Agency. Indeed, after the election of Giscard d'Estaing in May 1974, Gaullist pressure within the governing majority prevented him from bringing France into the IEA.

The energy crisis also had the effect of reversing the decline of American influence in Western Europe. Only the US possessed continental size and resources, minimal vulnerability to international economic disturbances, and the political, economic and military muscle to focus cooperative efforts at coping with the impact of the energy problems. Despite its efforts at autonomy, the French government found itself severely constrained by the facts of interdependence. These enhanced France's vulnerability both to oil producing Arab states on the one hand and to her European allies and the United States on the other.[24]

POST-CRISIS CALCULATIONS AND THE PROBLEMS OF NUCLEAR ENERGY

In the aftermath of the energy crisis, France faced fundamental problems of energy supply and price. The former meant overwhelming dependence on imported oil from the Middle East, the latter an immense burden in finding the means to pay for huge cost increases and to deal with the resultant balance of payments problems. In these circumstances, French energy policy options were severely constrained. By 1975, for example, oil constituted approximately 64 percent of French primary energy supply compared to 16 percent for coal, 10 percent for natural gas and 10 percent for hydro-electricity and nuclear power combined. (See Table 1.) Given France's resource scarcities, policymakers concluded that only massive development of nuclear power offered any significant long term impact. Accordingly, plans were established for huge increases in nuclear generated electricity to reduce dependence on imported oil. The 1974 Messmer Plan target was that by 1985 nuclear would provide about 70 percent of the country's electricity and 25 percent of its energy needs (compared with 7.8 percent and 1.6 percent in 1974), and 45 percent of total primary energy usage by the year 2000.[25] In the interim, a limit of 51 billion francs was imposed on imported oil for 1975 and efforts were undertaken to conserve oil and diversify sources of supply, as well as to increase French exports.

This nuclear policy appeared to offer a number of advantages. Not only would it reduce France's dependence on imported oil, and hence the vulnerabilities which this implied, but it promised to provide distinct economic benefits as well as a source of technological leadership within Europe and of potential exports elsewhere. However, the French had encountered difficult problems with reactor development in the 1960s, involving the domestically built graphite-gas reactor which used natural uranium to which France had ready access. Ultimately, the chief difficulty with this reactor design was not so much technological as economic. Following de Gaulle's resignation in 1969, France finally turned to American designed light water reactors (LWR), using enriched uranium (supplied by the U.S.) and built under license from the American firm of Westinghouse and its U.S.-France subsidiary, Framatome.[26]

The French also intensified their commitment to long-term development of fast breeder reactor technology (FBR). This breeder would yield fifty times the power of conventional reactors from the same quantity of uranium[27] consume as fuel highly toxic quantities of plutonium (otherwise usable only in nuclear weapons) produced as a waste product by the LWR, and generate additional uranium fuel for the LWR reactors. Without the FBR, France faced uranium resource shortages or exorbitant uranium price increases.[28] FBR development would lessen French dependence on American LWR technology and on imports of uranium, as well as solidify a position of world leadership in fast breeder technology which France claimed. Nonetheless, the breeder reactor posed certain problems, namely cost (considerably more expensive than the LWR), security (the risks of a plutonium economy), and time (only minor impact before the year 2000).

Within Europe, the French nuclear policy led to promotion by the Commissariat à l'Energie Atomique (CEA) of a large uranium enrichment plant, known as EURODIF. This project involved not only European partners (Italy, Belgium, Spain) but also a 10 percent investment by Iran.[29] Subsequently, France and West Germany agreed on joint research and development of breeder reactors and involved the Dutch, Belgians and Italians in plans to market breeder reactors in other countries.

This nuclear policy was supported by the major political parties in France, including the Communists, except that the *Parti Socialiste* advocated an eighteen to twenty-four month moratorium on nuclear construction to reevaluate the country's energy and nuclear programs. The largest trade union, the Communist-oriented CGT, remained pro-nuclear, but the program received considerable criticism from the Socialist-oriented CFDT. It cited unsolved problems of nuclear waste disposal, lack of public discussion and debate, absence of analysis of collective needs, safety risks for workers and the public, enhanced power for multinational corporations, dangers that a massive nuclear program would accelerate the development of a technocratic or even authoritarian state, and the overall social and political problems induced by nuclear 'gigantism.' However, the CFDT did not oppose nuclear development completely. It advocated less development of electricity, greater use of hydro-power and natural gas, maintenance of coal production at existing levels, energy conservation, and modification of the production process to reduce wasteful consumption. Like the P.S., it called for a moratorium for three years, in new nuclear reactor orders.[30]

The nuclear program also stimulated the bitter hostility of a growing number of French environmentalists concerned with the hazards of a plutonium economy, including potential terrorism, health risks, diversion of weapons-grade material, increased state centralization and nuclear waste disposal. This led to a major confrontation in July 1977, at Creys-Malville in southeastern France, over construction of the world's first breeder reactor for commercial electrical power production. As work began toward a goal of operation in 1983, 30,000 activists and 5000 French riot police converged on the site. The resultant battle injured scores and killed one demonstrator.[31] The environmental confrontation was complicated by the presence of foreign, particularly West German, demonstrators and a *gauchiste* component, but it raised the question of whether domestic opposition within France (for example as reflected in an ecologist vote temporarily reaching as high as 10 percent in some municipal elections), could delay the nuclear program. However, government use of public relations measures, and powerful centralized authority allowed it to avoid the extensive nuclear delays that occurred elsewhere in Western Europe and North America.

Fears of nuclear proliferation led to increased opposition from the Carter administration in the United States. Agreements by France to sell a reprocessing plant to Pakistan and a nuclear reactor to Iraq were particular subjects of concern. In 1974, France initiated preliminary bilateral nuclear plant agreements with Iraq, Iran and Libya, and in November 1975 the French signed an agreement with Iraq for construction of an enriched uranium research reactor. In

1976, Pakistan negotiated a contract for a nuclear reprocessing facility. Although the Libyan contract was never signed, the Iraqi and Pakistani contracts were, as was a subsequent reactor contract with South Africa. These offered outlets for French exports and technology, but in regions where diversion of nuclear materials for weapons development was a distinct possibility. However, in December 1976, some four months after Raymond Barre replaced Gaullist Prime Minister Jacques Chirac, official French policy became more cautious. In particular, the French government discontinued signing of bilateral contracts to sell reprocessing plants, but those with Pakistan and Iraq continued in effect.

French government policy remained ambiguous in assessing tradeoffs between nuclear development and the risks of nuclear proliferation. Prime Minister Barre told President Carter that France was aware of the dangers of nuclear proliferation, but felt that they had to be reconciled with what Barre termed the 'indispensable' development of nuclear energy.[32] Subsequently, however, the government sought to alter its contract with Pakistan to ensure that plutonium would not be diverted to nuclear weapons use. Pakistan refused, but in September 1978, under French pressure, the entire agreement collapsed.[33] Nonetheless, France continued its strong interest in the export of nuclear reactors and in the long-term development of the breeder reactor program—areas in which it continued to differ with the United States.

In the case of Iraq, France's second most important oil supplier,[34] President Giscard d'Estaing claimed that France could ensure that the nuclear fuel provided would be adapted exactly to the needs of the reactor and not diverted to other (i.e., weapons) uses.[35] However, that particular reactor utilized highly enriched (93 percent) uranium and Iraq received sufficient fuel (65 kilograms) to make nine or ten crude atomic weapons (if the material were diverted). In April 1979, as completion and delivery of the reactor were imminent, its vital core components were blown up mysteriously. This set back the schedule some two years and created the possibility that a reactor to run on a newly developed non-weapons grade fuel (7 percent enriched) might be provided instead.[36]

The nuclear logic of France's energy policy was also reflected in the fifteen-nation nuclear suppliers group. Although willing to cooperate in certain nuclear safeguard efforts, France took a less restrictive view than the U.S. on important issues such as reprocessing. Thus, in October 1977, the French government agreed to reprocess Japanese uranium fuel, beginning in 1985. Since reprocessing produces plutonium, which is usable for weapons as well as fuel, this ran sharply counter to Carter administration positions on nonproliferation.[37] Nonetheless it reflected French and Japanese concerns to ensure their own supplies of nuclear fuel.

The nuclear policy raised old dilemmas in new forms. While the major political parties—except the Socialists—favored nuclear development because it appeared to enhance France's national autonomy and economic security, many old constraints remained. Initial nuclear targets had been overly ambitious, and with the subsequent recession and an unexpectedly low rate of growth in energy demand, as well as limits of industrial capacity and some problems of technology and site selection, the 1985 target was reduced during 1976–79, from 25 percent of total primary energy to 20 percent.[38]

These revised nuclear energy targets appeared feasible. Nonetheless they involved new problems. The enormous costs of nuclear construction, for example, implied choices in resource allocation and hence reduced investment funds in other sectors of economy and technology. A unanimous report by the Finance Committee of the French National Assembly criticized the government for seriously underestimating the costs and consequences of the nuclear program. It noted that over four years the officially calculated cost per kilowatt hour (KWH) of electricity had nearly tripled and that these calculations systematically underestimated the likely costs. They also criticized the fact that the nuclear program would not guarantee France's energy independence because it relied upon American LWR technology, and that reactors could be exported only with American approval. Indeed, due to joint ownership arrangements, France could not control unilaterally all decisions concerning the EURODIF enrichment plant located on French soil.[39]

The nuclear program could not even be financed on an exclusively national basis. The quasi-autonomous French electricity company, EDF, had to turn to foreign sources for approximately two-thirds of the enormous sums needed to finance its nuclear program. It went to the U.S. commercial paper market where, in 1976, it became the third largest participant, after General Motors and Ford.[40]

In addition, serious questions were raised as to whether energy policy-makers were emphasizing the nuclear program at the expense of cost-effective investments in energy conservation, and (to a lesser extent) new forms of energy technology.[41] France has had a leaner energy economy than most of its industrial counterparts, consuming only 795 tons of oil equivalent per $ million of GDP, compared to 1031 for Germany and 1480 for the U.S.,[42] and actually managed to reduce oil imports by nearly 14 percent between 1973 and 1978.[43] Also it has had one of the most effective national conservation programs. Yet, total funds available to the *Agence pour les économies d'énergie* in 1979 were only 540 million francs ($123 million), compared to 12 billion francs ($2.7 billion) for nuclear investment,[44] even while France appeared likely to fall substantially short of its 1985 conservation objectives.[45] The reduction in French energy usage in 1974 and its lower than forecast subsequent rate of growth during 1975–77 may have owed more to important but one-time conservation measures than to major adaptations. Indeed, an important part of the energy savings may have been due to recession and lagging economic growth.

189

To be sure, the nuclear program did produce some real national advantages. Thus, France had become the best placed Western European country at all stages of the nuclear fuel cycle.[46] This implies some prospect of technological leadership and export competitiveness in nuclear industry. Yet uncertainties—political, economic, technical, and even psychological—remain over key aspects of the nuclear program. The goal of substantially enhanced national energy independence will also remain elusive.[47] Thus, even in 1985, France will depend on foreign sources for approximately 67 percent of her total national energy needs (including natural gas and coal, as well as petroleum).[48] Above all, the country will still face the increasingly difficult tasks of producing sufficient exports to pay for imported energy and of financing the remaining balance of payments costs.

In sum, its continued need for imported oil, its involvement in cooperative European relationships to develop and export costly nuclear technology and its profound economic, financial, investment and trade ties with the advanced industrial economies of the West (as well as with many developing countries), will continue to enmesh France in a web of interdependent economic, technical and political relationships.[49] The Giscard administration recognized this dependence explicitly, but the constraints on France remained so fundamental and structural that a more avowedly Gaullist or even a leftist government would have faced comparable or possibly greater restraints.[50] In essence, the energy problem has had the effect of reducing the overall economic and political resources available to a French government. Even an ambitious nuclear policy cannot enable France to transcend these facts.

GAULLISM, INTERDEPENDENCE AND THE ENERGY PROBLEM

Regardless of the policies of Fifth Republic governments, the demands of coping with energy problems, particularly in the post-1973 period, have increasingly circumscribed France's freedom of maneuver. These constraints have been intensified by the necessity for reliable sources of oil and its immense cost and the resultant needs to export and to attain balance of payments equilibrium, to develop and pay for costly nuclear technology and more prosaic but vitally important energy-saving measures, and to cooperate increasingly with countries of the European Community and other advanced industrial economies in seeking to manage the pervasive and interwoven monetary, economic, trading and investment aspects of the energy problem.

Policies of dirigisme and neo-mercantilism, in the sense of using state mechanisms to shape industrial and economic development, to a degree have permitted France slightly greater antonomy. But this autonomy is hemmed in increasingly by determinants outside the direct control of any French government. Indeed, their origins are not exclusively external. Although successive French administrations had the power necessary to control the energy sector, they gradually abdicated to the competitive fluctuations of the world energy market. By thus giving priority to minimization of energy costs over energy independence, particularly from 1967–68 onward, their policies contradicted de Gaulle's emphasis on national independence.[51]

In any case, the efforts to maintain some degree of state direction through such measures as influencing the national oil companies, mainingtain French domination over at least half the domestic market, building up French refining capacity, seeking economic or political control of foreign oil production equivalent to domestic consumption, and later maneuvering for bilateral deals with oil producing countries proved largely inadequate to ensure French energy autonomy. Nor is the nuclear policy, despite the ultimate benefits it may offer, likely to reverse these trends fundamentally.

The Giscard-Barre government began, in mid-1978, to modify at least slightly the long tradition of *dirigisme* in French energy policy. It did so by extending to the energy field certain measures of market-oriented liberalism—which it had begun to implement elsewhere in the French economy with by no means obvious success. These measures included some relaxation in the tight control over petroleum imports and marketing which the state had exercised since 1928 (provisions of which had occasioned complaints from the E.C. Commission in Brussels).[52] While the government still retained substantial control of the oil market, its actions earned the condemnation of a former architect of Gaullist energy policy, Jean-Marcel Jeanneney, who criticized this as readiness to abandon tools for structuring the petroleum industry in the national interest.[53]

The conflict between Giscardian liberalism and Gaullist (and pre-Gaullist) *dirigisme* was also evident in other ways. In August 1978, for example, in response to the decline of the dollar and resultant reduction of the franc price which France paid for its oil, the minister of economy, M. Monory, proposed to reduce the price of gasoline by 3 to 6 centimes per liter. While this proposal was comprehensible on anti-inflation grounds and as a response to domestic political criticism by the PCF of excess oil company profits, it conflicted with broader aims of reduced energy consumption. A few days later, prime minister Raymond Barre intervened to halt the reduction, while temporarily siphoning off the sum in question (500 million francs) to energy conservation purposes.[54] In another, more important example of this conflict of objectives, real electricity prices actually *declined* by approximately 10 percent from 1973 through Spring 1979.[55]

In areas outside the energy sector, domestic economic priorities were sometimes inconsistent with international energy policy imperatives. Here, too, the market-oriented liberalism of the Giscard government diverged from *dirigiste* precedents. Barre's objective to force many public services to change 'true' prices as well as to reduce the budgetary burdens of state subsidies resulted in steep public transport fare increases. In July 1978, for example, fares were raised on the Paris bus and subway system and fares on the national railroad were increased 15 percent. These price rises, particularly on the railway system, ran counter to energy consumption priorities to discourage the use of private cars. While gasoline prices remained high—the equivalent of approximately $2.30 per gallon of premium, as a result of high taxes—possible 12% percent per year rail fare increases are planned for each of the next five years.[56]

Even in the more circumscribed high politics area of foreign policy, French choices brought no more than mixed results. Thus, pursuit of the pro-Arab policy did not insulate France from worldwide oil pricing patterns. Indeed, France's share of total OECD exports to the OPEC market (including non-Arab states) actually fell from 10.3 percent in 1972–73 to 8.4 percent in 1978.[57] In addition, by mid-1979, in the aftermath of the Iranian crisis the French were paying the same 30 percent to 40 percent increased world oil price and facing the same troublesome economic consequences as other major oil consuming countries. More ominously, limited domestic energy resources, as well as the ensemble of choices made in the energy field, particularly in the nuclear area and in the lesser priority according to measures of energy conservation or of major commitments to new energy technologies, left France highly dependent on costly imported energy for the period to 1985 and beyond. Yet it was far from certain how advantageously France would compete in the international export market with the most advanced industrial countries, such as Germany and Japan, or with the most dynamic of the newly industrializing countries, in order to pay for the costs of imported energy. Exhortations by President Giscard and Prime Minister Barre notwithstanding, long term success was by no means assured.

CONCLUSION

Fifth Republic governments have been unable to overcome the constraints imposed by the external realities of the energy problem. If, on occasion, their policies have achieved slightly more room for maneuver than that obtained by their European partners, this has been a difference of degree rather than kind. And their energy policy choices (as in the 1960s) sometimes have had the ultimate effect of decreasing France's autonomy. Energy problems as a whole have made France more dependent not only upon energy producing countries of the Middle East but also upon the major advanced industrial states of the OECD. The Giscard government has acknowledged that France cannot go it alone, as in the President's December 1977 statement that 'We buy our oil at the international price, and in the event of a crisis or embargo, no country could protect itself all alone.'[58] A similar attitude characterized France's June 1979 call for consumer cooperation in the face of rising oil prices and for a general dialogue with oil producers. But such recognition apart, the resource constraints and accompanying political and economic limitations imply that

French governments, whether Giscardian, Gaullist or leftist, will find that their range of choices for an enhanced foreign role or ambitious domestic commitments has become significantly narrowed. Thus, the energy problem has had a profound impact on political and economic life in Fifth Republic France.

NOTES

*For their comments on earlier drafts of this paper, I wish to thank Marc Perrin de Brichambaut, Daniel Yergin, Donald Rothchild, Hans Maull, and Guy de Carmoy. I received support for this research from a University of California research grant and an International Relations Fellowship of the Rockefeller Foundation and used facilities kindly provided by the Atlantic Institute in Paris.

1. An otherwise thoughtful and perceptive book on the foreign economic policy of the Fifth Republic, Edward Morse's *Foreign Policy and Interdependence in Gaullist France* (Princeton: Princeton University Press, 1973), completed in December 1972, makes passing references to nuclear energy but devotes almost no attention to energy, oil, gas, coal, or natural resources.

2. Morse discusses de Gaulle's objectives and the use of planning in order to modernize France in ibid., p. 281.

3. Stanley Hoffmann's observation, while delivered in a broader context, is equally applicable to energy policy: '... the central problem is that of the meaning and possibilities of independence for a middle power, in an age not merely of giant states but also of transnational forces which reveal the limits of middle and small-power control far more cruelly than those of super-power autonomy.' *Decline or Renewal? France Since the 1930s* (New York: Viking, 1974), p. viii.

4. Horst Mendershausen, *Coping with the Oil Crisis: French and German Experiences* (Baltimore: Johns Hopkins University Press, 1976), p. 19; and Guy de Carmoy, *Energy for Europe: Political and Economic Implications* (Washington, D.C.: American Enterprise Institute, 1977), p. 56.

5. Dominique Saumon and Louis Puiseux, 'Actors and Decisions in French Energy Policy,' in Leon N. Lindberg (ed.), *The Energy Syndrome: Comparing National Responses to the Energy Crisis* (Lexington, Ma.: D.C. Heath, Lexington Books, 1977), pp. 136–37.

6. Ibid., p. 142, and N.J.D. Lucas, 'The Role of Institutional Relationships in French Energy Policy,' *International Relations* (London), Vol. 5, No. 6 (November 1977), p. 96.

7. Carmoy, p. 58; also Lucas, p. 96.

8. Saumon and Puiseux, pp. 143–4.

9. Ibid., p. 142–3. From 1960 to 1973, French energy consumption increased at a rate of more than 6 percent per year, compared to a West European average of 4.8 percent; in addition, the increase in the coefficient of elasticity of increased energy use with increased GNP went from 0.8 (1949–60) to nearly 1.0 (1960–70). Ibid., p. 125.

10. See ibid., p. 140.

11. Figures quoted from Mendershausen, p. 33 and Saumon and Puiseux, p. 119.

12. In addition to control or influence over the two major French oil companies CPF and ELF-Erap (later ELF-Aquitaine), the government controlled, via state-owned corporations, coal (Charbonnages de France), electricity (Électricité de France), natural gas (Gaz de France), and nuclear power (Commissariat à l'Énergie Atomique).

13. See the discussion of these aims in Mendershausen, p. 26.

14. John Zysman, 'The French State in the International Economy,' *International Organization*, Vol. 31, No. 4 (autumn 1977), p. 872.

15. For detailed figures, see Mendershausen, pp. 19–21.

16. A number of these points, as well as the discussion of the abortive 1971 mensures, are lucidly elaborated by Saumon and Puiseux, p. 144.

17. Morse, pp. 297–8; and Peter Katzenstein, 'Conclusion: Domestic Structures and Strategies of Foreign Economy Policy,' in *International Organization*, Vol. 31, No. 4 (Autumn 1977), p. 885.

18. From 1961 to 1972, France achieved an average growth rate in real GNP of 6.2 percent per year, compared to 5.1 percent for West Germany, 4.3 percent for the U.S., and 4.9 percent for the European Community. *Economic Report of the President*, January 1978 (U.S. Government, Washington, D.C., 1978). Table B–107, p. 380.

19. Saumon and Puiseux, p. 169.

20. Carmoy makes this point effectively. *Op. cit.*, pp. 37–38.

21. The comparative figure for Britain was 52.1 percent, for West Germany 58.6 percent and for Italy 78.6 percent. Source: British Petroleum Statistical Review of the World Oil Industry, 1973, in Louis Turner, 'Politics of the Energy Crisis,' *International Affairs* (London), Vol. 59, No. 3, p. 408.

22. For a detailed analysis of this crisis, see Robert J. Lieber, *Oil and the Middle East War: Europe in the Energy Crisis* (Cambridge, Ma.; Harvard Center for International Affairs, 1976), pp. 12 ff.

23. Exact calculations of oil supply reductions are complicated by the dates and measures used (e.g., stocks on hand, actual deliveries compared with forecast deliveries, comparisons with previous year, consumption, etc.). One of the most useful analyses can be found in Robert Stobaugh, Statement before the Subcommittee on Multinational Corporations of the Committee on Foreign Relations, U.S. Senate, on Multinational Corporations and Foreign Policy. 25 July 1974, mimeographed; and Stobaugh, 'The Oil Companies in the Crisis,' in Raymond Vernon (ed.), *The Oil Crisis* (New York: Norton, 1976), pp. 179–202.
Also see Romano Prodi and Alberto Clô, 'Europe,' in Vernon, pp. 91–112.

24. Avner Yaniv makes this argument in 'The French Connection: A Review of French Policy Towards Israel,' *Jerusalem Journal of International Relations*, Vol. 1, No. 3, spring 1976, p. 130.

25. Albert Robin, 'Une voie nouvelle pour couvrir les besoins en énergie: l'électricité.' *Paradoxes*, No. 26 (février-mars, 1978), p. 98. Also, *The Economist* (London), 7 September 1974.

26. Saumon and Puiseux, pp. 148–9. Also Guy de Carmoy, 'La politique énergétique française et l'option nucléaire.' *Etudes* (Paris), mai 1977, pp. 641–53.

27. See 'France's Position on Breeder Reactors,' French Embassy, Press and Information Division, New York, PP/78/2, January 1978.

28. Carmoy, *Etudes*, mai 1977, p. 649, and 'Les politiques énergétiques comparées de la France, de l'Angleterre et de l'Allemagne,' *Revue de l'Energie*, mai 1977, No. 294, pp. 319–20.

29. Carmoy, *Energy for Europe*, p. 60.

30. 'Pour une autre politique de l'énergie,' *CFDT aujourd'hui*, No. 29, janvier-février 1978, pp. 71–98.

31. See *The Economist*, 6 August 1977.

32. 15 September 1977. French Embassy, Washington, D.C., *France*, October 1977, p. 1.

33. See *Le Monde*, 25 August 1978 and *International Herald Tribune* (Paris), 5 September 1978.

34. In 1978 France's principal petroleum suppliers were Saudi Arabia (35.1 percent), Iraq (17.7 percent) and Iran (9.1 percent). See *Les chiffres clés de l'énergie*, Paris: Ministère de l'industrie, 1979, pp. 60–61.

35. 'Interview of Valery Giscard D'Estaing, President of the French Republic,' broadcast on 9 February 1978, on radio station Europe No. 1. French Embassy Press and Information Division, New York, 78/12.

36. See, e.g., *Le Nouvel Observateur*, 14 April 1979, pp. 142–145. Subsequent press speculation suggested the sabotage could have been carried out by Israelis, anti-Iraqui Arabs, or even the French.

37. In another area of U.S.-French differences, agreement on a U.S. veto over re-export and reprocessing of nuclear fuel is required under the Nuclear Non-proliferation Act of 1978. The Americans supply nearly half of Western Europe's enriched uranium fuel used in generation of nuclear power and most of the fuel used in research reactors. France, however, has obtained approximately half of it LWR fuel enrichment from the USSR and after 1980 will become self-sufficient through operation of the Tricastin enrichment facility.

38. M. René Monory, Minister of Industry, in budgetary figures presented to the National Assembly. *Le Figaro*, 16 November 1977, and 8 February 1979.

39. the Schloesing Report. See *Le Nouvel Observateur*, November 18, 1977. According to estimates from the Institut économique et juridique de l'énergie de Grenoble, the price per KWH of nuclear electricity (10.56 to 11.36 centimes) was near that of coal (11.6 centimes) and this did not include costs of dismantling the reactors nor of nuclear waste treatment. *Le Monde*, 29 November 1977. However, official French figures indicates that nuclear power holds substantial cost advantages over other sources of electricity. See, e.g., Robert Lattès, 'Quelle stratégie énergétique pour la France?', Commissariat à l'énergie atomique, (mimeographed), Paris, 1979.

40. Lucas, p. 115. Though EDF also achieved a 'mastery' of the market. Ibid.

41. See, e.g., François Harrois-Monin and Alain Ledoux, 'Economie d'énergie: la France est en retard.' *Science et Vie*, Vol. 129, No. 716 (mai 1977), pp. 100–105 and 162. The authors make a compelling case that the extent of energy conservation has been limited and that in the absence of much more substantial investments in energy saving measures, a far greater program of conservation in industry (where savings have been marginal), and ultimately some adjustment in life style, France will fall far short of its 1985 goals and will face grave energy problems of availability and price in the following decades.

42. Joel Darmstadter, Joy Dunkerly and Jack Alterman, *How Industrial Societies Use Energy: A Comparative Analysis* (Baltimore: Resources for the Future and Johns Hopkins University Press, 1977), p. 5. Figures are for 1972.

43. Calculated from OECD figures, based on imports of 2.55 mbd in 1973 and 2.20 in 1978. See *OECD Economic Outlook*, No. 24, Paris, December 1978, p. 118.

44. *Le Monde*, 9 May 1979.

45. The savings in 1985 would be 25 mtoe instead of 45 mtoe. *Le Monde*, 24 February 1979. Saumon and Pusieux argue that major conservation efforts, changes in energy priorities, and shifts in types of industry could reduce French energy needs by as much as one-third in the year 2000. *Op. cit.*, p. 167.

46. These include extraction of the uranium, enrichment, reactor construction, reprocessing, and fast breeder technology.

47. For more optimistic assessments of the nuclear policy, see Robert Lattès, 'Perspectives énergétiques mondiales: synthèse d'études parues en 1976 et 1977,' B.I.S.T., Commissariat à l'Energie Atomique (Paris), No. 226, November/December 1977, and his Hambourg Conference paper, 'Some Key Aspects of Energy Strategies in France,' 9 May 1979. Conversely, a pessimistic and critical analysis may be found in the articles of Roger Garaudy and *les groupes Espérance*, *Le Monde*, 4, 5, 6 and 7 May 1979.

48. *Les chiffres clés de l'énergie* (1979), p. 31.

49. Cf. the lament of a member of the CERES (the major left-wing *tendance* within the Parti Socialiste) that the huge nuclear program makes France dependent on foreign sources for uranium, capital, export of reactors and retreatment facilities, and technical knowledge. He argues that for an autonomous nuclear industry France must diversify its energy resources and slow the pace of its nuclear program. See Yves Durrieu, 'Nucleaire et indépendence nationale,' *Repères*, No. 48, December 1977, p. 76.

50. The subject of constraints on a leftist government is developed at length in Robert J. Lieber, 'Energy, Political Economy and the West European Left: Problems of Constraint,' in Leon Hurwitz, ed., *Contemporary Perspectives on EEC Integration* (Westport, Ct.: Greenwood Press, 1979).

51. Saumon and Puiseux, pp. 167–169.

52. The measures allowed the elimination of import quotas, removal of price controls by 1980, and abandonment of the requirement that more than 50 percent of the domestic market must be supplied by French companies. However most imported oil would still be delivered in French tankers and the state would continue to monopolize petroleum imports. See *Le Monde*, 1 September 1978 and *The Economist*, 2 September 1978.

53. *Le Nouvel Observateur.* 11 September 1978, p. 26. Jeanneney was Minister of Industry from 1959 to 1962.

54. *Le Monde*, 22 and 31 August 1978.

55. An official of EDF, in an interview with the author, Paris, 27 May, 1979.

56. *Le Monde*, 22 August 1978. In January 1979, the government's share of the 2.72 franc per liter cost of premium gasoline was 68.7 percent. *Les chiffres clés de l'énergie* (1979, p. 42).

57. *OECD Economic Outlook* (Paris), No. 24, December 1978, p. 118.

58. Televised interview of President Giscard d'Estaing, Paris, 14 December 1977. French Embassy Press and Information Division, New York, 77/164.

Gaullism and Collective Bargaining: The Effect of the Fifth Republic on French Industrial Relations

Janice McCormick

The ambition of the social policy of de Gaulle's Republic has been to discover a third way between capitalism and communism that would transform social relations in France, gradually replacing "the spirit and fact of class struggle."[1] The various programs—*participation*, *intéressement*, *politique contractuelle*—for achieving this goal have all been vague. The means were to be the corporatist organization of competing groups in society, and the result the harmonization or pacification of social relations. Yet, after twenty years, many social groups remain unorganized or lack access to the decisional structures of the state,[2] and social harmony has not resulted.

De Gaulle appreciated the need for predictable, peaceable industrial relations, for like many American leaders, he recognized that as industrial production plays an increasingly important role in modern society, the need for predictable industrial relations to guarantee stable production grows concomitantly. The American theorist Clark Kerr has argued that "industrial society quite generally is highly disposed in favor of law and order. Aggressive conflicts between capital and labor are considered both undesirable and largely unnecessary..."[3] As a result, some rules of the game are usually established to limit conflict, especially in the work place; these rules differ from country to country.

In France, collective bargaining has played a minor role in regulating industrial relations, baffling most American theorists who had assumed the practice to be a universal element in the industrial relations systems in advanced capitalist democracies. State intervention through legislation and regulation as well as unilateral employer decision-making have been the most important

197

means for determining the conditions of work in France. Collective bargaining agreements have rarely been more than an inventory of those benefits already granted by law, and they have never included real wages. Industrial relations were politicized because the state, not the plant was the arena in which most important decisions were made.

In the early Fourth Republic, collective bargaining was stifled under the weight of extensive state *dirigisme*. The Collective Bargaining Act of 1946 granted the state control over most working conditions, including real and minimum wage levels. The 1946 Act established a hierarchy of negotiation—a national agreement was obligatory in an industry (*branche*) before local or regional agreements could be discussed—and any agreement was invalid without the signature of the Minister of Labor. Consequently, only ten national agreements were signed and these were in small industries of minor national importance.[4] In 1950, government control was loosened: wages were made negotiable; the obligatory hierarchy of negotiations was eliminated; and plant-level negotiations were permitted. Regional representatives of the labor ministry met with management and unions in many key industries to aid in the conclusion of agreements, but the results were disappointing. Many of the agreements were seen as minimal for the industry at a national, regional or local level. They did not lead to subsequent discussion. Negotiated industrial relations on a regular basis remained rare.

After the stabilization of the Fifth Republic, the state intervened to incite both employers and unions to negotiate at all levels. In 1967 Prime Minister Pompidou set a precedent for encouraging negotiations directly. He invited the union confederations and the CNPF to begin discussions in five issue areas for the conclusion of national inter-industry agreements. Apart from the Matignon agreement of 1936 and the unemployment insurance agreement of 1958, agreements at this level had been rare. Since the late sixties, however, inter-industry agreements have almost replaced state regulation, resolving many issues previously left to legislators.   Other areas of collective bargaining changed during the Gaullist period: the collective bargaining law was altered to facilitate plant-level negotiations, and the ministerial powers to extend a particular agreement to other industries was broadened.[5] The state recognized that "employers' and workers' organizations being directly affected by certain legislation are well-fitted to decide how it would operate and that when changes are sought, they can be introduced more readily if they are wanted by the parties concerned than if they are imposed from above."[6]

Optimistic studies of the late sixties applauded the "renaissance of negotiation" in France, pointing to a trend across industry for new, creative, noninstitutionalized forms and procedures and more frequent negotiation sessions.[7] Although the cases where the changes had occurred were scattered (industry and plant level agreements had grown the least), these authors felt that

198

this new trend toward collective bargaining would alter the entire pattern of French industrial relations; by the mid-seventies, however, it was clear that the changes were neither as permanent nor as pervasive as had been predicted. More recent studies have concluded that important changes have taken place, but not everywhere; as a result, France has not one but several systems of industrial relations.[8]

A brief survey of French industries demonstrates that virtually all have legally valid industry-wide collective bargaining agreements, yet some are over 25 years old, while others are renegotiated every few years. In some industries, unions and management have not met for ten years, while in others, they meet monthly.

Remnants of the older authoritarian model of industrial relations remain, even where collective bargaining has been more successful: often wage clauses and at times the entire agreement remain minimal for the industry; inter-industry agreements have raised as many problems as, or have merely replaced, legislated solutions. Changes in the collective bargaining law during the Gaullist period have not stimulated bargaining at the company or plant levels, where industrial relations problems have a particular urgency. The Gaullist *association* and *politique contractuelle* experiments have not altered the French industrial relations system significantly. Instead, Gaullist France possesses an industrial relations system with varying practices and very unequal results from industry to industry. This essay attempts to examine relations in the workplace and the means for determining the conditions of work in the Fifth Republic in an effort to account for this heterogeneity.

In particular, it examines why collective bargaining traditionally has been difficult in France, analyzes the dynamic of the relationship between the Gaullist state, industry, and the unions and the impact of government policy on the success of collective bargaining. Has Gaullist policy made a difference in the role collective bargaining plays in French industrial relations? If *not*, as this chapter argues, why?

POSSIBLE EXPLANATIONS

In most of the industrial relations literature, the French system reflects an overreliance on the state to legislate or regulate the conditions of work.[9] Several theories have been advanced to explain this weak role for collective bargaining. These are convergence, cultural, and ideological unionism arguments.

Convergence theorists argue that all nations will develop similar social and political systems over time, and thus, similar industrial relations. They posit a common unilinear evolution of the infrastructure of all societies, with industrialization as the motor. Affluence created by modernization tends to undermine political discipline and ideological orthodoxy, [10] and unions discovering a common interest with management seek a regular business-like relationship with them.

The French case does not fit that pattern. In their efforts to explain French particularism—reliance on the state and ideological unionism—sociologists such as Seymour Martin Lipset cite incomplete modernization and industrialization. Strong ideological unions tied to communist parties are a result of the pressures of slow and incomplete industrial development and lead naturally to blocked negotiations in industrial relations.[11]

A second group of theorists assign "national culture" a prime role in shaping the social relations of any given country. Where collective bargaining is the principal method of determining the conditions of work, they argue, particular cultural characteristics and attitudes prevail: a willingness to compromise, a tradition of participation in and recourse to voluntary associations, and democratic authority relations in society. Since French society does not possess these traits, the role of collective bargaining is predictably limited. As a result of the French fear of face-to-face relations, organizational life is weak and the problems of the workplace are settled through state intervention: the tendency of unions and management to look to political action to resolve their problems is reinforced.[12]

A third major explanation blames the resilience of ideology for French exceptionalism. If collective bargaining is weak in French industrial relations, the evolutionary cycle of unionism is the explanation.[13] The union movement itself and its ideology and tactics at a particular historical moment determine the character of industrial relations. Revolutionary or politically ideological unionism is characteristic of an early phase of the union movement. In a later or more mature phase of unionism, business unionism, collective bargaining and economic action dominate. These theories argue that if France has no collective bargaining, immature unionism is responsible.

These theories, useful to a point, fail to account for certain critical features of French industrial relations, most notably for their heterogeneity. Collective bargaining is by no means absent from the contemporary French scene: it is the principal method for determining the conditions of work in *some* French industries, but not in others. One research team counted six formal meetings of unions and management per month in the chemicals industry. The agenda was varied, including discussions of reduction of the hours of work, wages, hiring, etc. [14] In the furniture industry, on the other hand, the major unions have boycotted meetings with management for over four years. Furniture employers recently divided their association in two by types of production; they wanted to negotiate separate contracts for two groups of industries. The unions refused to come to the bargaining table. Instead, wages and working conditions have been determined by individual employers. To explain this heterogeneity, each of the suggested variables must be examined individually. As we shall see, convergence, culture and ideology are not sufficiently explanatory.

The convergence arguments are problematic. France is no longer at an earlier stage of industrialization. The French GNP has grown considerably throughout the Fifth Republic; rapid economic expansion and industrial concentration have brought France up to the productive and per capita income levels of other European countries.[15] Yet, despite Lipset's prediction, the CGT is still the dominant union and is still tied to the Communist party. Since collective bargaining is growing in importance in some French industries, the convergence argument seems to be fulfilled at least superficially; but national income distribution as a causal variable does not seem to be sufficient. For the argument to be made that a lag in the French industrial structure is responsible for weak collective bargaining, an intensive comparative study of French industries and industrial relations would be necessary. The convergence theorists have not done this.

The various cultural arguments are also open to challenge. If collective bargaining has been preempted by government intervention, why is the French cultural pattern no longer followed in all cases? Do union and management attitudes and cultural characteristics in negotiating industries differ from those in non-negotiating industries?

The clusters of ideological and attitudinal variables should be diametrically opposed in industries where collective bargaining has had greater or lesser success. This is not so: collective bargaining has had its greatest success and most innovative results in industries like steel, glass, cement, and oil refining where the unions—especially the CGT—are the strongest. Industries, such as furniture, food processing, and wood products, that are weakly organized by the "ideological unions" tend to have little or no collective bargaining.

Specific plant investigations and interviews with French unions and management have led to conclusions that like ideology, attitudes toward collective bargaining vary little, even where collective bargaining results vary drastically. As in most other countries, French unions see collective bargaining as a major part of a larger strategy for obtaining benefits for their members. Management, too, favors negotiation in the abstract, though some employers feared "revolutionary unionism"—the CGT and the CFDT—whose aims they perceived as the destruction of the country's economic machinery.[16] Yet, those unions were the weakest where the employers' fears were the greatest.

Cultural, convergence, and ideological unionism arguments, at best, offer incomplete explanations for the past weakness of collective bargaining in *all* French industries or its present success in some. This paper argues that:

1. ideological trade unions do negotiate in good faith under certain conditions;
2. the cultural pattern has not been the major barrier to collective bargaining in French industry;

3. and finally, although most French industries considered "modern" by Lipset's standards do bargain collectively—while the "least modern" do not—this is not so much a result of incomplete modernization as a consequence of the French legal framework for collective bargaining. Only industries with certain characteristics can meet the conditions of that framework.

This paper argues that the legal framework for collective bargaining in France has made collective bargaining especially difficult. The state has failed to establish clear procedural norms defining who will bargain, at what level and how often. In many cases, instead of relying on collective bargaining, the state has simply arrogated the right to settle industrial questions with its own legislation. Thus, it has reduced the potential benefits of collective bargaining for both unions and management while raising its costs. As a result, only some industries have been able to establish a stable collective bargaining system.

Within the French legal framework for collective bargaining, what Dunlop has called "environmental factors"—technology, market and budgetary constraints, and power relations[17]—seem to be more important in distinguishing those industries where collective bargaining has been a success. Specific industrial characterics encourage employer unity perceived as necessary to the economic survival of the industry: high investment costs, greater industrial concentration, and an organized work force are the major stimuli for employer cohesion. Given the legal structure, such cohesion is a precondition for industry-wide collective bargaining. In industries whose structure is more dispersed, capital investment lower, and the work force less organized, employer unity is more difficult; as a result, so is collective bargaining. The legal and industrial structures are the primary determinants of the character of a particular industrial relations system.

In order to test this argument, the legal framework for collective bargaining must be examined closely first. What are the specific rules or procedures that would facilitate or impede collective bargaining?

Second, the industrial relations of several industries must be studied carefully. Union and management attitudes, ideology and industrial characteristics will be examined to determine how each might influence the success or failure of collective bargaining.

Finally, the correlation between the legal framework and the industrial structures must be demonstrated.

The present study, part of a larger project, will attempt to test these hypotheses.

ASPECTS OF THE FRENCH COLLECTIVE BARGAINING LAWS

The state may determine the form that collective bargaining should take, the substance to be discussed, or both. In the United States, the government has been most concerned with determining the form. The American National Labor Relations Act establishes the procedures for identifying the "appropriate bargaining unit"—usually a plant or company—and then for holding elections on a question of whether its employees wish to be represented by one or more petitioning unions or do not wish to be represented .[18] A union that receives a majority vote is entitled by law to recognition as the exclusive collective bargaining agent for all employees in that unit. France has no state-established structures to define the size and scope of the bargaining unit or the parties to the bargain. Instead, this is determined by the employer signature on the particular agreement: an individual employer may sign for his plant, or a leader of a trade association or confederation for all members of his organization. This legal clause makes decisions about the size and scope of the bargaining unit tactical choices of employers before they reach the bargaining table. The unions have only indirect leverage, political pressure on the state or the employer.

In the past, individual employers as well as trade associations in some industries—for example rubber and wood packaging—have based their continued participation in employers' associations on the nature of the agreements signed by the association. In some companies, a worker cannot know that his employer is a member of one of these associations and therefore that a particular agreement applies to him except through recourse to the labor courts.

As union representation is not exclusive, who will negotiate for the workers is a perpetual point of contention. Agreements signed by one union are binding on all employees within that bargaining unit irrespective of their union affiliation. Which unions will negotiate and which will sign are thus elements of both unions' and managements' strategies.

The major unions—CGT, CFDT, CGC, FO, CFTC—are legally recognized as nationally "representative" and therefore qualified to sign agreements binding for all. Other unions (company unions or the CFT) occasionally obtain recognition as "representative". In some cases, agreements have been signed by a union whose membership includes fewer than 3% of the workers in the bargaining unit. Conflicts between these minority unions, or even FO or CFTC on the one hand and the CGT or the CFDT on the other hand, are frequent and sometimes violent. This embitters the majority unions and defeats the purpose of collective bargaining. Instead of encouraging the development of collective bargaining, these legal provisions make it very difficult to institutionalize the parties to the bargain—which is important for stable collective bargaining.

The state extension procedure, unique to France, presents the same problems: instead of encouraging the organization of the employers and the unions, the state acts as their proxy. Following a specific procedure, the Minister of Labor can extend any negotiated agreement by decree to all employers and employees of a particular geographic region, or under more limited conditions, beyond that industry or region. Created under the Popular Front as part of an effort to establish uniform working conditions and incite employers to negotiate,[19] extension in fact had the opposite effect. In many industries, employers' associations will sign a national agreement only if it will take effect after the complicated and lengthy extension procedures have been completed and the decree signed. As many employers are not members of the associations, extension protects members from unfair competition from non-members who would not implement the agreement and who, consequently, would have lower labor costs; also, extension discourages membership in the associations, since non-members need not pay the costs of membership to receive the collective good—no competition in wage rates, working conditions of benefits. Often many clauses of the agreements—especially wage rates—are obsolete or have been improved by law by the time the agreement is extended. Thus, extension has become a crutch as well as a handicap for poorly organized professions, and at the same time a barrier to collective bargaining.

Finally, as mentioned by most analysts of French industrial relations, many benefits obtained through negotiation in other countries are obtained through the state in France—paid vacations, retirement benefits, etc. As the benefits to be had from collective bargaining are reduced, the incentive for the unions to press for negotiations is also reduced, while the incentive for political pressure on the state is increased.

The legal framework for collective bargaining in France has a multitude of other problems. In the end, it has tended to complicate the determination of the parties to the bargain, exacerbate problems of collective behavior for both unions and employers, and encourage further reliance on the state to solve problems of industrial relations.

To demonstrate the impact of this web of rules on collective bargaining, the problems of business-union relations in two industries will be examined. These industries with opposite characteristics—cement and wood products—exhibit varied collective bargaining procedures and results, enabling us to determine why some industries bargain collectively and others do not.

In the cement industry, collective bargaining procedures are institutionalized; employers and the major representative unions meet frequently to examine problems as they arise. The results of collective bargaining discussions in cement are often innovative; agreements deal with subjects not previously treated by law and in some cases real wage increases are negotiated.

In the wood product industries, the procedures are non-institutionalized or irregular: the timing of meetings for discussion is often erratic; the legitimacy of the negotiating partners is often questioned; and the meetings take place only in times of crisis. The results of negotiation are also mediocre: industry wage minima are closely tied to the SMIC and the conditions of work are those granted by law.

Collective bargaining agreements, union, management and national press articles, interviews with government representatives, industry managers, trade association leaders, union delegates and in some cases workers in the industries were consulted for material concerning collective bargaining procedures and results. Trade journals, shareholders' reports, government publications and other secondary sources were used to study the history of the industries' restructuring and production results.

THE CASES

The French cement industry, fifth ranked in the world, is composed of fourteen companies of which the top four control over 90 percent of the production. It employs approximately 15,000, is a capital intensive industry, and is considered by economist J. Chardonnet one of the most dynamic industries in France.[21]

The procedural norms for collective bargaining in cement closely resemble a pattern of continuous bargaining at the industry level,[22] and the results are among the most innovative in France. For example, cement was among the first to negotiate extended maternity leaves, task restructuring and real wage increases. A very elaborate structure of institutions brings together regularly the major representative unions—CGT, CFDT, FO, CGC—and the SNFCC (*Syndicat national des fabricants de ciments et chaux*), the cement employers' association. The *Commission paritaire plénière*, made up of 100 members, sets the agenda for discussions for the year. The *commission de négociation*, about 25 representatives, sets out the positions of the various groups on a particular problem. The *groupe d'etudes* negotiates any differences. Minimum wage rates are negotiated quarterly, and to reduce wage drift (which is very high in France), minima are gradually being set close to real wages.

The wood products industries stand in contrast to cement. The different sectors—wood packaging, semi-finished wood products, and finished wood products manufacturers—are united only by the raw material they work. The wood packagers manufacture cheese boxes, wine casks, fruit and vegetable crates, as well as other food packaging in wood. The semi-finished wood products industries supply construction and furniture industries with materials including plywood, particle and fiber board, pre-fabricated doors, walls and window frames. The finished wood products industries are the traditional crafts of wood floor making, carpentry, tools and other objects made of wood. Together these subsectors include about 100,000 employees.

Despite enormous diversity of products, structures and technologies, these industries have been united through their primary trade associations (such as the Union of Cheese Box Manufacturers, or the National Syndicate of Oak and Chestnut Floor Makers, etc.) in a national confederation, the *Confédération nationale des industries du bois* (CNIB). The CNIB has attempted to coordinate wages and industrial relations policy, but specific wage rates and benefits have divided the industries. The most recent collective bargaining agreement was signed in 1956, and is largely obsolete; the wage rate discussions have not fared better. Wages are among the lowest in France, and the minimum wage rates rise with the SMIC. Many subsectors have had serious problems over the legitimate representatives of both labor and management. Neither procedural nor substantive norms are institutionalized. Industrially and socially it is a *secteur délaissé*.

However, in one subsector of the wood products industries industrial relations are changing. The employers of the semi- finished wood products industries—plywood, particle board, fiber board, and industrialized carpentry (doors, walls, etc.)—withdrew from the CNIB in 1968 over its position during the May events; more heavily unionized, and thus affected during those events, semi-finished product employers responded to their workers' demands. In 1972, citing common problems of heavy investments, marketing, and exports which distinguished their subsector from the other CNIB subsectors, they formed the FILB (*Fédération des industries lourdes du bois*), adhering directly to the CNPF. Since 1972, this sector had made an apparently sincere effort to institutionalize collective bargaining procedures. Plywood, fiber and particle board are negotiating an agreement which includes a very innovative wage clause much like the wage scale negotiated but never implemented in the Parisian metals industries in the 1970's. The industrial relations system of the FILB industries is moving toward regular collective bargaining procedures and innovative substantive norms leaving behind its companion wood industries. How can we explain this shift? How did one industry overcome the legal barriers to collective bargaining?

Just as the employers are better organized in cement and in the FILB industries, so are workers. Less than 20% of the French work force is unionized,[23] but the cement industry figure approaches 75%. About 75% of all unionized cement workers belong to the CGT, about 15% to the CFDT and the remainder to the CFTC, CGC, and FO.

Due to the dispersed, rural and weakly-industrial character of most wood products industries, unions have had more difficulty organizing the workers. The FILB industries, especially particle and fiber board, are the most heavily unionized of the subsectors of the wood products industry.[24]

The problems with the French legal framework for collective bargaining have been resolved in cement, are beginning to be overcome in semi-finished wood products, and remain barriers to collective bargaining in all other wood products industries. Only industries with very particular industrial characteristics have been able to meet the conditions set by the legal framework for the institutionalization of collective bargaining.

The industrial characteristics of cement made employer unity essential for

economic survival of the industry. In the 1930's, this unity came at the initiative of the employers. Under Vichy and during the immediate post-war
period, the state assumed the functions of company reorganization, product
distribution, pricing, and investment financing. In the late 1960s, the
employers, with the urging of the banks, stimulated reorganization of the industry's only remaining disorderly market—the Paris region.

The French cement industry is homogeneous, highly concentrated and has
increased six-fold in production in the past 25 years.[25] It is highly capital intensive; cement has the highest per capita investments of any manufacturing industry after oil refining.[26]

Specific characteristics of the product are responsible for these high costs.
The raw materials from which cement is manufactured and their excavation
represent under 10 percent of the product's net cost, whereas the energy used
in the production process accounts for over 40 percent of the net cost. Large
firms can economize by automating the arrival of fuel to the kilns and augmen-
ting kiln capacities. Rather than risk the loss of the heavy initial capital investment, cement employers decided early to organize the market.

The first national organization of cement employers, formed in 1891, was a
confederation of regional associations to coordinate product markets and protect the industry against state intervention. To meet the demands of World
War I, the state reinforced the Chamber of Cement and Lime Manufacturers,
and the Cement Chamber became one of "the most advanced from an
organizational perspective; ...the Chamber grouped all of the primary associations and synthesized their work."[27] The wartime state not only sanctioned but
solidified employer collusion in the cement industry.

With the economic crisis of the 1930s, the construction boom collapsed. Faced with overcapacity, the federation of cement manufacturers took a new role
organizing market agreement among competing companies. Under the wat-
chful but approving eye of the state, the French cement cartel was created,
"destined to discipline a disorderly and ruinous competition by arranging for
the distribution of cement under the best transport conditions."[28] Within each
region, prices were set, production was reduced, and import quotas set by the
state to protect border areas. The first wave of "restructuring" had begun at
the industry's own initiative. The result was concentration and the disappearance of many small firms. One industry spokesman claimed that "the efforts of this well thought-out organization showed themselves rapidly and
durably: for the producers, the opening of more regular outlets and the
stabilization of prices with some slight rises in areas in which the decline had
been the greatest, for the consumers, the refound possibility of getting certain
estimates and the insuring of supplies in a balanced economy."[29]

Although the cement manufacturers association and its cement cartel were
formally disbanded in 1940, the cartel structures and trade association

207

representatives reappeared as the core of Vichy's *Comité d'organisation des ciments et chaux*. Their problem, however, shifted from overcapacity to under-capacity. The new priorities were rationing scarce resources and regulating regional prices, controlling the shipments and uses of the product.

Due to their activities during the Vichy period, several cement employers feared nationalization after the Liberation.[30] Several were forced to resign their posts, but their capital remained untouched. In the 1947 Plan, cement was a high priority among "the few critical sectors on which subsequent development of all other industries depended."[31] The *Fédération nationale des fabricants des ciments et chaux* emerged solidified. The state continued to regulate prices and shipments, but also provided financing for investments. The results were astounding: the industry further concentrated and production increased greatly to meet the post-war demand. Except in the North, parts of the East and Paris region, where there were intermittant price wars and financial losses among the smaller firms, the industry was relatively stabilized and dropped from sight as a high government priority.

Indicative of this stability, the national federation reorganized in 1954. The specific product chambers were abolished and a national center for economic and technical information was created. The stronger SNFCC was also less defensive.

Another wave of concentration took place after 1968, this time at the in-itiative of the industry and the banks.[32] The number of companies was reduced again through absorption by one of the four leading groups and competition has been reduced in the Paris region through an entente between the two top producer groups in the industry. Although neither group enjoys a monopoly of production in any particular region as in the past, there is litle competition bet-ween them. Each group is represented within the SNFCC where policy is coor-dinated and there is considerable interpenetration of subsidiaries.[33]

Changes in industrial relations in the cement industry echoed these changes in industrial structure. Due to a combination of union pressures and industrial imperatives, the organized employers decided very early to negotiate. After the passage of the 1936 laws regarding collective bargaining and arbitration, twenty-five regional agreements for manual workers and three regional agreements for technicians were signed.[34] Wage rates were determined regionally in relation to the regional cement price and the regional chambers negotiated separately any differences within their region.

After the enactment of the 1950 Collective Bargaining Act, negotiation began for new agreements for the industry. In 1952, three were signed: a na-tional agreement for all manual workers except those in the Lyon area; a na-tional agreement for all technicians and lower management again excluding the Lyon area; and a regional agreement for all cement employees in the Lyon area. Ciments Vicat, where wages and benefits were lower, was the major obstacle to a national agreement. But by the early 1960s Vicat had expanded outside the Lyon area and isolation no longer had advantages. Three national agreements were signed by 1963: manual workers; technicians; and engineers and supervisory personnel. Since then, national negotiations have been uninterrupted. Approximately ten supplementary agreements have been concluded and in 1976 a new, innovative national agreement was signed. Many social experiments have been undertaken in the industry, including autonomous work groups and early retirement programs.

But there are still collective bargaining problems in cement, especially in two procedural areas—the size of the bargaining unit, and which unions will bargain. In the 1960s many plant and company agreements were signed. Since 1968, the SNFCC has refused all plant-level negotiations, except those adapting national agreements to specific conditions. Employers felt that the unions were using plant-level negotiations to extract different benefits in each plant, then to push their extension to all others, in a strategy of "fragmentation-extension."[35] Although this assessment of union strategy is quite accurate, within the French legal framework for collective bargaining, the employers hold the key to determining the size of the bargaining unit in function of their own strategies. The unions' powers in this area are limited.

Given the strength of the CGT and the CFDT, it was obvious which unions would bargain in cement. In 1973, when one CFDT section rejoined the CFTC and asked to be present at all discussions and negotiation sessions, the CGT and the CFDT protested. The SNFCC was embarassed,[36] not wanting to make the negotiations more cumbersome or to be forced to sign an agreement with a union that represents a tiny minority. Nevertheless, the CFTC has remained present, protected by its legally "most representative" status.

In spite of these problems, the system of agreements is dense. High investments and the necessity of continuous production made the potential costs of not recognizing or negotiaton with the unions too high. The potential threat of a prolonged strike brought the SNFCC to the bargaining table. In general, "as investment per worker grows, management becomes more concerned with the consent of the employees who work with this investment";[37] collective bargaining and negotiation were the means that the cement industry chose for eliciting that consent, even with the so-called "ideological" CGT.

Just as the presence of certain industrial characteristics—high investments, concentration, and complex technology—made employer unity essential for the economic viability of the cement industry; their absence in the wood products industries has made employer unity and thus collective bargaining difficult.

The industrial characteristics as well as industrial relations of the wood products industries are diametrically opposed to those of cement. Wood products industries use heterogeneous production methods, produce diverse products and on the average, per capita investments are one half those of cement. The finished wood products industries have remained artisanal; over 90 percent are small workshops employing under ten workers. Since the post-war housing boom, industrialized production of floors, doors, windows, and walls, for prefabricated units as well as original construction has flourished, often displacing the skilled workshops. The wood packaging industries employ few skilled workers and often produce for farms in the vicinity. Due to competition from paper and plastic industries, they too are finding survival difficult. The semi-finished product industries—plywood fiber board, and particle board—are the most recent, industrialized and prosperous of the wood industries.

Employers in each trade were organized in separate, autonomous trade associations in the 1860s. Although many employers were not members, the number of primary wood and furniture associations registered under the 1884 law grew over 400 percent between 1893-1920. In 1920, 108,815 wood and furniture manufacturers employed 377,352 workers, and 200,534 artisans worked alone. According to one writer of the period,

> "this situation explains why the corresponding owners' associations for a long time have had a remote influence within the union organization; the isolated manufacturer and the workman are infinitely less accessible than the owners of large companies, for the collaboration and common exploration of professional questions; workers' questions and problems, moreover, hardly exist for them."[38]

Furniture employers united in one large confederation in 1921 for commercial expansion, but wood products manufacturers did not follow suit.

Those problems of employers unity—small plant size, and as a result less interest in common discussion of social questions and technological innovation—remain for many wood products industries fifty years later. The Vichy *Comité d'organisation* was the employers' first experience with unity and in the immedite post-war period the *Confédération nationale des industries du bois* (CNIB) a confederation of small trade associations, was formed.

From 1935 to the late 1950s, the wood industries were in crisis. One observer noted three reasons: the high price of wood, due to an excessive number of small, competing sawmills which for lack of timber were not working at full capacity; a drop in the use of wood, due to its higher price and competition from plastics and backward production methods.[39]

For consruction, cheaper substitutes were found in industrially synthesized wood—plywood, fiber and particle board—that could be produced using cheaper qualities of timber or even sawdust. While many traditional artisans of housing and housing interiors were still working with raw wood, the newer industries were driving many of them out of business. Plywood—which requires the least industrial transformation of the semi-finished wood products—was first made in France in the 1920s, but experienced its greatest expansion after the Liberation, with its wide uses for furniture, building carpentry, and construction.

Fiber board, made from wood pulp and pressed at high pressure with natural wood resins added, was introduced in France in the late 1930s and has remained the quasi-monopoly of one company, Isorel, whose name is synonymous with the product in France. Particle board, first manufactured in France with the product. Particle board, first manufactured in France in 1952, is made of small particles of wood mixed with a synthetic glue and pressed into sheets of varying densities.

The particle and fiber board industries require the highest investments of the wood products industries for the shredders, the presses and their automation, although the per capita investments are only a fraction of those of cement. Production is continuous, automated and the unskilled labor force is minimal.

With the new cheaper synthesized materials, the production of other construction materials was stimulated: doors, windows, interior paneling, and prefabricated homes and buildings, all were now being mass-produced to meet the increasing demand. On the other hand, the demand for decorative mouldings, and framings for interiors declined and many of these artisinal undertakings have disappeared. Those remaining are producing for a high cost luxury market. Wooden flooring has had the same difficulty surviving the competition offered by the newer, less expensive products, and is also now a luxury item.

The role of wood packaging industries has declined since the war. Lightweight wooden crates for fruit and vegetables are being replaced by cardboard and recyclable plastic; cheese boxes are suffering the same fate. Only the wooden pallet industry (wooden platforms for forklift mechanization of storage) has rapidly developed. The wood packaging industry employs 87 percent manual laborers and is technologically simple requiring little transformation; the wood is sawed or sliced and then nailed, stapled or glued together to its necessary form. This subsector has the largest number of companies (30 percent) and employees (22 percent) in the industry and makes only 18 percent of all the sales in the wood products industries.[40]

In the late 1940s the government and the unions were pushing for industry level negotiations. The CNIB urged its members to remain united: no plant agreements were to be discussed as long as there was no national sectoral agreement.[41] After the passage of the 1950 laws freeing wages and facilitating collective bargaining, the CNIB took the position that general clauses would be discussed by the Confederation for all subsectors; wages would be determined regionally by inter-wood industry agreements. As they were stronger in some regions and in some industries than in others, the CGT and the CFTC demanded one national collective bargaining agreement. In 1953, the Labor Minister summoned a Mixed Commission of unions, management and state representatives, which concluded that there would be one national agreement per subsector; wage rates would be regional and close ties would be maintained between subsectors to avoid "any stances that could disturb another industry."[42]

In the plywood industry and the mechanized wood industries (*travail mécanique du bois*) which include sawmills, all packaging industries except cheese boxes, and a few minor industries, two agreements were signed and extended in 1955–6. An agreement for industrialized carpentry was signed in 1956 but not extended. In the new fiber and particle board industries, collective bargaining had a difficult beginning. Industry level negotiations never went beyond the general clauses; instead most major companies negotiated their own agreements to adopt the general causes to the particular conditions of their plant and to set company wage and benefits policies. The few particle and fiber board industries that did not sign agreements applied either the TMB or the plywood agreement, since most manufactured these products as well.

By the mid-sixties, there had been few changes in the original agreements. Wage rates remained unchanged, although the employers association regularly recommended specific increases to their members. The particle board and fiber board industries continually tried to negotiate a national industry-wide agreement to equalize the labor costs among the companies, but due to the insistence of certain employers on the presence of the confédération française du travail the negotiations flourished only where the CFT was absent. Differences in labor costs among firms grew. In 1976, the FILB resolved the CFT problems and began to pressure reticent employer-members to negotiate with their unions. Discussions for industry-wide agreements have resumed, with considerable success.

In the wood packaging industries, the situation has worsened. Their federation was among the first to express dissatisfaction with the CNIB's negotiations. It adhered to the TMB agreement as a federation, withdrew several years later complaining that the different subsectors had different labor costs and therefore different positions on the wage increases. It decided to negotiate itself but litle has come of its efforts; it has refused the presence of the CGT and the CFDT at the negotiations, and no agreements have been signed.

The wood packaging federation (UNEB) then set out to define a coherent general industrial policy to respond to the crisis of declining demand. It called for the creation of industrial groupings of small firms to organize marketing and production to meet the crisis of the industry. Efforts of this sort have been partially successful in packaging as well as in other finished wood products industries. But this market organization is solving only the least critical of the industry's problems. Other serious problems remain: the general decline in demand for many products and consequent need for reconversions of its industrial activity; the need for technical progress and modernization of production

methods, and in some cases larger and more profitable plants. Market groupings do not address these problems. In such conditions, collective bargaining
can only be difficult.

Collective bargaining in the wood industries has had two different fates. In
those industries where investments and production costs are high and the work
force is more unionized—FILB industries—collective bargaining procedures are
becoming more secure and its results innovative. Where the investments—and
usually the plant size—are small, collective bargaining procedures and results
are poor; in these industries (finished wood products and wood packaging) the
future of collective bargaining is not bright.

Under a legal framework that emphasizes industry-wide rather than plant or
company-level bargaining, industries with characteristics similar to those of
finished wood products and wood packaging will continue to have difficulty
bargaining collectively. If collective bargaining has had a different fate in the
cement and semi-finished wood product industries, this is not due to more
positive cultural attitudes or ideologies; the ideological CGT and CFDT are the
major negotiators for workers. Nor is it directly because these industries are
more modern. Instead, collective bargaining is more institutionalized in these
industries because they are sufficiently well-organized and motivated to
establish their own collective bargaining procedures, and to overcome the barriers set by the French legal framework. Only through unity within their profession could they guarantee an equal market for labor and equal labor costs while
responding to union demands for participation in the determination of the
conditions of employment.

In other industries with other industrial characteristics, employer organization is more difficult and unions are weaker. These industries will never be able
to meet the terms of French collective bargaining law.

CONCLUSION

For more regular collective bargaining in industries with other industrial
characteristics, the legal framework would have to be altered. This, however, is
not likely to happen. Neither the government, nor the employers' association,
nor even the trade unions in the Fifth Republic have had an interest in such a
change. The Gaullist government, already relying on a shrinking electoral base,
is trapped by its social and class alliances; the Majority will not order small
employers to alter their industrial relations radically, as they are too important
for its political success. For similar reasons, employers have their own internal
divisions—smaller vs. larger employers, etc—and have more to gain by the
greater flexibility of the weakly institutionalized collective bargaining system.
Although the unions, especially the CGT and the CFDT, are weaker in some
respects under the present system, they also enjoy greater flexibility of action.
Under existing agreements, they enjoy the right to call a strike at the plant,

company or industry levels *at any time*, even before a contract expires. They can call for revison of the conditions of the agreement at any time. And the continuing importance of state intervention in industrial relations means that they can always use political as well as industrial pressure to achieve their goals.

If Gaullism has had relatively little impact on the establishment of negotiation in French industry, this may have been due to the lack of unions and management in such a change. More likely, it was never one of the real aims of Gaullism.

NOTES

1. Philip Williams and Martin Harrison, *Politics and Society in de Gaulle's Republic* (Garden City, New York: Anchor Books, 1971), p. 358.

2. Philippe Schmitter, "Still a Century of Corporatism?", *Review of Politics* (January, 1974), p. 85-132.

3. Clark Kerr, "Industrial Conflict and its Mediation," in *Labor Management in Industrial Society* (Garden City, New York: Anchor Books, 1964), p. 167.

4. Gerard Adam, Jean-Daniel Reynaud and Jean-Maurice Verdier, *La Négociation collective en France* (Paris: Les Editions ouvrières, 1972), chapter 6.

5. See Michel Despax, *Conventions collectives du travail, Traité du Droit du travail*, volume 7 (Paris: Dalloz, 1966, p. 48; and see also the discussion below of the characteristics of the extension procedures.

6. Yves Delamotte, "Recent Collective Bargaining Trends in France," *International Labor Review* (April 1971), p. 366.

7. See the work of Adam, *et al.*, and Delamotte, cited above.

8. Gérard Adam and Jean-Daniel Reynaud, *Conflits de travail et changement social* (Paris: Presses universitaires de France, 1978), p. 77.

9. The sources cited in footnotes 11 through 14 are good examples of this type of argument.

10. Clark Kerr, *Industrialism and Industrial Man* (New York: Oxford University Press, 1964).

11. Seymour Martin Lipset, "Socialism—Left and Right, East and West," *Confluence* (Summer 1958), pp. 173-194.

12. Michel Crozier, *The Bureaucratic Phenomenon* (Chicago: University of Chicago Press, 1964), p. 257.

13. See especially Robert F. Hoxie, *Trade Unionism in the United States* (New York: Appleton and Company, 1971); Selig Perlman, *A Theory of the Labor Movement* (New York: Macmillan, 1928); and Richard Lester, *As Unions Mature* (Princeton, New Jersey: Princeton University Press, 1958).

14. Adam et al., *La Negociation*, p. 24.

15. See the conclusions of J.-J. Carré, P. Dubois and E. Malinvaud, *La Croissance française: Un essai d'analyse economique causale de l'aprés guerre* (Paris: Seuil, 1972).

16. Interviews conducted with the leaders of the employers' federations, Spring 1977.

17. John T. Dunlop, *Industrial Relations Systems*, (New York: Holt and Company, 1958), p. viii.

18. Seyfarth, Shaw, Faiweatherand Geraldson, Attorneys at law, *Labor Relations and the Law in France and the United States* (Ann Arbor: Graduate School of Business Administration, University of Michigan, 1972), p. 206.

19. G.H. Camerlynck and Gérard Lyon-Caen, *Droit du Travail* (Paris: Dalloz, 1975), p. 570.

20. These industries were selected on the basis of a categorization of the dimensions of collective bargaining in Geoffrey Ingham, *Strikes and Industrial Conflict: Britain and Scandanavia* (London: Macmillan, 1974).

21. Jean Chardonnet, *l'Economie Française*, Tome II, *Les Grandes Industries* Part II (Paris: Dalloz, 1974), chapter 3.

22. This pattern is best described in Adam *et al.*, *Négociation*, chapter 9.

23. Jean-Daniel Reynaud, *Les Syndicats en France*, volume one (Paris: Seuil, 1975); see the description on pages 139-236.

24. The exact percentages of unionization were unobtainable, but the trade union federation leaders as well as managers in the industries all agreed on this point.

25. Chardonnet, p. 101.

26. Ministère de l'Industrie et de la Recherche, *Les Structures industrielles Françaises, 1973 Matériaux de Construction* (Paris: La Documentation Française, 197), p. 10.

27. etienne Villey, *l'Organisation professionnelle des Employeurs dans l'industrie française* (Paris: Libraire Félix Alcan, 1923), p. 37.

28. Robert Fabre, "l'Evolution de l'industrie cimentiére française sur le plan professionnel et technique," *Revue des Matériaux de Construction et de Travaux Publics* (November- December 1955), p. 24.

29. Fabre, p. 34.

30. René Domenger, "Les Trusts du ciment, *Economie et Politique* (January 1956), p. 57.

31. John H. McArthur and Bruce Scott, *Industrial Planning in France*, (Boston: Harvard University School of Business Administration, 1969), p. 406.

32. François Morin, *La Structure financiére du capitalisme français* (Paris: Calmann-Lévy, 1974), pp. 245-249.

33. Each of the top four cement groups have stock in minor cement companies; in 1978, *all* of the fourteen cement producers in France were at least partially owned by one of the big four.

34. Fabre, p. 26.

35. Christian Morel, "Les Stratégies du negociations dans l'Entreprise," *Sociologie du Travail* (October-December, 1977), pp. 362-382.

36. Their embarrassment was first admitted to me by a representative of the SNFCC. The trade union delegates openly acknowledged this to me in later interviews.

37. Clark Kerr, "Industrial Peace and the Collective Bargaining Environment," in *Labor and Management in Industrial Society* (Garden City, New Jersey: Anchor Books, 1964), p. 152.

38. Villey, p. 35.

39. "L'Industrie Française du Bois," *Notes et etudes documentaires*, Number 2073 (September 13, 1955), pp. 13-14.

40. Ministère de l'Industrie et de la Recherche, *Les Structures Industrielles Françaises: Travail Mécanique du Bois* (Paris: Documentation Française, 1975), p. 32-5.

41. *Caisses et Emballages en Bois*, Revue de la Fédration nationale de caisses et emballages en bois de france, (1949-1950); see especially the editorials.

42. *Caisses et emballages en bois*, (1955).

The Fifth Republic and Education: Modernity, Democracy, Culture

Paul A. Gagnon

PRELUDE: RESISTANCE PLANS

Under Nazi occupation, Frenchmen sustained themselves with visions of a new and just society, modern, competent and more democratic than France had known, with a national system of education that would reflect and promote that society. The first program to renovate public schools was set forth by a special commission of Charles de Gaulle's Algiers government in 1944 and took final form in the famous Langevin-Wallon proposal of 1947. Like most French programs for education, it was explicit about the purposes of schooling—preparation for work, for active citizenship, for personal cultivation—and about how each was to be made democratic.

Democratizing career education required open access to technical and professional training at all levels, and equal chances to succeed at it. The Algiers plan made secondary education free and universal, so that new talent could be drawn from 'the whole people.'[1] Similarly, the Langevin-Wallon project called for new technical and professional schools at the upper secondary and postsecondary levels, together with democratized universities and *grandes écoles*.[2]

Democratic schooling for citizenship and personal culture called for similar equality. The education of Frenchmen for public affairs and private life was to be equal in content and quality. No longer could secondary educaton be a matter of 'feudal caste,' said the Algiers Plan. France would have public secondary schools in which the ordinary worker would study history, logic and philosophy in order to 'comprehend all the great questions that life poses to man.'[3] To this end, they and the Langevin-Wallon committee proposed a common middle

216

school for all, to replace the system of primary education for the masses and secondary for the few which had persisted since the Revolution. But the Langevin-Wallon project was turned down and the Fourth Republic, of which so much was expected, made little progress.[4] In 1958, when Charles de Gaulle returned to power, educational reforms conceived under his wartime government fourteen years earlier had not yet been carried out.

THE FIFTH REPUBLIC: AN OVERVIEW

The Fifth Republic, as in other matters, put its greater authority and resources behind plans already developed under the Fourth. Its first twenty years produced drastic change in the look and substance of French education. The pace of rising enrollments and expenditures was unprecedented for France and among the highest in the Western world. When the Fourth Republic disappeared in 1958, French universities enrolled 180,600 students, up from 97,000 in 1945, from 135,700 in 1950.[5] Twenty years later, university enrollment was 820,000 and all postsecondary programs well over a million.[6] Secondary education was extended to age 16 universally, enrollment rising from 1958's 1,350,000 to more than 4,000,000 in 1977-78.[7] In 1952, in mid-Fourth Republic, the budget for public education at all levels was 2.2 billion francs, 7.21 percent of the total national budget and 2.02 percent of the gross national product. By 1958, the Fourth Republic had lifted these figures only to 4.85 billion francs, 10.3 percent of the total budget and 2.57 percent of the gross national product. France lagged considerably behind most industrialized countries.[8] Since 1958, French spending for education has reached 50 billion francs, amounting to 18.5 percent of the budget and 3.4 percent of a much larger national product, putting France (with Sweden, Canada, Denmark, and the United States) in the front ranks of expenses per capita.[9]

Other changes are also typical of advanced industrial societies since the Second World War. Curricular design and student choice have gradually shifted from traditional humanist subjects, Greek, Latin, philosophy, early history and literature, toward the social sciences, the natural sciences and technology, at upper secondary and postsecondary levels. More students from moderate and lower-middle income families complete the baccalaureate and enter higher education. Working class students, rural and urban, lag behind. Their numbers are higher, as expansion is universal, but they form only a small proportion of the school population above the age of sixteen.[10] Finally, in common with other advancing technological societies, the French have been hearing and repeating an instrumentalist rhetoric of education, American-style, which justifies schooling primarily as the open road to prosperity and personal advancement.[11] These trends were evident in the mid-1950s, when the needs of an expanding modern economy pressed themselves upon the educational planners of the Fourth Republic. As foreseen in Algiers, France was short of scientific and technical personnel, particularly at the middle levels of research, development and management.

By 1958, little had been accomplished except to crowd twice as many students into buildings and curricula little changed from those of the late Third Republic. Several scaled-down versions of the Langevin-Wallon reform had emerged since 1947, but the infirmities and distractions of the Fourth Republic, its shortage of revenue amid pressing needs, and the leverage of vested interests had defeated each one.[12] The task of the Fifth Republic, as de Gaulle put it, was to marry the twentieth century, lest France be its victim. But it would be a modern marriage of equality; France would remain France. Nowhere has this been more evident than in education. On the one hand, technological society dictated advanced vocational and professional training for much of the working population. In gearing her school system to this end, France resembled all other modern societies; she looked to them for models. But she pursued the two other purposes of education—citizenship and culture—in a jealously-guarded French manner, out of a tradition evolved from the legacies of the ancient and medieval worlds, the Renaissance, the Jesuits and the Revolution. At the turn of the century, Charles Péguy, patron saint of the Resistance, had spoken for it, that humanist, Christian Jacobinism, true to the past and the dead, embodying human virtues essential to any society fit to live in.[13]

HIGHER EDUCATION: REVOLUTION AND REALITY

As the Fifth Republic worked to bring Resistance plans to life, higher education drew the most attention, culminating in the events of May 1968 and the reforms that followed. The first decade of expansion in postsecondary education was ill-managed. The press of time and numbers, social demands and economic needs, made long range planning difficult. Change was contrived piecemeal, at close range, sometimes only weeks before autumn *rentrée*, only to be confused by further changes in rules and arrangements, building student and faculty frustration. The central figure in pre-1968 reform was Christian Fouchet, Minister of Education from December 1962 to April 1967, the longest tenure in the twentieth century. His main achievement was the long-awaited common middle school (the *collège d'enseignement secondaire*) in 1963, but what made news and trouble were his actions in higher education.

A major innovation was the law of 1966 creating the *Instituts Universitaires de Technologie* (IUT), offering two-year courses at the immediate post-baccalaureate stage in industrial and commercial studies to furnish middle-level technicians to all sectors of the economy. Adding a third branch of the French postsecondary system to the universities and *grandes écoles*, the IUTs were to draw off some of the students flooding the old arts and letters faculties in numbers far beyond the capacity of the universities to educate them or the job market to absorb them.[14] The IUTs started with 2,000 students in 1966–67, and grew to only 12,000 by 1968. They and other post-baccalaureate short programs enrolled 100,000 a decade later, but in the crises of the late 1960s they did little to reduce student demand for university places. Critics accused Fouchet and Gaullist technocrats of cheapening all higher education, of sacrificing French students to private profit.

Broader action was required to cope with the flood of new university students. Before Fouchet left office, university enrollment had more than doubled since 1959. Paris saw the greatest influx: from 78,000 students in 1960 to 137,000 in 1967 and 270,000 in 1977. Despite hurried alterations to old buildings and the opening of new campuses at Nanterre and Vincennes, facilities were rarely adequate. As Raymond Aron observed after the explosion of 1968, the mere fact of crowding such numbers, noise and activity into so little space could produce a certain delirium.[15] But Paris was not alone in its growth. Between 1960 and 1967 Aix grew from 15,500 to 29,000, Grenoble from 10,000 to 20,000, Bordeaux from 12,000 to 26,000, Lyon from 13,000 to 30,000, Toulouse from 12,000 to 28,000. The total university population rose from 215,000 in 1960 to 460,000 in 1967.[16] New university centers opened at Nantes, Orléans and Reims in 1961, at Rouen and Amiens in 1964, at Nice and Limoges in 1965. Faculty staffing quadrupled, from 6,200 in 1958 to 23,600 in 1968.[17] Budgets soared, but construction, equipment and personnel could not keep pace and complaints multiplied.

The centerpiece of university instruction, the large lecture, was discredited, as amphitheatres overflowed and hundreds were turned away; libraries were overcrowded, books inadequate, service slow or unavailable. Outside the sciences and selective *grandes écoles*, the student:faculty ratio reached fifty and more to one. The new rank of *maîtres assistants* relieved some of the pressure, but many young *maîtres*, low-paid, overburdened, chafing under professional autocracy, were bitter and communicated it to their charges. Fouchet struggled to find a means to limit entry to the universities and deflect students from the arts and social sciences into earlier specialization in the natural sciences and mathematics. He instituted a five-track baccalaureate examination, each track leading to a particular faculty, and wholly revamped the degree system, changing requirements and years of study, beginning with a new two-year post-baccalaureate course of introductory work for the first diploma.[18] These changes, and others affecting the *licence*, the *maîtrise* and the varied range of doctorates, were applied hurriedly to students already in line, further exasperating them and their parents, who saw the new requirements and the imposition of yearly in-course examinations as a series of new barriers to entry and success. Fouchet was attacked for diminishing the baccalaureate (not requiring the classics) and university degrees, and, on the other hand, for doing nothing to slow the scandalous rate of failure and dropping out at the end of the first university year, which reached 40 percent in 1967 and, the Left argued rightly, affected the children of lower class families most often.[19] The years 1966 to 1968 saw rising confusion and demoralization, worsened by delay and inconsistency in the administration of change. In a system where all was decided and implemented by the central bureaucracy of the Ministry, local efforts to adjust or mitigate were little help, and the appointment of Alain Peyrefitte as minister of education in 1967 was widely expected to mean overt, stringent selection for entry to all faculties.

Pre-1968 reform in higher education, then, was too limited to modernize the system.[20] But the revolution of expectations was not limited at all. The new economy of consumption, the rhetoric of equal opportunity, of open meritocracy, led very many young Frenchmen and their families to expect, in short order, what neither the economy nor the universities could provide. Graduates found that their hard-won degrees did not guarantee positions with higher pay and status and, in the economic slowdown of 1967 and early 1968, often led to no position at all. Worst of all, students were finding that study conditions did not offer them fair chances to earn, or demonstrate, their merit. For the new middle and lower-middle class youths in the universities, academic success or failure fixed them in place for life. Open access increased anxiety and inequality of result was 'far more glaring in a uniform system than in a diversified one.'[21] That such is the price of meritocracy was no comfort at the moment, for the rigidities and insufficiencies of the French university in effect denied equal opportunity to those who made a start in it. This was the common denominator of anger in 1968. Whatever the other motives for rebellion, and the wild array of demands arising in May, the egregious unfairness of the system furnished the foot soldiers of the student revolt and also explained the widespread sympathy of their elders, at least in the early stages, before the general strike and the excesses of student *enragés* threatened to change not only the rules but the game itself.

The university reforms launched by the Orientation Law of November 1968 and presided over by de Gaulle's new minister of education, Edgar Faure, were nicely articulated to isolate the extremists, to respond to the demands of the majority, both explicit and implicit, (better to study the feelings, not the words, of the angry), and render bearable the necessities of meritocracy.[22] Faure avoided the bad word 'selection' but kept Fouchet's devices for channeling and evaluating students. The desire to improve study conditions on the one hand and preserve national standards on the other has shaped official policy in higher education since 1968. It is open to the charge of inconsistency at best, hypocrisy at worst, but always of unwillingness to allow basic change. One critic sums it up: 'The Faure reform which was to have been the renaissance of the French university has, instead, found itself distorted in the university's restoration to its former self.'[23] Supporters of the Ministry retort that renaissance by its nature must imply a degree of restoration, an attempt to revive the best of the past by new methods, which, they say, Faure and his successors have achieved.[24]

Faure hoped to modernize the universities by organizing broad participation in governance, allowing local autonomy, encouraging interdisciplinary teaching and research, breaking mass universities and monolithic faculties down to units of human scale. France's twenty-three universities were divided into sixty-five university centers, and the five traditional faculties—medicine, pharmacy, law (including economics), letters (including the social sciences) and natural sciences—were organized into some 700 departments called UERs (*Unité d'enseignement et de recherche*). These were enjoined to strive for '*pluridisciplinarité*' connecting arts and letters with science and technology. Many do, most often around the social sciences, but others are merely smaller versions of the old faculties, each attached to a new university center, as at Paris, where most of the dozen new sub-universities have their own UERs in the standard disciplines.

On the principle of participation, each UER has a governing council, as has each university, with elected representatives of the different ranks of faculty members, of students by year of study, and of other university personnel. Several UERs and university centers organized themselves along ideological lines. Student participation was highly politicized and already by 1972 more than 70 percent of the eligible students failed to vote—some, *gauchistes*, on revolutionary principle, the rest out of indifference or because the demands of participation in time, energy and personal discomfort did not seem justified by the marginal influence they might exert.[25]

Each university was to have a certain autonomy in allocating its budget, in curriculum and research, teaching methods and grading. The Ministry kept the right to overrule local decisions, notably on faculty appointments. Under Article 20, which let the ministry define general requirements for national diplomas, successive ministers have reimposed central standards for examinations and grading. Those, like Faure, who had preferred American-style multiplicity of university diplomas deplore the return to centralization. But students and parents, particularly outside Paris, are wary of inequalities that decentralization might produce, in actuality and in the eyes of the world. Whatever the disadvantages of central standards, the French see them as guarantees of the diplomas' value, an equality of result necessary to fair competition. The uneasy compromise between local autonomy of means and national setting of ends satisfies nobody entirely, but is unlikely to disappear. French universities, as Michelle Patterson says, remain 'in quiet turmoil.'

French higher education has been loosened and modernized somewhat since 1968 but is not yet democratic, either in access or outcome. The *grandes écoles* survived the upheaval all but untouched. At the summit of the education

221

system, their mission is to prepare the highest cadres, the elites for public service and private business. Including certain commercial and engineering schools not always recognized as *grandes* by the others, they enroll 80,000 students, some 8 to 10 percent of all postsecondary education. Entry is highly competitive, by examination or on the basis of student dossiers. Most require two, three or more years of preparatory work in post-baccalaureate courses, some at distinguished Paris *lycées*, Louis-le-Grand, Henri IV and the like, others offered at university centers. Upper class male students with the necessary time and resources predominate in these *classes preparatoires* as in the more renowned *grandes écoles*—Polytechnique, Mines, Ponts et Chaussées, the Ecole Normale Supérieure. Drawing the heaviest fire of egalitarians is the Ecole Nationale d'Administration, founded in 1945 ostensibly to democratize the higher reaches of the civil service. Over half of those admitted to each annual entering class of 100 are graduates of the Institut d'Etudes Politiques at Paris. Graduates of ENA have been prominent in Gaullist cabinets and high administrative posts, and its abolition or absorption into the university system is mentioned frequently by the campaign platforms of the Left parties, which otherwise tend to skirt the issue of the *grandes écoles* (not a few Left leaders are graduates), or ask only—as the Algiers plan did—that recruitment be opened by drawing from democratized universities and from persons in service already.[26]

Access to and completion of university education itself, however, also remain much easier for upper class children. Repeated studies since 1968, both partisan and neutral, have shown that many factors, familiar to observers of higher education elsewhere, still reduce chances for all but the most talented working class students.[27] Even these start later and take longer than their upper class peers to complete a given course of study, because they must support themselves. Hence the widespread demand for student salaries or higher financial aid. In the short run, the only other way to equality would be to eliminate selection and evaluation altogether. Other nations, including the United States, have taken this way in certain sectors of higher education, asserting that schools can be different but equal. The French are not likely to follow. Too many, especially on the Left, believe that further deterioration of the universities would render them not democratic but irrelevant, leaving access to advancement all the more surely to those with inherited advantage.[28]

SECONDARY EDUCATION: EVOLUTION AND DEMOCRACY

All parties agree that democratic higher education is a matter of the long run, to be prepared well before the university, and the larger effort of the Fifth Republic's reformers has been directed to the secondary schools. At stake is not only an open and honest meritocracy, but the democratic and cultural purposes of schooling that the Resistance set. However lively the quarrels over universities and *grandes écoles,* these are, in the main, schools for the professions, old and new, genuine or jumped-up. As in most of Europe, postsecondary education is preparation for work. The general education of the citizen and the person must take place at the secondary level, at least for most young people, whose energies must soon thereafter turn to work and family.

The Algiers and Langevin-Wallon plans gave the new obligatory secondary schools the task of raising the level of general culture for all citizens to a point—and here the French are unique—that would clearly *disengage* the quality of their education from their level of employment, for all had the right to the best possible preparation for public action and for private cultivation, regardless of rank:

> In a democracy, where each worker is a citizen, it is indispensable to keep specialization from becoming an obstacle to one's understanding of the greater problems of the society and to insure that man is liberated from the limits of his own work by a broad and solid general culture.[29]

The ideal of the common middle school, free and obligatory for both sexes, as the way to democratize a republic emerged during the French Revolution. In it, Condorcet said, 'all citizens shall receive the instruction which can be given to all alike,' mathematics, natural history, ethics and the social sciences. But nineteenth century France extended free education only through primary school, and until the second World War the Republic kept two separate sets of public schools, the primary for the people, the secondary for the elite. Resistance plans recalled the reforms proposed by the Popular Front's minister of education, Jean Zay, himself a Resistance martyr. Zay's plan had been patterned after the long-discussed ideal of a band of teacher-veterans of the First World War who called for the common middle school under the name of *l'école unique.* Their campaign dominated much of the educational debate between the wars, failing in part because the term *école unique* allowed partisans to stir up the battle between clericals and anti-clericals.[30]

After the defeat of the Langevin-Wallon project in 1947, the Fourth Republic failed to pursue *l'école unique.* The primary schools added courses for several years beyond the primary certificate and some vocational schools were established, but the old bifurcation remained, even in the Ministry: the primary system, including teacher training, under one administration and the *lycées* (many with their own selective primary classes) under another. An attempt by the minister of education René Billères in 1956–57 to create two-year middle schools for orientation foundered on the opposition of secondary teachers, who accused him of wanting to 'primarize' the first two years of secondary education, to hold back the talented.[31]

The government of Charles de Gaulle began cautiously. The Berthoin decree reform of 1959 raised the school-leaving age from fourteen to sixteen, but allowed eight years for implementation.[32] A two-year cycle for observation and orientation was set up, but in the separate schools as they stood. 'Bridge Classes' in the third year (ages 13 or 14) were to facilitate transfer of able children to *lycées*, but proved ineffective. Still, one step led to another. The logic of universal education to sixteen obviously required massive new efforts at evaluation and guidance, and equality of chances and freedom of choice hardly could be offered to children from all social classes as long as they remained segregated in separate, unequal schools. In 1963, Christian Fouchet created the *Collèges d'Enseignement Secondaire* (CES), comprehensive lower secondary schools (*le premier cycle*) for grades six through nine (French classes *sixième* through *troisième*), destined to replace all other lower secondary instruction, whether in the grades added to the primary schools earlier (sometimes called the *Collège d'Enseignement Général*, the CEG) or in the opening years of the *lycées*. The new CES enrolled students into several ability tracks, ranging from the 'classical,' taught by instructors from the secondary system, to the slow or 'transition' sections, taught by primary *instituteurs*. Transfer from track to track was still not easy in the face of divergent curricula, standards and methods of instruction. The middle school 'had found its home but not yet its pedagogy,' that *tronc commun* of general studies for everyone that Condorcet had wanted.[33]

Since 1963–64, this last step has been taken. In 1963, the government decreed that all studies in the CES would be liberal (*la culture générale*). Vocational programs prior to the tenth grade (French *seconde*, age sixteen or so) were abolished or postponed. A uniform curriculum was instituted gradually for the four-year *premier cycle*, the tracks then varying only in methods and standards. The Haby reforms of 1975–76 discontinued formal tracking, leaving each CES free to employ its own forms of mixed-ability groupings.[34] In theory, the less able get extra weekly hours of *pédagogie de soutien* and the gifted, extra hours of *pédagogie d'approfondissement*. Neither function has been staffed adequately yet, and *collège* teachers have difficulty grappling with classes of mixed abilities. But in law and, to varying degrees, in fact, the Fifth Republic has accomplished what no prior French republic did. Secondary education is free and universal to age sixteen, in the common middle schools of the democrats' dreams, with a *tronc commun* of liberal studies, charged with evaluating and advising as objectively as possible all the children who pass through it. Over the past five years, some 35 percent of CES graduates have moved on to *lycées* for the course to the baccalaureate, whether classical, modern, scientific or technical, 40 percent have entered other upper secondary vocational schools, and the remaining 25 percent have entered the work force directly.[35]

The question posed universally is whether the vast new enrollment in French secondary schools is an educational advance or, as some critics have said of mass enrollment in American universities, merely demographic. To judge from the prescribed curriculum, it is educational, marked by the attempt, unique in the West, to preserve most of the subject matter content of the education for the favored few while offering it to ten times the number of students enrolled before the Second World War. In direct contrast to the American school system, the French have not decided yet that the influx of the masses necessarily dictates the abandonment of academic content and standards. They know that some will fail and others will turn away, but they pay this price to offer liberal education to everyone, for anything less would be undemocratic. The French consensus on what may be called humanist populism crosses party lines and is especially strong on the old Left, which insists that equal access to school must mean equal access to required subjects American educators have long dismissed as 'elite' learning.[36]

The core curriculum required of all children in the *premier cycle* best reveals what the French believe everybody ought to know.[37] It includes (1) four years of history of Western civilization, one year each for the Ancient World, the Middle Ages, the Renaissance through the eighteenth century, and the nineteenth and twentieth centuries; (2) four years of geography and '*éducation civique*' both of which begin with local matters and move outward through the years to the nation and the world, contemporary economic and social questions; (3) four to six hours a week of French language and literature for four years and three hours weekly of a second modern language (Latin has become optional; students may add it in the third year); (4) three weekly hours in the biological and physical sciences, three to four in mathematics, two in art and music; in a gesture toward enlarging the traditional concept of *culture générale*, two to three hours of manual arts and classroom study in applied science and technology. Options added to, not instead of, the core begin in the third year. The student must choose a third modern language, or Latin or Greek, or some form of prevocational course. Students who have chosen or been advised into the last find it difficult to reverse fields and prepare for the *lycées*. In sum, the required general education extends through the school-leaving age of sixteen, but differentiation for the upper secondary level and consequent career options begins at age fourteen, in the third year of the *collège unique*.

CRITICS AND PROSPECTS

Currents of critical opinion on French secondary education as shaped by the Haby reforms divide into three main categories: first, educational conservatives or traditionalists; second, the utilitarian, funtionalist innovators, mainly Center and Center Right in politics, frequently called 'Americanizers,' with good reason; third, the egalitarian innovators, mainly from the Left parties, social scientists, Marxist polemicists. Conservative critics are found in all parties and classes. Among them are many teachers, administrators, academicians and politicians from the Left, particularly in the Communist party and the teachers' unions, who believe that loosening course requirements or standards would betray the deepest interests of the new working class students, threaten hierarchies necessary to education, restrain the gifted and lower the quality of French learning and culture, not to speak of politics. Educational conservatives on the Left see the relaxation of the *tronc commun* and standards as a reactionary device to track the masses downward, 'in the American style,' some say, 'of giving them what they want!'[38] Traditionalists on the Center and Right see the same relaxation as the consequence of the Left's mania for egalitarianism, whatever the cost to other values or to French competence and culture.

They fear in common the erosion of their humanist mode of democratization by the forces of current popular culture, and by innovations being promoted by the other factions, utilitarian and egalitarian. They fear that innovators, especially French innovators new to modernization, assume too easily they can make changes without losing anything of value from the past. Curriculum poses a particularly complex problem of cultural ecology; the 'goods' in traditional culture are fragile, easily trampled in the rush to rationality and levelling.[39] They are critical of postponing Latin and adding social sciences at the expense of traditional subjects. They deplore the new notions of teaching the French language primarily as 'communication' and of cutting back literary studies. They doubt the wisdom of mixed-ability classes, preferring the tracks as more honest and also more helpful to children at all levels of ability. If not tracks, then standards must be guarded by fully-staffed *pédagogie de soutien* and *d'approfondissement*, by smaller classes, by free books and financial aid to lessen the outside burdens of lower-income adolescents. As the quality of the *collège unique* declines, even non-Catholic children will transfer to private schools. The new army of public school teachers is loosely trained, they say, lacking the proficiency and depth of culture to keep the young at their books.[40]

The other two modes of criticism are, of course, much more prominent, are nourished by powerful political and economic forces, and enjoy limitless coverage in the press and television. As the prevailing orthodoxies, they dominate debate and their spokesmen emerge on national study commissions and committees for reform, American-style.[41] Egalitarian innovators on the Left denounce French schools as hierarchical, authoritarian, closed in upon themselves, cut off from real life and their communities, and discriminatory against children of the worknig classes because they insist upon teaching, and measuring talent by, traditional 'bourgeois culture.' They point to studies showing that changes in secondary and university education have benefited the middle classes, that the number of workers' children reaching the baccalaureate has risen only marginally.[42] The third year of middle school is too soon, they say, to force students into course options that will track the rest of their lives. *Pédagogie de soutien* even at its best cannot overcome disadvantages afflicting working class children from the first year of school. At thirteen or fourteen, they are likely to see themselves, and be thought of by parents, teachers and guidance officers, as fit only for immediate employment or, at best, to pursue modest vocational training. Thus, democratization has not been served and nothing has changed. In sum, the schools are oppressive instruments of capitalism, designed only to shape pliant servants and consumers, to 'reproduce' the unjust existing order.[43]

Utilitarian innovators of the Center and Center Right charge that French schools are hierarchical, authoritarian, closed in upon themselves, cut off from real life and their communities (in part by a Leftist teaching corps), and unresponsive to the needs of modern, technological, consumer society. Like some of their Left counterparts, the functionalists consider the schools too traditionally academic, obsessed with imparting humanist high culture, bookish, abstract, and oriented toward the past. To Jacques Minot, there is a '*grand décalage*' between education and daily life, 'schooling is absolutely alien to our daily concerns' and 'independent of the society as a whole and of other societal systems.'[44]

The two streams of criticism have most in common the view that French schools are, in American jargon, 'isolated from life,' as though that ended the argument. Utilitarians satisfied with the established social order mean that schools do not prepare French children for useful lives in society as it is and as it will be improved by more of the same. Left critics insist that schools do not prepare children for life in the socialist, egalitarian society of tomorrow. Neither view allows education an autonomous role. Each demands that schooling be absorbed into, and serve directly, its preferred mode of production. Both, then, are instrumentalist in the name of progress and, as such, draw heavily on American notions for modernizing public education, which are legitimized by the steady stream of scoldings and demands for change that flows from the UNESCO, the OECD, the Council of Europe and Plan Europe 2000, whose managers, experts and publicists form something of an interlocking directorate with the peripatetic scholar-consultants of comparative education in the Western world. Without exception, their recommendations follow the latest American fashions in educational innovation.[45] Education must be 'industrialized' and made 'cost efficient.' Continuing education (*la formation permanente*) can equalize everybody's chances in life and allow the secondary schools to relax their emphasis on subject matter (most of which is 'obsolete' or soon will be) and to concentrate on developing attitudes—cooperation, creativity, economic rationality—and tools for later learning.

Bertrand Schwartz, whose writings have made him France's best-known proponent for both egalitarian and utilitarian innovation, exemplifies the approach. He sees the *tronc commun* as out of date; most subjects should be optional, the student choosing his own 'menu' out of his 'felt needs,' in one of many terms Schwartz borrows from American educators. Teachers should not

227

be trained in the traditional manner with emphasis upon academic subject matter, but for roles as counselors, motivators, mediators and coordinators of educational 'experiences' involving the daily work of the whole community. Schwartz' school of the future is not an autonomous institution but wholly absorbed in the societal system.[46] The danger conservatives see, of course, is that such a purely instrumental view of culture (history, Schwartz says, should be taught only insofar as it applies to current environmental problems) would destroy the best in French education that has not prevented educated French people from being creative, critical, communicative and productive.

In conclusion, an outsider can hardly predict the future course of French public education. The education planks of party platforms for the 1978 parliamentary elections were often ambiguous and inconsistent, torn between innovation and tradition.[47] What is the significance, to take but one example, of the Center Democrats' demand that the schools 'suppress elitism and recognize all subject matter as equally worthy?' If it means that applied science, technology and manual arts get a fair portion of curricular time within a *tronc commun* that remains heavy in history, science, mathematics and the humanities—and continues to be required of all—the Resistance ideal will be served. If, on the other hand, it comes to signify the principle on which American secondary education has operated for decades—traditional arts and sciences for the few (in private schools and college tracks) and 'Life Adjustment' for the rest—the ideal will have been abandoned.

So far the French appear to be working at a *juste milieu*, to open access and to modernize structures and pedagogy while keeping, as Crane Brinton hoped ten years ago, 'the best of the oldest classical tradition and its standards.'[48] They have not yet succumbed to unmixed utilitarianism or to fears of over-educating the mass. The very ambiguity of party platforms suggests recognition that the three ancient aims of education—for work, for public life and for private culture—are indeed disparate, requiring different, even opposite, modes of pedagogy seeking different results. That in pursuing their disparate aims schools must be conservative and radical at once, that they must serve both the collectivity and the individual, that they must be close to the world at some moments and isolated at others, are commonplaces to the French. This, and the pride in French culture that crosses all class and party lines, suggests that the Fifth Republic's version of educational democracy, 'founded on the work of the past but turned to new horizons,' may persist for some time.[49]

The Fifth Republic and Education

NOTES

1. Luc Decaunes et M. L. Cavalier, *Réformes et projets de réforme de l'enseignement français de la Révolution à nos jours (1789-1960)* (Paris: Institut pédagogique national, 1962), p. 261. This work includes an historical survey and texts of proposals from 1919 on.

2. Ibid., pp. 278-281.

3. Ibid., p. 261.

4. Ibid., pp. 136-204; Antoine Prost, *L'Enseignement en France, 1800-1967* (Paris, 1968), pp. 420-422.

5. Jacques Minot, *L'Entreprise éducation nationale* (Paris, 1970), p. 169.

6. Ministère de l'Education, *Tableaux des enseignements et de la formation* (Paris: Service central des statistiques et sondages, 1976), pp. 10, 29.

7. See Minot, *L'Entreprise*, p. 166 to evolution to 1969-70 and yearly *Tableaux* thereafter.

8. Prost, *L'Enseignement*, p. 487.

9. *Tableaux*, 1976, p. 15. Data to 1978 from the Ministry's Service des études informatiques et statistiques, 58 boulevard du Lycée, Vanves.

10. Monique Segré, *Ecole, formation, contradictions* (Paris, 1976), pp. 30, 95-110; Raymond Boudon, *L'Inégalité des chances* (Paris, 1973), pp. 83-87.

11. See Alain Gras et al., *Does Education Have a Future?* (The Hague, 1975); Bertrand Schwartz, *Permanent Education* (The Hague, 1974); Alfred Sauvy, *Access to Education* (The Hague, 1973), all volumes in the Plan Europe 2000 series; also OECD, *Educational Policies for the 1970s* (Paris, 1971); UNESCO, *L'Education et le développement scientifique, économique et social* (Paris, 1969); and the French Commissariat Général du Plan, *Rapport de la commission éducation et formation* (Paris, 1976), for the 7th Plan.

12. Jacques Natanson et Antoine Prost, *La Révolution scolaire* (Paris, 1963), pp. 45-66; W. R. Fraser, *Reform and Restraints in Modern French Eduction* (London, 1971).

13. Charles Péguy, *Notre jeunesse* (Paris, 1919); see *Oeuvres en prose 1909-1914 (Paris, 1958)*.

14. W. D. Halls, *Education, Culture and Politics in Modern France* (Oxford, 1976), pp. 216-218.

15. Raymond Aron, *The Elusive Revolution* (New York, 1969), p. 41.

16. C. Grignon and J.C. Passeron, *Innovation in Higher Education: French Experience before 1968* (Paris: OECD, 1970), pp. 118, 119; also *Tableaux*, pp. 321-327.

17. OECD, *Reviews of National Policies for Education: France* (Paris, 1971), p. 46. By 1975, faculty numbers were 38,220 (*Tableaux*, p. 319).

18. For a summary of the complex array of French degrees, diplomas and requirements, see Raymond E. Wanner, *France* (Washington, D.C., 1975), a recent volume in the World Education Series of the American Association of Collegiate Registrars and Admissions Officers.

19. The *grandes écoles*, on the other hand, have a retention rate approaching 95 percent. For the contrast, see OECD, *Reviews*, pp. 71, 72.

20. Grignon and Passeron, *Innovation*, pp. 86-113.

21. Stanley Hoffmann, *Decline or Renewal? France Since the 1930s* (New York, 1974), pp. 155-157, 465.

22. Aron, *Revolution*, p. 41. On the Orientation Law, see OECD, *Reviews*, pp. 72-80.

23. Michelle Patterson, 'French University Reform: Renaissance or Restoration,' in Philip G. Altbach, ed., *University Reform* (Cambridge, Mass., 1974), p. 136.

24. André G. Delion, *L'Education en France* (Paris, 1973), pp. 101, 102.

25. Michel Crozier, *La Société bloquée* (Paris, 1970), pp. 77-83.

26. Wanner, *France*, pp. 138-144; Halls, *Education*, pp. 221-231.

27. The most influential early study was Pierre Bourdieu and J. C. Passeron, *Les Héritiers* (Paris, 1954), which they followed with *La Reproduction: Eléments pour une théorie du système d'enseignement* (Paris, 1970). See also Noelle Bisseret, *Les Inéqaux ou la selection universitaire* (Paris, 1974) and OECD, *Educational Policy and Planning: France* (Paris, 1972), pp. 125-148.

28. Hoffmann, *Decline*, p. 463.

29. Decaunes et Cavalier, *Réformes*, p. 126.

30. John E. Talbott, *The Politics of Educational Reform in France, 1918-1940* (Princeton, 1969) is indispensable for the period and subject.

31. Decaunes et Cavalier, *Réformes*, pp. 196–200.

32. Ibid., pp. 391–410.

33. Prost, *L'Enseignement*, p. 424.

34. L. Leterrier, *et al.*, *Programmes, instructions* (Paris, 1977), pp. 7–24 for the text of the Haby law and subsequent elaborations.

35. Halls, *Education*, p. 97. More complete data may be obtained at the service des études informatiques et statistiques, cited above.

36. Natanson et Prost, *Révolution*, p. 125 ff.

37. Leterrier, *Programmes*, for programs of *premier cycle* which, aside from minor alterations, are still in force. The ministry also issues regular detailed descriptions in its series *Horaires, objectifs, programmes, instructions*, published by the Centre National de Documentation Pédagogique, 29, rue d'Ulm.

38. Interview with Jacques George of S.G.E.N.-C.F.D.T., October 1973 (Syndicat Général de l'Education Nationale).

39. Interviews with *collège unique* teachers and directors, and at the Institut National de la recherche pédagogique, rue d'Ulm, May 1978.

40. Same as above, together with interviews with parents, May 1978.

41. The Joxe Commission of 1971–72 and La Commission de l'éducation et de la formation of 1975–76, which helped prepare the 7th Plan, as examples.

42. Segré, *Ecole*; Boudon, *L'Inégalite*; OECD, *Educational Policy*, 125–148.

43. See, among the most recent Left critics, Louis Legrand, *Pour une politique démocratique de l'éducation* (Paris, 1977); C. Baudelot and R. Establet, *L'Ecole capitaliste en France* (Paris, 1971); Bernard Charlot, *La Mystification pédagogique* (Paris, 1975); Suzanne Citron, *L'Ecole bloquée* (Paris, 1971); Georges Snyders, *Ecole, classe et lutte des classes* (Paris, 1976); Pierre Juquin, *Reconsttuire l'école* (Paris, 1973), the approved Communist Party education platform, repeated for the 1978 campaign. For an extreme version of the 'reproduction' charge, couched in theoretical terms, Bourdieu et Passeron, *Réproduction*.

44. Minot, *L'Entreprise*, p. 15.

45. OECD, *L'Innovation dans l'enseignement secondaire* (Paris, 1978), pp. 112–117, for a veritable catalog of thirty-six recommended changes in the American mode. See also sources cited in note 11.

46. Bertrand Schwartz, *Une autre école* (Paris, 1977). See also his *L'Education demain* (Paris, 1973).

47. For party programs, see *L'Education* of 2 February 1978, pp. 9–27 and *Le Monde*'s special issue of its 'Dossiers et Documents' entitled *Les Elections législatives de mars 1978*, pp. 45–48.

48. Crane Brinton, *The Americans and the French* (Cambridge, Mass., 1968), pp. 183, 184.

49. The expression is de Gaulle's, in his *Mémoires d'espoir*, II Paris 1971, p. 171.

France's Cultural Anxieties Under Gaullism
The Cultural Revolution Revisited

Michel Crozier

AN UNEXPECTED STORY

For those readers who might be misled, the cultural revolution referred to is not the thundering radical hope of the Maoists but the title of a modest article this writer contributed to the journal *Daedalus* in 1963.[1]

The thesis could be summarized as follows: The intellectual as a torchbearer of humanity had been the hero of the late 40s and early 50s. But one should not have illusions about the alleged radicalism of the intellectual of this period. In manner and mode of reasoning he was an aristocrat who suddenly found himself out of place with the changing social patterns. The intellectual establishment was already being displaced because of the very success of the knowledge which was its product. This was due to the liberalization of social relations and social hierarchies for which these individuals fought. Such painful displacement was at the root of diverse intellectual upheavals and disarray. It had greater impact in France where the intellectual establishment has a considerable stake in a very conservative hierarchical society. But France—as other European countries at that time—was about to come of age. And her tumultuous ordeal might even have led to new social and intellectual discoveries.

The period 1958-1978 hardly lived up to these expectations. Surely there was turmoil. Admittedly, this had been an ordeal that had little to do with the peaceful end of ideology contemplated by Daniel Bell and many other Americans, yet there was no sign of a coming of age. What was particularly dismaying, the traditional intellectual leftist establishment not only resisted but conquered the media, exerted a tremendous influence on the public consciousness and became a form of parallel power under Gaullism.

In a sense, these facts may hold true only in appearance. One should inquire

231

about what kind of practical relations underlie successive intellectual modes. May not something be salvaged from the old thesis? Indeed, could a new thesis be drawn up to meet the actual state of affairs? This quite speculative paper shall address those questions.

First, I shall attempt to tell the story—at least as I perceive it—in a very rough sketch. At the same time, I shall try to relate it to my thesis of 1963. Finally, I shall conclude by speculating on the more basic questions.

But before entering the complexity of this chaotic period, I would like to present a few general remarks.

1. This was an unusual period in the tempo of change and the radicalism of the successive intellectual fashions. These fashions not only succeeded one another more rapidly than ever, also they opposed one another as much as they attacked the conventional world view.

2. Successive intellectual fashions were intertwined with another parallel rhythm, the rhythm of political activism: periods such as 1945-50, 1956-61, 1967-70, 1975-78 had been periods of political activism. In between, had been temporary lulls, (similar to the present), throughout these interwoven trends. Nevertheless, there was an overwhelming dominance of the left in French culture which can be contrasted with the reign of the Gaullists and moderates in politics.

3. Although the leftist cultural drift was overwhelming during the twenty year period there was a rapid left-wing acceleration crowned by May 1968. After the climax of 1968, came a period of deceleration.

4. May 1968 was a major cultural event that divided the period sharply. Prior to this singular event was still an era of cultural optimism; after 1968 pessimism became dominant, tempered only by millenarist hysteria.

5. The failure of the Left in the 1978 elections may be considered another major event in the future. It was prepared by a gradual disenchantment with millenarism and may even come to be viewed as an important stage in the "coming of age of French society".

I will divide this period in sections which exemplify the dominance of one or another of the prevailing intellectual fashions. This is necessarily arbitrary, especially since intellectual actors require a lengthy time of latency and work. Moreover, contributions have often become obsolete once they have made their major impact. Opposing contributions may also coexist even though only one fashion dominates in the trend-making intellectual set.

The dominance of a fashion is nevertheless an important element for understanding the intellectual debate, the pressure on intellectuals, the impact on students and on the public. Finally, it should be remarked that the media played a more important role in promoting the fashion than in the past. Ideas were brought to public attention much more rapidly. This in turn had an impact on politics.

THE GOLDEN YEARS MALENTENDU

The years of the Liberation had been dominated by political activism. Sartre and Camus were its heroes. Economic and social issues were translated into lofty intellectual debates. France's powerlessness could be transfigured by its intellectual prominence. The great powers could claim financial and military strength. Gallic supremacy, however, was moral and intellectual.

This came to an end when France's recovery made it possible for her to take charge of substantive issues. Mendès France's prodigious success in 1954 was a sign of this change.

The Algerian war years only partially marked a revival of old style intellectual activism. This era was the last glow of Sartre's intellectual magnetism. The manifesto of the 121[2] was one of the major instances of the prowess of intelligentsia. But the cultural exploit had no impact on politics or social events. It soon became clear that the battle was not to be waged in this arena. Problems were too serious to be left to intellectuals. Even Algerian nationalists did not trust their cumbersome allies, and they were all too happy to hold talks and subsequently negotiations with the more responsible French leaders. The last years of the Algerian War marked a period of political and cultural lull.

The younger generation that came to the forefront then was a mixed breed of student-union leaders, journalists, civil servants, and non-committed members of political clubs. The past had witnessed similar gatherings periodically. This one was especially crucial because of the demise of political parties during the early years of the Gaullist regime. Also, it was produced by the breakdown of social barriers and social relations, as exemplefied by the disappearance of hostility between Catholics and anticlerical forces which was so influential later in the building of the socialist party. This new breed associated not only with the liberal wing of the Gaullist government but also with the trade unions, young farmers and junior businessmen's associations.

The rather surprising non-catastrophic end of the Algerian war and the very successful repatriation of the European minority from Algeria may be attributed to these aforementioned groups as well as to de Gaulle. When instead of the chaos and fascism predicted by the radicals of the Left (without mentioning, of course, the disaster for western civilization announced by the radical right) France peacefully absorbed one million former colonists not only for her own benefit but, also for theirs, the political and cultural climate was bound to change. These were the golden years of the new intellectuals of the sixties.[3] Clearly, from 1962 to 1966 cultural fashion tended to be represented by the moderate Left. These were the years of a successful modernization of the "French ways" in the liberal "American pattern." The U.S. of JFK and the 'Best and the Brightest' was at a high point. These were the years of the John XXIII Catholic *aggiornamento*. France did not merely imitate and follow, but made contributions of her own. This was the heyday of democratic planning that was imitated in the UK and highly praised in the U.S. A strong liberal democratic breeze was blowing, but no warning announced the coming storm.

In the cultural world, the social sciences were the great beneficiaries of the change. There was now time to re-think old problems, away from the agitation and hysteria of impending doom. For the first time in years, day-to-day political events did not dominate. Political parties were out. Old style rhetoric was out. New thinking was very much in demand. Moreover, this time, the elites seemed opened to a new discourse.

The cultural answers to these demands were still very modest. French new-wave movies seem now hopelessly conventional. Democratic planning was a very moderate liberal version of traditional establishment patterns. It was believed at the time that social sciences were a tool for pointing out the more basic needs, problems and realities of everyday life, with which enlightened technocrats would be able to cope.

The misunderstanding was deep. Leaders of French society were searching for better relations with the public and not for challenging ideas. Change was slow, at least at the political, administrative and organizational levels. New social science jargon was used to replace the Marxist and radical phraseology but with no more than cosmetic consequences.

The cultural revolution I was discussing at that time did not take place in the manner I had hoped. Certainly there was an acceleration in the displacement of old-style intellectuals and the enlargement of the intellectual community; but it led only to a political and moral crisis within society; it did not impose new ways of thinking and acting.

THE FASCINATION WITH STRUCTURALISM

The end of this period of the conservative golden years (pre-1968) must be set apart, not only because one can already identify during these years the first themes that were to become the main arguments during the crisis: the conditioning of man by organization, workers' alienation, the existential drama of youth and middle aged executives' spleen, but also and much more importantly, I think, because it was dominated by a new and specifically French craze: structuralism.

Structuralism can be viewed as the extreme and radical formalization of social scientific arrogance. As such it came on the French scene as a complete surprise. Since French intellectuals had been as reluctant to accept modern social sciences as they had been to accept psychoanalysis, how is it that they became the most arrogant exponents of structuralism?

If one does not think in terms of cultural traits or linear history, it makes a good deal of sense. New converts are usually more fanatical. Misunderstandings in science and especially in the social sciences may lead to new discoveries or at least to impressive new theories. The French intellectual tradition is sufficiently strong to respond to outside challenges with new contributions. One can find at the same time in French structuralism an accommodation to the vanguard of the social sciences, an original answer to the challenging problems of these sciences, and a special French logical and even absolutist trend that tends to push the basic paradigm to its utmost limit. But fashion is not consciously made by intellectual leads, it depends on response. Why did the French intelligentsia react so ardently to people like Levi-Strauss, Foucault, and Barthes? Why did a whole literary school (the *nouveau roman*) develop around a structuralist paradigm?[4]

This is still part of the basic misunderstanding. French society was and is frightened by change. Intellectual change is more important for France than for other societies because intellectual mechanisms are more basic to its social fabric. The success of the social sciences, therefore, could be experienced as a challenge to the predominant modes of thought of our humanistic societies. The structuralist craze was a sort of exorcism. With structuralism one could at the same time reach the avant-garde of the social sciences—and practically reject its consequences since structuralism could not deal with present day problems. At least, this seemed to be the case. Levi-Strauss himself made a point of insisting that structuralism could deal only with 'cold societies', where change did not take place.

Curiously, the *nouveau roman* authors such as Michel Butor and Marguerite Duras went further, although nobody seemed to notice at first. The absence of man, i.e. the impossibility or meaninglessness of man's personal decision and free will, could not be read as science but as a romantic call for help. At that point, we were not far from the May revolution to which, of course, literary ivory-tower characters as well as arrogant scientists rallied in the most extreme romantic confusion.

THE THUNDERSTORM OF MAY 1968

To most Frenchmen and certainly to most intellectuals the May 1968 revolution was a thunderstorm out of a clear blue sky. Later of course, all the warning signs were seen to have been there. But who could have paid attention to them in the existing cultural climate? That a fashionable moviemaker like Godard made a success out of a provocative story[5] of Nanterre radical students had not disturbed any seasoned analyst of French mores and politics.

Many very good and convincing explanations of the crisis have been offered. In a sense they are all true since every crisis—that is breakdown or rupture—can develop only because of the conjunction of a number of unrelated and possibly contradictory elements. However, the distinctive feature of May 1968 was that it happened without reason, i.e. without conventional social or political reasons.

Especially from this distance, it seems that the 1968 events should be understood first of all as a cultural event, a crisis about the content of the culture and even more about the human relationships associated with it. This crisis has developed in all western countries and has had an impact even on the communist East. It is the coming to life of the problems discussed in my 1963 paper. Men need a new culture, new intellectual instruments. Our economic progress, our social developments already have disturbed our nineteenth century bourgeois culture. But culture has always been conservative and the change of cultures may become revolutionary. I had used the term as a figure of speech and it turned out to be almost a reality.

What is specifically French in May 1968 is its dramatic quality. Everything was well arranged and played within six weeks: *"unité de temps, unité de lieu,"* an extraordinary neat clinical tragedy and at the same time the immediate association between culture and politics. In no other country has the playacting of culture become the central event, not only of politics but even of national consciousness.

Even if May 1968 revealed the problems of a society in search of a new more useful culture, if it gave vent to its cultural anxieties, it did not assist directly in obtaining realistic solutions or constructive steps leading to solutions. It raised problems so climactically that no one could escape listening. It offered a dream-like stage on which utopian solutions could be played out. But when the dreamers awoke the problems remained.

Thunderstorms, of course, always provide a sort of necessary relif. This one did not fail to do so, although in a deep and subtle way. It imposed some degree of modesty on our social establishment. To some extent, it changed the human relations game. It became possible for young people to assert their freedom to take alternatives. It enabled more people to communicate more openly across traditional boundaries of professional logic and ideology. Furthermore, it weakened the old cultural establishment substantially.

Yet as a structuring event in culture and politics, its basic impact has been essentially regressive: it brought back to life artificially a ghost that had disappeared in the late fifties, the intellectual as torchbearer. The story of the next ten years was mainly the tale of the gradual recovery from the blow it represented for culture. This is why the cultural climate has been pessimistic all these years.

What did May 68 bring us?

First of all the return of an old hero—the revolutionary. But in a different way. No Winter Palace was stormed. Instead of the professional revolutionary, the new hero expressed revolution as a way of life. His appearance was much more cultural than political. Second, a strong association was established between culture and revolution. Revolution was a way of culture, even a culture itself. And culture could not be anything but revolutionary.

Of course, the majority of intellectuals did not subscribe to such dreams, but their logic led to such reasoning. Most left-wing intellectuals, that is most intellectuals at the time, insisted that politics was everywhere, that everything was political and that culture was the main battlefield.

A third basic trait has a completely different nature. This was the colonization of the media by avant-garde culture. Media that had been ignoring the universities and the social sciences, seized upon the event and created the new fashion. They did not do so with any special intention, although the response was both good and profitable. But journalists, traders in ideas, were deeply perturbed by the crisis themselves. They were the target of attacks, as well as possible actors in the movement. A cause, a real cause for justifying one's calling was at hand, while traditional constraints could not be enforced.

This change in the media had very far-reaching consequences. First, it gave the cultural world a much broader platform. It unified the cultural universe temporarily, and gave intellectuals a wide audience. A new public was born. Second, it had a decisive impact on politics. From 1968 on, the logic of French politics has been leftist, according to which you could always beat your competitor by outflanking him on the left. This logic was not concocted by the media. But it dominated only because the media made it possible.

THE MAD YEARS OF ANTIPSYCHIATRY

From 1968 to 1972, French politics can best be understood as the slow and difficult but constant process of returning to normalcy. The basic pattern of social control had been shaken deeply and the traditional social bards could no longer be trusted as they had been. Any day, some group of hard-headed skilled machinists in some remote town might refuse to listen to their union leaders. Because they happened to occupy their plant at the right moment, the whole industrial system might collapse again. The rank and file would not trust their leaders; those leaders, in turn, could not afford to take risks. Bargaining was not possible, for its results might be challenged immediately. Industrial relations were, of course, not the only hazardous problem. Churches, universities, schools, in fact all cultural institutions were equally vulnerable.

In order to effect a return to normalcy throughout the country, authority became overly cautious, patient, at times even understanding. Liberals (intellectuals or civil servants such as Prime Minister Chaban-Delmas' aides, Simon Nora and Jacques Delors) often had their own way. They were ideally suited for such tasks. They tried to exploit the situation to promote their own ideas, but usually to little avail. They were not supported by the cultural and political wave and the establishment used them as sparingly as possible.

However, culture took an entirely different course. While politics in this period was the politics of cautious liberalization, even the major left wing parties: both the Socialists and the Communists made many attempts to seem respectable. Culture was dominated by a radical hysteria even greater than the slogans of May 1968. Rarely has the divorce been so deep between political and social action on the one hand, and the intellectuals, on the other. Not that intellectuals retreated to their own ivory tower. On the contrary. The more they became part of the action, the more estranged their problems became from the world of politics and social and economic life.

If politics contained a longing for an immediate return to normalcy, to be achieved with the overall complicity of all parties, culture was deliberately lagging behind, fighting its own battle for its own stakes.

At the distance of a decade, that time was the mad years of antipsychiatry.[6]The leftist logic, which was their dominant logic, went ahead unchecked by constraints. Antipsychiatry was only one aspect but it was most flamboyant, especially in a country that had always been cautious if not backward in this domain.

Basically, the mad years were dominated by a highly unusual mixture of institutional fights and fashions whose basic cultural content was radical, yet showed no discernible coherence.

These years, following the 1968 shakeup, marked the disintegration of a number of key cultural institutions. Not only were churches, universities and secondary schools affected, but research institutes and public and semipublic agencies as well (this especially held true in the area of urban problems). Psychiatric institutions were the hottest battleground, perhaps because the problems being dealt with there run the deepest in modern consciousness. To these should be added jails and legal institutions.

As to content, the intellectual fashions were only partly convergent. Superficially, the main feature was the triumphant comeback of Marxism. This took several forms: the humanist approach of Henri Lefebvre whose triumph was absolute but limited to the period of revolution itself; the austere approach of Louis Althusser whose rigor was supposed to be proof of scientificity; the many nonconformist varieties whose so-called openness did not prevent them from esotericism. Poulantzas was the new star of these diverse trends.

But behind the lip service paid to Marxism, the real driving force of the period was a general, almost hysterical, revolt against authority, which took several forms and exploded in the most varied domains but always eclipsed the more traditional political rhetoric.

Lacan was the first guru of all these trends, but here again his works which predated 1968 were more revered than used practically. There was a triumphant return to Freudianism, but the new heroes, especially Deleuze and Guattari, were more in line with far-out educators, encounter group gurus, adamant opponents of authority than were disciples of Freud [7].

A place apart should be given Michel Foucault, whose influence may prove to be the most lasting because it was more complex although not esoteric, and much more open to evolution and change. Foucault, who was more solidly and scholary rooted in history, was the first intellectual leader in the fight against asylums and prisons. But he already possessed a more sophisticated view of contemporary and human relationships and was to develop it in increasingly realistic terms.

During these years, two views prevailed whose overwhelming dominance could be found in intellectual boookshops not only in Paris but everywhere in France.

1) Authority is the Problem, and Power is intrinsically evil.

2) Progress is achieved only by wresting new rights for the individual from Authority.

Not only were they written about in countless books and brochures, but also debated in innumerable educational groups.

When viewed from this distance, the tremendous upsurge of intellectual activity during this period is impressive. This was, in a way, a general *aggiornamento* of French culture, at least in as much as it dealt with human relations. These were also the years of sexual liberation. Culture was understood to be providing answers—admittedly simplistic—to all the new anxieties and queries of modern man overwhelmed with his new-found freedom.

Yet if France is compared to other countries, in the final analysis, this difficult coming of age was achieved at a rather low social cost. Italy experienced much more disorder in the adjustment to a similar challenge of modernity. France seemed to have followed a much more puritanical and restrained course. Hysteria was restricted to cultural argument. Acting out was limited and kept under control in the intelligentsia's labs, under the tolerant benevolence of a lofty State.

Fashion not rooted in experience brings conformism more rapidly. This was the price paid by French society. But one wonders which is worse: the tamed aspect of intellectual hysteria turning to conformism, or the risks of such hysteria turned loose for lack of social control.

In any case, whether viewed from an institutional or a cultural bias, the lessons learned during the period do not seem to meet in any way either the aims of the movement, or the demands of society, or even scientific possibilities.

WAITING FOR GODOT AND THE RETURN TO NORMALCY

Only a few years later, everything seems to have faded away. Culture is a battleground no more. The equation ''culture equals revolution'' appears strange, if not absurd. Avant-garde theaters have returned to Shakespeare and universities to scholarship. Progressive TV directors are promoting a fashionable revolt against the Communist party.

The latest craze has been the new philosophers i.e. a group of the 68ers who have come full circle, from radical revolution to a harsh questioning of all that

239

revolution stands for. Certainly, culture has not become dominated by a political right wing or even by moderates, but the leftward drift has stopped and the pendulum has begun to swing the other way.

This is all the more surprising since the years 1975—1978 were years during which an impending victory of the Left was anticipated. That was to ultimately bring about in France, if not the millenium, at least the beginning of a new era. Never had there been such serious enthusiasm for change. Virtually all the promises and cherished goals of 68 were to be fulfilled. Yet even before the final failure, the cultural movement was shifting to the other side of the spectrum.

What happened?

The unpredictable conjunction of two movements made this fundamental reversal of the trend possible: first of all, the "recuperation" of the ideas of May by the establishment, Secondly, the internal collapse of the new Left in whom the last hopes of the 68ers had dwelled.

A continuous theme of the students of 68 was their fear of being "recuperated". However naive this obsession, they were quite right. For they were to succumb at least, according to their own definition and quite rapidly. Precisely because they refused to understand a world they pretended to deny, they could not resist very long. But the co-opting process was unexpected and may offer clues for understanding the significance of the movement as well as the period of restructuring that followed.

The 1968 generation was no more enlightened than preceding ones. Indeed, because of the complexity and turmoil of the time, it was bound to be less consistent and even resilient. Political gullibility had been a sort of second nature of the 68ers.

Very few members of this generation could maintain uncompromisingly radical positions. Their obsession with concrete practical deeds which had been the source of their strength very soon became their weakness. The outside world did frustrate them most effectively. The reality they were supposed to rediscover became more and more trapped in rhetoric.

In the first place, they were co-opted by the Communist party. Radicals were superb at triggering agitation. But they could not exploit the events they provoked. C.P. militants gradually discovered how useful these potential allies could be when handled properly.

Conversely, the Communist militants became attractive to the 68ers because they were getting things done. Further, they seemed to have a principle of reality in this disturbed world. Despite the fact that one of the earliest main targets of the students' revolt had been the Communist party, it became the first pole of attraction for the disenchanted radicals. Indeed, the Party found in them a new source of vigor that helped it modernize and become a force for its latest drive for power.

But the Socialist movement three or four years later became an even more powerful recuperating agency. This time it was not a party or a church which imposed a ritual together with behavioral constraints. Rather it was a very general undifferentiated hope which did not oblige one to abjure one's own faith. The *Programme Commun* was a prodigious solution for maintaining the May spirit. Ostensibly a practical and realistic rupture, it could be interpreted in all possible ways; moreover, it had enough ideological appeal to appear protected from the stigma of "impure" politics. The whole French left-wing intelligentsia (i.e. a great majority of the French) awaited the victory of the *Programme Commun* like the two tramps waiting for Godot. Not only did the '68ers find a place in the fold, they were its driving spirit. Finally, life was to be changed. Whatever the shortcomings of politicians, the movement would drive them in the right direction.

Meanwhile other struggles also played a "recuperating" role. The ecology movement which began much later than in the U.S. represented another opportunity, a way of life, a satisfactory answer to the existential dilemma. The women's movement played a similar role. Both movements could be as radical as possible and yet had the virtue of being concrete, "here and now" fights, while at the same time they were socializing ventures forcing people to interact, to negotiate, to compromise.

If "recuperation" seems to be a reasonable adjustment process whose theoretical difficulty resulted from the young Frenchmen's obsessions with ideological purity, why did it fail to bring about a victory of the Left and a new deal in French politics?

This is not the place to speculate about the reasons for the political failure of the *Programme Commun*. But what should be explained is the change in the trend which antedates the election by at least two years.

Why did the existing consensus of all the hopes and dreams for which people had fought so hard begin to lose its appeal? Why did people reject so quickly without really giving it a try—the solution which they had professed to be the only possible substitute for revolution, yet without reverting to their former radical position?

Two successive events exemplify that change. Consider, first the resounding response to the publications of Solzhenitsyn and the discovery of Soviet dissidents; second, the astounding success of an unprecedented fashion: the new philosophers.

Solzhenitsyn's final victory was to force the Western World to face up to the repressive and sadistic nature of the Soviet regime. This was not in itself a French event. But it played a major role in the French context. Solzhenitsyn's appeal to French intellectuals and especially to '68ers was felt deeply. It exposed in extremely concrete terms the contemporary drama of freedom and anti-authoritarianism. According to many studies of individual motivation, this is a major and enduring preoccupation for most Frenchmen. Therefore, again, the Left was forced to face the impossible choice of freedom versus revolution. And despite the efforts of leftist leaders, this appeal finally made counter revolution appear to be a decent alternative. Following a spate of dissillusionments: Cuba, Vietnam, Cambodia, Portugal, here was a new cause which could be understood as really pure. Not only was it counter revolutionary as regards dogma, but in concrete, even physical terms, it challenged the arch hero and taboo, Lenin.

The new philosophers'[8] success was the logical outcome of Solzhenitsyn's breakthrough. Their rhetoric and prose has very little substance. The contribution of this group has been important only in contradicting most stereotypes of the "mad years." What seems decisive and yet extremely puzzling is the reason for their success within the Left. Solzhenitsyn had a hard time breaking through. *Le Monde* consistently tried to minimize his appeal. Only one year later, this was not at all the case with the new philosophers whose access to the influential public was immediate. Although they were adopted quickly by the Giscard clique, they were not denied access by the powerful gatekeepers of *Le Monde* and *Le Nouvel Observateur*, and were launched in what can be viewed with hindsight as a major press campaign.

Why did the media change? Why did the public jump on the bandwagon?

Because of a simple combination of the following: internal weakness, fear and anxiety. The risk of the P.C. come to power was actually feared. France's existential drama seems to be the impossibility of acting out revolutionary dreams. As in Pagnol's famous play of the 30s, the infuriated radical who is the hero looks to his companion to stop him from going too far. 1968 was a perfectly pure revolution whose only flaw was that it did not take place. Finally, so was the *Programme Commun*. It was waiting for Godot to the extent Godot did not come.

To return to the media, the gatekeepers were internally divided, fearful of the Communist party, and guilt-ridden because of their constant compromises. In 1977, this group of '68 youngsters (the new philosophers) were not a threat; they looked like insiders rather than enemies. And the public cheered because it was tired of the Left-wing revolutionary stance, because it had second thoughts about the possible outcome of political change. A new era of realism was at hand. Props were no longer necessary. The '68 movement was socialized more in keeping with the traditional values of French society than with the naive hopes of the movement.

THE STATE OF THE UNION

Comparing the cultural world of 1978 with the early 60s the extent of change is not striking. The professional establishment has resisted extremely well. The great engineering and professional schools still train a small elite through harsh selective processes. The influence of ENA is greater than ever. On the other hand, philosophy as the rallying cry of the cultural pundits has almost recovered its former significance. Moreover, the Ecole Normale Supérieure's boarders do not feel guilty about enjoying their cultural primacy.

Everything is more or less back to normal. True, the churches, the universities, even secondary education have not regained their equilibrium. But again, even among them, the mood temporarily at least, is one of restoration. And the legacy of '68 seems to be, in the long run, only a singular disturbing and revealing accident. Cultural life is beginning to be replenished at its source. The novel may even flourish once more. Stories and plots are in demand, and writers may even enjoy writing.

Social sciences have come of age only very partially. But history has kept its promises. The international success of the new French school of historians, its institutional expansion with the Ecole des Hautes Etudes en Sciences Sociales have made it the temporary leader and standard bearer of all the social sciences. But its leadership is quite partial in this chaotic field. Sociology and political science are hampered by their own institutional weaknesses and paralyzed by their incapacity to accept minimum standards of scientific evidence. Economists have been stirred very much by the vigor of the political debate. But they too have gone from one misunderstanding to another; and they have not gone substantially beyond skillfull rhetoric. As in sociology, original contributions are few and they are not yet supported by the intellectual milieu.

Nevertheless, something has changed, in the cultural climate if one takes the long view. First, parochialism has decreased along with the inferiority complex counter-balancing it. Of course, this is especially noticeable as regards the U.S. French intellectuals feel perfectly at ease with American approaches and fashions. There is less emphasis on a French tradition or some specific French know-how. Leftwingers no longer use Marxism or radicalism as protection against North American or Anglo-Saxon capitalist fashions. In counterpart, one no longer finds very many zealots of the new American managerial creed. The American giant has fallen down. Its moral crisis has stamped it out, at least for the immediate present.

Secondly, taboos, especially sexual taboos, are gone. Intellectuals felt they were on fire in the early 60s, but they had to learn the difference between the freedom of the happy few and the general exposure of the great many. The French had to learn to express themselves more candidly and to remain ''cool.'' The disappearance of all traditional restraints has forced people to change their behavior and learn coolness.

Third, human relations have become more direct. Coolness as regards words and feelings may have brought more warmth in concrete relationships. The main regulator of behavior now is a growing sense of humor of which Claire Bretecher, the cartoonist of *Le Nouvel Observateur*, is the best example.

Bretecher's mission for the last four years has been to teach her public to consider its own rituals, illusions, and fancies from a distance. Her tremendous success has been a sort of cultural counterpoint to the waiting for Godot years. Its pretentious leftwing types, especially women, argue loftily and ponderously the radical creed but behave as much as ever in the bourgeois manner. They do not even have to be "recuperated" because they never left.

WHAT ABOUT GAULLISM?

Notice that I have managed to discuss all these twenty years without mentioning the name of de Gaulle or referring to Gaullism or Gaullist institutions. Yet, everything took place during those Gaullist years. Moreover, the regime was not neglecting the cultural milieu. On the contrary, it certainly placed culture high on the list of its ambitions of grandeur. Yet it seems to have made little impact. The regime had little influence on culture. The new crop of cultural fashions had no influence on politics. (Indirectly, of course, the manner in which intellectuals behave may be important for politics and the direction of society.)

In any case, Gaullism does not seem to be relevant for understanding this period, at least from a cultural point of view.

Why? The fact is puzzling. How is it that such a powerful State with an impressive father figure did not bring its influence to bear in the cultural world?

Estrangement and aloofness may be partial answers. De Gaulle's strategy was primarily to maintain himself as an aloof figure, to impress people by his distance from events and problems. Respect and estrangement may be two sides of the same coin. By forcing people to respect him and the State, de Gaulle obliged French intellectuals to keep their distance. Frenchmen already had been accustomed to the divorce between culture and practical politics. They managed quite well in freely discussing existential problems while being well protected by a benevolent state[9].

Tolerance may finally have been the General's contribution to French culture. To be sure his tolerance bore the mark of a lofty Gallic disdain. Yet it was very welcome in this country of religious ideological warfare.

THE CULTURAL REVOLUTION REVISITED

When one now tries to assess the meaning of this long period of intense intellectual activity and controversy, a sense of chaos emerges. It is a story of sound and fury. Radical fashions not only succeeded one another but coexisted without rhyme or reason in a senseless confrontation. All the contradictory tendencies pointed out in my 1963 article have seen the light of day. All the possible attitudes have been worn and discarded in facing up to the contradictions of the situation. The diagnosis of a crisis was well borne out. Reality, however, has gone far beyond my words. As yet, there has been no conclusion, nor successful revolution, i.e. no passage from an earlier equilibrium to a new one.

Those remarks require another qualification. That the crisis was serious is certain. But in another sense it was managed rather well. More specifically, society has been able to withstand this crisis without apparent loss. The cultural crisis erupted, was recognized, threatened the fabric of society briefly. It prompted a number of moral readjustments, but society has not yet been affected, basically. Moreover, if one compares France with other western societies, the French experience was not the worst, as many had predicted earlier. A tremendous spectacle was made out of the contradictions of modern times, but people did not kill each other. Violence was kept to a minimum. No wild risks were taken, and altogether it seems that Frenchmen—even French intellectuals—behaved quite properly according to a civilized tradition.

But what did the crisis achieve? The balance sheet here is not clear. In 1963, I argued that we were engaged in a decisive learning process. Some learning indeed has taken place in human relations. Frenchmen are somewhat less tense, more open, even cooler in their debates. Young people may be more willing to talk to one another and even to adults. But it is different to argue now that this learning process has ended or even that it has been accelerated. The diagnosis, however, should be more qualified if one moves from the area of human relations to intellectual culture.

True, let me reiterate that without abandoning its own parochialism the French culture milieu has learned to accommodate itself to the intellectual environment where it is again active and well at ease. It has not progressed in a decisive way as regards modes of reasoning, but more sophistication is possible now or even required when discussing complex human problems, and some sensible gains have been made in intellectual relationships. They have become simpler and more direct. Intellectuals may not have recognized the challenge of their increased numbers and the concomitant inevitable loss of status, but they tend to adjust to it intuitively.

Curiously, what has finally survived more strongly than ever is what has been attacked most strongly, and what I had diagnosed as the weakest—the institutions. I have noted the resilience of the strong cultural power centers which may have changed partially, but basically in order to reinforce themselves.

If I was correct in 1963 this sturdy resistance may herald more problems and a revival of crisis in the future. If one could venture a prediction, however, it seems that we now come to the quiet part of the cycle after years of activism, i.e. we may expect a period of respite analogous to the period of the Golden Years. But the basic problems have not been solved. Not only the opposition between moral arrogance and short term technocratism remains crystallized in the old institutions but it is now re-enacted and expanded on a broader scale in

245

the basic opposition between the world of communication expertise and the world of action, responsibility and scientific endeavor. These two worlds need each other, although they work on their own completely independent regulations. The world of communications just became emancipated in France during the crisis, and its unregulated freedom is bound to exacerbate confrontations.

In this respect an important change may have been achieved, but it was unexpected and undesired. As in the U.S. the communication experts—the media people—are presently the most important influence in the cultural world. More and more they will be central in the process of change, and will be the key actors in any new crisis. But new thinking is required to understand this other game.

NOTES

1. Michel CROZIER: "The Cultural Revolution in the New Europe," in S. Graubard, ed. *A New Europe?* Boston, 1964.

2. Manifesto sponsored by French intellectuals giving support to those refusing to serve in the Algerian War.

3. I borrowed the term from Diana Pinto whose remarkable thesis on the comparative development of sociology in France and Italy is essentially based upon such a diagnosis. See D. Pinto *"Sociology as a Cultural Phenomenon in France and France and Italy: 1950—1972"*, Ph.D. dissertation Harvard University, Cambridge, Mass, 1977.

4. Admittedly the first major novels of the *nouveau roman* antedate the success of structuralism. The success of the *"nouveau roman,"* however, occurred virtually in the same years. Literary critics as well as authors themselves were soon openly advocating the structural point of view.

5. La Chinoise

6. Felix Guattari and Gilles Deleuze belong to this group.

7. Although this is not the place, the story of the Ecole Normale's vagaries should be carefully related and the "normalien" complex analyzed. Most of these disputes raged among *normaliens*, of whom Bordieu was another guru.

8. This group includes: André Glucksmann, *Les Maitres Penseurs* and Bernard-Henri Lévy, La Barbarie a Visage Humain.

9. The long fight of Sartre trying hard and yet failing to be put in prison is a good case in point.

The Fifth Republic in Europe[1]

A. W. DePorte

Every French government since World War II has pursued a common set of goals in its European policy: to have a voice in all decisions affecting France; to achieve status in European and Atlantic affairs at least equivalent to that of Great Britain and ahead of that of the Federal Republic of Germany; to assert some form of French leadership in Europe; to maintain the country's security against threats from the East; and to promote other specific French interests, particularly economic.

The successive phases of French policy under the Fourth and Fifth Republics are thus characterized less by their goals than by the means chosen in changing international circumstances to try to achieve them. France's policy, like that of all European countries since World War II, has had to be mainly reactive to developments in an international system created and dominated by the cold war competition of the superpowers. But the new system, though its fundamental structure has been stable, has been far from static. The United States and the Soviet Union have constantly tried to improve their positions relative to each other, and the European states have been able to pursue their own objectives in the interstices of the shifting and uneasy relations between the superpowers. The system has been challenged most persistently by France, the European state which was least reconciled to dependence on the superpowers and most determined to bring about change within—or even beyond—the postwar structure of power and status in Europe.

France's struggle against the new order of things began even before it was established. The 1940 defeat removed France from the ranks of the great powers—those which had to be taken into account in important international decisions. General de Gaulle, refusing to accept this disaster as anything but temporary, managed by extraordinary stubbornness and political skill during World War II to recover for France at least the outward trappings of great power status: a permanent seat on the United Nations Security Council and an oc-

247

cupation zone in Germany. De Gaulle's achievements provided the starting point for postwar French policy. His failures provided the agenda for his successors.

Notwithstanding de Gaulle's efforts, France had not achieved the status he sought. The Big Three met without France in 1945 at Yalta, Potsdam, and Moscow. The United States and Great Britain carried their wartime special relationship into peacetime and continued to exclude France. After 1946, France had little choice but to take its place in the emerging Atlantic security and economic system. But the Fourth Republic was no more reconciled to its status than de Gaulle. It pursued his goals by other means, most notably by launching, in 1950, the imaginative policy of European integration through the Schuman-Monnet plan for a coal-steel pool. In this way it hoped to enhance its diminished voice in world councils and its claim to status by speaking for the six partners—and particularly the Federal Republic of Germany—as the one nominal great power among them.

This policy of magnification has been followed by every French government since 1950 in pursuit of the goals they shared. De Gaulle took it up—though distinctly in his fashion—as the central element of an effort which over eleven years used every asset of skill and national power and seized every opportunity presented by changing international circumstances to establish once and for all France's clear right to participate in the management of all world problems—that is, to reclaim its place as a great power.

A key word in this definition of de Gaulle's supreme goal is "participate." His rhetoric obscured this fact by suggesting that his main objective was to remove all serious limitations on France's freedom of action in international affairs, whether imposed by colonial encumbrances, economic weakness, or dependence on foreign states. De Gaulle himself, of course, was clearly not very much inhibited by the constraints which he claimed shackled France. Even so, he had reason to be concerned about them. No doubt he feared that his successors might be less resolute in defending France's interests if he did not disencumber them in advance from dangerous ties. Also, he had in mind to reconcile the "ferments of dispersion"[2] of a defeated and divided people not only by giving them a tolerable place in a world they had led and lost but by convincing them that despite the defeat of 1940 and the rise of the superpowers they were still masters of their fate. But in this case as in others we must be careful to consider de Gaulle's actions as well as his words, which played an important part in his policy but not always to reveal it. Too much weight has been given to his constant talk of national independence, as if that were an absolute objective beyond discussion and compromise. If de Gaulle derided and resisted Atlantic and European integration, he did so as part of his campaign to participate in Atlantic, European and global decision-making on his own terms. The independence he sought was not splendid isolation but the reverse, a recognized hand with the other great players in the international game.

Fixed in his goal, de Gaulle was a supreme opportunist in his means, adapting his policies as circumstances not of his making permitted or required, above all in his all-important dealings with the United States and the Soviet Union. The first phase of his diplomacy took place largely in an orthodox cold war framework defined by the then current relationship of the superpowers; the second, from 1963 on, was a bolder movement toward overcoming the consequences of the cold war in Europe. In both phases he challenged the postwar European system. Had he succeeded in his first effort, the balance of power within the Euratlantic subsystem would have changed to France's advantage. Had his second effort been successful, the fundamental structure of the bipolar system and the division of Europe would have been dismantled, or put on the road to being so.

At first (September 1958) de Gaulle tried to restructure the Western bloc by proposing a tripartite directorate to manage the cold war globally, as Roosevelt and Churchill had managed the many theaters of World War II. Whether he expected this to be accepted or negotiated, he knew then, and always, that the status recognition that he craved for France could be accorded only by the US as the greatest power in the world—a fact he never doubted—and the most important participant in the web of military, political, and economic relationships in which France, however independent he proclaimed it to be, had no choice but to participate.

When the Americans refused this direct proposal, de Gaulle did not terminate France's military integration in NATO at once. Nor did he do so even when the Algerian war ended (July 1962) or his political mastery of France was reaffirmed at the polls (fall 1962). Since, obviously, he could not have foreseen the Cuban missile crisis and the detente that followed, it is not surprising that his security policy and diplomatic moves toward the United States and the Federal Republic during the four years that followed September 1958 continued to reflect cold war premises. But he must have had still other reasons for not dis-integrating France from NATO, for he waited another four years—until 1966—to do so.

No doubt de Gaulle really feared the encroachment of American control on French independence through the alliance and wanted to be rid of it as soon as it was no longer necessary to France's security. But he believed also that NATO, precious to the US as its main instrument of hegemony in Western Europe and to the FRG as its main bulwark of security, provided a hostage which he could threaten if the Americans persisted in refusing France what they had denied in 1958. During eight years, therefore, he reduced French cooperation step by step in a kind of water torture intended to make the United States think again about the price it might have to pay to preserve France's role.

We can never know whether France might have been kept in the NATO military structure on terms that were compatible with its effectiveness and respectful of de Gaulle's status goal because the American government would not negotiate. It did not believe he wanted to bargain and did not want to do so itself for fear of strengthening his ability to undermine the Euratlantic edifice altogether. De Gaulle at last predictably removed France from NATO's military system, but only when it became clear that neither persuasion nor coercion would lead the US to give France the status he wanted. By then, international circumstances seemed to open up an even more dazzling prospect for French policy to hold before the Germans and others: reunification of Europe from the Atlantic to the Urals by dismantling of the two-bloc system and ending superpower hegemony. If the US would not bargain to keep France in the Western grouping, the Soviet Union might bargain to take it out. If France could not obtain a satisfactory role within the European system, it might achieve an even greater one by helping to disrupt it.

After the Cuban missile crisis, de Gaulle was convinced that the chances of a Soviet attack on Western Europe were almost negligible, because of changes in the Soviet system, Soviet preoccupation with China (which he recognized early), and Soviet respect for American power. He knew that, whatever he did, the US could not withdraw its protection from France while continuing to guarantee Germany and other neighboring states, for France had no frontier with the Soviet bloc and no bilateral quarrel with it. If he did not withdraw France from NATO integration until 1966, and if he then emphasized continued loyalty to the Atlantic Treaty and to the Alliance, it was because he wanted not isolation but leverage, on his allies and the Soviet Union. Therefore, France continued after 1966 to participate in the North Atlantic Council and in certain other Alliance activities and to maintain its forces in Germany. De Gaulle's purpose was to lead the other European allies, not cut France off from them; reduce American power but not eliminate its still essential presence in the European balance; induce the Soviet Union to negotiate by opening the prospect of dismantling the Euratlantic system but only if the Russians would make reciprocal moves in the East.

Thus, adequately covered against a negligible danger, de Gaulle began to argue that the West Europeans no longer had to pay the price of political and economic dependence on the US in order to maintain protection which the Americans, in their own interest, could not withdraw, and which, in any case, was both less needed and less dependable than before. Insofar as there was a residual danger of Soviet attack and a legitimate doubt about the efficacy of the American guarantee, the French *force de dissuasion* would be there, in European hands, to trigger nuclear war, and thereby deter the USSR.

At the core of this new French policy, as of de Gaulle's European policy at all times, was the Federal Republic. On French-German relations depended, in the words of his foreign minister, "the evolution of the entire continent, the question of how the new Europe would be organized, what sort of lasting balance would be established, in short, what would be the future of our country placed as it is in the world."[3] De Gaulle therefore tried at all times and by all means to "weave a network of preferential ties"[4] with the West Germans as France's main partner in a Western European bloc which would eventually be able to deal as an equal with the United States and the Soviet Union. During the Berlin crises (1958–60 and 1961–62) and up to the end of the Adenauer era, he tried to persuade the Germans that the United States might negotiate away their interests in a "new Yalta" by which Europe and Germany would remain permanently divided and under the control of the two superpowers. These arguments had some appeal to Adenauer, and in the dawn of detente following the Cuban crisis he and de Gaulle seemed to be the last of the cold warriors. Yet de Gaulle failed to establish a Franco-German nucleus to counter US policy. The Franco-German treaty of January 1963 seemed for a moment to represent the consummation of his hopes. But Adenauer could not line up his country in what seemed in the circumstances (after de Gaulle's veto of British entry into the European Community) a challenge to the American-led system. With American blessing, the German parliament sterilized the political thrust of the treaty by adding a preamble to the ratification law which reaffirmed Atlantic orthodoxy. A few months later Adenauer was replaced by the ostentatiously Atlanticist Ludwig Erhard.

De Gaulle reversed his line almost at once and began to suggest that Germany's hope for reunification lay in detente between the two halves of Europe, a detente to which Bonn could contribute by loosening its ties with Washington. Looking beyond the unsatisfactory Bonn government of the moment, he believed the tide...of German politics was beginning to flow in this new direction and that Franco-German relations and French leadership of Europe could flow with it.

It seems clear that de Gaulle's policies toward the Soviet Union were to a considerable extent arrived at, whether wishfully or cynically, as a by-product of other calculations. His initial cold war orthodoxy served his purposes with respect to the United States and the Federal Republic. So did his shift, after 1963, from a rigid to a more open approach toward the Soviet Union when circumstances beyond his control or foresight changed. In this phase, he argued that Soviet policy was evolving and that "detente, entente, and cooperation" was possible in Europe—provided that the European countries, and especially the Federal Republic, followed France's lead in emancipating themselves from dependence on the United States, the *sine qua non* of a parallel loosening of the Eastern bloc. The USSR might eventually agree to a settlement on a basis other than the *status quo* of a divided Europe—and divided Germany—but only if the Western European states played their own part in dissolving the blocs rather than waiting, rigidly and hopelessly, for the USSR to give up its satellites to an American-dominated Western bloc or, worse, for the two superpowers to reaffirm their joint condominium over Europe.

By visiting the Soviet Union in 1966, soon after taking France out of NATO integration, de Gaulle made his Atlantic policy appear not as the tearing down of established institutions but as part of a constructive effort to bring about a settlement of frozen postwar European problems. De Gaulle's long-range vision for Europe was not very explicit beyond the eventual withering away of the Eastern and Western blocs in some reciprocal manner. He had in mind, not an early settlement, but a long process of contacts and negotiation in which France would be a central player. De Gaulle did not seem to exclude the United States from this process or think that American or Russian influence would disappear from Europe. But he wanted to encourage the West Europeans to take initiatives themselves, to talk to Moscow bilaterally, and to come to feel that they should not and need not rely on US diplomacy to take advantage of the new opportunities opening up in Europe. Thus de Gaulle was involved in a long-range campaign of European consciousness-raising.

But it was clear even before 1968 that neither the Federal Republic nor the other European Community members would accept French leadership in East-West or other matters if that meant distancing themselves from the United States. De Gaulle never brought any of them to accept this, notwithstanding his often ingenious use not only of the prospects for detente but of every available strategic, political, trade and monetary issue—which were many—to try to arouse in them a sense of separateness from the United States. His failure cannot be attributed only to their resentment of his peremptory unilateralism. Rather, it proved how small that sense of separateness was, notwithstanding serious policy differences between the US and some European allies on a range of important problems.

There is more to de Gaulle's failure even than rooted West European attachment to the United States and the refusal of the Soviet Union to provide substance for his dreams by loosening its grip on Eastern Europe. As an opponent of the European *status quo* and the division of Europe, de Gaulle could not fail to see that his policy pointed to a reopening of the German question if not ever to the eventual reunification of Germany. He certainly had no reason to wish that the West Germans would miss this implication of his views. Of course, de Gaulle also believed that the Germans would have to sacrifice more to reunification, should it even be feasible, than their dependence on Washington. Among other things, they would have to accept the Oder-Neisse frontier (he said so publicly as early as 1959) and continued non-nuclear status. But in favoring German-Soviet bilateral talks and at the least a reawakening of German interest in reunification, de Gaulle may have risked France's security for a sterile show of leadership, or, as Edward Kolodziej has put it, subordinated national interests to pursuit of systemic change.[5] This was a bold policy with which the other West European governments, less ambitious than de Gaulle and therefore less willing to take risks, did not agree. They saw his attempt to reduce American influence in Europe as likely to lead not only to a local French hegemony, which would in itself be less welcome to them than American because less useful, but to the possibility over the longer term of

252

releasing the Germans, united or not, from dependence on the US, the most important of the constraints placed on them and assumed by them since the war—a prospect the West Europeans found less attractive still. Of course de Gaulle might have done without the support of the smaller European countries if he could have won the West Germans (and eventually the Russians) to his ideas. But he did not win them, even when the Kiesinger-Brandt "Grand Coalition," more solicitous of France, replaced Erhard in October 1966. In the attempt, de Gaulle completed the diplomatic isolation of France in Western Europe which his NATO and common market policies had began.

Compared to the grand policy of relations with the United States, the Federal Republic and the Soviet Union, de Gaulle's dealings with the European Community were second-level, exploitative and defensive. Apart from wanting to ensure maximum benefit for the French economy, especially agriculture, de Gaulle was interested in the EC mainly as the framework for a special relationship with the FRG and as a possible vehicle for forming a French-led political bloc based on the Franco-German entente. Hence, he accepted the Rome treaties readily when he returned to power. But his hope to establish a confederal political as well as an economic community came to nothing, after three years of negotiations, not because his proposals for structured political consultations were so repellent in themselves (the EC members have since moved in that direction) but because the other five in different degrees correctly saw in his plan a desire to establish a European grouping conspicuously apart from the US.[6]

Once de Gaulle's hope to use the EC for his own political ends faded, his limited positive interest in that structure declined also. There remained a desire to ensure economic benefits and avoid further supranationality. In 1965, therefore, he created a major crisis in the belief that the Commission and the other members were trying to force France to accept greater central powers for the Community authorities as the price of establishing the system for financing the Common Agricultural Policy (CAP), or simply to avoid honoring their commitment to do so. The French reaction seemed so virulent that many concluded that France's membership was no longer compatible with the continued survival of the Community's institutions in their integrated form.

As it turned out, either de Gaulle was bargaining for the best terms or he backed down from his original position when confronted by the opposition of the five. But they too backed away from some of their more advanced positions. In the end, the institutions survived, the details of the CAP were worked out, and de Gaulle not only stopped the proposed enlargement of the Commission's and the European Parliament's roles but also blocked implementation of the treaty clauses providing for less-than-unanimous decisions by the Council of Ministers. De Gaulle's legacy in this area was one of the more ironical facets of a career filled with ironies. For all his hostility to Brussels, the EC existed only on paper when he took office in 1958 and was a flourishing economic union when he departed the scene. Yet he clearly bears some—though not all—of the responsibility for damping the "European spirit" and preventing further institutional evolution. By doing that, he perhaps blocked the growth of an institution which, even short of an improbable federal union, might have posed a challenge more serious than his own to the structure of the Euratlantic subsystem.

De Gaulle's intellectual agility and well cultivated capacity to shock and amaze concealed for many years his failure to establish a firm partnership with Germany, or secure the leadership of a coherent European bloc, or take even a first meaningful step toward negotiating the end of the cold war division of Europe and the superpower hegemony over it. The determination of the superpowers to maintain the *status quo* in Europe and the acquiescence of the European countries (whether satisfied, resigned, coerced, or skeptical of alternatives) in the international structure in which they lived were little affected by de Gaulle's far-reaching and diverse attempt to change things. The six-day Middle East war in June 1967 probably showed him that the forces arrayed against his hopes were overwhelming, outside Europe but also in it. He lost his dream of reducing the dependence of states in all areas, including Europe, on the superpowers. War reaffirmed the dependence of Israel on the Americans and of the Arabs on the Russians, that is, the polarization of the Middle East. Worse, it brought the United States and the Soviet Union into direct collaboration to end the conflict and prevent its spread. The Glassboro meeting of President Johnson and Prime Minister Kosygin in July, welcomed by many as a step toward peace and detente, was a black day for de Gaulle. The superpowers, having confirmed the *status quo* in the Middle East, now seemed likely to do so in Europe at a "new Yalta," thus checkmating his policy of "detente, entente, and cooperation" from the Atlantic to the Urals. It is not fanciful to speculate that de Gaulle's virulent hostility to Israel and politically pointless behavior in Quebec in August can be traced to the sense of impotence and defeat laid on him by the events of that summer.

De Gaulle's failure was completed in 1968 with the domestic upheaval in May, which undermined his international prestige by revealing the internal weakness of his rule, and the Warsaw Pact invasion of Czechoslovakia in August, which showed again that the Soviet Union's permissiveness with respect to change in Eastern Europe was much too limited to sustain the hopes he had nourished. This turned out to be a spur to a new kind of German Eastern policy which in sharp contrast to both Adenauer's and Erhard's accepted and ratified the postwar *status quo* in the hope of ameliorating and in the long-run perhaps modifying it. But this was the antithesis of what de Gaulle sought. His dream of gradually loosening both the Western and Eastern blocs was shattered by Soviet determination to maintain control over Eastern Europe. The detente built by the Federal Republic and the United States on that fact was not de Gaulle's detente. From the point of view of foreign policy, his resignation from office in April 1969 was an anticlimax.

In the last few months of de Gaulle's rule, however, there were several shifts in his policy that allowed his successor, Georges Pompidou, to implement his campaign slogan of "change within continuity" without having either to stand pat on second-phase Gaullism or abandon his link to the General's practice and followers. In face of the flattering courtship by the Nixon administration and the monetary difficulties caused by the May "events," de Gaulle executed a rapprochement with the United States. He and his chief of staff also began to tone down the implications of their doctrine of *tous azimuts*, which had seemed to place the United States on the same plane as the Soviet Union in France's defense planning. Finally, de Gaulle made a cryptic gesture toward Great Britain which, whatever its purpose, perhaps reflected a wish to extricate France from the deadend to which his European policy had led. Pompidou followed up all these leads. Despite official emphasis on a new "Mediterranean policy" (itself a retreat from de Gaulle's attempted global reach), his most important policies were directed to improving relations within Western Europe and with the United States.

Even if Pompidou had not wanted to lead France out of its isolation he would have found that its diplomatic latitude from 1969 on was overshadowed by the important negotiations which the new American and German governments were pursuing with the Soviet Union. France's hoped-for role as a broker in detente was bypassed. The French government had no choice but to back Willy Brandt's *Ostpolitik* but could not avoid being nervous about its possible costs for France's special position in German affairs and even for French security. Perhaps de Gaulle's successor was more relieved than disappointed when the Soviet-German negotiations ended by confirming rather than changing borders and alignments in Europe.

In any case, Pompidou devised a European policy to advance traditional goals by a new combination of means that would be attractive not only to the other five members of the EC but, at home, to the old Gaullist supporters whom he hoped to keep ("continuity") and the centrists he hoped to add to his coalition ("change"). The core of his approach was to maintain as close a relationship as possible with Bonn—a fixed French priority—while seeking reinsurance by moves toward London and Washington. His single most striking departure from Gaullist orthodoxy—dropping the French veto on Britain's accession to the European community—reflected all these considerations. But he did this, probably, not so much because he feared the economic power of the Federal Republic and wanted the UK to help balance it within the EC (on the contrary, France in those years hoped to catch up with the FRG) as because he understood that France could not achieve its goals in Europe unless it ended its alienation of the Five, centered most specifically on the veto. Pompidou must have known that he could not hurl threats of breaking up the EC with the same abandon as de Gaulle. He would have to negotiate for several things that France wanted.

Pompidou's call in 1969 for completion, enlargement and deepening of the community suggested the range of the bargain he was proposing. One goal was very precise: completing arragngements for financing the common agricultural program—a policy of major national and political concern for the French government. The other five, of course, wanted enlargement. The third panel of Pompidou's triptych was the most interesting and long-term. Deepending meant a return to de Gaulle's idea of structured political cooperation among the EC members, but outside the EC machinery, without integration, and without the paraphernalia of treaty and secretariat which de Gaulle had wanted to underline the importance—and distinctiveness— of his "European Europe." To this end (as well as for domestic reasons) Pompidou abandoned the theological debate between federalism and confederalism which de Gaulle had relished to his cost. Deepening meant also a bold—and, as events showed, premature—initiative for a European monetary and economic union to be achieved by "confederal" rather than integrationist means.

Pompidou thus conducted a very active European policy, but its objectives—though not its context—were more like those of the Gaullist first phase than those pursued between 1964 and 1968. In his Mediterranean policy, Pompidou's courtship of the Arab states, Eastern and Western, was still wrapped in the rhetoric of disengaging the sea from superpower competition and presence. But, despite occasional talk of developing a "European will," restructuring the European or even the Western systems was not expected. The slackening of consciousness-raising efforts against the United States, the dropping of the veto on British admission to the Common Market, the pursuit in the EC of practical benefits for the French economy—in these and other ways Pompidou made clear that he was promoting French interests and leadership within the fundamental East-West division of Europe which de Gaulle had tried to change. By those standards, Pompidou could claim solid policy successes. France again entered into constructive contact with its European partners, inside and outside the community. The process of political dialogue was launched among them. And, perhaps because Pompidou's France was more accommodating in these and other ways, the Nixon administration gave it marks of status that its predecessors had refused to de Gaulle. The French government could not but be gratified that important decisions affecting the Western monetary system were taken at French-US summits (the Azores in December 1971, Iceland in May 1973).

For Pompidou, as for his predecessors, the effort to develop common policies among the members of the community pointed to a long-term goal of strengthening Europe *vis-à-vis* the United States within the Western bloc. Perhaps he even hoped that detente might someday help France recover its leadership of Europe. But the man who said that the US military presence in Europe was normal clearly understood that a policy of trying to disengage Western Europe from the US in order to disengage the Soviet Union from Eastern Europe was, even in the high noon of East-West detente, and would be for a long time sterile, self-isolating and even dangerous.

Perhaps because Pompidou's final illness coincided with an acute international atmosphere, four years of Pompidolian pragmatism gave way in 1973-74 to an upsurge of the true Gaullist spirit when his foreign minister, Michel Jobert, responded with a biting defense of Europe's, and France's, autonomy to the American government's attempt to define a lasting relationship with the Europeans on American terms (the "year of Europe"). The Yom Kippur war seemed a perfect occasion for European consciousness-raising of the classic Gaullist style. France had little trouble persuading the EC members to move in the direction of Arab positions. But the energy crisis imposed a *de facto* cooperation between the two sides of the Atlantic to which France could offer no alternative that the other Europeans found realistic. The dramatic clash between the United States and France at the Washington energy conference in February 1974 ended with the isolation of France and the acceptance by her eight partners of Henry Kissinger's plan for dealing with the energy problem. Three months later Pompidou was dead, Valéry Giscard d'Estaing was president, and the winter flowering of Gaullism was over.

French particularism in foreign policy has faded further under Giscard, as compared not only to Pompidou's last months but to his rule as a whole. Giscard made his priorities clear in his first press conference, which dealt entirely with internal affairs. Indifferent success in his efforts at reform and political realignment as well as persistent economic difficulties have not led him to follow de Gaulle's precept of using a vivid foreign policy to compensate for—or conceal—domestic troubles.

Without being grandly ambitious or dramatic, Giscard's foreign policy has nevertheless been active. France has continued to cultivate as close ties as possible with third world countries. It has been fertile in proposing forums for discussion of north-south issues such as the Conference on International Economic Cooperation, the Euro-Arab dialogue and structured European-Arab-African Cooperation. It has led the European Community toward a more pro-Arab policy—not difficult in face of OPEC's power—and aligned itself with the critics of the Israeli-Egyptian peace treaty. Africa has been for Giscard what the Mediterranean was for Pompidou—the main arena for France's extra-European role—and has provided some policy successes (the small military operation in Shaba province in spring 1978, for example, carried out—a departure in itself—in open collaboration with the United States).

But in Europe, always the focus of French policy, the diminution of prospects for an active detente policy has left the French government even less latitude than under Pompidou to pursue the disintegration of the two-bloc system, and it has not tried to do so nor talked about this as a policy goal, even distant. France's relations with the Soviet Union have been testy and sometimes even contentious. For a moment (June 1978) Giscard, who in 1977 had criticized the United States' human rights policy for jeopardizing detente, seemed to be writing off detente by insisting that the Soviet Union respect the *status quo* everywhere if it wanted detente in Europe. He later backed off from this (perhaps because he became convinced that the US still remained committed to detente despite human rights and alarums in Africa) but the French-Soviet "privileged relationship" is visibly thin of political content. French relations with the US, on the other hand, have continued to improve. It is perhaps only a small exaggeration to say that France is competing with its closest partner, the Federal Republic, for a "privileged relationship" with the United States, if only to preclude what Fred Bergsten has called US-German "bigemony."

France under Giscard has not been a model ally for the US, any more than it ever was or is likely to be. This is not, as is sometimes thought, because he has been constrained by his Gaullist supporters (whose relative influence on policy has waned steadily) but because he and almost all French citizens now share a consensus on maintaining French "independence" *vis-à-vis* the US and NATO, however defined in detail. French positions on the Middle East, arms control, monetary and energy policy and other issues, often expressed vigorously, continue to irritate Washington. But France has not tried seriously to strengthen its own leadership in Europe by taking advantage of the weakened US leadership that has coincided with Giscard's regime. On the contrary, this has perhaps made it more attractive and easier for Giscard to deal with the US, reinforcing the tendency to practical cooperation which economic difficulties have made essential for both governments.

The realism with which Giscard has approached the US was expressed with daring frankness by Foreign Minister Sauvagnargues:

> Problems between the United States and France, as between the United States and Europe, result from the requirements of the facts. These are the disparity between their respective power, a disparity which on the part of the United States implies, I would say, both reticence and moderation and on the part of the less powerful partner, the desire and the concern not to provoke useless difficulties and not to inflate uselessly the inevitable differences.[7]

On the whole, the United States has responded as Giscard might have hoped to this unaccustomed recognition of its power and leadership. It has shown respect toward France; has accepted the institutionalization of the Western economic summit, first proposed by Giscard in 1975, as a normal part of the international scenery; and has even taken part in a smaller four-power summit (at Guadeloupe, in January 1979) which is not so different from the arrangement de Gaulle proposed in 1958. The change in the American position (accepting such a meeting notwithstanding the unhappiness of the other European allies—and Japan) is at least as striking as the change in France's policy (accepting the Federal Republic into the inner circle).

French rapprochement with the United States has not removed the traditional impulse for a European policy aimed to provide near-term benefits, particularly economic, and to strengthen the inevitable longer-term hope for some redistribution of influence within the Western system to Europe's, and France's, benefit. Europe, Giscard said, should not be a void on the map. The most striking aspect of his European policy is the ever more visible partnership with Germany. Of course, Giscard, like his predecessors, has not neglected to underline the essentiality of the FRG's non-nuclear status and the fact that France, but not the FRG, was an extra-European power. He has also called for strengthening the French economy and French conventional forces to balance Germany's better. The partnership was thus not equal in the French view and the inequality was to France's benefit notwithstanding the FRG's greater economic weight. But it has been no secret that Giscard and Chancellor Helmut Schmidt have formed a team on whose agreement the policies of the European Community depend. They felt themselves strong enough to launch the European Monetary System (EMS) bilaterally, without reference not only to Italy and the smaller EC members but to the UK as well. And they were right. Giscard's suggestion (February 1976) that an enlarging community might need a small inner-core directorate has had no formal result so far, but in practice the balance of influence in the community in the late 1970's swung perceptibly to the Big Two when they agreed.

They, and the community in their wake, have agreed on a new effort at monetary union, admission of new members, direct election of the European parliament, and regular political consultation—and sometimes policy concertation—at the highest level. They have not agreed on arms control policy in Europe nor have they tried to add a security dimension to their own or the EC's agenda, which Giscard said could be considered only when political independence had been achieved. Indeed, he was bold enough to strengthen his own argument by adding that the Soviet Union would not like such an effort and that many allies still preferred integration with the United States—a statement that was accurate enough but that reflected a degree of compliance with the wishes of others not likely to have been calmly admitted in public by de Gaulle or even Pompidou.

The Giscard government's candid admission of the limits of its foreign policies obscures its successes. If the place of France in the late 1970's is measured against the goals all postwar French governments have pursued, the balance sheet has many positive elements. France's security is as reasonably maintained and its economic interests—as the French understand them—as reasonably promoted as could be. The British-American special relationship that vexed the Fourth Republic and de Gaulle has waned, along with British influence. France is a leader of Western Europe, but it shares that function in a

The Impact of the Fifth Republic on France

complex way with the Federal Republic and the United States. France participates in constant European, Western and four-power summits, though
whether they add as much to its influence or prestige as de Gaulle believed is
questionable.

But the most fundamental policy goal of both the Fourth and Fifth Republic
remains out of reach. In a television interview given in February 1978 Giscard
claimed that

> France has a voice in all the major international debates which, as you know, was not
> always the case.[8]

But this is not so. The French government would like very much, for example,
to participate in Middle East peacemaking but, so far, it does not. France does
not participate in the arms control negotiations of the superpowers and is not
bound by their agreements, but their choice of detente or tension affects it profoundly. The superpowers remain on their high perch above all others. The
two-bloc system they maintain in Europe encadres all French policy. De
Gaulle's most far-reaching ambition—to end this state of things—is not only
unachieved but is no longer even pursued by the French government, which
lives not uncomfortably in the European and Atlantic structures it cannot
change.

Yet why should Giscard's policy be judged by de Gaulle's ambitions?
Though de Gaulle's successors have now led the Fifth Republic longer than he
did, there is still a strong inclination to measure their achievements by his objectives. But his success in Europe was not so considerable that his heirs did not
feel obliged to pursue classic French policy goals by quite different means.
There is no realism, therefore, in condemning Giscard for not having established French leadership of Western Europe or put the two-bloc system in Europe
on the road to dissolution. It is doubtful that any French government could do
these things. Perhaps those are to be praised most who understand the facts of
international life and act on that understanding.

NOTES

1. This chapter includes material from the author's book, *Europe Between the Superpowers:
The Enduring Balance* (New Haven: Yale University Press, 1979), with permission of the Press.
2. Charles de Gaulle, *Mémoires de Guerre, I: L'Appel, 1940–1942* (Paris: Librairie Plon,
1954), p. 1.
3. Maurice Couve de Murville, *Une Politique Étrangère 1958–1969* (Paris: Librairie Plon,
1971), p. 235.
4. Charles de Gaulle (trans. Terence Kilmartin), *Memoirs of Hope* (London: Weidenfeld and
Nicolson, 1971), p. 173.
5. Edward A. Kolodziej, *French International Policy Under De Gaulle and Pompidou* (Ithaca:
Cornell University Press, 1974), p. 585.
6. The elementary and fundamental question was to know whether the Europe we wanted to
build would be European or Atlantic. Couve de Murville, p. 100.
7. Address to the Anglo-American Press Association, Paris, July 11, 1975.
8. French Embassy, Press Information Service (78-12), p. 3.

Consensus, Confusion, and Confrontation in France:
The Left in Search of a Defense Policy

Michael M. Harrison

THE GAULLIST SECURITY MODEL AND A PLURALISTIC LEFT

One of Gaullism's most significant legacies has been a compelling ideal of national security and defense based on the abstract concept of independence.[1] This doctrine has been necessarily flexible and often ambivalent, in application if not in conception. Its rhetoric has ranged from the advocacy of a tripartite Western oligarchy in the 1958 Memorandum to an embrace of extreme defense autonomy and quasi-neutralism between 1966 and 1968, although a pragmatic collaboration with the Atlantic Alliance on terms set by France has been the prevailing pattern of national security ties.[2] Whatever aspect of this flexible policy is emphasized for domestic or international reasons, its essential premise was that a state or government without maximum feasible independence in defense cannot define its priorities in other arenas of importance to the national interest, and will consequently be incapable of coherent national action and international cooperation to promote the state's interests.[3] Although this perspective can be interpreted narrowly and unrealistically, it amounts primarily to a reasonable emphasis on the integrity of national decision-making as one means of guaranteeing maximum leverage in an interdependent and often hazardous international order.

Once subject to acrimonious disputes within France, the fundamental premises of the Gaullist security model seem gradually to have attained the status of a broad national consensus that sets the terms and parameters of debates over contemporary issues. Thus it commands the respect of Giscard d'Estaing and the neo-Atlanticists of the center, as well as the more or less enthusiastic allegiance of socialists, Gaullists, and communists closer to the ex-

261

tremes of the French political spectrum. The evolution of the left is particularly striking. It has embraced the symbols, rhetoric, and even the instruments of Gaullist security policy as potentially useful vehicles for socialism. This has not been true during most of the Fifth Republic and represents a significant change by left-wing parties. Recent developments are perhaps most remarkable as far as the French nuclear force is concerned, for one of the few issues commanding a consensus among left groups during the 1960s was their opposition to a national nuclear force and their attachment to vague disarmament or arms control schemes as alternatives to the *force nucléaire stratégique* (FNS).

Much of the French left also seems to have accepted the Gaullist design for a special kind of independent French membership in the Atlantic Alliance, one that retains flexible ties to the Alliance itself but eschews direct links to the integrated military organization. For the socialists, such a position is the culmination of an erratic evolution in Alliance policy. The old SFIO had been one of the promoters of the Atlantic Alliance in 1949, became disenchanted with NATO during the Fourth Republic traumas of the 1950s, but remained loyal enough to join Francois Mitterrand and the Federation of the Left in proposing a motion of censure over the partial withdrawal from NATO in 1966. Even then, however, the Federation's position was ambivalent, notable more for opposition to de Gaulle's isolated and nuclear-centered defense policy than for its warm attachment to the American coalition itself. A subsequently more critical socialist position on the Atlantic Alliance (discussed below) did not, however, quite bring them around to the point of view of the communists, who had vehemently opposed the Treaty in 1949 and later held the Soviet position that NATO was an aggressive and militaristic capitalist arrangement, a threat to the socialist bloc and an instrument for suppressing the working classes within the Atlantic states. Despite their criticism of nuclear weapons, communist opposition to Gaullist foreign policy was always somwhat awkward and hesitant because they perceived advantages in General de Gaulle's opposition to an American-dominated West, in his resistance to the supranational aspects of European cooperation, and in his audacious pursuit of a detente policy with the Soviet Union and the East bloc.[4] Thus, the principle of independence from debilitating international constraints, and the characteristic Gaullist challenge to a hegemonic Western bloc, appealed to the communists while they gradually gained approval by a more radical Socialist party. By 1972, then, communists and socialists could capitalize on the Gaullist achievement and agree to tolerate, perhaps only temporarily, membership in a capitalist alliance on the basis of maximum independence and autonomy.

A gradual and partial reconciliation to de Gaulle's defense policy has been difficult and awkward for a left long accustomed to simplistic criticism and posturing that usually betray unwillingness to confront its own confused priorities. Socialists and communists alike have been unable to overcome fully their own ineptitude in handling security issues, and have thereby reinforced widespread doubts about the maturity, competence, and intentions of leftist parties and elites. Despite the common Gaullist approach of the major left parties, security policy was one of the many unresolved issues within the left alliance and often surfaced to reveal starkly divergent perspectives on France's international role, her alignments, and her status within an interdependent Western capitalist order. Debate over security policy is always heated in France because the issue has such high symbolic value for French elites. This case, however, was particularly controversial, being linked to a dramatic leftist challenge to the domestic status quo and to France's general attachment to the Western capitalist system.

The left's congenital inability to set priorities has doubtless been exacerbated by intra-party divisions and sometimes radical fluctuations in socialist and communist assessments of domestic and international situations. Abrupt shifts in the views of the French Communist party (PCF) may reflect uncertainties inherent in a recent independence within the international communist movement, and an inability to find a comfortable relationship with either the Soviet Union or the West that is also compatible with the shifting priorities of national communism. Despite its awkward handling of many issues, in defense affairs the PCF does seem to be guided by a consistent antagonism toward French association with Atlantic or West European security institutions—a stand that is perfectly compatible with general communist hostility to economic and political dependence on the West. Because the communists often cannot attack directly all the instruments of Western capitalist interdependence, they sometimes focus on defense and security issues as a metaphorical arena for exposing the party's most congenial international choices. Thus, for example, the particular French communist ideological paradigm and a habit of relying on Soviet analyses of the international situation often lead the PCF to embrace Soviet security perspectives, even though this may conflict with the party's recent commitment to define its own domestic and international priorities.

Although communists and socialists have both provided evidence of ill-defined or contradictory perspectives on West European security, the Socialist party (PS) faces the distinctive problem of managing diverse and often combative internal factions. Thus, PS elites have difficulty producing coherent policy because, on defense and most other issues, the party is awash with different viewpoints and postures that only sometimes coincide with its "official" majority-minority divisions.[5] Francois Mitterrand's leadership doubtlessly compounded this problem, because he held the party and, until 1977, the left alliance together through a cultivated plan for ambiguity, indecision, vacillation, and dissimulation. In security matters, at any rate, Mitterrand often appears uncertain of his own attitudes and interests.

ELUSIVE THREATS AND HOSTILE ALLIES

The stormy alliance between socialists and communists was based on the Socialist party's post-1971 commitment to an anti-capitalist philosophy emphasizing the socio-economic factors of domestic and international politics. Socialist security perspectives shifted closer to a communist framework as traditional diplomatic and military interpretations of international threats were superseded partly by a neo-Marxist analysis asserting that the structure of international politics and of international dominance and dependence is primarily a product of economic relations and the international division of labor.[6] Given their values and this analytical framework, socialist elites could sympathize with communist sensitivities to the potential costs of international economic interdependence and its severe restraints on an audacious domestic program deemed incompatible with the Western system. The principal threats to French independence, especially under a leftist regime, were identified as international capitalist financial and market instruments acting in alliance with the strongest capitalist powers, the United States and West Germany. This situation posed an awkward dilemma for PS security policy, because the actions most hostile to a socialist France were expected to emerge in the context of relations with ostensible partners and allies.

Most post-war French governments have been exceedingly wary of dependence on an American-dominated West, and have sought to limit the restraints and piece together maximum leeway and independence. The left certainly ascribed a more pervasive and insidious hostility to France's close allies than any of these governments, including even de Gaulle's at the brief zenith of his policy of independence and grandeur from 1966 to 1968. This perspective was a prominent feature of the new PS until perhaps 1975, when the party's leadership and policies shifted to the right temporarily to emphasize more moderate approaches to international economic and political issues. By 1977, PS international policy was based on the assumption that a socialist-dominated left government could secure the international concessions necessary for a domestic transition to socialism. Thus it might avoid drastic ruptures in a period of serious economic disruption and decay. The communists, on the other hand, retained their "socialism in one country" perspective dictating multiple ruptures with many international capitalist restraints and rigid controls of others by a state-dominated socialist system.[7] The communists' preference for national economic self-reliance was accompanied by stress on defense autonomy compatible with relative isolation from the West, just as the socialist refusal to countenance a break with the Western international economy was complemented by a greater insistence on maintaining basic ties to the Western allies and avoiding moves that could jeopardize a fragile Western system. These divergent assessments of leftist international policies reflected the distinctive electorates of the parties, and especially socialist sensitivity to the

important part of its public which was leery of dramatic and risky policy initiatives.[8]

In a decade dominated by economic issues, military threats have not usually
preoccupied left leaders. The inconveniences of Western economic interdependence did, however, sometimes evoke public discussion of military interventions or pressures from France's ostensible allies.[9] The PCF has never
doubted that the only significant imperialist threats to France emanate from
the United States and West Germany.[10] Socialist party defense experts also
cited an independent national defense as the best guarantee against such
pressures and the argument sometimes extended to indulgent speculation
about how to ward off American or West German armed forces.[11] Although the
idea of Western military pressures was perhaps useful to the Socialist Party in
convincing anti-nuclear militants to tolerate a French nuclear force, or in competing with the super-nationalistic rhetoric of the Communist party, it is difficult to believe that such extreme notions were ever taken very seriously by
socialist elites. They realized that their most pressing problems are bound to
arise in the context of mutual Western economic dependencies relatively un-
susceptible to direct military pressures.

Until the left alliance collapsed, the issue of a Soviet political-military threat
was treated gingerly by Socialist party leaders. This was in deference to communist sensitivities and a consequence of socialist preoccupation with instruments of economic intervention that naturally diverted attention from the
East. Thus the dominant opinion in the PS seemed to be that the Soviet Union
was essentially defensive, compensating for an inefficient economic system by
building up exaggerated military power. The left wing of the PS was especially
determined that the specter of Soviet military imperialism should not again
divert the socialists from their ideological goals and induce them to compromise with Western capitalism. The PS also had an intrinsic interest in
minimizing East-West tensions that might jeopardize a detente environment
conducive to the political success of the left.

This situation was changed somewhat by mounting tensions within the
Union of the Left, and the generally cloudy atmosphere of East-West detente in
light of continuing Soviet internal repression and the remarkable expansion of
Soviet military power. The Socialist party thus became more sensitive to the
arguments of its own right wing and particularly of Robert Pontillon, until
1979 the secretariat's expert on international affairs, who had long insisted that
Soviet inability to use sophisticated political-economic instruments of
hegemony made crude military power an attractive weapon for Soviet leaders.[12]
In November 1977, the PS *bureau exécutif* agreed on a defense platform singl-
ing out the U.S.S.R. as the only power to conduct hostile military actions in
Europe since World War II, against Hungary and Czechoslovakia. This was
given as the principal reason for continuing to adhere to the Atlantic Alliance,

a rationale bound to antagonize the communists. While PCF relations with Moscow had deteriorated significantly, Communist party leaders still seemed unable to imagine a Soviet threat to a democratic and socialist France; nor could they contemplate the use of military force or deterrence against the homeland of the communist revolution.

These divergent perspectives emerged most clearly in debates over French nuclear strategy, but they were also readily apparent in different and often fluctuating alliance commitments, especially the Atlantic Alliance. After abandoning the SFIO's basically pro-NATO views, the new Socialist party originally adopted the more antagonistic standpoint of its young radicals and ambitious cadres, who asserted that "for France membership in the bloc of the Atlantic Alliance does not signify a guarantee of security, but offers an additional facility for her economic colonization by the United States."[13] Nevertheless, the 1972 Socialist party program accepted the Gaullist solution to Alliance membership and did not urge outright withdrawal, pending the dissolution of both military blocs. In negotiating the Common Program, the reluctant pragmatism of the PS prevailed over the communist stand for full withdrawal from the Alliance. This major communist concession was concealed in a vague statement that committed a left government to "respect for France's existing alliances."[14] Greater emphasis was placed, however, on a left government's determination to pursue a resolutely independent policy toward all political-military blocs, and to work for a European collective security system that would render such alliances obsolete.

During the ascendancy of PS moderates, the party defense convention in January 1978 reaffirmed this commitment to the Atlantic Alliance in much more positive terms and seemed to offer it as a guarantee against irresponsible leftist ruptures with the Western international order.[15] Reflecting new enthusiasm for the Atlantic security connection, Mitterrand cited approvingly the Gaullist precedent of maintaining basic Atlantic ties and even insisted that "the Americans ought to know that we will be loyal allies, if there is a war and if this war is provoked by the desires of outside powers."[16] This accommodation to the Atlantic Alliance was doubtless prompted by an inclination to avoid unnecessary international confrontations, particularly during a vulnerable transition to socialism under a future left regime. Another factor favoring "detachment without disengagement"[17] was the flexible Alliance membership de Gaulle carved out after 1966—permitting political-military relations with the United States and NATO to vary by government composition and substantive disagreements over issues. Charles Hernu, the leading PS defense expert, has commented favorably on the general NATO trend toward a looser structure, noting that allied governments can now engage in dialogues over security issues without facing the constant threat of submission to an American-dominated military organization.[18]

Despite a more favorable position on the Alliance, the Socialist party constantly reaffirms its anti-Atlanticist and Gaullist credentials by resolutely opposing any form of reintegration into the NATO military structure that might compromise the independence of France's defense system. Thus, the PS has been careful to rely on the Gaullist precept that France must retain essential autonomy in military affairs, to avoid being dragged into a conflict where French interests or responsibilities are not at stake. This stand is not surprising, because no French political leader of importance directly challenges the withdrawal from NATO integration, although Giscard d'Estaing's Atlanticist tendencies have made him vulnerable on this issue and subject to frequent attacks by communists, socialists, and ardent Gaullists.

While the leftist parties have sustained agreement on the issue of NATO integration, their original pact in favor of Alliance membership seems tainted by communist reservations that tend to invalidate it. Georges Marchais told the Central Committee on 27 June 1972, that the PCF had not really revised its basic judgment that the Atlantic Alliance (and the EEC) was a vehicle for "imprisoning our country in the imperialist system under the direction of the United States." The use of foreign and military policy to liberate France from "the class imperatives of the world imperialist system" remained a fundamental communist goal and was a first step toward the aim of gradual French disengagement from the Atlantic Alliance.[19] After signing the Common Program, then, the Communist party lost no opportunity to bemoan the Alliance and suggest that French interests would be served by renegotiating the Atlantic Treaty's provisions to minimize French contacts with Western allies.[20]

For some time, socialists and communists concealed their basic disagreement on the Alliance with a superficial commitment to work together for the eventual dissolution of both military blocs. This perspective was compatible with a long-standing French hostility to a bipolar order that limits the independence of middle-range powers and subjects all states to the twin dangers of superpower conflict or condominium. Despite an agreement to encourage the more pluralist international system traditionally identified with French interests, the communists seemed to go much further than the socialists and interpreted their bloc position as a tactic for chipping away at French alignment with the West while establishing new and eventually decisive ties to the East and the radical third world. The 1972 Marchais report, for example, cites the PCF policy of "independence toward any political-military bloc" as simply another version of its position on disengagement from the Atlantic Alliance.[21] During the 1977 renegotiations to update the Common program, the communists proposed a non-alignment policy involving treaties of non-aggression and renunciation of force with the East. The PS rejected that outright because it implied French neutrality.[22] The PCF apparently still adhered to his strategy in March 1978, when Marchais insisted that "France ought to practice a policy founded on the rejection of alignment—of any alignment with anyone whatsoever."[23] The PCF's abandonment of political ties to the socialists after the 1978 elections was accompanied by a revival of such intense nationalist and neutralist policies that, for all practical purposes, it renounced its previous concessions regarding the Atlantic Alliance.

The communists included a perspective of neutrality within the Gaullist security model because of the "*tous azimuts*" position adopted by de Gaulle briefly at the end of 1967. But neutrality and a drastic reversal of alliances were not part of de Gaulle's security repertory, even though by the mid-1960s he may have perceived the need to combat a nascent American global hegemony by offering support to the Soviet Union and the third world. De Gaulle's most characteristic formula for an ambitious transformation of the international system involved the construction of a French-led European bloc, united and independent of the superpowers. The left failed to agree on this issue. The communists are fundamentally opposed to any West European corporation with a political or military dimension, and suspicion of Socialist party toleration for some future EDC evidently contributed to communist intransigence during the 1977 Common Program negotiations. Indeed, a pro-European bias exists within the Socialist party, where the right wing has emphasized a formal PS commitment to European unity and even envisages a military dimension to this cooperation. The party's other flank, around CERES, has resisted this commitment on grounds that the European Community is unlikely to foster socialist goals,, might sabotage a socialist program in France, and cannot become an economic or political-military counterweight to the United States. The Socialist party as a whole has rejected such stark pessimism and clings to more ambivalent views that include a strong rhetorical commitment to European cooperation and a reluctance to favor political-military collaboration that might encourage the emergence of a West European bloc.

Perhaps the only conclusion to be drawn from these diverse and contradictory attitudes is that the Socialist party, at least, offers no grand alternative to the contemporary international security structure—other than somewhat worn rhetoric that an avant-garde socialist France is bound to stimulate renovation of the international system. For its part, the PCF's recent and uncertain commitment to a democratic and pluralist political system for France, and apparent adherence to the Italian communist perspective on a pluralist international communist system, have not been accompanied by commitments to France's Atlantic and European roles. Instead, it betrays a persistent and fundamental antagonism toward the status of ally and partner in the framework of the West.

NUCLEAR WEAPONS, DETERRENCE, AND EUROPEAN DEFENSE

De Gaulle's most concrete legacy and guarantee of French independence was the *force nucléaire stratégique*. The most visible symbol of France's grandeur seems no longer likely to be jeopardized by a left regime, due to shifts by both major left-wing parties. Mitterrand's 1965 presidential program condemned the notion that France could have a full defense system of her own, particularly one based on a small nuclear force that was "ineffectual, costly, and dangerous." The force, it said categorically, should be dismantled.[24] By 1972, however, the program of the radicalized Socialist party had become more ambiguous—it mentions "renouncing" the nuclear force along with a "reconversion of atomic industry," but the only genuine commitment was to "interrupt the construction of the *force de frappe*" by halting atmospheric nuclear tests.[25] Socialist reservations about jettisoning France's nuclear deterrent system immediately nearly broke up negotiations on the Common Program that year, until a compromise was reached to "renounce" the nuclear force and halt construction, but to make no precise schedule or commitment to dismantle. By 1974, the left's position had become sufficiently muddled for Mitterrand to state that development of the nuclear force was not his first priority but he had no intention of liquidating existing armaments without international guarantees. These subtle and glacial changes in socialist attitudes resulted from patient work by Charles Hernu and his group of defense experts, who since 1971 had been urging Mitterrand and the party leadership to accept at least a "minimum deterrent force" against unknown future threats, and particularly "to ward off any risk of aggression against the construction of a socialist society as long as the blocs have not disarmed."[27] Hernu's position gradually gained acceptance among the party elite, so that by November 1976 a meeting of the *Comité directeur* seemed to reflect a consensus that the nuclear force was indispensable to the independence of a socialist France.[28]

An evolution in thinking was also characteristic of the PCF, which abandoned its once-fervent opposition to French nuclear weapons. Envisaged by some communist defense experts since at least early 1976,[29] the somewhat abrupt change in policy came in May 1977 in the form of a report to the Central Committee. In it, Jean Kanapa argued that only the nuclear deterrent protects France against external aggression, due to the weakness of her conventional forces.[30] The communist rally seemed to stem from a realization that nuclear weapons could be useful in convincing the socialists to sever ties with NATO military organs and redirect France's entire defense system away from its preferred targeting on the Soviet Union. Both socialists and communists must also have perceived that public accommodation to the FNS was a politically-astute means of placating and even seducing a bourgeoisie attracted by Gaullist symbols of independence. Also, it could reassure the most sophisticated and technologically-oriented military cadres that the foundation of France's defense would not be discarded summarily by a leftist regime.

Many of the advantages of the new position were, however, undermind by the left's inability to come to terms honestly and directly with the conclusions and recommendations of its own experts. The Socialist Party bore great responsibility, partly because Mitterrand continued to be troubled by a profound moral reservation about nuclear weapons that reinforced his characteristic political prudence. Also, Socialist Party militants have strong pacifist, anti-militarist, or anti-nuclear sentiments that became more vocal and complicated decision-making for party elites.[31] These factors figured prominently in the 1977 renegotiation of the Common program, when the parties at times seemed to agree to maintain the FNS pending the outcome of a major French initiative for general nuclear disarmament. The socialists, however, could not take a definitive position and fed communist suspicions by insisting that a clear commitment would have to await a socialist convention on defense scheduled for late 1977. Also, Mitterrand's last-minute proposal for an eventual referendum on the nuclear force was interpreted by the communists as yet another example of PS indecision and evasion. It confirmed fears that the PS would be an unreliable government partner, constantly inclined to outflank or undermine the Common Program and the PCF with Gaullist-type public appeals.[32] The ill-considered referendum idea evidently contributed importantly to the breakdown of the leftist alliance.

All along, the communists were understandably annoyed that the Union of the Left's policy on such an important issue was unsettled because the Socialist party could not sort out its internal disagreements. Later socialist discussions continued to betray a rather uncertain commitment to the FNS and the principle of national deterrence. The CERES joined the PCF in insisting on firm support for the strategic force as a basis for relative autonomy from the United States. But the strong anti-nuclear element in the party, which cut across the major factions, resisted an unqualified commitment and insisted at least that the national territory be de-nuclearized by relying solely on the submarine part of the deterrent. This group remained quite hostile even to the concept of an independent nuclear force and seemed to prefer a stronger dependence on the Atlantic Alliance and the American nuclear guarantee.[33] Mitterrand, while criticizing the CERES position, and sometimes seeming to accept the anti-nuclear arguments, did nevertheless support the decision in favor of maintaining the FNS pending the outcome of a major socialist international disarmament campaign. Approved by the party national convention in January 1978, this reversal of previous socialist positions finally gave the left minimal consensus on the nuclear issue.[34]

Leftist mores require that such a radical departure from the ideological aversion to nuclear weapons be presented as a temporary aberration until the world comes to its senses and agrees to a general disarmament program. Communist and socialist elites may be genuinely committed to this viewpoint, which has helped them justify these policies to suspicious and even hostile militant opinion. Thus, the Socialist party could "solemnly" announce "that it is ready to renounce nuclear arms" and seek "a world conference on disarmament or, failing that, a conference of nuclear powers."[35] Other measures proposed by the socialists included severe restraints on French arm sales, measures against disseminating nuclear technology, terminating the French nuclear testing program, and French participation in arms control forums such as the Geneva and MBFR talks. Although particular communist and socialist positions differed, a strong mutual interest in this theme was perhaps the most coherent element of left defense policy and naturally received priority attention by both parties.[36]

Although the left could achieve a certain consensus on arms control and disarmament because of its characteristic addiction to utopian projects, on more practical and immediate issues such as the structure and strategic orientation of national defense, it had trouble finding a basis for agreement on eventual government policy. The structure and development of the FNS is a lesser problem, because the Gaullist inheritance of a triad of strategic forces could be altered without fatal damage to its deterrent value. The FNS has three components, the oldest of which are the thirty-six aging Mirage-IV aircraft dispersed over seven bases, each carrying a nuclear charge of seventeen kilotons.[37] These plans are supposed to remain in service until the late 1980s, but their vulnerability to modern air defenses gives them dubious value already. The second component consists of eighteen S-2 ballistic missiles in two squadrons at hardened sites on the Plateau d'Albion in Haute-Provence. The most important branch of the French deterrent is the five missile-launching nuclear submarines in service or undergoing trials. In Fall 1978, Giscard bowed to Gaullist and other pressures and approved plans to construct a sixth submarine, which will not become operational before the mid-1980s.

Socialist policy on developing nuclear weapons have been marked by some prudence and hesitation because, until early 1978, the party as a whole had not officially reversed its position on renouncing the FNS. The PS Commission on National Defense had, however, already indicated a preference for concentrating on modernizing the submarine fleet and substituting an independent alert system for the present dependence on the NATO network.[38] In January 1978, the party agreed that a left government should "renounce" the Mirage force and consider abandoning the land-based missiles in the event of significant developments in reciprocal disarmament projects. The Socialist decision to give up the Mirage component of the FNS was singled out by Mitterrand as an example of the party's willingness even to engage in "a form of unilateral disarmament" and induce other powers to follow the French example.[39] Nevertheless, he insisted that the party "will not destroy the atomic arsenal and, by maintaining it intact, and not only intact, we will carry out the technical modifications required by the advance or progress of technology ..."[40] The PCF Central Committee has accepted the full French triad and also urges technological innovations such as satellite and air-borne radar systems.[41] During 1977 negotiations, the PCF argued for the goal of full independence from NATO detection systems, while the socialists maintained that, for the time being, the situation was one of reciprocal dependence that would not interfere with the autonomy of French military decisions in a crisis.[42] The discussions did, however, seem to indicate agreement on eventually finding a means of independent warning against aggression.

The complexities of finding a nuclear deterrence strategy for a left-wing medium-size power have posed one of the most vexing problems for the Union of the Left, not so much because of technical issues of appropriate weapons systems and targeting requirements,[43] but because of the political implications of particular strategies. Left parties may, however, find some comfort in the ample precedent for contradiction, confusion, and inspired ambiguity in strategic thinking under the Fifth Republic—even though a certain degree of evasiveness is justified in deterrence strategy and has probably enhanced the value of the FNS. Gaullist doctrine essentially rested on the argument that a small, independent nuclear force was a valid proportional deterrent against attack by larger powers when it posed the threat of causing "unacceptable damage" to an aggressor. De Gaulle never made clear whether he accepted the extreme argument of General Gallois that such a threat was sufficient in itself, without the additional menace that the smaller power might trigger a nuclear exchange between superpowers because of the alliance system. The latter view, developed by General Beaufre under the rubric of multilateral deterrence, seems to have been the actual strategic doctrine of de Gaulle and his successors because they have all depended for security on both the FNS and the Atlantic Alliance. Also, the existence of a semi-autonomous French nuclear force has enhanced the security of Western Europe, because it serves as an additional factor of uncertainty and risk in the context of European theater deterrence.

Apart from its function as a potential trigger that reinforces Western European theater deterrence, Gaullist doctrine also emphasized the force's utility as a vehicle of neutrality if a French government were to decide to remain apart from an armed conflict in which its national interest was not engaged. The need to preserve maximum freedom of decision in such cases preoccupied de Gaulle most and led him to disengage from NATO and build a nuclear force. This was the more nationalistic aspect of French strategic thinking. It led to the short-lived Ailleret notion of a *"tous azimuts"* defense in 1967–8, in which French neutrality was conceived in the framework of a global nuclear deterrent and full political independence. No practical measures were taken to fill in the doctrine, however.

A summary explanation of Gaullist views has been necessary because socialist and communist thinking on such issues is largely derived from them, emphasizing one or the other as is most convenient for the broad political and security goals of the party. Recourse to often narrow interpretations of Gaullist security policy has also been useful for attacks on Giscard d'Estaing's modifications, which de-emphasize a rigid national deterrence in favor of collaboration with Atlantic allies. The principal socialist concern seemed to be for a return to absolute deterrence, eliminating or at least restricting plans for preliminary engagements of non-strategic forces and restoring the FNS deterrent function of ensuring that a European conflict involving France would escalate rapidly. Also, they have stressed the corollary Gaullist theory that the FNS may serve to protect France against unwilling involvement in a European conflict because "it is an arm of neutrality."[44] This position is reconcilable with previous defense policy. Nevertheless, the concept of neutrality is flexible enough to set the stage for a shift from merely preserving a capacity for non-involvement in a crisis, to a more ominous political definition of armed neutrality sometimes attributed to the Ailleret strategy of "*tous azimuts.*"

This issue blossomed during 1977 and contributed to the escalation of conflict between socialists and communists. The PCF interpreted the Common Program agreement on military strategy, which mentioned a capacity "to oppose any aggressor whatsoever," as the equivalent of a neutral position with no pre-designated enemy or target. The communists were essentially pursuing their interest in adjusting targeting plans and strategy away from the Soviet bloc. The socialists proved unwilling to jeopardize the Atlantic Alliance tie by giving the West "equal time" along these lines. Mitterrand did "not perceive the necessity of pointing our missiles at our own allies."[45] Although it revealed significant differences in the bloc perspectives and alliance interests of the leftist parties, the argument ended inconclusively in a mutual willingness to consider the feasibility of abandoning all pre-designated targeting for the nuclear force.[46] The socialists later seemed unwilling to go even this far, probably because a truly neutral FNS in the hands of a left government seems incompatible with membership in the Atlantic Alliance, which, by its nature, commits allies in priority to a military engagement against the Warsaw Pact. In general, the Union of the Left's contradictions and indecisiveness seem likely to undermine the credibility of a small nuclear deterrent controlled by an unstable leftist government.

Another dilemma for the left has been France's ambivalent strategic ties to her European neighbors and, by implication, to the NATO system for conflict on the Central Front. The issue became prominent because government policy changes favored early French participation in the forward "battle of Germany," to be fought along NATO guidelines stressing conventional defense and relatively late escalation to selective use of tactical nuclear weapons. The new French position was announced in spring 1976 after long presidential reflection under the influence of the subsequent Chief of the General Staff, Army General G. Méry. He described his concept as an "enlarged sanctuary" around France, where conventional defense forces could intervene in crises and military conflicts.[47] According to Giscard d'Estaing, the government no longer assumes the existence of two distinct security zones in Europe as far as France is concerned. In the event of a conflict, "... there will be only one space, and the French space will from the beginning be in the zone of a battle which will be general."[48] As a consequence to this new perspective, although the ultimate French freedom to decide whether to participate is still formally intact, NATO contingency plans based on French participation probably have been upgraded and expanded on the assumption of closer collaboration in terms of tactical battle plans.

Even without more detailed information or precise knowledge of the Ailleret-Lemnitzer Agreements on French-NATO military cooperation, the Barre government seems to have gone far beyond its precedessors in strategic theory. The Méry-Giscard doctrine is not a simple extension of previous plans for French actions beyond the frontier in Germany, because guidelines developed under de Gaulle and Pompidou restricted such actions to brief, small-scale engagements, perhaps involving tactical nuclear weapons and intended primarily to avoid a premature firing of the strategic nuclear force itself. Recent plans do not appear to be linked directly to the FNS, whereas they do bring over-all French defense strategy more in line with American flexible response guidelines for European defense.

Apart from widespread and necessarily contradictory speculation about Giscard's Atlanticist and "European" intentions, the left has been troubled most by the prospect of French collaboration in large-scale conventional and tactical nuclear warfare in Europe—a possibility that grows stronger with any French accommodation to NATO flexible response plans. The Tactical Nuclear Weapons (TNW) issue is particularly sensitive because almost any plans for their use are bound to extend the escalation process, detract from absolute national deterrence, and involve France in allied defense plans. The Giscard-Méry strategy alters previous guidelines by seeming to stress TNW utility as "an instrument of battle" as well as deterrence, so that the Pluton's function as a trigger for the FNS is now less prominent.[49] However, France has not developed coherent and precise plans for using her TNWs, any more than NATO has for its American-controlled weapons. The French position remains particularly ambiguous because the Pluton is to be used only on German territory, yet Paris cannot relinquish national control over the weapons so the Pluton regiments must remain in France. Whatever their current status, the propensity of the Army's tactical arms to engage France in European defense cooperation, and in the controversial "forward battle," has made the left extremely reserved and pessimistic about this weapon's future utility to a socialist government. Naturally, the Communists have insisted that the TNWs remain on national territory and uncoordinated with NATO planning. Hernu has branded the Pluton a "dangerous toy" of de-sanctuarization that could turn Europe into a nuclear battlefield.[50] At their 1978 convention on defense policy, however, the Socialists failed to arrive at a clear position on this question. Despite insistence on maintaining the Gaullist heritage of defense autonomy and absolute deterrence, the party rejected amendments warning France against a "harmonization of her strategy with that of the United States in Europe."[51] Given the confusion that has surrounded recent leftist defense debates, and the upheavals within the Socialist party itself, it is impossible to say whether such actions indicate an actual socialist shift toward forward defense and more European military cooperation.

TOWARD A PROFESSIONAL ARMY?

This analysis indicates that, despite important disagreements between parties, the left based a broad security design for France on the Gaullist model of an independent strategic nuclear force and defense system, relative autonomy from allied military blocs and a diminished intention of participating in major European conventional or tactical nuclear battles. This perspective implies a different conventional army structure than that of Giscard d'Estaing's government, whose 1977–82 military program aims at reinforcing the operational capacity of the Army for both European and extra-European actions. Recent reforms regroup five divisions attached to the *forces de manoeuvre* and, combined with other branches of the Army, create a core of eight armored divisions and a number of smaller and more mobile infantry divisions.[52] This armed forces policy deviates from the Gaullist design of the 1960s primarily in its emphasis on an important conventional capacity for extended battle, rather than the relatively minor role of testing an aggressor's intentions to attack French territory and thereby trigger the strategic nuclear deterrent. Nevertheless, the president's 1977–1982 defense program will reinforce the trend, initiated under de Gaulle, toward a reduction in the size of the Army as it is transformed into the more streamlined force required for modern warfare.[53] Although the government has declared consistently that it intends to maintain the principle of universal military service, such develops inevitably raise the possibility of evolution toward a professional or semi-professional army.

Such a prospect poses an awkward dilemma for the left, especially the socialists, whose recent defense plans tend to downplay massive conventional defense capabilities despite the fact that both communists and socialists have adhered to the traditional Jauresian prescription for a nation-in-arms model of mass conscription. This position stems from the longstanding feeling that a conscript military force is the best guarantee against external military imperialist adventures and is also protection against the internal use of the Army to suppress the democratic republic or the left itself, or otherwise take repressive measures against the working class. Socialists and Communists insist on a conscription force rather than an all-volunteer or professional army, because the former is safer for the republic, for democracy, and for ensuring that an elite *armée de métier* is not used by the right to seize power someday.[54]

Despite this emotional and formal commitment, a close examination of PS plans for the conventional force structure indicates that they may not long resist the trend toward some kind of professional army, while an entirely different type of para-military service would replace the classic system of conscription.

275

The party Commission on National Defense envisages two main branches for the armed forces in addition to the FNS: *Force d'appui et d'intervention* (FAI) and a *Force de mobilisation populaire* (FMP). The former would be a much shrunken version of the existing conventional combat units, but made up of professional volunteers. This small force would intervene abroad on behalf of the allies, protect the FNS, or meet enemy units penetrating French territory.[55] The size and composition of the FAI is unspecified, particularly since some socialists seem to envisage duties in Germany or around the Mediterranean, while others see it as a force of marginal importance in relation to nuclear weapons and the FMP. Judging from socialist reactions to recent French military interventions in Africa, such extra-European activities would not cease altogether under a left government, although direct military assistance to conservative states would be reviewed and probably halted.[56]

The *Force de mobilisation populaire* is the most innovative element of the socialist defense project, perhaps because it emerges so clearly from socialist ideology and the *autogestion* model of society that would replace the bourgeois state and class structure. The FMP would serve as the symbolic replacement for the mass army, because all male citizens would be required to participate in it. Based on the six-month military service prescribed by the Common Program, the FMP would be a home guard on the Yugoslav or Swiss models, creating a large reserve of trained manpower for defense and related duties. The active forces would be organized around participants' residences or workplaces and involve them in intensive military instruction during their period of service. Eventually, the entire barracks system would give way to these home-based units. Their main military function is envisaged as organizing and directing popular resistance against threats or aggression aimed at the national territory; they might also give domestic support for FAI actions. Links between the two organizations are not entirely clear, however, and would have to be defined over the many years it would take to put the new defense structure in place.

Apart from a kind of popular deterrence and resistance to external aggression, the extreme left of the PS apparently envisages more political activities for the FMP reserve units. Noting that the Army could not remain neutral in a state engaged in profound social change, the CERES defense group foresees that the "*groupes militaires de base*," or reserve units, could be composed of politically "advanced" individuals willing to engage in civil defense, education, and, one wonders, perhaps surveillance activities.[57] Despite such chilling speculation, socialist proposals for adapting the French tradition of a nation-in-arms to the requirements of a modern defense organization are worth careful attention—particularly because France has experienced great and costly difficulty already in moving halfheartedly from one model to the other. Recurrent demonstrations among conscripts and widely-noted malaise among French military professionals suggest discontent within the Army that has not been quelled or addressed adequately. To the extent that French left-wing ideology has been partially responsible for maintaining a shaky commitment to the nation-in-arms, it is encouraging that the Socialist party has been reassessing its inherited dogma and searching for creative alternatives that would still permit active citizen participation in national defense.

CONCLUSION

This analysis has suggested that the thrust of leftist defense and securicy polity in France has been to adapt to the Gaullist model. The essential aim of this model was to restore a certain autonomy of decision in defense, largely through an independent military system based on a nuclear force, a semi-autonomous national defense strategy, and a carefully controlled and restrained set of relations with French allies. Apart from this core of Gaullist security policy, the model is flexible and ambiguous enough to appeal to a variety of groups and interests who can select the aspects that serve their purposes best. Within the left, the cornucopia of Gaullist policies and postures furnishes ample material to suit the often divergent and clashing interests of the various actors and their explanations or justifications have resorted increasingly to the Gaullist security model as a guideline or point of reference.

The left's embrace of Fifth Republic-security policy is not surprising, because in this arena de Gaulle represented attitudes and views widely shared by French elites and generally appealing to the nation as a whole. He synthesized and organized the incoherent security policies of the Fourth Republic to present a compelling but flexible vision of independence. This accomplishment lay the foundation for a national consensus on defense that had eluded previous regimes. The achievement described here suggests that de Gaulle was not the idiosyncratic leader he is sometimes made to appear. Nor was he an anachronism focusing on outmoded and irrelevant security issues while neglecting more important develops of national or international political economy.[58] Apart from his clear attention to such matters, he was preoccupied with the potential costs of military dependence and subordination in a nuclear age. Also, he saw nuclear weapons as an available and relatively inexpensive means of maximizing independence and acquiring some leverage over the international security system. Precisely because France's influence in non-security arenas seemed weaker than her potential leverage over European regional defense, de Gaulle doubtless seized upon military power as a compensating factor. Thus a strong defense system could increase French status and prestige, traditional elements of power. Also, they could be a source of leverage in a newly complex international system in which states are not only mutually dependent, but find that dominant influence in the context of one arena can be manipulated to compensate for weaknsses elsewhere. De Gaulle perceived a key relationship, or linkage, between the economic and security arenas and judged that a strong national defense could help minimize the potential costs of dependence across a spectrum of issues.

The left in France has been particularly concerned with the consequences of international economic interdependence, and has seized on the Gaullist defense legacy as one tool for limiting and managing the many constraints of the international system. Certainly, this accords with de Gaulle's intentions. On the other hand, while de Gaulle's search for independence in the 1960s entailed a certain autonomy and distance from the American-dominated Western security system, this autonomy was always partial and carefully controlled to avoid irresponsible damage to the West or France's own interests. Nor was the Gaullist challenge distorted and exaggerated by ideological attachment to a radical alternative model of socio-economic organization on the domestic or international levels. In many respects, the French left has offered this kind of challenge and has therefore posed a more serious risk of eventual disruption and fragmentation than did de Gaulle. But one of de Gaulle's other accomplishments was to lay the foundation for a more flexible and pluralist order in the West, one which may be able to accommodate and even thrive on the often innovative ideas offered by the left in France and elsewhere.

NOTES

1. This paper incorporates material from earlier studies written for the Lehrman Institute in New York City and the Washington Center of Foreign Policy Research at the Johns Hopkins School of Advanced International Studies.

2. On the changing nature of France's Alliance relationship under two republics, see my study: *The Reluctant Ally: France and Atlantic Security*, Baltimore: Johns Hopkins, 1981.

3. Perhaps the best statement of this Gaullist perspective is the epilogue to Maurice Couve de Murville's *Une Politique étrangère, 1958-69*, Paris: Plon, 1971. See also Stanley Hoffmann, *Decline or Renewal? France Since the 1930s*, New York: Viking, 1974, and Edward Morse, *Foreign Policy and Interdependence in Gaullist France*, Princeton: Princeton, 1973.

4. For discussions of Communist policies and perspectives, see: Annie Kriegel, "The French Communist Party and the Fifth Republic," in Donald L.M. Blackmer and Sidney Tarrow, eds., *Communism in Italy and France*, Princeton: Princeton, 1975, pp. 69-86; and Ronald Tiersky, "Le P.C.F. et la détente," *Esprit*, no. 2 (February 1975), pp. 218-241.

5. See Vincent Wright and Howard Machin, "The French Socialist Party: Success and the Problems of Success," *The Political Quarterly*, Vol. 46, no. 1 (January-March 1975), pp. 36-52; and Jean-Francois Bizot's *Au Parti des socialistes: Plongée libre dan les courants d'un grand parti*, Paris: Bernard Grasset, 1975. The radical CERES minority obtained 25.4 percent of the votes at the Pau Congress in February 1975, 24.21 percent at Nantes in June 1977, and 14.4 percent at Metz in April 1979.

6. This discussion simplifies the diversity of views in the PS, although the positions described correspond to the attitudes and rhetoric of many party leaders. See Richard Gombin, "Le Parti socialiste et la politique étrangère," *Politique étrangère*, no. 2 (1977), pp. 199-212.

7. For a concise communist critique of the PS that reveals the PCF's own attitude, see Daniel Debatisse, "La Crise internationale, réalités et prétextes," *Cahiers du communisme*, (December 1977), pp. 32-43.

8. On these elections, see: *Le Monde* Dossiers et Documents, *Les Elections législatives de mars 1978* (March 1978).

9. This kind of discussion was most prominent during Kissinger's administration of American Foreign policy. See Charles Hernu's *Soldat-Citoyen: Essay sur la défense et la sécurité*, Paris: Flammarion, 1975.

278

10. Jean Marrane, *L'Armée de la France démocratique*, Paris: Editions sociales, 1977. This official defense policy statement of the PCF cites only Western threats to France.

11. Such notions are discussed even by moderate Socialist party military experts such as General Becam. See *Repères: Le Cahier du CERES* (April 1977), esp. p. 32.

12. See Robert Pontillon's "La Défense nationale francais dans son environment international: Contribution au débat sur la politique de défense," *Comité directeur* des 6, 7, novembre, 1976 (mimeo).

13. From the program of Mitterrand's *Convention des institutions républicaines Un Socialisme du possible*, Paris: Seuil, 1970, p. 96.

14. Parti socialiste, Parti communiste, Mouvement des Radicaux de gauche, *Programme commun de gouvernement*, Paris: Flammarion, 1973, p. 85. On this more radical period in Socialist party foreign policy, see my article "A Socialist Foreign Policy for France?" *Orbis*, Vol. XIX, no. 4 (winter 1976), pp. 1471-1498.

15. See *Le Monde*, 11 November 1977, for the text of the motion finally approved in January 1978.

16. *Le Monde*, 10 January 1978.

17. The phrase is from Pontillon's report, cited, p. 10.

18. Charles Hernu, "Faut-il assurer la sécurité de la France? Crises et menaces—perspectives du Programme common," Parti socialiste, *Comité directeur* des 6 et 7 novembre, 1976, p. 14 (mimeo).

19. See the Marchais report in Etienne Fajon, *L'Union est un combat*, Paris: Editions sociales, 1975, esp. pp. 95-96.

20. See Jean Kanapa's report to the party Central Committee, in *Le Monde*, June 24 1976.

21. Fajon, cited, pp. 96-97.

22. See the communist proposals in: Parti communiste francais, *Programme commun de gouvernement actualisé*, Paris: Editions sociales, 1978, p. 143; also, Mitterrand's statement on the matter in *Le Monde*, 24 February 1978. For the PCF view of the 1977 negotiations, see: Pierre Juquin, *Programme commun: L'Actualisation à dossiers ouverts*, Paris: Editions sociales, 1977.

23. See the Marchais interview in *Le Monde*, March 3 1978.

24. From Mitterrand's "Seven Options" of the 1965 presidential campaign, in: Pascal Orley et al., *Les Chemins de l'unité*, Paris: Tema-éditions, 1974, p. 100.

25. *Changer la vie*, p. 206.

26. See Mitterrand's statements, *Le Monde*, 4 and 16 May 1974.

27. Hernu, *Soldat-Citoyen*, p. 55.

28. See the Pontillon and Hernu reports,. Jean-Pierre Chevènement's contribution to this meeting reflected the fact that the party's left-wing elites were mostly in agreement. See: "La Conception d'une défense indépendante dans la stratégie du Programme commun," November 1976 (mimeo). Also interesting is the forthright discussion of the party's new perspective by Gilles Martinet, "Les Socialistes et la bombe," *Le Nouvel Observateur*, November 22 1976.

29. The possibility was first raised in public by PCF defense expert Louis Baillot, at the *Fondation pour les études de défense générale* in April 1976. *Le Monde*, 18-19, 20 and 23 April 1976; *L'Humanité*, 19 April. Until May 1977, the most forthright communist statements in favor of the FNS came from Jean Elleinstein, the party's leading "Eurocommunist," *Le Monde*, 10 November 1976.

30. See a summary of the Kanapa report and Jacques Isnard's analysis in *Le Monde*, 13 May 1977.

31. For example, see the debate between Jacques Huntzinger and Dominique Taddei in *Faire: Mensuel pour le socialisme et l'autogestion*, nos. 21/22 (July-August, 1977), pp. 7-16. Also, Taddei's article in *Le Monde* on 7 January 1978. *Le Nouvel Observateur* (22 October 1977) reported that PS militants were hostile to nuclear power in all forms by 48 percent to 42 percent.

32. See, for example, the Marchais interview in *Le Monde* on March 3, 1978, Marchais' statements in *L'Humanité* on 9 August 1977, and Juquin, cited, pp. 46-47.

33.   The amendment submitted by this group was defeated. It stated that "in the only foreseeable hypothesis of a territorial intervention of the USSR in Europe, Western solidarity is infinitely more of a deterrent than a specifically French threat," (*Le Monde*, 8–9 January 1978.)

34.   The leadership's's resolution was approved by 68.2 percent of the federation mandates voted at the convention.

35.   From the defense motion text, in *Le Monde*, 15 December 1977.

36.   See the communist suggestions in Marrane, cited, and in *Programme commun de gouvernement actualisé*, cited.

37.   Another 26 Mirage-IVs are out of service or used for reconnaissance work.

38.   Hernu's 1976 report, cited, also recommends construction of a sixth submarine. For the PS Defense Committee's brief recommendations, see *L'Armée Nouvelle* September 1974 (mimeo).

39.   *Le Monde*, 15 December 1977.

40.   *Le Monde*, 10 January 1978.

41.   The Kanapa report also favors a sixth submarine and specifies that the Mirage-IVs should not be replaced as they wear out.

42.   *Le Monde*, 26 July 1977.

43.   These complicated problems are mentioned here only in passing. See Geoffrey Kemp's *Nuclear Forces for Medium Powers*, parts I and II, London: International Institute for Strategic Studies, Adelphi Papers nos. 106 and 107, 1974.

44.   Hernu, *Soldat-Citoyen*, p. 156.

45.   *Le Nouvel Observateur*, 18 August 1977.

46.   See Marchais and Mitterrand in *Le Monde*, 9, 10 and 12 August 1977. The PCF also proposed abandoning the anti-city targeting strategy for the FNS, but quickly backed down under socialist criticism. Communist proposals for a no-first-use of nuclear weapons commitment met a similar fate.

47.   Général d'Armée G. Méry, "Une Armée pour quoi faire et comment?" *Défense nationale*, Vol. 32 (June 1976), pp. 11–36.

48.   See the President's speech to *L'Institut des hautes études de défense nationale*, in *Défense nationale*, Vol. 32 (July 1976), pp. 5–20.

49.   This was partially confirmed by government strategic guidelines (*Le Monde*, 7 May 1976), although officials have recently reemphasized the trigger function of TNWs. (See remarks by defense minister Yvon Bourges, *Le Monde*, 17 June 1978).

50.   On the Pluton, see Hernu's 1976 report, p. 6; also his *Chroniques d'attente*, cited.

51.   *Le Monde*, 10 January 1978.

52.   The most thorough study of the Gaullist military structure is Lothar Ruhl's *La Politique militaire de la Ve république*, Paris: Presses de la Fondation nationale des sciences poltique, 1976. On changes under Giscard, see his speech and that of General Méry (cited above), and *Le Monde*, 10 June 1976, and 5 May 1978.

53.   The new army organization should result in a net decrease of about 20,000 men by 1980, from a total of 330,000 men in 1976. All branches of the French armed forces had 505,000 personnel in 1976. (*Le Monde*, 17 November 1976).

54.   Hernu, *Soldat-Citoyen*, p. 162. For communist plans, see Marrane, cited, and discussions in the PCF newsletter, *Correspondance Armée-Nation*.

55.   See "La Force de mobilisation populaire," *Repères*, No. 42 (April 1977), pp. 39–46. On the general problem of conscription in France, see Michael L. Martin, "Conscription and the Decline of the Mass Army in France, 1960–1975," *Armed Forces and Society*, Vol. 3, no. 3 (spring 1977), pp. 355–406.

56.   While the communists have condemned French interventions on behalf of moderate African regimes, socialist responses have reflected contradictory attitudes within the PS. See, for example, Rocard's critical stand on the Zaire affair in the spring of 1978, and Hernu's subsequent disavowal of the Rocard position (*Le Monde*, 16 and 25 May 1978).

57.   See the discussion in *Repères: Les Cahiers du C.E.R.E.S.*, no. 47 (November 1977).

58.   This is the view of Edward Morse in *Foreign Policy and Interdependence in Gaullist France*, cited.

The Fifth Republic
at Twenty

Stanley Hoffmann

This chapter will discuss two sets of problems. One is the role played by the Fifth Republic in the transformation of French society, the other is the state of French political culture. In both instances, the main purpose is to try to pull together threads provided by the essays in this volume.[1]

STATE AND SOCIETY, REVISITED

Change

The economic and social transformation of France—the liquidation of the stalemate society—was already underway when General de Gaulle returned to power. One of the main goals of the new institutions was to provide France with a state that could pursue economic modernization and handle the resulting social costs with maximum efficiency and minimum friction. This, and the need to end the Algerian drama, explains the shift from the weak parliamentary regime of the Fourth Republic to the hybrid system of the Fifth, engineered to provide the Executive with a combination of the advantages of a presidential system and of a stable parliamentary one.

There have been many shifts of economic policy in twenty years. At some moments, as in 1968 and 1973-6, the government, buffeted by events, has seemed to stagger from one extreme to another, from rigor to *relance* back to rigor, or from expansion (and inflation) to restrictive monetary policies back to expansionary measures and again to restrictive ones. But two continuous mottoes inspired General de Gaulle's drastic financial and economic measures of 1958 as well as the policies followed by Raymond Barre: industrialization and competitiveness.

As a result, France has witnessed the simultaneous appearance of phenomena that had characterized industrialization during the first wave of the industrial revolution (England) and the second (Germany, the U.S., Japan), and the more recent features of advanced industrial society (sometimes called post-industrial society). On the one hand, France presents a new industrial map (thanks especially to the spread of industry into the South-East). The French have experienced a progression of economic rationality. A nation that had remained predominantly a country of small towns witnessed the rapid growth of cities and planned the development of new ones. On the other hand, intellectual capital was given new importance—to use Daniel Bell's notions, 'knowledge' was recognized as more important than property, managerial skills were acknowledged as essential, and a huge new tertiary sector of services and executives grew next to the old one of traditional commerce and artisanat.

These changes in the ecological and scoiological map of France are well-known. The old structures are fading away. The agricultural population now represents only 9.6 percent of the active population, and the biggest losses have been among small family farms (1 to 5 hectares). A real 'capitalist' sector has developed in rural France, and even the rest of French agriculture depends far more on the national and European markets. The development of an industrial-urban society has changed the composition of the top bourgeoisie. It shows an increasing importance of managers, and indeed a growth of the business community (and of the representatives of large businesses within it), as compared to the previously prevalent noncapitalist bourgeoisie of the professions. There has also been a rapprochement between the traditional quite separate '*antichambres*' of the bourgeoisie. By contrast with Alain's 'petits,' both the petite bourgeoisie of wealth and that of prestige consist now primarily of wage-earners, because of the vast increase in the number of technicians, *cadres* and engineers, and of the decline in the number of small entrepreneurs and employers. The hierarchy of prestige is beginning to change: being a school teacher (or even a *lycée* professor), or a lawyer or a small civil servant no longer clearly gives one more status than being, say, an insurance company executive, a '*cadre*' in a factory, or an engineer. The working class has become more differentiated. Not only has its standard of living risen; its way of life has become more like that of the bourgeoisie. Labor mobility has increased. A new underclass or proletariat is composed mainly of immigrant workers. In other words: the French social structure resembles that of its neighbors.

Deep changes in attitudes and behavior have accompanied this transformation. The most striking has been a national conversion to growth. To be sure, it was most visible among French elites (including those of the Left, as reflected in its Common Program of 1972); opinion polls have shown that the public has had many misgivings about some by-products of growth in France, such as inflation, dislocations, inequality, pollution. It may well be, as Volkmar Lauber argues,[2] that the average Frenchman saw growth as the right strategy for the nation only because that was the best way for the individual to survive and improve his lot in a system he did not control, and he might have preferred a far less competitive, more humane, and above all less rapidly changing one. Nevertheless, no important fraction of the French political class and union leadership has come out for a 'British approach'—a smaller rate of growth in a more equalitarian society. Only intellectuals (whose prestige, so high in the old *bourgeois* France of lawyers , property-owners and teachers, was fading in the new France of executives and *énarques*) have shown strong longings for the way of the British or the utopia of Ivan Illich. One of the most visible differences in behavior between pre-war France and France today—the drive toward consumption, the rush toward individual material improvement—would not have been conceivable without growth. The stalemate society stressed 'moderation,' the avoidance of luxury and conspicuous consumption, distrust for the materialistic cravings of 'the masses.' These notions have been revamped and preserved by those intellectuals who denounce the consumer society; but these are minority views, a protest against the dominant trend.

Another new attitude is the quest for, and expectation of social mobility. Like the drive for consumption, it means release from former inhibitions, an expression of long repressed demands. Instead of slow individual ascent, *par le travail et par l'épargne*, there is a desire for rapid collective social promotion, as reflected in the tremendous increase in secondary and higher education attendance, as well as in the eagerness for continuous education (*formation permanente*).

These changes have produced a new outlook on life and work. The French remain exceedingly hard working: the average length of work per week is higher than in most EEC countries, and work continues to be seen primarily as a necessity and a means, rather than as an end in itself. However, yesterday's end, in a society whose economic growth was either low, or slow to benefit the bulk of the people, was above all security. Security remains important, but the end has become a better life. Hence, there has been more concern about leisure and travel, greater attention to the quality of work, and greater resistance to the kind of work over which one has no control or which is enslaving and monotonous. Those who could afford it have become owners of their principal residence and seekers after a secondary one in the countryside. A kind of flight into the future—a hope that it would vindicate one's sacrifices and hardships during one's own lifetime—has been wedded to a fear of staying in the same place or even falling behind in the rat race. This desire for a better life has also bred impatience with such obstacles to it as authoritarianism in social organizations or the old 'social controls' (to use Crozier's phrase)[3] that enforced repression or compression in personal or social life. The family has become much more permissive and less hierarchical without losing its importance, and indeed has developed new modes of solidarity between generations.[4] Its transformation and that of the Church both reflect and reenforce this new set of attitudes.

Despite the vast upheaval which the liquidation of the stalemate society has entailed, and despite the appearance of some pockets of anomie—unemployed young workers precariously living on dole, as '*assistés*,' or gangs of adolescents roaming in Alphaville-like suburbs between empty spaces and drab housing projects—there is less anomie than in the United States. The social fabric remains tighter and tauter for reasons that are partly ecological (density or population), partly social and political (less geographical mobility and a denser network of administrative regulations). But the modes of social integration in the stalemate society and in present-day France are not at all the same. Integration in the stalemate society was ensured both by society and by the state. Society took care of it through a mix of common values (including the acceptance of slow individual social ascent) and of mainly primary institutions which transmitted these values, and submitted the individual to a battery of restraints: the family, the Church, the primary school system (whose values were either explicitly Christian minus God, or a lay and 'scientific' version of Christian morality), the small family enterprise. The values were largely national (nation-wide as well as patriotic),[5] but the locus of integration was local: France was a congeries of *pays*, of small areas that set the horizon of the small farmer, or the limit of the small businessman's clientele, or of the *notable*'s influence. The state contributed to integration, even though its functions were limited, in three different ways: 1) The republican ideology, a blend of liberalism, democracy and national pride, was spread by the highly decentralized electoral and the highly centralized school systems. 2) Within the regime's orthodoxy as well as outside it were separate political ideologies that provided links among the innumerable cells into which, as Zeldin has noted,[6] French society was divided, and which would indeed have tended toward Tocqueville's nightmare of disconnected self-centered individuals and islands without those ideological bridges or cements. 3) A remarkable system of mutual complicity and deterrence existed between the agents of the state and the *notables* in France's network of local government, which fitted each area's needs and wishes into the rules of the state.

Integration today is a very different sort. In society, the role of common values has declined. This is not very surprising, since the kind of bourgeoisie from which they emanated has changed profoundly, as have the 'social controls' which used to enforce them. Instead of relying, in order to ensure its safety, on a set of apparently universal principles and standards that served as criteria of exclusion, as targets for social ascent, as tests of entrance, and as mechanisms of assimilation, society relies much more on the attractions of material progress or (when growth slows down or stops) on its superior economic performance as compared to most countries especially those where the proletariat is supposedly in power. Institutions such as the school and the Church still play an integrative role, but not primarily as carriers of values: as functional institutions that dispense useful skills. Indeed, integration today is more functional than substantive. Its success depends on the internal cohesion and efficiency of the institutions that perform it: large enterprises of industry or banking, *collèges* and universities, state-run agencies of social security and welfare. Integration is also increasingly assured by voluntary associations, whose numbers, membership, diversity, and capacity of collective action have grown, and which range from *associations de quartier* and PTA to business, farmers' and labor unions. The Church's other role in contemporary social integration is to serve as the original inspiration or institutional matrix of many of these associations. The locus of integration is much less local. Many functional and voluntary organizations have a nation-wide scope, and the role of national radio and television programs cannot be ignored. Yesterday's communication networks were primarily regional, and carriers of values; the core was the newspaper. Today's are national, and their message is far less clear.

The role of the state has changed, too. Here again, functional ties tend to replace substantive ones. There is no explicit 'Fifth Republic' ideology beyond the celebration of efficiency and economic modernization, and the old competing ideological glues are dissolving (more on this later); but there is a formidable extension of state functions and operations. Again, the focus is national rather than local. The delicate network of '*isolats bureaucratico-corporatistes*' described by Pierre Grémion[7] has been replaced by a national scheme of bureaucratic decision-making that empties local government of much substance. One more change must be noted: yesterday *both* the social and the political modes of integration tended to inject national or nation-wide values and rules into the '*isolats*' with which they dealt and which they accepted as givens. Today, the *social* modes of integration tend toward diversity, even though the horizon is no longer local: instead of local cells tied together by common ethical codes, and by rules laid down by Church and State, large enterprises and associations fragment society along functional lines. But *political* integration not only continues to strive toward unity, it tries to squeeze society into a double corset of centralization—the one which results from the extension of state functions, and the one which consists in the predominance of the bureaucrats over the notables. Thus, the state's efforts collide with the tendency of society to diversification, and with society's emancipation from previous controls—just at the time when the state's ideological message has become far vaguer, except insofar as it celebrates the preeminence of the state over society—another factor of collision!

Yes, the state has been the incubator and promoter of the new economic and social order. Why it decided to liquidate the old one is by now familiar. The men who took over after 1944 formed new teams with new values. They were convinced that the old system had been responsible for France's fall. They were determined to build not only a new society but also a new state, to replace a Republic that had essentially been the guardian of the stalemate society (through tariffs or quotas at the border, through protection against competition, defense of *'les petits,'* maintenance of a huge if inefficient rural population, acceptance of cartels, and manipulation of the tax and education systems) with a state that would neither accept the social status quo nor persist in the mediocre bureaucratic routines that had infuriated both Monnet and Debré. They used for this transformation some of the assets which the old values and structures had produced: on the side of supply, the willingness to work hard and long, the skills of the labor force and of the engineers trained in the primary and technical schools, the large amounts of savings that could be mobilized for investments; on the side of demand, the old peasant and bourgeois concern for acquisitiveness, which could be oriented toward consumption, and the rebirth of nationalism after the Resistance. There existed already a powerful state machinery, as well as a tradition of public intervention in economic and social affairs. The former could now be fueled with Keynesian principles, and the latter turned from protectionism to *dirigisme.*

The state did more than remove obstacles to pent-up demands for individual products, gadgets, apartments, or cars, more than allow France to catch up after the delays, lags, and regressions that had hampered French economy and demography in the 1930s and early '40s; its demographic policies, nationalizations and planning, its decision to open France's borders within the Common Market, amounted to a clear choice for industrialization and for the modernization of agriculture. Both were carefully supplied with private and public investments. The state deliberately fostered the new industrial map. It changed the countryside. It made a massive 'rural exodus' not only possible (now that the peasant leaving his farm could see clear prospects of *embourgeoisement,* rather than having to fear proletarization, as in periods of slow or no growth and excessively rigid *barrières* and high *niveaux*) but also often necessary (since the cost of modernization for small farms could become unbearable or a crushing debt), and even advantageous through indemnities. And it made the transformation of those who chose to remain on the land profitable, through a system of aids to economic development and social promotion. Social security, public housing, wage policies aimed at stimulating demand for consumer goods (without endangering the competitiveness of industries) integrated the workers at least partially into the new society.

To reach these goals, the state resorted to three tiers of levers. It had at its disposal the network of public instruments ranging from the *Trésor,* to the nationalized banks and enterprises, and to the use of *Grands Corps* as tools of economic guidance; it built up the solemn exercise and rituals of planning—an experiment in institutional learning; and it worked out what is sometimes called 'neo-corporatism,' the complicated symbiosis between the state on the one hand, organized social groups on the other, which allows the state, as the dispenser of subsidies, favors and power, to orient these groups and to carry out policies which cannot be enforced by bureaucrats alone. This state of affairs is symbolized by the large number of high civil servants, trained to believe in the leading role of the state, who move from the bureaucracy to positions in the private sector, whereas only a few business leaders occupy positions in public or semi-public enterprises.[8] The symbiosis has been doubly uneven; first, because it has worked well only with the CNPF and the FNSEA (admittedly of enormous importance)—not in the relations between the state and the shopkeepers or even small business, or between the state and the labor unions: secondly, because in this new game of mutual complicity, played for very high stakes, it is not always clear who was actually orienting whom.

Much of this had been undertaken long before the Fifth Republic. But the brief period of '*Tripartisme*' under de Gaulle, in 1944–45, was the matrix of both the Fourth and the Fifth Republics; and the main difference between the two regimes lies in the inability of the Fourth to give clear priority to the task of economic and social transformations, because its institutional set-up allowed distracting tasks (such as colonial wars) and social groups that were being squeezed out by the new policies (such as the shopkeepers or the *bouilleurs de cru*) to interfere with the modernization. Moreover, the new French industrial revolution did not become apparent until 1955: the great debate provoked by Mendès-France in 1954 had been over alleged French stagnation and the state's lack of support for productive undertakings. Starting from the common aspirations of the Liberation era, what the Fourth set in motion but could not keep on course has been pursued relentlessly by the Fifth. Future students may see a great deal of continuity in the apparently discontinuous history of post-war France and also may decide that that era had come to an end sometime around the mid or late 1970s. For a number of reasons, the great transformation that was decided after the Liberation has been completed. The rural population is unlikely to decline much more (and the governing majority is unlikely to allow it); the era of rapid growth with an ever increasing labor force (through demographic factors, repatriation of *colons*, and immigration of foreign workers) is over; the main concerns for the future are unemployment and the cost of energy. Industrial reshuffling and bloodletting (euphemisticaly called *redéploiement*), not expansion, and breathing more life into small and medium-sized towns, not urbanization, are the new objectives. The Fifth Republic at twenty must now cope with the product of its own, and of its predecessor's policies, during a time of troubles for all advanced industrial powers.

Problems

We must therefore turn to the problems which society poses to the regime. Before examining their nature, it is important to note their various origins.

Some problems are residues from the past—from the very society that has been replaced. After all, the post-war transformations have taken place within the matrix of this society. Three important residues can be listed. The first—a hardly perennial—is the traditional style of authority, with two components: resort to superior authority to solve conflicts, and the fear of arbitrariness and resulting resistance to superior authority. The most superior of all authorities, the state, has been the agent of transformation. Although economic modernization has led to some increase in the capacity of collective action of voluntary associations and functional organizations, the prime mover has been the state precisely because—after the Liberation—it had a quasi-monopoly of the means of collective action—accepted, indeed bolstered by the only possible challenger: the labor unions. To the extent that the Gaullist state has an ideology, it is that the state is the sole definer or diviner of the national interest, i.e., of the state as entitled to its monopoly. The result, inevitably, has been a crippling of the new forms of collective action—either because they have been deliberately resisted by the state (as in the case of consumer defense, whose repression in turn leads to the failure to satisfy some needs: for better organization of leisure, for better housing or more efficient telephones, for instance) or because they could not develop as fully independent associations, but have become, at least in part, instruments of the state. This, in turn, activates the subjects' tendency to distrust and rebellion, already nurtured by the changes in attitudes and behavior listed above. In a society that is less a sum of individual or family actions than the old one, and which, like all modern industrial societies, requires a modicum of *concertation*, of cooperation among organized components, such resistance can be highly damaging, and lead not only to a variety of explosions (strikes by labor unions, civil disobedience by shopkeepers) but also to inflation.

Two other residues from the original matrix have not been eliminated either. One is inequality, including the system of educational and civil service 'castes,' a very wide scale of wages and a complex hierarchical differentiation of personnel in enterprises. It also entails an educational hierarchy that not only distinguishes (as all societies do) between general education (plus the higher vocational instruction that builds upon it) and technical training, but separates these two populations at an early age and gives clearly inferior status to the latter. The other residue, from an era when agriculture rather than industry was seen as the condition of France's survival and influence, is a certain deficiency in the aggressiveness of business. Its leaders remain, more than elsewhere, the somewhat haphazard products of either heredity (family firms are still numerous) or *pantouflage*; the state had to encourage mergers, and the drive for exports also requires strong state bracing. Nor is competition seen any more willingly than in the past as the healthy norm within the business community; again, the state has to induce it.

Some of the problems are partly or wholly new. They are partly new, when caused by something that cannot be described as simply a residue. Some pre-existing values or institutions have gained new functionality, a new lease on life (e.g., the *Ponts et Chaussées*, described by Thoenig),[9] and now conflict with new trends that move in the opposite direction. Whereas the notion of the state as the repository of the general interest is a residue that goes back to the Old Regime, the specific French form of centralization (the subordination of all other rules to those that emanate from the center) not only has been preserved, but has blossomed and bloomed in post-war France because of the enormous increase in the functions of the state, and (especially in the Fifth Republic), because of the decline in the role played by the deputies in the drafting and adpatation of the rules. Similarly, the desire to have rights and privileges codified so as to protect places in the social hierarchy has been strengthened and given enormous new leeway by the diversification of society and the acceleration of the tempo of change. But centralization collides with the very complexity of French society and with the growth (however stunted) of forms of collective action; and the desire for enshrined security is not easily compatible with the acceptance of growth and consumerism: for security can be conceived more easily through stable statuses and fixed shares of a well established pie, than in a free race.

Finally, an entirely new set of problems results from the process of industrialization itself, and from the recent international economic crisis: in a sense, what is new is whatever is not purely French. Yet, these are not always the least burdensome problems; adjusting to the competition from the industrializing Third World and to the increase in oil prices, lasting unemployment, especially among the young, and the social security deficit (which plagues all welfare states) are now the top issues on the government's agenda.

The problems themselves fit into four categories: efficiency, equality, authority, legitimacy—the last resulting from the first three. There are, of course, contradictions among them. One could argue that the problems of efficiency could best be solved by reenforcing some authoritarian features of French society, or by allowing even more play for inequality (for instance by not sheltering weak industrial or agricultural productions that are not competitive on world markets, or by discouraging wage increases or by reducing social security contributions that weigh heavily on the costs of production). Conversely, it was argued *ad nauseam* during the 1978 election campaign that some measures advocated by the Left against inequality, or by the Socialists against authoritarianism, would destroy the efficiency of the economic system. These contradictions, which create policy dilemmas, do not prevent the four groups of problems from existing simultaneously. The regime's priorities may change, depending on who is in power, but it cannot neglect any one of them.

Efficiency

For the last three years most attention has been concentrated on problems of efficiency. Some have been put into sharp relief by the recession, and, therefore, are not peculiar to France, but France has been hit particularly hard for a number of reasons that *are* French. First, since fall 1973 there is a new awareness of a double dependence on the outside world, after the proud years of Gaullist claims for independence. De Gaulle and Pompidou had wanted to reduce French dependence on the U.S. They had promoted French industrialization through a policy of cheap energy, which led France to reduce (not without social dramas) its production of coal, and expanded its imports of oil from the Middle East. The 1973-4 crisis revealed that French industrial power was economically and politically at the mercy of OPEC and that France could not convince its EEC partners to define a common energy policy independent of that of the U.S. nor make bilateral deals nor switch easily to domestic alternatives to imported oil. Secondly, the very importance of the post-war conversion to growth, the way in which, for the elites that promoted it—and even for those who challenged official policy—growth had become the prerequisite either of 'transformation without risk' or of 'greater social justice without trauma,' made the sudden downfall of the production curve a disaster. Pompidou had learned from the explosion of 1968 the need to keep the pie growing (even at the cost of some inflation, whose impact on external payments could be taken care of through devaluation); for social tensions had to stay within manageable limits. Indeed, his whole policy was to rely on the trickle down effects of industrialization, with the state essentially coping with its victims and limiting their number.[10] Thirdly, French industrial expansion had remained particularly vulnerable to recession or economic slowdown. The industrial labor force had grown, but less than in comparable countries, the conquest of export markets was recent and fragile, and the range of exports was much narrower than West Germany's; with industrialized powers, the balance of trade was in deficit; any slowdown could not fail to worsen the deficit of the social security system; and there was the nagging problem of inflation.

Before the recession, inflation had been an occasional goad to French expansion (since it wiped out much of the debt incurred by businessmen or farmers, and provided the state with rising revenues) and a recurrent threat to French competitiveness. Hence the tendency of economic policy to oscillate between two poles. One was priority to anti-inflationary policies, so as to preserve competitiveness abroad as well as the currency exchange rate—but at the cost of a degree of social compression (through wage controls, or through priority to collective equipment over individual consumption), and of a certain slowdown of investment and growth, as after the stabilization plan of 1963.[11] The result was the 1968 explosion. The other pole was a loosening of wage policy, efforts to raise the lowest wages, easier credit for industrial expansion, the acceptance of a rate of inflation much higher than in Germany—but the result was a threat to French competitiveness, or to the stability of the franc (hence to the prospects of European monetary unification), or to the balance of payments. The headache became a nightmare when France began to experience stagflation: the persistence of inflation amidst a recession. With oil constituting a huge portion of the cost of French imports, the harmful effects of inflation on the balance of payments could not be offset through devaluation; but the fear of a deterioration of the balance, as well as the experience of the new wave of inflation following the limited *relance* of September 1975, made Raymond Barre reluctant to stimulate internal consumption. The very persistence of inflation has forced the government to take drastic measures aimed at making French industry more competitive—a policy that accepts the closing down of inefficient enterprises and a very high rate of unemployment—but these measures, at least initially, risk perpetuating inflation since they entail a deregulation of prices at a time when enterprises function below capacity, i.e., with a high rate of fixed costs per unit of production. The large budget deficit suggests that the fight against inflation is not the overriding priority, but trying to reduce it by curtailing public investments or incentives to industrial expansion could provoke a new recession without affecting inflation; and trying to reduce it by cutting subsidies and aid to needy social groups could provoke widespread unrest. No government has been able to nail itself to either pole, to pursue to the end the logic entailed by either choice. Even under the Barre plan, until 1979 the standard of living of the average French household had increased, and wages had risen faster than production. Production and investment have been subordinated to the priority of external balance without internal social explosion—in the hope that production and investment will rise again once the industrial shake-down has been achieved. To reduce inflation, the government seems to count on external discipline to be imposed by the new European Monetary System, and assumes that it will be more effective than the earlier monetary 'snake' which France had to leave twice.

Inflation not only complicates the problems created by the economic downturn, but is also one of the main problems of efficiency. Whatever its economic strategy, its policy on wages, public rates and prices, the regime, except in its first years, has been plagued by seemingly unquenchable inflation (and by a plethora of explanations for it). Recently, the problems of efficiency of French industry have been discussed the most ardently. They are caused partly by the survival of old values, partly by new methods in the service of old habits. Concerning the former, most French wealth has continued to be invested in houses or land, not industrial stocks (hence the recent government decision to encourage such investment by reducing taxes on savings that are used to buy shares—one more of the measures that seem to have limited effect). While the hierarchy of prestige has shifted—the most sought-after curriculum in high school is mathematical, no longer literary—technical training has not

291

been revalued. It remains frequently of low quality and meets student resistance. As a result, the number of industrial workers with a professional degree is much lower, the number of non-worker employees in factories much higher, than in West Germany. In 1971, half of France's workers were unskilled and semi-skilled.[12] Nor have industrial wages, especially at the bottom, been high enough to attract proportionally as much manpower to industry as in West Germany.

New methods in the service of old habits have brought about the high cost of state-led modernization. The state has often succumbed to the old French fascination with technological skill rather than profitability, or reenforced the industrialists' dislike of competition and their tendency to rely on crutches provided by the state—although the nature of the crutches has changed, and the initiative has passed to the state. Several French indictments have been added to the criticisms made some years ago by Americans.[13] They deal with a multitude of errors. There have been errors in orientation, both in advantages provided by the state for investments in land or houses or for credit to commerce rather than to industry, and within industrial policy itself, as in the vast amounts of public funds spent on advanced technologies that proved unprofitable. These were abandoned, or—when they were not, as with the Concorde—have proved disastrous, both financially and by diverting money and research from less ambitious but probably more marketable attempts, such as a bigger Caravelle. Another error in orientation was the effort to shore up and expand the French steel industry, which resulted in a vast excess capacity, in a danger of collapse, and in the need for the state to take over the industry to reduce its debt, put it on a new financial basis and prepare its reorganization. These measures, and the subsidies to help retire or relocate surplus workers, not only go against the 'new liberalism' of industrial policy, and show its limits, but also add a heavy burden to the state budget. There have been errors also in inciting enterprises to merge, out of a conviction that French industries were weak because of their size rather than the structural flaws having to do with management, with the division of labor in the firm, and with authority relations. Many 'national champions' merely cumulated the weaknesses of their components, and added new factors of rigidity and tension.

Above all, errors have been inherent in the method adopted by the state to promote French industrialization—the state as regulator, financier and supporter of industry. Through subsidies, the granting of fiscal advantages, various kinds of loans and loan guarantees, low interest policies, occasional measures of protection from external competition, and, most importantly, the manipulation of credit and the control of prices, the state has tried simultaneously to reenforce, however artificially, the competitiveness of industry, to aid sectors in trouble (such as steel or shipbuilding), to ensure full employment and to limit inflation. Often, the results have been distressing. Price controls have not been effective against inflation; indeed, they have worked against price reductions, stifled competition, made it more difficult for enterprises to constitute reserves during good periods, or hampered their investments and reenforced the firms' tendency to rely on loans rather than their own resources. The greater effectiveness of price controls on industrial goods, by comparison with commerce, has diverted entrepreneurial initiatives away from industry. Industry, having gotten used to living in a state-woven cocoon, has often failed to make the structural adjustments necessary to survive in a world of free competition. Gradually, the cost of the cocoon has become prohibitive, especially during the economic slowdown. The state could not go on without feeding inflation through an ever-rising deficit, and sooner or later being forced to return to protectionism in order to preserve whole sectors that had stopped being competitive despite state help. Even partial removal of the cocoon has revealed the degree to which the state's industrial policy, and the soothing effect of inflation in allowing the survival of inefficient enterprises by reducing their burden of debt, had fostered uncompetitive sectors. These cannot stand up against industrial imports from Third World countries to France or against the exports of other advanced industrial nations.

The new policy of price deregulation draws lessons from past errors, and tries to let competition decide which sectors can survive, which firms are too weak to be saved. It encourages industries to restore profit margins big enough to spur lagging investments. However, several problems make a return to efficiency through economic Darwinianism dubious. One, deregulation and competitiveness are not synonymous. Price increases may become a substitute for the solution of problems of management and structure within the firm, and in particular for attempts at productivity gains or at conquering new markets. Two, a relance of investment depends on demand more than on present prices and profits; and future internal demand, amidst spreading unemployment and without governmental stimulation, is likely to be 'morose;' indeed, investment after picking up for a few months, dropped in Spring 1979. It has risen again, but the new policy, announced in the Summer of 1979, of keeping the standard of living from rising, will not improve matters. Whether France can gain a sufficiently large share of foreign markets to rely on external demand is unsure, given the serious weaknesses in the composition of French exports. Three, the policy cannot be carried to the end of its logic: if free competition were to cause too many bankruptcies, unemployment would leap and investments would drop further, and for deregulation to lead to a drastic redution of the burdens of enterprises, it would have to be accompanied by a politically unacceptable reduction in purchasing power and by a financially intolerable reduction in taxation and social security payments.

The maintenance or increase of state and social security taxes, the decision not to lower the existing average level of purchasing power (and indeed to improve somewhat the purchasing power of those at the bottom of the wage scale), the unconditional deregulation of industrial prices may combine to create a situation in which firms could try to survive—as before—in conditions of less than perfect competitiveness, and continuing inflation, unless all sources of outside help are cut off. But here comes a fourth problem: deregulation does not end the state's industrial policy, it shifts the emphasis—from support to big, often inefficient enterprises, to encouragement for small and medium-sized ones, for new forms of energy and advanced technologies, for industries that would reduce imports of products that can be manufactured in France, and for industries capable of breakthroughs on foreign markets. This amounts to an intended switch from an ineffective to an effective industrial policy. Yet, the same cause—reliance on state support—might produce the same effects—bad habits, detrimental to the health of French industry, and consisting, paradoxically, of excessive fiscal or industrial policy demands *by* the state, and excessive industry dependence *on* the state. Thus, the problem of state-led modernization is double: stopping the process creates formidable costs for society, comparable to the sudden removal of drugs from an addict, but continuing it has high costs also.

Problems of efficiency are not limited to industry. The state cocoon is even thicker in agriculture, as John Keeler's essay shows. One again, the results are mixed. The transformation of French agriculture has been celebrated as a great success for the regime; even more than in the state-business symbiosis, it has led to new attitudes by and roles for the farmers' organizations, to a passage from a highly defensive to a dynamic conduct, from frantic concern for high price levels to an interest in modernizing production and organizing markets. Yet, state-induced modernization has had drawbacks here too. High prices stopped being the alpha an omega of farm policy, but they have been used as the carrot of transformation: 'if you modernize, I—the state—will fight in Brussels for prices to help you pay for modernization and to ensure outlets for your products among our partners.' Once again, the policy has made French agriculture competitive artificially: the productivity of the Dutch or German farmer is much higher, the reluctance of France's partners to keep subsidizing an inflationary Common Agricultural Policy that breeds periodic food surpluses is growing, and the policy has kept afloat mediocre productions that may not, after all, survive the competition of Spain, Portugal and Greece, once they join the Common Market. Aid to the farmer's income rather than to productive investments has fed inflation, notably by encouraging the acquisition of land and the rise in real estate prices. Also, it has failed to promote the development of an adequate food industry: the French balance of trade in this sector is negative.

Problems of efficiency abound in French commerce, where the state, after a brief attempt at encouraging competition in the days of the *circulaire Fontanet*, has returned to traditional protection of *les petits*.[14] The problem is not that the new methods have failed to destroy old habits of inefficiency and of reliance on outside saviors, but in the persistence of old methods. Indeed, the new 'liberal' policies, we are told, shall be applied with great prudence—if at all—in the realm of commerce. Its antiquated nature is a major factor of inflation. Both in commerce and in agriculture (unlike or far more than in industry), coping with inefficiency would mean eliminating or hurting masses of voters of the majority.

Finally, problems of efficiency plague the state itself. Enormous new tasks—industrial and agricultural renovation, urban development, social welfare—have been undertaken by preexisting institutions. To be sure, 'neo-corporatism' allowed the state, one-eyed at best, to substitute the eyes of its organized subjects for its own on the long journey toward modernization. But not only have its companions sometimes tended to take it where *they* wanted to go (to preserve existing uncompetitive positions, or bolster those activities on which the leadership of these organizations rested), often they have needed its help too much to be able to divert it from its errors (as in the case of Fos). These mistakes result from the nature and organization of French bureaucracy. As Ezra Suleiman points out,[15] those who shape the state's policies are not really technocrats, they are '*polyvalent*' managers with limited expertise in matters of production or distribution or urbanism. Moreover, the services in charge of economic policy are badly fragmented. There are frequent rivalries along functional as well as territorial lines, between ministries and public or semi-public enterprises, and between all these and professional organizations endowed by the state with the power to distribute aid. Hence the frequent opposition between the *Trésor* and the ministries that are supposed to supervise industry, commerce, agriculture or public works, and that often become spokesmen for their clientèles, or the pulverization of state aid to industry, agriculture or research (which often leaves the state at the mercy of its beneficiaries). Other effects are the inconsistencies that result from extreme stratification and poor communications, the difficulty—well illustrated in Alain Peyrefitte's book—of getting bad decisions reversed, the strangulation of initiative by bureaucratic hierarchy—it took 22 operations over two years to launch the construction of a college. The traditional instruments of French bureaucracy have been minute financial control, and regulation. Despite the ambitions of Monnet and his successors at the *Plan*,[16] these instruments of dubious effectiveness have prevailed over the attempt at broad orientation which planning represented. And while price deregulation tries to undo some of the damage, an end to state financial and credit control is hard to foresee—especially as long as private investments are meager and inflation runs high; it must be remembered that the '*déplanification*' of recent years did not mean a return to a free enterprise economy; and the French bureaucracy, whose numbers have doubled in less than 25 years, is not likely to remove itself from the battlefield.[17]

Equality

For many years before the government raised issues of efficiency (however selectively), the opposition had drawn attention to the problems of inequality. The intensity of the ensuing discussion had several causes. The process of modernization itself—rapid growth, consumerism, social mobility—had fostered in the public a revolution of rising expectations. But it was accompanied by a fear of a rollback, or at least of falling behind others in the race. In other words, the very speed and size of the transformation could not fail both to arouse the desire for *homeorhesis*—for stability of the hierarchy of statuses and rights—and to damage that hierarchy. Not only, as Tocqueville has noted, does improvement itself lead people to become most upset by injustices they had long accepted, but also they improve unevenly, and some groups that are better off than before in absolute terms, note that others have done even better. The differential effects of inflation, and differences in regional opportunities, hav exacerbated this feeling.

A second cause was the 'French' specificity of the process of modernization: everywhere, it collided with, and had to proceed within, old structures of inequality that served as barriers or dams separating the many from the few. A comparative study of French and West German enterprises[18] has shown the greater spread of wages in France; in education, until recently, secondary schools provided different *filières*, leading students to different career patterns from an early age; and, in higher education, the fundamental cleavage persists between Universities and *Grandes Ecoles*. The civil service has a clear hierarchy both between the national bureaucracy and local government, since the former has a monopoly of expertise, and within the national civil service—indeed among ENA students themselves[19]–between the members of the *Grands Corps* and the other functionaries. (The two kinds of inequalities are connected; while Suleiman in his essay points out rightly that the existence of the *Grands Corps* is an obstacle to decentralization, centralization itself may make the *Grands Corps* necessary because of their 'polyvalence').

A third cause of the emphasis on inequality is political. After all, who is *La Majorité?* Both *l'Etat UDR* and Giscard's state are dominated by an elite of rather narrow recruitment, in which high civil servants largely of high bourgeois (indeed, often high civil service) family origin play a decisive role not only in the bureaucracy but in the political class, and work closely with, or move on to occupy positions of leadership in, the business community.[20] And the years of expansion witnessed an *affairisme* comparable to that of the Second Empire, especially in urban speculation, and the rise of sudden fortunes.

The main manifestations of inequality are well known. Recent studies have shown its scope in the distribution of incomes and of wealth.[21] Real income per household doubled between 1960 and 1976, and the gap between the richest and the poorest wage earners' income after taxation narrowed in the '70s. The income of the poorest elderly has risen faster than that of all other categories as a result of government policy and the income from stocks has barely increased, but it remains true that among 100 households the tenth from the top has an income ten times larger than that of the tenth from the bottom, that one-half of all wage earners receive less than 3000 francs a month and that (before taxation) the 10 percent who are best off represent 30 percent of the total income; and the scale of wages goes from 1 to 15.[22] In recent years, two categories have been hit hard: the unemployed, despite attempts to guarantee their income for a while, and large families, whose allowances have risen more slowly than other incomes. Unemployment has risen faster than in the rest of the EEC for many reasons, it is likely to endure, especially as the imperative of competitiveness may result in the gradual 'informatisation,' i.e., substitution of computers for manpower in industries and services. Wealth is even more concentrated than incomes: the 10 percent best-off own one-half the total wealth, despite some 'deconcentration' due to a wider spread of housing property (which, however, remains unevenly distributed, since the national average of house ownership was 50 percent in 1975, but only 28 percent among workers). The 1 percent of the population with the highest declared incomes possess 11 percent of the total wealth; the 5 percent who own the biggest fortunes possess 26 percent of the total—as much as the 69 percent at the bottom. Inequality in wealth is greatest in land, houses and stocks.

Inequality in taxation takes a variety of forms. In recent years, direct taxation has come to represent a bigger share—23 percent of state taxation. Consumption taxes are down at 55 percent, but this is still a formidable factor of inequality since they weigh more heavily on the poor. The government has tried to eliminate some glaring deficiencies. In 1978, it reduced the 'special deductions' in the income tax legislation that had been granted to no less than 89 categories of wage earners (the list reads like one of Jacques Prévert's poems); in 1976 and 1978, bills were passed to tax capital gains, but are riddled with derogations and exemptions (which, once more, favor the acquisition of houses and protect rural property). They do not make clear whether the central idea is merely to catch various kinds of speculators living off capital gains, or to catch large numbers of regular activities that had remained beyond the reach of the income tax. The latter continues to display two huge dents: the system of '*forfaits*' for agriculture as well as for three-fourths of industrial and commercial incomes and two-thirds of the incomes of the professions, and the very high rate of fraud among members of the professions, industrialists, and merchants. Taxable income constitutes only 40 percent of total income. The politically motivated effort of the government in recent years to unify the conditions and rates of salaried and nonsalaried income tax payers introduces a new source of favor for the latter. Inheritance taxes produce only meager returns, because of a combination of exemptions, fraud, and low rates in direct succession cases. A commission of civil servants made a strong case for reform in early 1979, with little effect so far. Capital itself remains untaxed, despite suggestions that come not only from the Left.

In education, the post-war process of democratization has taken place largely within the bourgeoisie and petite-bourgeoisie. An official report, a few years ago, indicated that, out of 100 students in higher education, 32 came from the category of 'cadres supérieurs et profession libérales,' 10 from among workers, whereas, in the age group of 15–24, the proportions were 6 percent and 40 percent respectively.[24] The Haby reform of secondary education has created a *collège unique*, but the *filières* continue, in fact, in the higher grades within the *collège*, and the remedial programs to even out the students' future opportunities seem not to be widely enforced. In higher education, the principle of non-selection (free entry to all who have the *baccalauréat*), instead of being replaced by a rational procedure of diversified selection, has been altogether breached in a variety of places (medicine, Technological Institutes) and replaced in fact by a rather savage process of elimination at the end of the first year or first cycle of studies; this process and the fear of unemployment after university studies result in a large number of drop-outs, particularly among students of working class or small employee origins.[25] Here, as in other areas, inequality is actually a factor of inefficiency and waste of human resources.

This is true in various professional activities. In the civil service, the 'caste system' gives to certain groups the triple advantage of restricted access (through highly selective competitive examinations), of job security at the top for life, and of possibilities of *détachements* which, for instance, allow simultaneous pursuit of a political career; this results in a waste of the careers of less fortunate civil servants, whose horizons remain limited and whose mobility is minimal. Agriculture has three different farming systems: the very large, mechanized farms whose mode of production compares with that of American farmers and which have been the chief beneficiaries of the regime's efforts and favors; small family farms that remain profitable through improved machinery and technical training; and small farms that are in debt so heavily that their future is bleak. This division is largely the result of the FNSEA's own composition and of its symbiosis with the state; the third and poorest sector has been 'captured' by the FNSEA's rival, the MODEF. As Henri Mendras has pointed out,[26] the regime's policy, endorsed by the leaders of the farmers' largest organization, has deprived the 'rural world' of its old independence: the farmer now depends both on the state for credit and subsidies, and on the EEC for exports; but another result has been (as we have seen) very uneven efficiency, and a clear hierarchy between the rich, the dependent survivors, and those whose dependence threatens their survival as farmers. Within the labor force, inequality operates, again, in many ways. The uneven network of collective bargaining agreements produces vast differences in wages and working conditions among branches and among regions, as well as between large and small enterprises. Another major difference has developed between 'protected' workers, covered both by this network and by legislation, and the underclass of immigrants, whose position is much more precarious, and is becoming even more so.

Studies of social mobility in France conclude that economic transformation has not noticeably loosened overall rigidity: there remain 'considerable limitations of upward movement within the working class,' 'the 'distance' travelled by the socially mobile tended to be short,'[27] and most movements have taken place within a class rather than between classes. In the depressed labor market of recent years, rigidity has increased. The social origin of ruling groups—business leaders, top civil servants—shows little democratization. The drive for collective social ascent, noted above, helps to explain the frustrations experienced by those who thought that the school system, or the great collective organizations of work (in industry or in the tertiary sector) would serve as social elevators, and, also, the further shock suffered when the economic slowdown made the post-education job market look bleak, and threw large numbers of workers and *cadres* out of their jobs.

Authority

The conflict between the new features of French society and the residues of the past is most apparent in the realm of authority. The rush to consumption, the development of voluntary associations aimed at protecting the interests of citizens as consumers of goods or of services, have provoked a new demand for representation and participation. It has collided both with the position of the state (whose bureaucracy continues to see itself as representing the common interest and resents pressures or 'usurpation' by private groups) and with the attitudes of unions, which claim to represent their members both as producers and as consumers. The drive toward collective social mobility, as well as the rise of voluntary associations, fosters resentment against the authoritarian features of many organizations which ensure functional integration: the schools and universities, the enterprises; hence frequent clashes, say, between unionized researchers, and the state that finances and tries to orient research, or between unions of '*cadres*' and the *patrons* of their firms, or between non-FNSEA farmers and the formidable apparatus of authority and power the FNSEA has organized with the state. Many years ago, Crozier described France as a *terre de commandement*.[28] The Fifth Republic has witnessed a variety of challenges to or tests of *commandement*, precisely because superior authority seems to protect existing hierarchies, castes and privileges, and also because, in a society where horizontal organizations multiply for collective action, they are bound to clash with the logic of vertical institutions such as the state or the enterprise. This clash has been made even fiercer, and more concentrated, by the weakening of traditional authority in two of its earlier bastions, the family and the

Church, which have preserved their influence only by changing their style of authority and, in the latter case, by changing its previous ideology.

Yet, many bastions remain. In the business enterprise, not only but two formidable residues of authoritarian rule subsist. One is the *patronat* itself, which has (far more than in West Germany) preserved, as principles for the organization work, criteria of authority or hierarchy. These are presented as impersonal rules of management, in accordance with the French style of authority; this sharply reduces the autonomy of the workers (and also of the *cadres*). The *patronat*'s lack of enthusiasm for labor unions inspires its distrust of union delegates (many of whom continue to be fired), and its preference for bodies in which the workers elect representatives (*comités d'enterprises* and *délégués du personnel*, whose functions are consultative only). And the business community has remained—successfully—opposed to any kind of co-management: the mild recommendations of the Sudreau committee of 1975 have not been enforced. The other authority is that of the state, whose omnipresence in bargaining results in large part from the refusal of each side: workers and business, to accept fully the legitimacy of the other. Traditional and contemporary factors account for the role of the state: the state, repeatedly, had to invite the parties to bargaining at the summit (Matignon agreements of 1936, Grenelle agreements of 1968), and has reserved for itself the exclusive right of interpreting legal provisions, in a country where the state traditionally settles much that is given over to collective bargaining elsewhere. Moreover, the government has found it necessary to try to control wages, either directly, in the vast public sector, by fiat, or indirectly, in the private sector, by pressure on the business community. As a result, collective bargaining rarely deals with real wages.[29]

These two forms of authority combine to limit the scope of any 'contract policy' such as the one launched in 1969 or the one begun in 1978. For often business cannot be obliged to initiate talks, nor the bargainers to deal with issues (such as compensation for unemployment) that are settled by law or must be resolved by unanimous agreement of all unions at the national level. Since the level of negotiation is itself a stake in the struggle, there are few agreements at the plant level: unions do not want them because they are often weak there. But centralized bargaining contributes to the worker's lack of control over the organization of work, as well as to low unionization especially to the unions' failure in small enterprises or with unskilled and unemployed workers, and to their domination by representatives of big factory workers and of civil servants. This produces the tendency which the CFDT leader has called '*tout-à-l'Etat, tout-à-la-loi.*'[29] Janice McCormick's essay has shown that bargaining succeeds best where both sides are well organized, but the divisions among unions and the low rate of unionization contribute to perpetuating a latent tension between the desire of the workers not only for a better lot but also for a decline in the weight of authority that constrains them, and the highly centralized nature of the system—both within the plant and outside.

The same tension exists in the school system, between students and teachers or administrators. Reform is difficult in the secondary schools because the teachers themselves are attached to the status quo; here, paradoxically, the desire for equality within each stratum of civil servants reenforces authoritarianism, since the teachers prefer the present situation, in which they depend on the distant ministry in Paris (where decisions require the consent of their representatives), to one with both greater autonomy of each school—hence greater power for its head—and a greater role for the parents or the students themselves. In higher education, the 'autonomy' granted to each university by the 1968 law has turned out minimal: financial power still rests in the ministry, the statutes of the different categories of university employees as well as the graduation degrees are defined, and appointments to teaching positions are made, at the national level. Recently, the minister has systematically strengthened the *Recteurs*, agents of the state, against the elected university presidents; she has now eliminated the last vestige of university leeway in the selection of professors. Crozier's model has been at work here: René Rémond, the former president of the University of Nanterre, points out that autonomy was fought by students, teachers and unions alike—all preferring to deal with the state: 'everything happens as if nobody wanted to be responsible.'[30] It works even more perfectly in France's system of scientific research, cut off from society, bureaucratized, fragmented, uncompetitive, and a permanent battlefield between strata as well as between researchers and officials.[31]

Indeed, the most important reservoir of *commandement* remains the state itself, in three essential respects. The first is the management of the economy. As noted above, the 'participatory' exercise of planning has dried out. What produced the gradual disenchantment and withdrawal of union representatives was less the futility of planning itself, than the economic policies (stabilization plan) followed by the government—policies which sharply circumscribed the significance of the *plan*. Already during the preparation of the Fifth Plan, the government decided some of the major issues: household consumption vs. public expenditures, consumption vs. investment. Later, the government dealt with corporate groups outside the planning mechanisms; the results were the various contracts between the state and businesses, the symbiotic relation with the FNSEA, the 'contractual policy' of Chaban-Delmas with the unions. Planning required a kind of universal *transparence*, and also risked diluting the power of the state. 'Neo-corporatism' allowed the state to deal with each group separately, and each group to pursue its own strategy. *Le commandement à la française* had never meant the pure and simply imposition of authority on the subjects; it always entailed bargaining. But it ruled out openness and universality: it encouraged *ad hoc* deals behind the façade of general rules. Planning shrank in procedure and in scope. Procedure was reduced primarily to the bureaucracy; scope was limited by abandoning even the pretense of dealing with the whole economy and with qualitative as well as quantitative goals. *Etatisme*, an old tradition, had prevailed over the *concertation* that Monnet had wanted to borrow from America's wartime experience. This happened for traditional reasons—the state is the only recourse when social groups seem unable to cooperate (and the state's behavior as the legitimate expression of the common good reenforces in turn the groups' reluctance to deal with each other directly and their tendency to turn to the state)—and because of the nature of the *Majorité*—a mix of *étatistes à la Debré* suspicious of pressure groups and determined to act through the state, and of *libéraux* whose enthusiasm for planning has never been high.[32]

Secondly, in local government, centralization has been reenforced enormously because of the relative decline of both elements of the old local symbiosis: the préfets, dispossessed of much authority by the new central administrations for economic and social development, and the local notables, representatives of districts or activities in decline or of small communes deprived of means. Only big city mayors can still play a role, but primarily in negotiation with Paris officials rather than with the préfet. Precisely the fragmentation of the communes makes proposals aimed at increasing their powers futile. Real powers could be exerted only if two conditions were met—a far more drastic reform of local taxation and a forcible *regroupement* of communes, which mayors resists (thus perpetuating the hold of the state). Moreover, mayors do not want to give up the protection which their powerlessness and dependence on the state give them, both from their electorate (or municipal councils) and from responsibilities.

Thirdly, in the central institutions of the state, authoritarianism has been strengthened by two major shifts. One is the decline of Parliament. The National Assembly, January – July 1978, sat for 220 hours and voted 38 bills and 620 amendments, as compared to 1016 hours and 881 bills for the U.S. House of Representatives.[33] MPs have no staff, only limited ways of forcing the government to change its bills and no real means of investigation (see the essay by John Frears). Scrutiny and control over foreign affairs and defense are minimal. The Fifth Republic has expelled Parliament from its position as the agency to define and express the general will. With the rise of the Presidency and the reduction of the legislative domain, this function has moved to the Executive. In reality, particularism had always characterized parliamentary behavior under the previous two Republics; the main function of the deputies and senators continues to be protection of their constituents' interests. But the stability of the governments, and the fact that they now clearly emanate from and depend on the president makes the parliamentarians' task much more difficult: in the frequently hidden bargaining between them and the civil servants, the latter now occupy the dominant position.

The other shift is the new intimacy or interpenetration between the top bureaucracy and the executive, the end of the relation of mutual tension between a cabinet composed essentially of politicians supervising the bureaucracy, and professional civil servants removed from politics. Career patterns have changed: not exceptionally, an ambitious young man starts with ENA, continues in a *cabinet ministériel*, becomes a minister—and later looks for a seat in the Assembly or a *mairie* in the provinces. It is not only stability, it is the shift from a *République des professeurs* to a *République des fonctionnaires*[34]—from a regime in which ministers not only needed parliamentary support but came from the parliamentary class, to one in which they are chosen by the president, frequently come from the civil service, and end up 'colonizing' the Assembly—that explains why the balance between Parliament and executive has changed (one extreme imbalance having led to the other) and also why the delicate equilibrium between the political and the administrative classes has been broken. Yesterday's center of gravity lay in the fragmented political class, which reflected the constituencies. This reduced the meaning and the weight of centralization. Now it is for real.

Among the effects of this increase in the weight of the state—in addition to the endless debate over decentralization, and the wealth of disagreements about its levels and scope—are two that the regime now faces. One is the problem of elitism. The old system of territorial government, described by Crozier as *contrôle croisé*,[35] always was elitist: a civil service elite acted in close connection with an elite of local elected and functional notables, and their process of joint decision left out most citizens. However, today either there is no more *contrôle croisé*, or indeed any *contrôle*: the state elite has free hands; or else the notables with whom it deals—those of the CNPF or FNSEA, or of various lobbies—are not elected representatives. The state elite is far more powerful, given the scope of the state; and the other elites with which it works are less democratic. Moreover the state elite is, if anything, narrower: with the decline of the influence of the *Ecole Normale Supérieure* as a 'pool' of top civil servants (outside academia) and the rise of ENA, the '*boursier*' element that had played such a role at Normale has largely vanished.

The other problem is that of voluntary associations. While they have multiplied, they still have to fight to have their legitimacy acknowledged. The defense of group interests against arbitrary or damaging public action is traditional; but joining forces to do voluntarily what public action is empowered to do or considers to be within its own domain remains problematic. Voluntary associations have frequently met strong resistance, not only from the state, but also from local government, already limited in scope and means, and distrustful of citizens whose activities seem to interfere with its own.[35] Failing to dislodge and replace the state or local government, many associations become pressure groups aimed at obliging public authority to take desirable measures—thus confirming its privilege. Moreover, since they often have trouble obtaining sufficient financial support from their own members, or from people who hope to benefit from the groups' activities without paying for them, occasionally they depend on subsidies from the very powers they pressure and denounce.

A last, vast pocket of authoritarianism has been the French Communist party—indeed, one of its inside critics, Louis Althusser,[37] has shown the extent that its internal organization and procedures reproduce those of the state's bureaucracy and army: all the decisions come from the top, the leadership is chosen by cooptation, its policies are carried out by an army of *permanents* who have no role in decision-making, and instability exists only at the level of the members, whose numbers and composition fluctuate rapidly, but not at the top. Widespread dissatisfaction over the way Georges Marchais has decided considerable programmatic changes (from dropping the dictatorship of the proletariat to endorsing France's nuclear force) and over the tactics he followed toward the Union of the Left until its defeat in March 1978 has opened a great debate and provoked a challenge to authoritarianism within the Party. Protest against the way it has been run is inseparable from the painful review of past positions (such as its relation to the Soviet Union). Clearly, the party's leaders are determined to avoid the kind of repression that could exacerbate the challenge and the review, and to prevent them from going too far.

This is a delicate exercise. It may lead either—as it has so far—to a drop in militancy, and electoral support, without any deep transformation of the party's structure, or, if the leaders' control should falter, in an internal democratization of the one remaining authoritarian Church. In the near future, the former outcome remains more likely, but even that marks something of a retreat: not only because of the losses described, but also because the preservation of hierarchy is accompanied by a great deal of ideological uncertainty or inconsistency. Many old dogmas have been discarded, a peaceful and pluralistic road to socialism was being offered, the Soviet model was no longer accepted *en bloc*, but was being picked apart. Yet, the party wants to remain Communist; its organization and style of action are unchanged; it wants to avoid anything that would look like even a temporary acceptance of the capitalist economic system and social order in France or the capitalist world economy abroad; it still calls the Soviet and East European balance sheet positive; and both his relentless war against the Socialists and the advent of "Cold War Two" have led Georges Marchais back to Moscow. The party's priority remains its relation to the Socialists—i.e., its role in the Left—rather than its relation to the majority—i.e., its role in the system as a whole. It still calls for a Union of the Left, while reverting to older anti-Socialist (yet contradictory) formulas such as union *à la base* and *Union du peuple de France*. It has not succeeded in defining clearly a 'French' way to Communism (nor did its revisionism ever go so far as its Eurocommunist colleagues in Italy and Spain). How long will *this* Church be able to preserve its authoritarianism, if its old creed crumbles? Or will authoritarianism keep rescuing the faltering dogmas, as it always has so far?

Legitimacy

This zone is delicate, with contradictory indications. On the one hand there are broad elements of a consensus. In the realm of economy and society is the general endorsement of growth and modernization. Indeed the present harsh medicine of industrial policy is being attacked not only by the Left but by Gaullist defenders of a fast *relance* of domestic production, and justified by the government as the necessary prelude to healthy and stable growth. While the two major unions, CGT and CFDT, speak a far more ideological language than their German or British counterparts, their behavior with respect to bargaining and strikes cannot be deduced from their general stance. Indeed, since March 1978, the CFDT has engaged in a serious effort at collective bargaining. In the political system, the regime has survived a cascade of tests, and a clear consensus on the quasi-presidential system exists. The Left itself made rather few proposals for changing it during the long campaign for the legislative election of 1978, and the Socialists pointed out that they saw no reason why a victory of the Left would oblige the president to resign. The Left's greater acceptance of a system it denounced so vigorously while de Gaulle was centering it ever more in the Presidency may have something to do with Left-wing successes in local elections. Pragmatism is rising in the electorate, which shows a sober concern for the reality principle. It contributes to explaining the repeated defeats of a Left that continues to have trouble ordering its priorities and calculating the costs of its programs, and it appears in polls that reveal far less ideological cleavage in the public than in the political class. Insofar as the legitimacy of the political order rests on the democratic election of the president, from whom, in de Gaulle's eyes, all authority emanated, the public can be said to have endorsed the system; and so has the opposition itself, by presenting its most prestigious leader in the 1974 election.

Yet signs of fragility remain, bits of evidence of doubts about the legitimacy of various parts of the social order. The economic system is far from being accepted by all. This is visible in the partial failure of the *politique contractuelle*. Jacques Delors, its inspirator, had hoped that bargaining bouts could clearly separate realms for negotiation (such as wages or working conditions or technical training) and realms excluded by ideological divergence. But even discussions on bread-and-butter issues soon raised forbidden issues—the *statut* of the enterprise, the national model of development, the future of declining branches, the organization of work. In the determination of these issues depend wage policies or the handling of matters internal to the firm; indeed, to agree on wages without dealing with the deep causes of a firm's troubles may divert the attention of the workers from a far more important issue—their future, as employees of a firm that is in difficulty because a whole branch of activity is threatened. Thus, even 'local' issues cannot be disconnected from the question of power either in the firm or in economic planning and policy. The depth of disagreements about the legitimacy of a system based on profit and that functions through an alliance between business and the state, has made any incomes policy impossible and obliged the state to arrive at it obliquely by controlling prices and grants and thereby forcing the *patrons* to control wages. This depth also manifests itself in the continuing popularity of anticapitalist themes, both on the Left and on the Right. Recurrent Gaullist calls for participation recognize that the present organization of enterprises and of workers-management relations leaves much to be desired; on the left, both the drive for more sweeping nationalizations and the ideal of *autogestion* challenge the legitimacy of private profit and the right of the capitalists to run or to choose the managers of firms.

Nor is there any profound legitimacy in the present educational system: the secondary school reform reads more like an uneasy truce between conflicting cultural models than like a clear choice, and in higher education the government's efforts to adapt universities to France's economic needs, to move students toward, so to speak, marketable curricula, have met with sullen resistance from the students and shrill opposition from many teachers. As in the economic realm, the problem of purpose—what should be society's aims—remains unresolved. There is one difference here: not all those who oppose a market or capitalist orientation have socialist or communist inspiration; often, it is the old cult of prowess and dislike for any kind of material consideration, a lingering tendency to oppose the spiritual and the practical, that persists.

How deep is the legitimacy of the regime itself?[38] The figures of electoral participation are impressive, but a formidable impatience—*ras-le-bol*—with bureaucracy is expressed in diffuse or occasionally mass violence. Support for a *Majorité* that has contributed to making the state the part-time master of all activities and ceremonies, indeed of most communications, is evident, but also, the state is either resisted or colonized by its subjects. They resist reforms other than those of individual mores: taxation, regional reform, incomes policy; they resist acceleration of change: the CID-UNATI's revolt and the *loi Royer*, or the university before 1968; they cling to *droits acquis* (for instance within the huge civil service of education) and they resist authority. And the state is the captive of its own personnel—*Grands Corps* or teachers' unions or unions of postal and telephone workers—and frequently of its own clients, as in the case of steel, or winegrowers. All parties, by contrast with pre-war France, accept broad responsibility by the state for economic progress and social welfare, and old divisive issues such as the Church and its schools, or constitutional reform, have virtually disappeared. But what the Left and the Right want the state to do is not at all the same. Even though the Left has at least two potentially very conflicting *projets de société*, and perhaps three—a command economy in the hands of the state according to the Soviet and East European model which the French Communist party has specifically not repudiated, *auto-gestion* which owes a great deal to pre-Marxian Socialists, and good old Social-Democracy—all three differ quite radically from the *Majorité*'s acceptance of the status quo, whatever nuances may exist between the more liberal and the more dirigiste and protectionist versions of that acceptance.

This range of disagreements within the political class is obviously greater than in West Germany, in Britain, or in the United States. To be sure, the public may be less polarized (voters for the *Majorité* might often prefer more of an attack on inequality and authority than was promised by the programs of Provins, in 1973, and Blois, in 1978, and more *dirigisme* than Barre uses in coping with the recession; many Left voters probably would have been better satisfied with specific and plausible reforms than with a deluge of imprecise calls for a new society). But this divorce between the electorate and the political class will not be overcome easily. The fragility of the regime, despite its stability (the two are not the same, as the Shah of Iran would now recognize), results from the exclusion of 40 percent to 50 percent of the population from the policy process *for so long*, at a time when this process shapes their lives; and the part of the political class which represents them has views of the economic and social order that differ profoundly from those of the political rulers who have, so far, run and been identified with the regime. The legitimacy of the regime will not be established firmly, until it has been tested by the election of an Assembly different from the political orientation of the President, and until it has become clear, either that such a coexistence is possible, or that the conflict can be resolved within the framework of the Constitution.

In other words, full legitimacy requires the possibility of an *alternance*. But there are two large obstacles. One is the weight of the Communist party in the Left. It prevents the Left from winning; it makes it impossible for the Communist Party to accept a stronger Socialist party capable of gaining greater support than the Communists in the new lower middle classes of urban, industrial France; and it condemns the Socialist party to a difficult choice between a Leftist strategy that has insufficient popular appeal and keeps the ideological pot boiling within the party, and a break with the Communists that would make them, once again, the unchallenged representatives of the ideal of change, the sole heirs of Utopia, and the Socialists hostages of the Right. The other obstacle is the weight of the past on the Socialist party, which precludes a 'centrist alliance,' between it and Giscard's UDF. (While a return to proportional representation would liberate each party from its bond to its more radical partner, such a move within the present constitutional system would be a sure

307

recipe for renewed instablity; and a return to PR accompanied by the creation of a purely presidential system would sharply reduce the powers of the president and the authority of the executive).[39]

Lovers of French political paradoxes can find one more here. The Left's own set of political contradictions keeps the Right in power—the fiendish rivalry between Communists and Socialists, the fact that the Leninist party organized for the conquest of the state has succeeded primarily as a '*contre-société*,' that the party that wants to 'change life' has succeeded better as an electoral machine than as a school for *autogestion* in society, the fact that neither has, anymore or yet, a clear view of the ideal social order. But without successful *alternance*, the regime will lack a final proof, and display not only the kind of 'bipolarization' that results quite naturally from the presidential election and the electoral system, but also the extreme polarization—camp against camp, however deep the rifts within each—which the lack of *alternance* encourages. The Left's weakness ends by being a weakness for the regime as well.

Once more, effectiveness must be distinguished from legitimacy. The regime, as a set of political institutions, has been effective. It has, for twenty years, produced a stable blend of France's monarchic and democratic traditions, and of parliamentary and presidential types of democracy. But this has been the case only because the president controls the parliamentary majority (which explains why the issue of the dual executive, and of a possible conflict between its two heads, has failed to arise: either the Prime Minister was an active chief of staff, who left when the circumstances required it, or else a political rival of the president, who could be forced out precisely because he belonged to the same party or majority). Would the blend be as effective, and the 'dyarchy' so clearly hierarchical, if the president no longer controlled Parliament? Only if the answer were yes, could the synthesis be both effective and legitimized. What had gradually given the Third Republic its legitimacy was its centrism—the fact that the Republicans in power *were* the center, and governed alternatively with moderate left and moderate right support. The inefficiency of the regime undermined it (as a set of political institutions, as the agent of economic and social order, as the guardian of the nation's interests in the world) after World War I. The effectiveness of the Fifth has been due largely to its *not* being centrist, i.e., to its clear-cut majority representing one side of the political spectrum (although, to preserve its hold on the electorate and prevent the divide from being too deep, its presidents, especially de Gaulle and Giscard, in different ways, tried to appeal to voters of the Left, in foreign affairs or through reforms). This leaves a question about the regime's legitimacy, because of the prolonged exclusion of the other side, and because of a difference between the effective functioning of the institutions, and the effective handling of the nation's problems. The latter might well, as Giscard used to suggest, require 'governing at the center,' but this is meaningless, for it is increasingly difficult to govern *at* the center with a majority not *of* the center in a country that, indeed, no longer has a center. The Third Republic had one center party (the Radicals), the Fourth at least two (the Radicals and the MRP); by now the Fifth—having, through gradual *ouvertures*, incorporated the Center into the Majority—has none: the Socialist party wants to be of the Left (or even to be the Left); the federated U.D.F., dominated by Giscard's In- dependent Republicans, is clearly conservative, endorsing the existing economic and social order, preferring a dose of economic liberalism to *dirigisme* and notables to populists.

A CULTURAL REVOLUTION?

What is Culture?

To what extent have the changes in French society and in the French political system, which these essays have examined, transformed French culture? The answer to this question must begin by separating two levels. Culture may mean either of two very different sets of factors.

One level is a specific group or subsystem within the social system: the in- telligentsia, i.e., the producers and diffusers of knowledge and ideas. The French intelligentsia has had sharp characteristics, analyzed, with some malevolence, by Tocqueville.[40] They have tended to pose problems in moral and universal terms, to think 'for all mankind' (even when their own knowledge, curiosity and concern were limited to France), to want to be the guides and consciences of their society. Since the Enlightenment, when they emancipated themselves from the double hold of the church and the king, they have, starting from France's specific political and social problems, raised all the issues of liberty vs. authority, equality vs. liberty, representation vs. participa- tion, reform vs. revolution that are the warp and woof of political philosophy as well as of French political history. Their stance and their ambitions have been imitated elsewhere: a Solzhenitzyn challenging Soviet leaders and addressing them as if he were spiritual power castigating temporal rule, reproduces the stand of Hugo facing *Napoléon le Petit*. This tradition made intellectuals, fre- quently, the earliest members of the Resistance.[41]

Now, is this tradition changing? There have been two signs, in opposite directions. In the last great generation of the traditional intelligentsia—that of Sartre, Malraux, Camus, Bernanos, Merleau-Ponty, Simone Weil—while the style of argument remained as sweeping as ever, the specificity of French pro- blems, which had fed all the debates until the late thirties, seemed to get lost in the debates about the human condition. Inversely, during the 1960s, the tradi- tional style itself seemed to vanish. After the apparent uprooting of great debates about universal values from the French soil, a new generation was giv- ing up great debates altogether. The intellectual seemed to repudiate ideology, to want to influence society as an expert, not as a conscience, to deal with policy, not with all mankind, to help France adapt to the 'post-industrial' era, not to overhaul it or to defend stoically its dying traditions. This was the era of the social scientist (or social engineer, but experimentally—not in the grandiose mode of Comte's philosophy of history), and America seemed to be the model. Michel Crozier's famous 1964 essay heralded the new age.[42]

Culture can be discussed also in a much more general sense and at a higher level, as when anthropologists refer to the culture of a whole society. In the second sense, a national culture is the sum of those values, attitudes and conducts which are, on the one hand, *permanent* or lasting enough to define the originality of a given human group as compared to others, and *compelling* enough (or internalized enough) to provoke or to exclude specific responses, unless deliberate and successful institutional modification takes place or new learning occurs. I have sometimes been accused of 'cultural determinism,' or of explaining all things French through culture, as defined here. The charge is false, both because I am not a determinist, and because culture is not, in reality, easily separable from economic, social and political factors. In particular, culture is itself the product of historical experience, profound enough to shape people's values and responses lastingly, and of structures and institutions that mold their behavior. 'Culture' does not eliminate the need to study specific class relations, ideological traditions, institutional networks, etc. . . , and is no substitute for the explanations of behavior they often provide quite fully. But after all structural explanations have been offered (especially when the structures are quite comparable to those of other countries), there remains something specific and irreducible to the other explanations: 'culture' quite properly comes in there—if only to show how, precisely because of its resilience and strength, it sometimes can distort institutions that were supposed to foster a different mode of conduct, or shape class relations in a singular way.

For a nation as for an individual, culture is what has been learned. The individual learns at home and in school, but carries it beyond the family and the educational system. Similarly, the lessons a nation has learned, the values that have become so widely accepted as to form a common social or political code, the patterns shaped by its legal, political and social institutions constitute a kind of collective second nature that is likely to be carried, in space and in time, beyond these matrices. Precisely because structures embody and shape culture, writers like Crozier conclude that the way to modify a culture is through 'institutional investments,' in the form of new rules of the game or of new games. However, because of culture's relative or residual autonomy certain kinds of institutions prove hard to change, or changes get diverted from their goals, with the old rules or games neutralizing or, as the French say, 'recuperating' the new ones. 'Culture,' like other sets of data, is heterogeneous: the values and behavior patterns that compose it are not equal in importance, some prove far more amenable to economic or institutional change than others, which (like the French style of authority) seem to survive through drastically different economic, social and political systems. One task of the scholar is to distinguish among the various ingredients of a national culture, and try to understand why some components seem almost beyond manipulation; and if the answer appears to be the persistence of certain kinds of institutional patterns that have been constantly present in all these systems, one still must account for the survival of those institutions, while all others were changing.

Precisely, the question to be asked at this level is: how much has French culture changed, given the vast transformations of France's economy, social system and political institutions—the passage from a largely rural, ideologically deeply divided, legalistic rather than 'productivist' society, to an industrial society dominated by considerations of efficiency and production. Have the past twenty years witnessed a mere adaptation of the old cultural model, which has ensured its survival, or is the model changing? If so, can the features of the new model be identified already?

The Intelligentsia

Let us begin with the intelligentsia, discussed by Crozier in his witty and benevolent essay. Most striking is the decline of political thought—but not in the form he had foreseen fifteen years ago. Indeed, one of the many meanings of May 1968 was a perfervid repudiation of 'social engineering': the walls of Nanterre and the courtyard of the Sorbonne were filled with sardonic attacks on 'tamed' sociologists or on their copulation with the state bureaucracy. It also was a grand if thoroughly confused reassertion of utopia. However, even the Utopias of May 1968 were remarkably unpolitical: they praised escape from the horrid real world, toward those beaches buried under the cobblestones. Insofar as they were political at all, they merely brought to the surface garbled, dimly remembered and badly assimilated memories of the past. True, in the aftermath of May '68, and in reaction to the regime's entrenchment and consolidation, Marxist thinking, which had undergone a crisis in the late '50s and early '60s, recovered its hegemonic position in the intelligentsia. Yet, the reborn Phoenix had little to say about France's political problems and future. It performed a critical rather than constructive function, and, in a strange way, ushered forth *an ère du soupçon* rather than a reflection about solutions to France's problems.[43] On the one hand, it mainly provided a vocabulary for the analysis and a stance (or a kit) for the repudiation of current practices and abuses, especially in the form of smart (or smart-alecky) unveilings of the ruling classes' lingo, collusions and assumptions, *à la* Bourdieu. On the other hand, it seemed less concerned with thinking through the problems of reform or revolution in a complex advanced industrial society, than with denouncing false solu-

311

tions that had been tried abroad: proud Gods that had failed in the USSR, or modest Gods that had failed in Britain and Scandinavia. While the Left political class rallied around, and later quarrelled about its Common Program, the Left intelligentsia opened fire on the Stalinist heritage, the bureaucratic oppression of Soviet state socialism, and the poverty of achievements of social-democracy. If any new model was offered, it was *autogestion*, but the huge issues raised by extreme decentralization and maximal participation in a society where efficiency, planning and coherence have to be ensured by the market (which these writers disliked) or by the state (which they distrusted), and which had become part of an open international economy, were not being faced adequately. *Autogestion* was an ambiguous symbol—anticapitalist enough for foes of capitalist society who were having serious doubts about the Soviet model, and libertarian enough for people who resented not so much private control of the means of production and the profit motive, as the authoritarian structures of capitalism in France. It was a Sorelian myth, with all the attendant weaknesses.

During this period, behind the neo-Marxist façade, many intellectuals actually turned away from politics and from the present. Sartre buried himself in his *face-à-face* with Flaubert. Structuralism wanted to do away with man as the subject and proclaimed the predominance of structures over men (rather than acknowledging that the structures might have been patterns, or even deliberate constructs, produced by men's thoughts and deeds). Lévi-Strauss, Foucault, Althusser were busy showing that history is only an epiphenomenon, that men do not make it, and that the role of the intellect is to explain the rules that shape us. Sometimes, this shifted from an indictment of the irrelevance of history to an attack on modern history, on the contemporary world. Lévi-Strauss repudiated it explicitly, Foucault launched a series of studies of modern incarcerations and obsessions, Deleuze and Guattari described the modern Oedipus as a victim of capitalist schizophrenia. They seemed to 'desire' (to use one of the fashionable words) either an escape into societies without history, or pure release.

Then, two new waves arrived. First came the New Philosophers. They reacted against Marxism, and have succeeded (for how long?) in making it unfashionable and *rétro*. Inspired by Solzhenitzyn, but unwilling to follow him into his own brand of thinking, they have done little more than rediscover the themes of Camus' *Rebel*. They are against revolution because it makes History the master and crusher of Man. But Camus had some ideas or images of ideal political communities and knew that not all political orders are equally evil. His latter-day *émules*, who see themselves as libertarians, show more than a streak of nihilism in refusing to do anything but denounce the evils of Communism and the lies of Socialism, and in failing to help the 'victims' of power, for whom they claim to speak, discriminate among regimes. Indeed, so strong is

312

their reaction against seeing the social and political realm as the arena of salvation and seeking an earthly millennium, that they go overboard in the opposite direction, reject as futile or dangerous any rigorous attempt to think about this realm, and, in their photogenic show of disembodied moralism, either, objectively (as *Pravda* would say) albeit tacitly endorse the status quo, or explicitly give it a pseudo-philosophical underpinning provided by a hasty reading of Montesquieu. All this is done in the most traditional style: these anti-prophets prophesy. They exhibit the very same intellectual *hybris* as the one they deplore in Marx or Hegel. For instance, they write modern history as if all its evils had been the unmediated consequences of the pronouncements of political philosophers, as if Marx had founded the Gulag. Most classically, they oscillate between, and often combine, an esoteric style that establishes their profundity and distance from the mass, and a cultivation of the media that give them a certificate of *maîtres à penser*.

Next came the New Right. The sudden celebrity of writers who had been around for a while also testified both to the power and to the short attention span of the media, quickly tired of the New Philosophers' antics. Here again the original impulse is anti: the New Right repudiates egalitarianism. Here, as in May 1968, one finds a mishmash of leftovers, warmed-up over a fashionable stove—sociobiology *à la française* now, theories of alienation and reproduction (Godard plus Bourdieu plus Lefebvre) then. Maurrassian scientific pretensions, Nietzschean derision of Christianity, echoes of Nazi celebration of pagan and Barbarian races, and of Nazi calls for a hierarchical, heroic united Europe, a familiar contempt for America, (the melting pot and Mecca of consumerism), above all a thoroughly unexperimental, unscientific, dogmatic extrapolation from animal biology to human societies: the brew smells like an *autodafé* of old notions from the Right, ten years after the Left Bank's funeral pyres of old notions from the Left. The scum of both new waves of the late '70s tosses about the old cultural envelope, but without its former substance; the old skin, with its moralism, universalist pretenses and claims for the intelligentsia *qua* ...*Normaliens*, covers a political vacuum. Is this impoverishment of thought—which did not begin yesterday—a temporary phenomenon, is it linked to a prolonged period of 'primacy of economics?' Is it, as Régis Debray asserts, the result of the media's magnetism in seeming to provide thinkers with a new way to fulfill their old ambition of spiritual leadership, but at the cost of substituting spectacle for reflection, and aphorisms for argument? Is it the manifestation of a larger cultural change? But if so, what does the reappearance of the traditional style mean?

National Specificity

With respect to the larger meaning of culture, what is left of French specificity? This 'specificity' had been linked, for a long time, to a certain type of society that is now gone, and to another important component of French political culture: the will of its political elites to preserve a major role in world affairs (a will which, in the 1930s, suffered a temporary eclipse whose fateful effects produced a major reaction in the Resistance and after the war). Elements of continuity and change exist in both domains.

Within the French polity—to use the Crozier-Friedberg terminology—new games are being played in the economy and in the political subsystem: the dynamics of industrialization and of the institutions of the Fifth Republic have resulted in such profound changes as the increasing dependence of the French economy on foreign trade, and prolonged political stability without tyranny. But two important factors of continuity combine to produce one significant result. First is the survival of the 'bureaucratic phenomenon,' with a wider scope and fewer checks and balances than in earlier Republics. The traditional style of authority had been shaped largely by the state since the Old Regime, and preserved by all regimes since then (although with important oscillations between authoritarian and libertarian poles—the *contrôle croisé* being an instance of the latter). It prospered precisely because the state, after all, created modern France twice: first, when as Tocqueville had shown, the dying Old Regime, the state of the Revolution and that of Napoleon put the stalemate society into place, and, again, when the Fourth and Fifth Republics liquidated it. Thus, one must distinguish between that 'creative destruction,' and the set of institutions and practices that have served and continue to serve as the backbone of French society. The four problems discussed above all relate in one way or another to the state. Also, the change in political institutions that has transformed the party system and the attitudes of the French toward their constitutional order, particularly toward the Executive, must be distinguished from the overall relationship of the citizen to a state that continues to appear remote, external, far more bureaucratic than participatory.

This tension between the present social order and the 'bureaucratic phenomenon' is new. The traditional style of authority was fitted perfectly to the stalemate society, with its small and narrowly open elites, its hierarchical system of education, its limited associational life, the emphasis of its values and structures on self-sufficiency (including a restricted role for the state). This style, dangerously stretched by the state's expansion, fits far less well the society which the state has now helped create and which increasingly resents and needs to open up the castes that ran it before. This society possesses a far less elitist system of secondary and higher education, and performs a wealth of collective activities that have become hard to control from above and outside. Leviathan has become, and is felt to be, a Frankenstein.

The second lasting feature is clearly a residue from the class relations of the stalemate society (but these were shaped already by the class relations of the Old Regime!). The partial material integration of the working class into

314

'bourgeois society' does not include acceptance of the capitalist order by a majority of that class, nor has it led to relations with the business community that allow for smooth cooperation on fully institutionalized modes of conflict. Also, the 'bureaucratic phenomenon' intervenes, because the extensive role of the state in the economy often transforms the contest between workers and employers into a contest between workers and State, and because the partial dependence of a not especially dynamic business community on the state makes the latter an inevitable participant in these struggles.

The combination of these two features results in the *partial* survival of ideological politics. One profound change in French political culture is the 'deideologization' of the Right with respect to the political and social order. One achievement of the Fifth Republic has been the creation of a coalition of social groups that extends from the modern business community and farmers, to shopkeepers, artisans or peasants who are being dislodged by economic change (yet prefer the Majority's mix of free enterprise and state direction to the Left's potential mix of state command and drastic democratization). These are indeed the objects of the Majority's solicitations: a kind of modern Toryism that makes the Majority a combination of 'declining classes' *and* modern sectors, not around political or social ideology, but around mottoes such as 'you've never had it so good' or (more recently) 'you'll be far worse off with our adversaries.' To be sure, the Right remains divided into two political factions, and more than nuances separate the RPR from the UDF. The former is more populist or plebiscitarian as well as more *étatiste*, the latter shows far more sympathy toward all that is between the people *en masse* and the state: intermediate groups, notables, elites. But their electorates and their parliamentary groups have few basic differences; all have reformers and conservatives.

This 'pragmatism' does not fully extend to the Left, its parties and its labor unions. The persistence of ideology there cannot be explained only by its long exclusion from power; after all, the German SPD wisely converted to pragmatism to end its own. It can be attributed to the combined effect of the style of authority and of class relations. The key issue remains the reintegration of the working class into society, both for the Communists who call themselves *the* party of the working class, and for the Socialists who want to keep their working class base and enlarge it at the CP's expense (or for the CFDT, which does not want to leave the bulk of the unionized workers to the CGT). In a society whose political mode is not participation, 'face-to-face' compromises and *décrispation*, but the familiar concatenation of impersonal rules from above, and either resistance to or pressures on the state from below, opposition tends to become ideological. Ideology is a weapon in the struggle, a fence built around the enemy's domain and a bargaining ploy to extract concessions through intimidation, without conceding much or sharing responsibility in return. Not because the Left has been dominated by intellectuals is its 'discourse' ideological. French intellectuals have been ideological for the same reasons that have fostered, and continue to foster, ideological thinking in the whole French left—which includes a Communist party that never let intellectuals dictate its style or program, and labor unions in which blue collar workers or the so-called new working class elements have been far more important than intellectuals in shaping policy. Today, paradoxically, left wing Catholicism has joined the ideological currents that have competed traditionally on the Left. Its roots go back to Lamennais; its dialogue with Marxism has been intense; its vigor contrasts with the quasi-disappearance of Right-wing Catholicism and the flabbiness of the liberal-Catholic tradition that irrigated Christian Democracy but barely sprinkles the fading Center.

On the Left, the struggle between two logics is striking. One is that of the new institutional system. As in other countries, *electoral* polarization (by contrast with what happens under pure proportional representation) incites each camp to seek votes in the middle, i.e., to become a 'catch-all' force, to blur the distinction between defense of the status quo and advocacy of drastic change through varieties of reformism. The other is the traditional logic of *ideological* polarization. Equally striking is that, so far, the latter has prevailed (and kept the Left out of power): the CP has starkly sought to preserve the image of a truly revolutionary party, to keep the workin class at the core of its organization and programs, and to maintain its grip on the CGT. The new Socialist party has been so busy trying to work out a 'correct' ideological formula that it has failed to incorporate sufficiently new kinds of demands—from women, or ecologists, or youth groups—that have much more to do with the concrete issues of present-day France than with the heady debates around *autogestion*, nationalization, or the primacy of economics. Only the CFDT, since March 1978, tries to combine toughness and pragmatism.

If the factors of continuing specificity create France's problems, how can they be changed? A second nature is not easy to change. 'Institutional investment' has risks. If the effort seems too radical (as, strangely, de Gaulle's 1969 reform of territorial government appeared to many beneficiaries of the present scheme), it is likely to frighten all those who benefit from the status quo or from whom (as in the reform of enterprises) the 'new game' would require far more of a commitment to cooperate and co-manage than the present game, which protects their freedom to act separately. If the effort is radical, it may indeed be destructive: this argument has been made again and again against election of regional assemblies by universal suffrage, or the setting up of truly autonomous and competitive universities, or a German-type *Mitbestimmung* for enterprises. But if the reform effort is too timid, the old rules will not be disturbed, the reform will be absorbed. This happened to the reform of territorial government in 1964 and the regional reform of 1972; or it will prove of minimal significance, like capital gains taxation—or, one might argue sacrilegiously, the creation of ENA. Precisely because so many players are tied to the existing games, few want the risks and responsibilities of change (even on the Left: coming to power would require coping with and managing a formidably complex society whose problems cannot be resolved by ideological formulas; remaining in the opposition has the advantage of saving one from the tragic dilemmas, 'agonizing reappraisal' vs. 'making a mess of things').

The necessary is, alas, unlikely: a method of change both gradual and general. General change is necessary because the various games are linked. The study, mentioned before, of hierarchy within French and West German firms shows a clear connection between, on the one hand, the wider scale of wages and higher number of (better paid) non-workers in French firms, and, on the other, the internal management of the latter, the French educational system, and the division of labor in France. Similarly, the problem of efficiency in industry cannot be solved by deregulation alone, but, as the best French student of the subject has noted, requires *both* greater freedom of the employer to lay off employees, and greater efforts at workers' participation.[44] In theory, Albert Hirschman's notion of institutional change through deliberate disequilibria is appealing,[45] since it requires action only in one well-chosen sector; but it cannot work well unless the effects, and especially the unintended ones, of the original impulse can be controlled. Michel Crozier's strategy of change is more appropriate.[46] It focuses on investments—in men, knowledge and experiences—and on the key areas of *blocage*, but begins with the weaker spots and leaves aside the hopeless cases and the unassailable fortresses. Clearly, general change cannot be introduced all at once: there will never be enough psychological and financial resources; the state of the economy and of the political forces will never be idyllic enough to pursue all necessary reforms at the same time.

The necessary changes would be a fine blend of three concepts: participation, liberalism, mobility. In local government—especially at the regional level—in enterprises, in the educational system, there is a need for more *autogestion*, a wider diffusion of responsibilities, autonomy from the Leviathan, to reduce the jurisdiction of the State, allow the expansion of voluntary associations, enlarge the scope of collective action, just as, at the top, there is a need to increase Parliament's powers of inquiry and control (as opposed to censure). Participation would entail a return to and democratization of politics. Liberalism would aim at untying enterprises to remove the cocoon or crutches to which they have become accustomed, to promote initiative, competition and *autofinancement* (but since all things are connected, liberalization ought to be, in turn, tied to the firms' efforts both toward internal managerial improvements in order to restore clear lines of authority and to wipe out what Crozier calls the 'eiderdown effect,' and toward reducing inequality and developing workers' participation); comparable measures could be taken for agriculture, the health services and the universities. The role of the state in business-labor relations should be reduced also, to strengthen collective bargaining. Mobility would aim at enlarging the elites, in particular by promoting wider access into the civil service, removing the barriers that impede circulation within it (or between it and the rest of society), reducing the privileges of the *Grands Corps*, and integrating into the university system the *Grandes Ecoles* that train the top elites.

This is not likely to happen. Not only, as Crozier and Freidberg warn, is any society (especially when already buffeted by economic change) unwilling to undergo too much change. But the effects of any change are increasingly difficult to predict: sociologists, after having advocated various reforms, now focus on the mushrooming of 'perverse effects', the results either of the social limits of growth or of the fear of personal accountability.[47] Moreover, a coalition of forces interested in any of the reforms hinted at would be difficult to find and the actors concerned surely would tend to prefer the status quo. Why should the state commit hari-kari? Why should business accept a drastic change in the organization of the firm? Why should unions accept partial responsibility for the performance of the economic system? Finally, neither the Majority nor the Opposition offers a coherent reform plan. One side proposes marginal improvements, timid variations of familiar themes; the other side suffers from a plethora of '*projets de société.*'

Indeed, in the absence of 'gradual general reform,' the Majority's method of small adaptations is the most likely to persist; they might ease some tensions even if they are more cosmetic than profound (as in the splitting of the finance ministry into two, or communal reform). But the meaning is clear: it preserves a cultural system whose functionality is increasingly questionable—and that lasts mainly because no intellectually and politically convincing alternative has appeared.

If the survival of much of France's specificity is the source of trouble at home, the problem abroad lies in shrinking French specificity. Many features of France's political culture have been tied to France's role in the world. This role supported and vindicated the intelligentsia's pretense to universalism. The French state, the spider at the center of the bureaucratic cobweb, had been built largely in response to external challenges. But precisely in that area the losses have been greatest—even though de Gaulle's key ambition was to restore France's dynamism and pride so that she could 'marry her century' and play a leading role with renewed vigor. One more paradox is not only that the internal success of the effort has made France lose some distinctiveness, but, as one European middle power among others, she shares in the loss of a world role that all European powers have suffered; and insofar as the 'specific' features that have survived inhibit her economic transformation somewhat and keep her from reaching the apparent goal of all the Fifth Republic's presidents—catching up with Bonn—the loss is even greater. Moreover, given the economic crisis and its effect on a nation that opened its borders in order to be capable of playing a major role abroad, the problems of efficiency and competitiveness are now so acute that France must do what, as de Gaulle said with commiseration, the Germans had to do after 1945: concentrate on the material tasks of domestic recovery.

De Gaulle accomplished many things in foreign affairs. He eliminated costly burdens. He modernized French instrumentalities for independence *and* influence—the *force de frappe*, the policy of cooperation with former colonies. He pursued an acrobatic course of deliberate ambiguity: independence yet alliance, détente while belonging to the West, being an advanced industrial and capitalist power and yet championing the Third World. However, the search for distinctiveness suffered severe setbacks, in Western Europe and in Prague. De Gaulle's successors launched a patient new quest for distinctiveness. Pompidou sought it first in a European *relance*, later in resistance to Kissinger's domineering methods. But the *relance* was plagued by the old Gaullist contradiction between two forms of national action: insistence on free hands (or resistance to transferring authority to Brussels), and desire for a 'European Europe' that France would lead. It was also bothered by the contradiction between choosing the road of monetary union to build such a Europe and preserving a domestic political base through economic policies widely divergent from Bonn's. Resistance to the U.S. became an exercise in isolated futility during the oil crisis. In turn, Giscard has sought 'specificity' first in so-called *mondialisme*, later in Africa, constantly in Western Europe. But if *mondialisme*, or its new version, the Euro-Afro-Arab *trilogue*, means playing a key role in the North-South dialogue, France simply does not have enough economic weight: among the industrial powers, Washington and Bonn matter; and if it means disarmament, the exercise is academic. As for supporting moderate regimes in Africa, it has built-in material limits and is not well coordinated with France's own new policy in Southern Africa. In the EEC, Giscard has been more successful in promoting diplomatic cooperation and common stands, but often at the cost of accepting the lowest common denominator, and without quite resolving the old Gaullist tension nbetween independence and joint action.

Today, despite the constantly modernized *force de frappe*, France's place in the world faces four issues. One is the shrinking of a distinctive role. Giscard was a chief instigator of the new European Monetary System, aimed at protecting European currencies from the divagations of the dollar; but this system also constrains domestic economic and social policy maneuvers, in a country with fewer reserves and a weaker currency and economy than West Germany. The Common Agricultural Policy is in trouble. Also, the problem of conventional defense in Europe being raised again, French leaders, despite their future neutron bombs, confront the reality of drastic unpreparedness because of the priority given to nuclear deterrence, and the necessity of rapprochement with NATO; the remaining distinctiveness, now that French policy on nuclear pro-liferation has changed, is arms sales. The second issue is the renewed battle over Europe: Giscard's acceptance of the popular election of the European Parlia-ment and a generally far more *communautaire* attitude within the EEC have revived Gaullist fears that, without eternal vigilance, the Common Market, so frustrating a terrain for French leadership, could all too easily become a war machine to destroy French distinctiveness. They have revived, among Com-munists and some Socialists, fear that the EEC could also tie France's hands with respect to domestic change. In other words, because many see the Com-munity as a possible set of handcuffs for France, the European issue reinjects a factor of ideology, even within the Majority—although once more the political class seems more agitated than the electorate, whose mood during the election campaign for the European Parliament was well-disposed indifference, and where only the Communist voters are predominantly hostile to the EEC.[48]

Third is a striking lack of any 'national ambition' of the kind de Gaulle deemed necessary to preserve France's cohesion. Assuredly, the world stage is not the focus of the ambitions or even the attention of the French. Fourth, the 'tyranny of the outside,' of external interests and ideas over French affairs, a tyranny de Gaulle tried so hard to abolish, reappears (just as Moscow's grip over the French Communist party toughens) in the form of the imperative to export, to compete, to cope with the changes of the world economic system. And France, in this respect, is squeezed between the dynamism of West Germany and Japan, and that of the new industrializing powers of East Asia and Latin America, where French exports are few and unlikely to grow unless France opened its borders more to imports from these countries—a threat to many traditional French industries. Moreover, renewed high tension between Washington and Moscow might force France to choose between giving up the ghost of détente, i.e. returning to "Atlanticism", and rather perilous or futile solitude, should its EEC partners prefer to cling to Washington.

With sharply felt limits to France's independence, few opportunities to exert leadership, and no head of state with de Gaulle's prestige and ambition to allow him to tell others what is right, the French therefore must turn inward, if only to try to reduce once more the tyranny of the outside. The loss of *external* specificity weakens further the appropriateness of the *internally* distinctive features, whose usefulness is not only questioned inside, but can no longer be justified as external necessity, and indeed may hamper France's position in the world. For domestic change to become both possible and positive, it must be undertaken by the political class—precisely because cultural transformation re-quires institutional reform, and the adoption of laws and policies for modifying old patterns of behavior or breaking obstacles that surviving features still raise against the new values or attitudes evident since the war. Therefore, we must end with a last look at that class. It has its own specificity and resilience:

throughout much of the Third Republic, it may have been less deeply divided than the public (whose ideological splits were manifested on election days, after which the representatives could their own games), while today's public is less divided than the political class. There are several reasons for pessimism about its ability to cope with France's major issues.

The first lies in the institutional system. It makes the Executive the motor, and somehow reduces the political class to being merely a chorus of bravos and boos. Of course, the executive's role is to shape support for its programs, but complications result, in part from the duality of executive leadership. The president tends to behave as the leader of all the French, the man in charge of the future, and insofar as this is *his* stance, his role in mobilizing such support is necessarily distant and indirect: the task is left largely in the hands of the premier, whose concern is with the present. This was less true of Pompidou than of de Gaulle and Giscard—precisely because Pompidou tended not to look too far ahead. (His first premier did, and found himself gradually strangled.) Even if the president decided on an imaginative and realistic course of reform (which the present incumbent has not done) and tried to rally support for it in the political class, there are two more reasons for skepticism.

The first is that three of the four major parties are in crisis. The Communists face a loss of voters—admittedly not the first, nor their primary concern, but serious enough, as it affects their oldest strongholds and reflects the decline of many industries in which it was basedd. Also, they face internal *contestation*, and uncertainty about doctrine and course. The Socialists agree on a stance—'resolutely Left'—but sputter and splinter over program, priorities and people. The Gaullists are united insofar as they feel threatened as a group, but suffer from a rift between militants, often of lower middle class or worker origin, who push a populist and nationalistic course of action (closer to the RPF than to President de Gaulle who accepted the EEC and gave priority to a strong franc), and parliamentarians who represent an electorate that is hardly distinguishable from the UDF's and highly susceptible to seduction by Giscard, as the 1979 European election demonstrates again. The split separated those who, feeling threatened, would like to say 'no' to Giscard, and those who, from the same feeling, believe (for reasons similar to those of Giscard around 1967, when *he* was a reluctant partner in de Gaulle's majority) that it is better to say '*oui mais.*' This rift is making Chirac's position unenviable. His shrill anti-European campaign cost the RPR much of its electorate, but a more 'balanced' position is akin to acknowledging impotence, and this too may push toward the UDF rather pragmatic voters who seek to vote *utile*. The UDF has no troubles, being the President's *masse de manoeuvre*—but that deprives it of a real program.

The second reason is that no possible combination or condition offers much hope for a combined attack on the problems of efficiency, equality and authority. The present majority rates high on the first of those problems because it has made possible the transformation and modernization of the country. But Barre's success remains in doubt, and on the second and third counts, the Majority is at least part of the problem. The Left, united or disunited, obviously looks like a better bet on equality, but its stand on problems of authority is confused, and it has not convinced the public that it would do well with issues of efficiency. The possibility of a centrist combination inspires skepticism: a boldly "reformist" Socialist president is unlikely to meet with UDF enthusiams, it would take a sudden leap in his political imagination for Giscard to devise, in a second term, a strategy that could get Socialist endorsement, and the cooperation of those two false centers, should it occur at all, is most likely to lead to the same failure on all three counts as that of the Fourth Republic's third force.

Under these circumstances, a cloud will keep hovering over the legitimacy of the social and political order. For its first ten years at least, the transformation over which the regime presided had a guiding purpose: France's presence, power and influence in the world. Now an internal purpose is needed to accomplish the cultural transformation that is still incomplete. But for the time being, *on ne voit rien venir*. This may explain why the old style of the intelligentsia survives; it also both explains and is partly caused by, the fact that this intelligentsia seems to be turning its back on the concerns expressed in these essays.

NOTES

1. This essay is my fifth attempt at drawing a balance sheet. My previous evaluations are in: S. Hoffmann, Charles Kindleberger, J. Pitts, L. Wylie, J.-B. Duroselle, F. Goguel, *In Search of France*, (Cambridge: Harvard U. Press, 1973); S. Hoffmann, *Decline or Renewal?* (New York: Viking Press, 1974); the postface to its French version, *Essais sur la France* (Paris: Seuil, 1974); and the preface to *Sur la France* (Seuil, 1975).

2. In addition to his paper in this volume, see his Ph.D. thesis, *The Economic Growth Controversy in France*, to be published.

3. See his contribution to *The Crisis of Democracy* (co-author with S. Huntington and J. Watanuki), (New York: NYU Press, 1975).

4. See Louis Roussel, *La famille après le mariage des enfants* (Paris: Presses Universitaires, 1976) and the research of Jacques Lautman.

5. See Eugen Weber, *Peasants into Frenchmen* (Stanford: Stanford U. Press, 1976), and Patrice Higonnet's remarks about the significance of French spelling and grammar in: "France: Literacy and Revolution," *Times Literary Supplement*, 13 October, 1978.

6. In his conclusion to *France 1848-1945*, Vol. II (Oxford U. Press, 1977), p. 1169.

7. *Le pouvoir périphérique* (Paris, Editions du Seuil, 1976).

8. See P. Birnbaum et al, *La Classe dirigeante française* (Paris: Presses Universitaires, 1978) ch. 2.

9. See Jean-Claude Thoenig, *L'ère des technocrates* (Paris: Ed. d'Organisation, 1973).

10. On Pompidou, See Alain Peyrefitte, *Le mal français* (Paris: Plon, 1976) and Jean Charbonnel, *L'aventure de la fidélité* (Paris, Seuil, 1976).

11. See Alain Prate, *Les batailles économiques du Général de Gaulle* (Paris: Plon, 1978).

12. See Jane Marceau, *Class and Status in France* (Oxford: Clarendon Press, 1977), p. 35.

13. See John A. McArthur and Bruce Scott, *Industrial Planning in France* (Boston: Division of Research, Grad. School of Business Administration, Harvard U., 1969); Robert Gilpin, *France in the Age of the Scientific State* (Princeton: Princeton Univ. Press, 1968); Alain Cotta, *La France et l'impératif mondial* (Paris: Presses Universitaires, 1978); and Christian Stoffaës, *La grande menace industrielle* (Paris: Calmann-Lévy, 1978). See also Gabriel Mignot, "Industrie Francaise: diagnostic et propositions," *Projet*, no. 136, June 1979, pp. 717-730, and the "rapport Hannoun" divulged in September 1979.

14. See Suzanne Berger, "D'une boutique à l'autre: changes in the organization of the traditional middle classes," *Comparative Politics*, October, 1977.

15. See his *Elites in French Society* (Princeton University Press, 1979) and "The Myth of Technical Expertise," *Comparative Politics*, October 1977.

16. See Jean Monnet's *Mémoires* (Paris, Fayard, 1976), Ch. 9-10.

17. See the chapters by J.-J. Bonnaud, Jack Hayward, Francois Jobert and Bruno d'Arcy, and Louis Nizard on French planning in: Jack Hayward and Michael Watson (eds.), *Planning, Politics and Public Policy* (Cambridge: Cambridge U. Press, 1975); the chapter by C.A. Michalet, N. Jéquier and J. Hayward in Raymond Vernon (ed.), *Big Business and the State* (Cambridge: Harvard U. Press, 1974); and E. Friedberg in M. Crozier et al, *Où va l'Administration française* (Paris: Ed. d'Organisation, 1974). See also *Huitième plan: options* (Paris, Documentation Française, April 1979).

18. For a summary, see M. Maurice, F. Sellier and J.-J. Silvestre, *Production de la hiérarchie dans l'entreprise*, a brochure from the Laboratoire d'économie et de sociologie du travail.

19. See J.-L. Bodiguel, *Les anciens élèves de l'ENA* (Paris, Presses de la Fondation Nationale des Sciences Politiques (FNSP), 1978).

20. See Pierre Birnbaum, *Les sommets de l'Etat* (Paris, Seuil, 1977).

21. See A. Babeau and D. Strauss-Kahn, *La richesse des Français* (Paris: Presses Universitaires, 1977) Robert Lattès, *La fortune des Français* (Paris: J.C. Lattès C.E.R.C., *Les revenus des Français* (Paris: Ed. Albatros, 1977); and C.E.R.C., *La patrimoine des Français* (Paris, Documentation Française, 1979)

22. See *Le Monde*, 8 March, 1977, p. 21; also, the articles by F. Méraud, *Le Monde*, 4 April, 1978, and his earlier *Rapport de la Commission des inégalités sociales*, Paris, 1975.

23. See *Statistiques et études financières*, no 353, "L'impôt sur le revenu en 1976," and the summary in *Le Monde*, 28 Nov., 1978, p. 25. The income tax represents only 5.5 percent of available income; 84.5 percent of taxable income in 1976 was provided by wages and pensions, 1.3 percent only by farm income and 10.6 percent by the income of businessmen, shopkeepers and artisans. 6 percent of taxpayers have declared an income superior to 70,000 francs; these represent 79 percent of the income of the professions, 59 percent of the income from interests and dividends, and 45 percent of industrial and commercial income. Between 1965 and 1973, the fiscal burden carried by wage earners has increased, that of the professions has decreasd.

24. Rapport Méraud (see footnote 22).

25. See the articles by Bertrand Girod de l'Ain on higher education in *Le Monde*, November 13-18, 1978.

26. *Le Monde*, 13 September, 1977 (pp. 1-2) and 14 September, 1977 (p. 2).

27. Jane Marceau, *op. cit.*, p. 35, 86.

28. In *Esprit*, December 1957.

29. Edmond Maire in *Le Monde*, August 18, 1979, p. 15. On all that precedes, see G. Adam and J.-D. Reynaud, *Conflicts du travail et changement social* (Paris: Presses Univ., 1978); and Janice McCormick's unpublished Harvard Ph.D. thesis, 1979.

30. *La règle et le consentement* (Paris, Fayard, 1979), p. 446. On the new system for appoin-

ting professors, see *Le Monde*, Aug. 16, 1979, p. 14, and Aug. 17, 1979, pp. 1 and 6.

31. See my study: OECD, *La politique des sciences sociales en France* (Paris, OECD, 1975).

32. See Y. Ullmo in Hayward and Watson (footnote 17); I have also learned much from a paper by Peter A. Hall, *French Etatism vs. British Pluralism*.

33. Michel Tatu in *Le Monde*, 5–6 November, 1978, p. 1.

34. See P. Birnbaum, *op. cit.* in footnote 20, Ch. IV.

35. See M. Crozier and E. Friedberg, *L'acteur et le système*(Paris, Seuil, 1977), Ch. VIII.

36. See *Esprit's* issue of June 1978, "La démocratie par l'association?"

37. See his articles in *Le Monde*, April 25—28, 1978. See also Annie Kriegel, "P.C.-P.S..: les causes de la rupture," *Commentaire*, no. 3, Automne, 1978. I am in debt to a working paper by Jane Jenson and George Ross, "The uncharted waters of destalinization," 1979.

38. For a view that differs somewhat from mine, see John Frears, "Legitimacy, Democracy and Consensus," *West European Politics*, vol. 1, no. 3, Oct. 1978, pp. 11–23.

39. For a different view, see G. Vedel, "Réflexions sur la représentation proportionnelle," *Commentaire*, No. 3, automne 1978.

40. And more recently by Régis Debray, *Le pouvoir intellectuel en France* (Paris, Ramsay, 1979).

41. See H.E. Kedward, *Resistance in Vichy France* (London, Oxford University Press, 1978) and my review of it in the *The New York Review of Books*, 9 Nov., 1978.

42. "The Cultural Revolution" in S. Graubard (ed.), *A New Europe?* (New York: Houghton Mifflin, 1964).

43. See my essay, "Fragments floating in the here and now," *Daedalus* (American Academy of Arts and Sciences) winter 1979, pp. 1–25.

44. Stoffaës, *op. cit.*

45. See his *A Bias for Hope* (New Haven, Yale University Press, 1971).

46. See his book, *On ne change pas la société par décret* (Paris, Grasset, 1979).

47. See Raymond Boudon, *Effets pervers et ordre social* (Paris, Presses Univ. 1977) and Fred Hirsch, *The Social Limits to Growth* (Cambridge, Harvard University Press, 1976).

48. See the SOFRES survey analyzed by Jacques Julliard in *Le Nouvel Observateur*, 23 July, 1979, pp 29 ff. 49 percent of the people questioned think that France's membership in the EEC is a good thing, only 9 percent think it a bad thing. Among Communist sympathizers, the proportions are 23 percent and 33 percent, among Socialists 49 and 8, among UDF sympathizers 71 and 3; the surprise concerns the Gaullists: 65 and 5!

Appendix

Dialogue, Michel Debré and Conference Participants*

Questioner 1 asked whether the founding fathers of the Fifth Republic had profited from the lesson of the Weimar Republic that a presidential and parliamentary system cannot exist together long. He asked if a conflict between a president and a prime minister would not lead to the eventual dissolution of the Fifth Republic or at least of the executive branch.

A.. The question is valid. I have often asked the same thing, and I was not the only one to do it. It seems to me that the answer is as follows: The appearance must be distinguished from the substance, especially in making comparisons with the Weimar Republic. The heart of this matter is knowing whether the possible difficulty between a president of the Republic and a prime minister is a question of the men or of a change of regimes. The 1958 constitution no more prevents the consequences of a crisis between two men than do other constitutions. We can play at 'political fiction' by imagining a victory by M. Mitterrand's supporters in the 1978 parliamentary elections. With a very large majority, Mitterrand certainly would have sought the departure of Giscard d'Estaing in order to provoke a presidential election. That already happened in France under the completely different system of the Third Republic when M. Herriot did not want to be prime minister under President Millerand. The large majority of the Assembly supporting such a man would make a government impossible and the president of the Republic would have the choice of dissolving the Assembly or stepping down. Under the previous constitution, the only

*Following his speech of June 10 (see above pp 1–14), M. Michel Debré responded to questions posed by conference participants. The session continued the following morning and ended with a standing ovation. The transcript of the session was edited by M. Debré and translated from French by Paula Lieberman and William G. Andrews.

possibility was stepping down. Perhaps it is better to give the President of the Republic the right to ask public opinion to judge the opposition's conduct. Probably, if M. Mitterrand had won a very large majority, 54–55 percent, and had refused to form the government, he would have compelled Giscard d'Estaing to step down and there would have been a new presidential election. But if the majority had been very weak, and, as a consequence, M. Mitterrand had not been certain of being elected president of the Republic, he would have agreed to be prime minister, and we would have entered what I have called the 'second reading' of the constitution, that is, a reading in which the president of the Republic has the constitutional rights, but the government, with the majority of parliament, takes charge. Therefore, I believe that conflicts between men can be resolved, but a conflict cannot be prevented from arising. It seems to me that the American constitution avoids that by the brevity of the presidential mandate. That is, if Congress has a majority completely hostile to the president, there will be an election soon—but, in the meantime, there is the impression from the outside that the American government does very little. A conflict between a majority electing a president and another majority electing a congress is always a problem, but once again, on this point, I do not see how institutions can prevent changes in the electoral body or the ambitions of men. When I say that the constitution has become legitimate, it signifies, for example, that the worst thing would have been for a Mitterrand to compel Giscard d'Estaing to step down in order to become president of the Republic himself and five years later for a change in the majority to give the position to a M. Chirac who would force Mitterrand to resign in his turn.

Questioner 2 asked the speaker to comment on allegations that the results of the legislative elections in France were distorted by gerrymandering of the election districts.

A. I accept only half of your observation. The districts were established in 1958 with truly as little political consideration as possible. A very old rule in France requires that each department have at least two deputies and, because many departments have lost population, disequilibrium among districts has developed since 1958. But the design of these districts, with very rare exceptions, was established without ulterior motives by politicians. But demographic evolution has been considerable in the last twenty years. The Parisian area and the area around Lyon have increased considerably in population and other departments in the center of France have decreased. And that is why, moreover, in imitation of the English, I have always asked that the districts be reviewed every twenty or twenty-five years. Except for the vicinity of Lyon, I was not listened to. (This is not the first time.) And for two reasons: To begin with, there are all those who would like to reintroduce proportional representation and who wait with satisfaction for the districts to appear worse and worse in relation to the evolution of population. And then, naturally, there are those who are strongly attached to the present outlines. Finally, there is a last reason—which I do not accept—that the creation of new districts would favor the Communist party in certain cases. The experience of these twenty years of Gaullism, makes it possible to demonstrate that even in the districts said to be Communist, the Communist candidates can be beaten and that the fear of Communism should never be used to alter institutions. But you are right; if the present legislature does not revise the constituency boundaries, that is, about thirty of them—no more, but that is a lot—there will be a problem of the quality of representation. In conclusion, I must insist on the fact that the last elections were not only a success for the majority in terms of seats. They were a success, also, in terms of votes and the opposition could not say that it would have won if the constituencies had been different. That could have happened, but in fact, the elections of March 1978 were a success for the majority independent of the design of the constituencies.

Questioner 3 asked if the distribution of power between the assembly and the executive branch of government as provided by the French Constitution might permit a situation similar to the recent development in the United States in which the legislature imposed restraints upon the executive with respect to foreign policy.

A. Toward the end of my speech, I expressed a very personal opinion that the presidential regime leads to an Assembly regime at the same time and to a situation—in which the United States has often been found—with a president having one policy and a Congress in which the majority wants another policy and tries to impose it. What I call the Assembly regime imposes decisions on an executive. I believe that the parliamentary system avoids what you have just said, because the government is supported by the majority of the Assembly. More likely is the situation recently evoked in which the President of the Republic has one opinion but the government, having the confidence of the Assembly, has another. But conflict in a parliamentary system, if there must be conflict, is not between the executive and the legislature. It is between *the head of state and the prime minister.* I think that is better and, under the French constitutional system, if the president of the Republic believes that the prime minister and the majority of the Assembly are wrong, he can dissolve the Assembly. In certain cases, he can call on the people for a referendum. That is, for very important matters, the President of the Republic has the possibility of recourse to arbitration, but in the examples that you give, under the French constitutional system the Assembly cannot take a position different from that of the government. But there can be difficulties between the government and the president of the Republic.

Questioner 4 expressed the opinion that M. Jacques Chirac advocated an interpretation of the French Constitution tending toward a strict and renovated parliamentarism such as M. Debré had proposed in 1958. He asked if M. Debré considered this position fair and if he found that, at the moment, Mr. Chirac is taking the position that M. Debré took twenty years ago.

A. If I had come ten years ago, to celebrate ten years of Gaullism instead of twenty, you would have asked me if M. Giscard d'Estaing did not espouse good parliamentarist principles with regard to presidential power. And I would have answered 'yes.' And then, M. Giscard d'Estaing became president and he became presidentialist. I am convinced that M. Chirac is parliamentarist. I believe that if he were president, he would be presidentialist. As I said, two interpretations of the constitution are possible. The presidential interpretation is possible only if the majority of the Assembly derives from very nearly the same majority of voters that designated the president of the Republic. Therefore, the president of the Republic is, in fact, the head of this majority. That has been the case since the beginning of the Fifth Republic. In 1967, the majority was four or five seats. In 1973, about twenty seats. But, a majority has always identified willingly with the president of the Republic or, in any case, as at the present time, agrees to regard the president of the Republic as the head of this majority. So, the presidential interpretation prevails. In the case brought up just now, one can very well imagine, as I have said, a parliamentary regime almost like the English. I have always maintained that the legitimacy of the republic in France does not have too pronounced a presidential affirmation. As much as I have always fought against the excesses of the Assembly regime, I am persuaded that French society wants an active parliament. In order for parliament to be active, the government must be a government truly responsible to it, and parliament must not have the impression too often that decisions are made outside it, indeed outside of the government, consequently outside the authority responsible before it. I am, therefore, quite firm about the idea of a president of the Republic rather close to a constitutional monarch. Nevertheless, because I know my country well, the monarch could have an important role in matters of defense and in foreign affairs. But I believe that too much power in domestic policies, the economy, social policies, and in matters of education is a poor gift to bestow on the presidential function. In saying that, I am not completely in agreement with the present interpretation. I have always said that both readings of the constitution are valid and that both had been envisioned before the drafting of the constitution. Nevertheless, the parliamentary reading was certainly more easily accepted to 1958, and the election of the president of the Republic by universal suffrage beginning in 1962, gave the presidential reading an importance that, without doubt, had not been evaluated as clearly before the drafting of the text.

Questioner 5 asked the speaker about his thoughts on the current trends in national defense policy.

A. I have certain criticisms and, at the same time, I am obliged to acknowledge what all countries know, that is, the tragedy that long years of inflation represents for a budget, consequently for defense policy.

I have a critical attitude that I have not hidden. The nuclear deterrent force required, still requires, choices and modernization. I believe that for a country like France the effort toward a credible deterrent policy in the coming twenty years will proceed through the development of nuclear submarines. And that is the essential point, in view of the fundamental nature of credibility in matters of deterrents. During the last five years, this priority has been set aside in many regards. Not that it has been abandoned but we have wanted to do too many things without really taking into account what was essential. That is my principal criticism. After all, a country like France and even a country like the United States, suffers from the consequences of inflation. Inflation has very grave effects on a budget such as the military budget, and in particular on personnel costs. When I was responsible, as minister, for the defense budget, my objective was that half of the budget, and no more, should be allocated to personnel and the maintenance of armies. To spend more than half of a military budget on maintenance and personnel is to ensure that in the coming fifteen or twenty years materiel that is insufficiently updated will become obsolete. I specify expenses for personnel and for maintenance and operation. Inflation increases ordinary expenses and the cost of new investments. It is a problem for all the budgets of western nations from the richest to the least rich. At the present time, aside from that basic criticism, what worries me is that the budget for personnel and operations is in the process of attaining and even surpassing 60 percent of the total. That figure denotes, in the long run, the certainty of obsolescence of equipment. Only countries like the Soviet Union or Eastern Europe, by continuing to pay their personnel poorly, succeed in maintaining their budgets and in assuring that increases in the budget are increases of potential and not only increases in personnel. And that touches on a problem that has worsened in the last four or five years and that, if inflation continues in all the western democracies, in my opinion, will have very grace consequences for our defense capacity.

Questioner 6 asked the speaker about his views on the proportional representation electoral system. In particular, he asked for his comments on the argument by Raymond Aron that the electoral system in use in France at the present time encourages bipolarization between the Union of the Left and Gaullist-Giscard coalition.

A. I want to repeat something that I said yesterday. I admire very much the arguments for proportional representation that come from the United States or England, in particular from England, because the English have an invariable principle which consists of never even considering the idea of proportional representation for themselves, but of giving proportional representation to all the countries they leave, in order to be sure that the governments in those countries will be weak! Proportional representation is fatal to authority. And democracy—and you are an example of it, all the Anglo-Saxon countries are examples—democracy lives by the existence of a majority. And Anglo-Saxon law gives the electoral system the character of a fundamental institution. So, the political parties must adjust to this electoral system. In France, the first republicans, in 1848 and in 1871, understood that perfectly. They used this simple balloting system, with several variations, which provides that the candidate with the most votes is elected. In France, we have lost this simplicity for reasons that are not recognized. Napoleon III invented the two-ballot system, so that he could put up a false Republican candidate on the first ballot [to split the Republican vote] in order to ensure the success of the Bonapartist candidate on the second ballot. After the establishment of the Republic, the Monarchists, who were divided into Legitimists and Orleanists, wanted two ballots in order to run two candidates on the first round and withdraw the less favored of them for the second round. That suited the Republicans who were also divided and who wanted to behave in the same manner. That is how the electoral system became a game for political parties and has not been treated as a principle in France.

My first answer, which is an answer of political philosophy, is that the electoral system is not a game. The electoral system is a principle. It is a basic principle of legitimacy for republican government. And to tamper with it, not to consider it simply as leading to the designation of an elected official in the easiest possible manner is to plunge into a debatable process. That is my first answer.

My second answer will respond exactly to your question, that is, to the articles by Raymond Aron and Maurice Duverger. Both say that proportional representation is a very bad method of balloting. But Raymond Aron says that, as the President of the Republic is elected by universal suffrage, it may be amusing to contemplate proportional representation for the Assembly. And Duverger says that although proportional representation kills democracy, it is the only way at present to separate the Socialist party from the Communist party. Therefore, I find that Raymond Aron and Maurice Duverger, with all the respect and friendship that I have for them, have exactly the same state of mind as Napoleon III or the Monarchists, when they worsened the method of balloting for secondary reasons. As far as the argument of Raymond Aron is concerned, I say that proportional representation results in having the deputies chosen by the party leaders. When the deputies are chosen by the party leaders so are the ministers, and the president of the Republic will lose very rapidly the real power to nominate his government. I add, as Professor Hermens whom I cited yesterday explained very well 40 years ago, that proportional representation kills the right of dissolution, because all the important party militants are certain of being elected. Thus, dissolution does not frighten them. Moreover, except for a tidal wave toward the end of the regime as, for example, when Hitler came to power, dissolution results in a change of only 1, 2, 3 percent. The problems are not changed. During the Fourth Republic, elections did not make big changes. Consequently, proportional representation would modify the 1958 constitution very profoundly, by reducing the power of the head of state, who will no longer be free to designate ministers and whose power of dissolution will lose its capacity for dissuasion. As for the argument of Maurice Duverger, I say if proportional representation is truly necessary in order that the Socialists leave the Communists, it has very little credibility. It should be necessary, therefore, as some say, to have proportional representation for all local elections. That is, powerlessness should be generalized. It is typically, and that is what I reproach, placing the electoral system at the disposition of the parties in order to give these parties a reason to exist. If the Socialist party wants to take a stand and if it really needs a new electoral system in order to take that stand, that means that it is unfit to do so. This electoral system should allow the party to want to become dominant. And I find it very curious to hear it said, as is said today, that bipolarization is bad. One cannot want a majority and regret bipolarization at the same time. The two things are tied together. I heard someone say only yesterday that the Communist party has changed as a result, in part, of the majority electoral system, which leads to coalitions down to the grassroots level and that proportional representation would restore the much blunter character of the Communist party. And if a hand is offered to the Socialist party, a fist is offered to the Communist party. That is the other side of the coin. Under these conditions, I am extremely severe toward proportional representation. But, as I said, in the manner of the English or of you Americans, I am ready to praise this electoral system for all countries, except my own.

Questioner 7 asked three questions. The first concerned the extent to which the constitutional reform projects of the *Comité général d'Etudes* foreshadowed the constitution of the Fifth Republic. The second concerned the circumstances and conditions in which the CGE worked. The third concerned the speaker's recollections of his first meeting with General de Gaulle near the end of World War II.

A. The first question is rather difficult and immodest for me to answer. In 1943, the constitutional work of the Comité général d'Etudes was entrusted to me in concert with Pierre-Henri Teitgen, who has left the political scene now but who was a minister under the Fourth Republic. The general ideas for consitutional reforms adopted by the CGE, which was made up of six to eight men, were very close to those of the 1958 constitution for the reason that I was the principal initiator in both cases. As I said yesterday evening, these ideas were: a head of state whose authority would not be derived from an electoral college composed of parliamentarians, and who has appropriate powers, especially dissolution; secondly, a parliamentary regime where the government directs the work of parliament and before which it is responsible with mechanisms for avoiding the abuse of responsibility, that is, of instability; thirdly, a majority electoral system. The deliberations of the Comité général d'Etudes were a little unusual because the meetings were never long and, in consequence, when I was charged with presenting a text, since we were all friends, the others agreed that I was right. Therefore, the draft was accepted. I cannot say that collective thought was very profound. But the ideas were real and, for example, the adoption of proportional representation by General de Gaulle for the election of the Constituent Assembly at the insistence of all the political parties was the beginning of a rather sharp dispute because I found that politicians who had been members of the Comité général d'Etudes or close to it abandoned rather quickly the principles they had adopted. But, if you compare the texts of 1958 and 1945, you will see the same plan rather clearly with an addition that is, properly speaking, the Gaullist addition, the referendum. General de Gaulle conceived of the referendum in order to be well informed on public opinion with respect to himself and to national issues. This is a rather curious sentiment, but I felt it in my very first conversations with the General in 1944—General de Gaulle was not confident of his legitimacy. Since 1940, he had lived far from France. The years 1940–44 had been terrible. He had not been in contact with leaders of the Resistance movements until the end of 1943 and had been deceived by them. For two years, he had watched the rise of the Communist party inside France and, as a result, wondered if his personal legitimacy was truly an historical or a political phenomenon. Thus, for him the referendum were an opportunity for a dialogue. The second idea, which is not strictly personal, is precisely the fact that the political scene in France has never had the clarity of the English or American political scene with two large parties. Because of that, the system of coalitions of parties and all the phenomena connected with it, that is, the ties of each party headquarters with interest groups, the referendum creates a sort of screen for important matters and gives public opinion a capability to decide without having to delegate to party leaders as intermediaries, at least for essential matters. This second aspect of calling for a referendum is not insignificant, not only for General de Gaulle but especially for the French people, and I would say even for the republicans, who saw during the early part of the twentieth century, a sort of deviation by political leaders relative to public opinion. Many actions taken by the Third Republic were decided or rejected by a majority of deputies even though public opinion ran in the opposite direction. For example, it is very certain that the anticlerical struggles, or indeed, another example, the refusal of the right to vote for women—whether positive or negative actions—expressed the positions of the party leaders. If public opinion had been consulted, there would not have been anticlerical struggles and women would have had the right to vote. I think of these two examples because they are typical. Therefore, quite apart from the person and the personal legitimacy of the General who was very desirous of this popular support, the referendum truly has been the constitutional mark of Gaullism, as I told you rather briefly yesterday. Even the Fourth Republic was obliged to write it into the constitution, naturally under conditions that deprived it of all value. The referendum is typically Gaullist as an institution.

The other two questions are more personal. The Comité général d'Etudes de la Résistance was an organism. *Now*, it is called an 'organism.' In fact, it was a meeting of men that two distinguished people had wanted; one of them is still living and the other died tragically. Jean Moulin was the one who died, as a result of unimaginable torture in 1943, about the same time of the year as now, in June 1943, thirty-five years ago. The other was François de Menthon who retired from political life after having been a Christian Democratic leader. Toward the end of 1942, these two men thought it well that there be a new conscientiousness about political, economic, and social problems shortly after the Liberation. Naturally, constitutional questions were posed. Those in London and Algiers thought that the Resistance would furnish the men and ideas since those in London and Algiers were principally soldiers. Jean Moulin agreed. Moreover, there was a new phenomenon in 1942 as a result of the entry of the Communist party into the Resistance after the 1941 invasion of Russia by Hitler. Jean Moulin and François de Menthon considered the Resistance movements to be political infants compared to the Communist party and they were profoundly right. They were occasionally unruly infants, not always having a clear understanding of consequences. Moreover, Jean Moulin wanted the entire Resistance movement, which was very diversified, to become united doctrinally around General de Gaulle. At that time, Jean Moulin and François de Menthon created a committee of four men: '*Primus, Secondus, Tertius,* and *Quartus.*' These four men added one or two men, of whom I was one. Then, in 1944, two or three more joined. This is very difficult to explain to the younger generation because these discussions of economic problems or of the post-Liberation period were surrounded by a very great concern for secrecy, both because the organism itself had problems that could not have been revealed usefully while it was in full battle and, especially, because most of those who participated in the Comité général d'Etudes were members of Resistance movements and, as such, were followed. Thus, the meetings were clandestine, rare, but this is what happened: In the six months that preceded the Liberation, the ranks of the Resistance leadership were decimated by the Gestapo. And others, including de Menthon himself, left to become ministers in Algiers. In the void created by the arrests and the departures, the Comité général d'Etudes seemed like the sort of organ that could be a kind of arbiter and could be consulted. In fact, in the six to eight last months, it became an organ of reflection somewhat at the disposal of the Resistance movements, very much so of the Algiers government's clandestine mission to Paris. At that time, the role of the Comité général d'Etudes had evolved into something rather different from what had been foreseen fourteen or fifteen months earlier. It had become less an organ of study than a sort of organ for deliberation and counsel.

I met General de Gaulle for the first time on the 20th of August 1944. I was not using my name because I was emerging from clandestine life; France was not liberated and my family was still in a zone occupied by the Germans. Naturally, it is a very great date for me. More than a year before, the General himself had charged me with appointing departmental prefects for the Liberation. Even though I had exchanged messages with him, I had never met him.

I can recount two anecdotes for you.

The first is that I committed an error of protocol. General de Gaulle thought that a commissioner of the Republic [regional prefect] should await the head of government at the boundary of his region. I was emerging from clandestine life with great difficulty and I went to meet General de Gaulle, but not exactly at the point where I should have. Naturally, he said nothing to me, but his associates told me immediately.

The second, occurred before Paris was liberated. The General was making his way toward Paris on the heels of the American soldiers and of those from the Leclerc division. I was accompanying him. We arrived in the city of Mans. General de Gaulle's arrival had been announced by word of mouth. There were no newspapers, only a few printed sheets which were distributed very little because transportation was lacking. The London radio was not easy to hear because the electrical current was cut often. The fighting had caused a lot of destruction. Therefore, the news that General de Gaulle was going to pass through circulated by word of mouth. We arrived in Mans at nine o'clock an evening in August. It was still daylight, but the light was fading bit-by-bit. In spite of the absence of press and radio, there was an enormous crowd. The General's car, an old car, had to slow down. Groups of men and women leaned on the car. A woman with tears in her voice threw flowers to the General and, in her emotion, cried out: '*Vive le Maréchal.*' The whole crowd that surrounded her seized her and threw her back. The General turned to me and said, '*Comment voulez-vous qu'ils se retrouvent.*'

Questioner 8 reminded M. Debré that he had said the preceding day that there had been a profound change in the recruitment and selection of political personnel in France and compared this to a comment by Alain Peyrefitte in *La Mal Français* that the students of the *Ecole nationale d'administration* immediately after World War II came from the same social categories as those who had attended the *Ecole des sciences politiques* before the war. He asked M. Debré's opinion on this apparent discrepancy.

A. I do not understand well. The problem is a bit different, the problem of the ENA and the problem of political personnel. Alain Peyrefitte—it happens even to ministers—is wrong. It is absolutely clear that the situation has not changed overnight. I know Alain Peyrefitte because I was the one who advised him to prepare for the competitive examination in 1945. Alain Peyrefitte was in the first class at the *Ecole nationale d'administration* and, it is very difficult to imagine, that despite the war and the fact that the examination was limited to war veterans, that social recruitment changed all at once. Nevertheless, I should tell you that in that group of students were many who had never taken the competitive examination and in ordinary times, would never have taken it. But, later on the *Ecole nationale d'administration* came to have two entrance examinations and these two entrance examinations profoundly modified the evolution of things, since the second examination is open to all those who have no other credentials than having held some public office, even the most modest. The change from the past has been very great! A two-volume work on the *Ecole nationale d'administration* appeared about two months ago. I wrote the preface, which required a lot of work, a rather long period of reflection on the past and of preparation. The first volume is on the historical aspect and the second is on the social origins of the students. And you will see changes. A point on which I often disagree with sociologists is that social advancement occurs sometimes all at once and sometimes in two generations. If one wants to know if a higher civil servant came from the working class or the present class, one must not be content with looking at his father and his mother, one must look at his grandfathers and grandmothers also. Moreover, when someone is described as the son or daughter of a civil servant, that may mean the son or daughter of a mail carrier or police officer, modest occupations, and the father and mother of the mail carrier or police officer may have been very far from public office. Of course, one's ideas on advancement must be modernized continuously, but I tell you, as I told Peyrefitte, his judgment is superficial. I have a whole series of cases which demonstrate well that continuous renewal is underway. Of course, this phenomenon is common to all countries. In the army, a considerable number of officers are sons of officers. At the university, a considerable number of professors are sons of professors. In government service, a considerable number of officials are sons of officials. This tradition should not be regretted for it contributes to the strength of a country. Modern countries that develop a tradition from father to son acquire strength and a sense of the state that are part of the value and the legitimacy of a regime. Therefore, tradition and a continuing effort at change and improvement must be combined at one and the same time.

The problem of political personnel in the Fifth Republic is completely different. Two phenomena are important. I mentioned the first phenomenon briefly yesterday. It is not new in France and I believe that it has been known in other countries as well. After periods of great difficulty, political careers are launched by men whose orientation has been set by those very trials. French political life has known such periods. Just after the Second Empire, the young generation of lower and middle bourgeoisie who had fought against Napoleon III for noble motives became involved in politics and furnished the fine generation of political leaders in the years 1880 to 1900. This did not happen after World War I for a reason which had enormous influence on the destiny of France: the Hecatomb. That war cut down an enormous number of young men including, naturally, the most courageous. In spite of the great tragedy of World War II and the fact that among those who died were, naturally, the best and the most courageous, the slaughter was less. After that war, French political life in all the parties was enriched by the emergence of political personnel forged by the trial. The Republican personnel forged under the Second Empire wanted revenge for the shame of Sedan. The generation of political men who issued from World War II wanted revenge for the tragedy of 1940. Outside of such periods, political life attracts men who have different motivations, either ideological or personal. Certainly, the generation that is thirty to fifty years old today and the one that is younger, do not have the same motivations.

The second point is very particular: The evolution of French society has changed the character of the advancement accorded by political office. Thirty or fifty years ago, certainly more than fifty years ago, political office was a double promotion for a provincial doctor or attorney or business executive and for their wives. It was a promotion because it allowed him to go to Paris. Also, it assured an improved social station. Today, that has ended. The standard of living for physicians and attorneys has risen. Becoming a member of parliament brings a certain reduction of income. As for coming to Paris, he has opportunities for that every day, not to mention that, with radio and television, the former isolation of Paris from the provinces has disappeared. Thus, for a great number, doctors, attorneys, heads of companies, political office is no longer a promotion. Is it even a promotion for the trade-unionist or the teacher? Yes, it is, but one must be aware of the second phenomenon, security. Those who are engaged in a liberal profession or an industrial profession must give up that position to hold political office. In case of defeat later, he will find it very difficult to recover his means of livelihood. Whereas a civil servant—since we do not have the same system as the English, where election requires resignation—simply takes a leave of absence and returns to his position again if he loses his political office. Therefore, civil servants are very numerous in political life—teachers, civil servants from all categories—because there is no risk. And even if that just barely represents a promotion, in any case it is not a leap in the dark. Thus, I think that the analysis of the modification of political personnel should rest on these two points. First, it is a new generation which has not known hardship and, therefore, its motivations are different. Secondly, the aspect of promotion that political office might represent is limited by the higher standard of living that many careers offer and by the insecurity that it may present. Moreover, one of the things for which I reproach the proportional representation electoral system is that it leads to such security that political office becomes a career. It is sort of escape from risk. Thus, this electoral system as was seen under the Fourth Republic, leads to a change in political personnel: it professionalizes political office and this mutation produces profound changes in the origins of the personnel.

Questioner 9 asked about Georges Pompidou's 1968 resignation as prime minister and the circumstances of the 1969 referendum, especially why de Gaulle had added secondary questions to the referendum.

A. Since 1966, General de Gaulle had wanted to change prime ministers. But the results of the 1967 elections were rather poor. The Majority won by only four or five seats. It was difficult to change prime ministers, especially because

M. Couve de Murville, whom the General was thinking of, had been beaten. I advised General de Gaulle not to give the impression that, in changing prime ministers, he was acknowledging the defeat of the government. I may have been wrong. But defeat could not be admitted, thus the prime minister had to be retained. In fact, General de Gaulle reproached M. Pompidou for being too conservative. However, it was a curious reproach. He had been chosen in 1962 partly to allay the fears of a large number, it seemed, who reproached me for having made too many reforms; thus, he should not have been reproached for wanting to appease everyone too much by not launching any reforms, especially with respect to 'participation.' The events of May 1968 crystallized this judgment. I may add that General de Gaulle, without hostility toward Pompidou, had the feeling that he had a choice between two attitudes: either to step down or to take upon himself again the entire governmental leadership. If he decided not to step down, he had to have a prime minister who would be a very loyal collaborator, in such a way that he could control personally the forces of government more than he had in the previous two years. Those were the reasons for the change in 1968.

As for the second question, the 1969 referendum was an error.

The mechanism of that referendum, the psychological mechanism, was the following: General de Gaulle had been hit hard, not so much by the events of May 1968 as by the difficulty of taking affairs in hand again. I always took the position that he had judged the behavior of the French people in the events of 1968 much too severely. All things considered, all those or almost all those on whom he could count remained steadfast and faithful. It was easy to see that those who had been weak were weak by nature. Thus, I found the severity of this judgment much too uniform, especially regarding the political class (as was often the case with him). We forced on him dissolution rather than the referendum, and he had kept a certain feeling of frustration over that. As always, he wanted to be sure that the French people supported his legitimacy and he felt that the deputies had been elected much more from fear of adventure than for himself. He had then, as it was said, a '*referendum rentré.*' Some day, if I have time, I shall write about the feelings I experienced then, because this period left me with a lot of bitterness—I remember this bitterness today in particular because I came to the United States; I was minister of foreign affairs at the time; I came to Washington for several days. The referendum was imminent, even its date was practically set. I was sure of defeat. In the conversation, talks, discussions that I was obliged to hold I pretended that nothing was wrong, but I felt a great deal of sadness deep inside. A grave error had been committed. The error lay in this: the ideas in vogue. When the minister in charge of preparing the referendum bills on regionalization and on the new Senate went to explain the contents of the text to local authorities everywhere, in Brittany, in Provence, in Alsace, he was applauded by his audience, from the Socialists to the Conservatives. Everyone applauded the idea that power and money were going to be given to them, and the minister returned to Paris and at each meeting of the Cabinet said, 'It's unheard of, how well these ideas are being received.' Many other ministers went into their districts talking to mayors, to general councilors, telling them about decentralization, about participation, that they would get more power, that they would get money. Naturally, they were received with open arms. There was a real difficulty that was seen as secondary, but I thought that it was grave. It was to add a reform of the Senate, which represented the loss of certain advantages for some. That aroused less enthusiasm. However, as long as the political problem was not posed, the atmosphere among the elected officials remained warm. Whenever, in lax times, a question of dividing up the authority of state or the state itself is raised, democrats seem quite willing—and this is not a phenomenon peculiar to my country if I understand the recent referendum in California—to come very close to destroying the State or the resources of the state. So, all the *notables* liked that so well that they said to each other, 'From now on, we will be kings.' Too few of us said that, when the choice was presented, people who were against the regions, like me, would vote 'yes' because the General asked for it and that people who favored the regions but who were against the General would vote 'no.' In other words, there would absolutely not be a vote on the ideas, but on the political choice. But, I should say that too few of us spoke this language, not so much because of General de Gaulle, but, because of the general atmosphere. The prime minister, M. Couve de Murville is a model gentleman, a model man, in my opinion, morally perfect. He explained to the General that it was difficult and when the General said to him that he was wrong, M. Couve de Murville was too loyal and polite to say to the General, 'No, it is you who are wrong.' I was loyal also but less polite than M. Couve de Murville. M. Marcellin, minister of the interior, was also less polite. But, except for M. Couve de Murville with a lot of politeness and M. Marcellin and myself with less politeness, all the ministers were persuaded that they heard enthusiasm from the mayors, from the county councillors. That was how we went into the referendum and the referendum was scarcely decided upon when it became obvious that the people who had been the first to want regionalization, even the parties that had been the first to want to suppress the Senate, suddenly opposed regions and suppression of the Senate. The Communist party has never stopped saying that the Senate should be suppressed. Yet, from the moment that suppression was proposed, it was scandalized! The Socialists and political leaders like M. Pleven, who were categorical on the necessity of regionalization, as soon as there was a political choice to make, were against regions. So, the phenomenon was clear. In a week, everything that had been said for four months fell into dust, as I had feared. In that atmosphere, secondary things were discussed: was one question needed, two questions ... I might add that another error was committed; the text of the bill was written so that only experienced jurists could understand it. The bill was truly difficult for an ordinary citizen to read.

At one moment, for several days, General de Gaulle considered cancelling the referendum. I was very favorable to his cancelling it. But, there is a phenomenon I warn you against if you ever occupy important positions. You should distrust associates who say, 'You are right. You cannot lose.' It is much better to have associates who say, 'You are wrong ... You are going to lose.' Far too many of the General's associates said to him, 'You are right. You must not retreat.' I had another point of view. But, at that very moment General de Gaulle surely said to himself, 'We will see for certain if the French have the audacity to break the historic contract that has bound me to them.' I will not tell you about the last conversation I had with him on this subject, but I can tell you that I do not favor voting on historic contracts in elections, without a very good reason. I told him so. Then came the defeat that I had foreseen for months. The truth is that General de Gaulle took the results of the referendum very badly, *very* badly. And his sadness was profound. He saw it rightly as revenge, revenge of all those who had been his adversaries, who had clung to him in difficulties and who abandoned him now. I telephoned him in the night and his remarks were bitter. The next morning it was all over. It is true that he suddenly gave the referendum a very high place. 'The French people broke the contract that bound me to them. Therefore, I regain my liberty.' But, this sort of romanticism that Malraux has described, came to his mind in the final three weeks. At the outset, the General wanted approval for a great reform. I want to make one last point on this subject. That reform and referendum dealt with the problem of regionalization. Regionalization, as one senses it in the remarks and some of the speeches of General de Gaulle, placed him in a very difficult position. In fact, as soon as one embarks upon regionalization, to talk about the authority of the State is very easily seen as a contradiction. He was less sure of himself at the end because the regionalization bill was, in fact, rather ambiguous. But, these technical concerns had been erased by the political choice and almost no Frenchman, except those who had spent their lives around certain senators and their anxieties, voted on the bill. They voted as a political choice and this political choice demonstrated two things. First, it demonstrated that General de Gaulle all alone and at the end of his era succeeded in carrying more than 47 percent of the French with him, with him alone; that was extraordinary, exceptional. But also, the coalition, going from the entire Left to an important fraction of the Center and the Right, wanted to turn the page and had seized this occasion to do so.

Possibly that departure of General de Gaulle was the best for history, because contrary to his reputation outside of and even inside France, I have not known a man so anxious to represent freely-expressed popular will, a man more concerned with tying the legitimacy of power to national acceptance. Because the nation did not give him a majority, he retired. All things considered, from the point of view of history and from the point of view of his person in history, this departure is likely to appear as a sign of republican grandeur. In any case, in the profound regret that it gave me, that it gave many, it was an important consolation to see the example given by a man who held all power and had the capacity to use it. He laid everything on the line—his person, his prestige, his authority—and accepted the verdict of the people.

Contributors

William G. Andrews: Professor of Political Science and SUNY Faculty Exchange Scholar, State University College at Brockport

Bela Balassa: Professor of Political Economy, The John Hopkins University, and Consultant, The World Bank

Suzanne Berger: Professor of Political Science, Massachusetts Institute of Technology

Michel Crozier: Senior Research Professor, Centre National de la Recherche Scientifique, Paris, Director, Centre de Sociologie des Organisations; and Director, Post-graduate School of Sociology at the Institut d'Etudes Politiques de Paris

Michel Debré: Member of the French National Assembly and former Prime Minister of France

A. W. De Porte: Director of the Office of Research for Western Europe, U.S. Department of State. The views expressed in his chapter do not necessarily reflect those of the Department.

John R. Frears: Senior Lecturer in Politics, Loughborough University, Great Britain

Paul Gagnon: Professor of History, University of Massachusetts at Boston

*Peter A. Gourevitch:*Professor of Political Science, University of California at San Diego

Michael M. Harrison: Assistant Professor, School of Advanced International Studies, The John Hopkins University

Stanley Hoffmann : Douglas Dillon Professor of the Civilization of France and Director, Center for European Studies, Harvard University

John T.S. Keeler: Assistant Professor of Political Science, University of Washington

Georges Lavau: Professor, Institut d'Etudes Politiques, University of Paris I, and Director of Studies and Research, Fondation Nationale des Sciences Politiques, Paris

Janice McCormick: Research Fellow, Graduate School of Business Administration, and Research Associate, Center for European Studies, Harvard University

George Ross: Associate Professor of Sociology, Brandeis University, and Faculty Research Associate, Center for European Studies, Harvard University

Ezra N. Suleiman: Professor of Politics and Director, European Studies Committee, Princeton University

Index

Index

Index

Middle East War of 1973, 184
Millerand, Alexandre, 328
Mitbestimmung, 320
Mitterrand, Francois, 93, 95, 97, 103, 106, 108, 109, 157, 262, 263, 266, 269, 270, 273, 296, 328, 329
Moch, Jules, 93
Mollet, Guy, 93, 96, 97, 98, 104, 108, 113
Monnet, Jean, 286, 295
Monod, Jérôme, 71, 173
Monory, René, 191
Moulin, Jean, 336
Mouvement dex Sociaux-Libéraux, 71
Mussolini, Benito, 92

NATO, 29, 36, 105, 249, 250, 258, 262, 266, 267, 272, 272, 273, 274, 296, 297, 298, 323
Napoléon, Louis, 82, 333
Napoleonic Wars, 1
National Assembly, 6, 10, 12, 15, 23, 48, 49, 50, 51, 52, 55, 58, 59, 60, 62, 70, 71, 102, 124, 189, 306, 330, 331, 333; Commission des Lois, 57; Committees of Enquiry and Control, 57; Conference of Presidents, 55; Propositions de Loi, 49, 54
National Labor Relations Act (U.S.), 202
Nationalist-Loyalists, 86
Nationalists, 83
Nazi Reich, 92
Nicoud, Gérard, 168
Nixon, Richard M., 256
Nora, Simon, 237

OECD, 127, 185, 192, 227
OPEC, 183, 184, 192, 257, 290
ORTF, 36, 78
Old Regime, 289, 317, 318
Ortoli, François, 30

PCF, 88, 93, 94, 95, 96, 97, 98, 99, 100, 103, 105, 16, 109, 110, 111, 112, 113, 115, 191, 263, 265, 268, 271, 273, 296. See also Communist Party
PCF Central Committee, 96, 103, 110, 267, 271
PR, 31. See also Republicans
PS, 88, 94, 98, 99, 100, 102, 103, 106, 107, 109, 111, 112, 115, 263, 264, 265, 266, 267, 271, 275, 299. See also SFIO and Socialists
PS Commission on National Defense, 275, 299
PS Epinay Congress, 105, 106, 107, 111
PS National Secretariat, 103
PSI, 112

PSU, 94, 107, 108, 109, 110
Paris Commune, 109
Parliament CMP, 51,
Patterson, Michelle, 221
Péguy, Charles, 218
Peyrefitte, Alain, 69, 78, 220, 295, 337, 338
Pinay, Antoine, 21, 28, 29, 37
Pinay-Rueff Plan, 124
Pisani, Edgard, 28, 107
Pivert, Marceau, 109
Plevin, René, 341
Pluton, 297, 298
Poher, Alain, 17, 102
Pompidou, Georges, 10, 17, 19, 21, 23, 24, 25, 26, 28, 30, 31, 33, 36, 39, 40, 41, 50, 51, 52, 60, 84, 85, 86, 87, 92, 98, 110, 148, 164, 165, 184, 198, 255, 256, 257, 259, 274, 290, 297, 322, 324, 340
Pontillon, Robert, 265
Popular Front, 104, 109, 113, 203
Poujade, Robert, 84
Poujadists, 150
Provisional Government, 37

RGR, 94
RPF, 81, 32. See also Rally of the French People
RPR, 100, 169, 318, 325
Radical-Socialist Party, 101, 111, 113, 115. See also Radicals
Radicals, 9, 94, 96, 97, 102, 110, 312. See also Radical-Socialist Party
Ramadier, Paul, 113
Rally of the French People, 5. See also RPF
Regional Missions, 76
Regionalization Conferences, 76
Rémond, René, 304
Republicans, 74. See also PR
Resistance, 4, 82, 222, 336
Right, 95, 98, 115, 226, 309, 310, 317, 318, 342
Rocard, Michel, 71
Rochet, Waldeck, 92
Roosevelt, Franklin D., 249
Royer Law, 169
Ruffenacht, M., 55

SAFER, 142, 144, 154
SFIO, 95, 96, 98, 106, 107, 109, 113, 266. See also Socialists
SMIC, 204, 206
SNFCC, 205, 208, 209
SPD, 319
SUAD, 154, 155
Sartre, Jean Paul, 233, 313, 315
Savary, Alain, 98

345